TV SOCIALISM

Console-ing Passions: Television and Cultural Power
Edited by Lynn Spigel

Anikó Imre
TV SOCIALISM

Duke University Press | Durham and London | 2016

© 2016 Duke University Press
All rights reserved
Designed by Heather Hensley
Typeset in Chaparral Pro by Westchester Publishing Services

Library of Congress Cataloging-in-Publication Data
Names: Imre, Anikó.
Title: TV socialism / Aniko Imre.
Other titles: Console-ing passions.
Description: Durham : Duke University Press, 2016.
Series: Console-ing passions : television and cultural power |
Includes bibliographical references and index.
Identifiers: LCCN 2016005266 (print) | LCCN 2016008076 (ebook)
ISBN 9780822360858 (hardcover)
ISBN 9780822360995 (pbk.)
ISBN 9780822374466 (e-book)
Subjects: LCSH: Television broadcasting—Europe, Eastern—
History—20th century. | Socialism—Europe, Eastern— History
—20th century. | Television broadcasting—Social aspects—
Europe, Eastern. | Television programs—Europe, Eastern. | Tele
vision and politics—Europe, Eastern.
Classification: LCC PN1992.3.E8 I47 2016 (print) | LCC PN1992.3.E8
(ebook) | DDC 791.450947—dc23
LC recordavailableat http://lccn.loc.gov/2016005266

Cover: Irena Dziedzic, hostess of *Tele-Echo*, in 1965. TVP/PAP—
Zygmunt Januszewski

CONTENTS

vii   Acknowledgments

INTRODUCTION   Why Do We Need to Talk about Socialism and TV? 1

PART I   GENRES OF REALISM AND REALITY

CHAPTER 1   From Socialist Realism to Emotional Realism 27

CHAPTER 2   Tele-education 40

CHAPTER 3   Crime Appeal 66

CHAPTER 4   The Great Socialist Game (Show) 83

CHAPTER 5   Postsocialist Ethno-Racial Reality TV 108

PART II   GENRES OF HISTORY

CHAPTER 6   The Historical Adventure Drama 133

CHAPTER 7   Postsocialist Nostalgia and European Historical Drama 155

CHAPTER 8   Commercials as Time-Space Machines 173

PART III   GENRES OF FICTION

CHAPTER 9   Women and TV 187

CHAPTER 10   Socialist Soaps 199

PART IV	GENRES OF HUMOR
CHAPTER 11	Socialist Comedy 227
CHAPTER 12	(Post)socialist Political Satire 242
AFTERWORD	Afterward 257

261 Notes
299 Bibliography
311 Index

ACKNOWLEDGMENTS

I am grateful to Lynn Spigel, editor of the Console-ing Passions series, as well as to Ken Wissoker and his editorial team at Duke University Press for responding so encouragingly to my pitch for a book on socialism and TV and for being so patient through the inevitable changes to the project. Feedback from the two anonymous reviewers was equally honest, thorough, and supportive.

The initial concept grew and flourished over the past five years thanks to my fortuitous involvement with the (Post)Socialist European Television History Network helmed by the one and only Daniela Mustata. I have gained an enormous amount of knowledge, inspiration, and pleasure from collaborating with our chief co-conspirators, Ferenc Hammer, Lars Lundgren, Sabina Mihelj, and Irena Reifová, including regular meetings in Europe and North America. In fact, one of the most beneficial aspects of writing about socialist television has been the unique spirit of sharing that characterizes this emerging area, which stems from the realization that the field can only be cultivated collectively. I am especially thankful for the professional generosity and friendship of Alice Bardan, Christine Evans, Heather Gumbert, Ferenc Hammer, Simon Huxtable, Judith Keilbach, Sabina Mihelj, Dana Mustata, and Zala Volčič. The symposium

"Television Histories in (Post)Socialist Europe," organized by Lars Lundgren in Stockholm in 2013; the conference "Television in Europe beyond the Iron Curtain," organized by Julia Obertreis, Sven Grampp, and Kirsten Bönker at the Friedrich-Alexander-Universität Erlangen-Nürnberg in 2013; the workshop "Networking the Networks," led by Andreas Fickers at the EUScreenX Conference: Discover Europe's Audiovisual Heritage in Rome in 2014; and the conference "Unlocking Television Archives," organized by Daniela Mustata with the generous support of FIAT/IFTA and the Romanian TV Archives in Bucharest in March 2015, gave me precious opportunities to test arguments and gather feedback.

I owe a great deal to Tim Havens and Kati Lustyik, who bravely undertook the idea of editing the first ever book on popular television in (post)socialist Eastern Europe and coaxed me into joining the editorial team. I am also grateful to each contributor to the collection *Popular Television in Eastern Europe During and Since Socialism*, which was published by Routledge in 2012.

Friends and other comrades in the broader television and media studies field whose writing, vision, and advice left an imprint on the book include Mark Andrejevic, Huub van Baar, Péter Bajomi-Lázár, Sarah Banet-Weiser, Jerome Bourdon, Paulina Bren, Charlotte Brunsdon, Jan Čulik, Michael Curtin, Nevena Daković, Sudeep Dasgupta, Alexander Dhoest, Andrea Esser, Nitin Govil, Petra Hanáková, Julia Himberg, Jennifer Holt, Ágnes Jenei, Henry Jenkins, Jeffrey Jones, Alex Juhasz, Nadia Kaneva, Marsha Kinder, Pia Koivunen, Nataša Kovačević, Marwan Kraidy, Shanti Kumar, David Lloyd, Kasia Marciniak, Vicki Mayer, David Morley, Rachel Moseley, John Neubauer, Aine O'Healy, Tasha Oren, József Orosz, Laurie Oullette, Lisa Parks, Sandra Ponzanesi, Yeidy Rivero, Kristin Roth-Ey, Ellen Seiter, Sharon Shahaf, Bev Skeggs, Aga Skrodzka, Joe Straubhaar, Petr Szczepanik, Serra Tinic, Annabel Tremlett, Ginette Verstraete, Patrick Vonderau, Helen Wheatley, and Matteo Zachetti—among many others.

For providing an environment most supportive for research, much credit goes to my colleagues at the School of Cinematic Arts of the University of Southern California, particularly Dean Elizabeth Daley, Vice Dean Michael Renov, and especially my previous department chair, Akira Lippit. The spirit of previous chairs Marsha Kinder and the late Anne Friedberg will always guide my intellectual pursuits.

My interest in television grew out of and was shaped in the course of teaching. I thank all those students at USC who participated in class, challenged me, and suggested further material to watch and read, and whose doctoral work I have had the privilege to follow closely. Among the latter, a very special thanks goes to Maria Zalewska, who first volunteered to help me with collecting Polish material for the book and then became a most excellent research assistant.

I am not a trained historian or ethnographer and am therefore heavily indebted to the assistance of archivists and historians who helped me access and make sense of materials in Budapest at the Open Society Institute Archives, the National Széchenyi Library, and the Hungarian Television Archives. Kata Palyik at the National Audio-Visual Archives (NAVA) came to my rescue many times and became a trusted friend with a pulse on politics as much as on TV. I also learned a great deal from the state of the media and public life from chats (over tea in the winter, beer in the summer, and email year-round) with Péter Bajomi-Lázár, Anna Borgos, Péter Dunavölgyi, Yvette Feuer, Ágnes Jenei, Zsuzsanna Kozák, and Mária Takács.

I am grateful to the Hungarian television professionals who willingly shared with me their thoughts and memories about TV during long conversations and email exchanges: Endre Aczél, Noémi Dankovics, Gergő Olajos, József Orosz, Ilona Pócsik, László Szabó, Katalin Szegvári, and István Vágó. Péter Dunavölgyi deserves credit not only for painstakingly documenting and archiving the history of Hungarian TV, year by year, indeed, day to day, but also for sharing his findings openly and generously. Péter became a one-person archive at a time when official Hungarian policy has moved toward restricting research access. He is truly one of the unsung heroes of television history.

This book was written during a turbulent time in my life. I don't think my master's swim team will ever realize how much of my sanity and daily survival I owe to our regular practices. Even more indispensable has been the support and love of close friends and family. Thank you, especially, Wendy Eisler, Yvette Feuer, Nitin Govil, Julia Himberg, Szabolcs Imre, Zsófia Imre, Zsuzsa Kozák, David Lloyd, Tim McGillivray, Ellen Seiter, and Zala Volčič. This book is dedicated to my greatest accomplishments in life, as they like to refer to themselves: Finny, Simon, and Fergus.

INTRODUCTION

Why Do We Need to Talk about Socialism and TV?

This book is not simply about socialist television. It is, however, very much about socialism *and* television. Socialism does not only designate a historical period here. It is also key to uncovering pieces of a globalized TV history that complement and challenge mainstream Anglo-American TV histories on the one hand and question some of our received wisdom about the Cold War on the other. Throughout, the emphasis falls on how television and socialism function as windows into each other. What do we learn about socialism when we examine it through the medium of television? And what do we learn about television as a global medium when we take into account its operation during almost four decades of state socialism in Europe? To answer these questions, I foreground the temporal continuity between socialism and postsocialism, as well as their joint historical roots in presocialist eras, and explore the geographical and cultural interconnections around television within a Europe embedded in a globalized media network.

I see "socialist television" as a necessary construction whose geographical boundaries stretch beyond the Soviet Empire and whose histories are both anchored in presocialist cultures and continue into postsocialism, never in isolation from the world of liberal capitalism even in the most isolated places and times. As Heather Gumbert writes in her history of early East German television, the historical experiment of socialism is so profoundly rooted in the history of modernity that socialism and liberal capitalism cannot be disentangled.¹ But the ultimate goal is far from assimilating the history of Eastern European socialist TV into that of Western European social democracies. It is, to borrow Sabina Mihelj's words, to think of socialist television "as a specific subtype of modern television, designed to promote an alternative vision of modernity, modern belonging, economics and culture."² Socialist TV certainly registered the socialist system's failures. Equally important, however, it also recorded its forgotten successes, reminding us of the viability of visions that diverge from the current monopoly of neoliberal capitalism on what constitutes the good life.³

Why is "socialist television" a *necessary* construction? Over the past four decades, television studies have created influential paradigms that span multiple disciplines and methodologies. However, the field has remained mostly confined to American and Western European academic hubs and developed with reference to television systems embedded in capitalist economies: the commercial system that has dominated television in the United States, the public service broadcasting system that dominated Western European and Commonwealth states until recently, and various combinations between the two. This book introduces television during and after state socialism in the former Soviet satellite states into television studies. Conversely, it introduces television studies into academic fields concerned with socialist and postsocialist Eastern European cultures and the Cold War in general. This dual merger requires that socialist television be conjured into legitimacy first before we can refine and deconstruct its parameters and evaluate how it changes the parameters of global television and (post)socialist studies.

While socialist television as such needs to be construed practically from scratch, socialism as an ideology and world system itself has been rapidly forgotten, delegitimized, or reduced to nostalgic clichés since the 1990s. To mention just one example, in 2013 the American television network FX released *The Americans*, a drama series created by former CIA agent Joe Weisberg. Set in the 1980s, the series portrays a Russian couple living a double identity as undercover KGB agents who masquerade as perfectly assimilated suburban Americans. The publicity image on the show's website features the couple, played by Keri Russell and Matthew Rhys, in the style of a communist propaganda poster. They stare into the bright communist future with the blind commitment of the brainwashed, holding weapons across their chests as if ready to defend their ideology at a moment's notice and at any cost, framed by the familiar halo of Leninist sun rays (brought to you by Coors Light in prominently placed ads across the screen on the FX site). As I began watching the show, it quickly turned out that the creators had little interest in the Soviet Union other than as a background that triggers American nostalgia for the Cold War. The Cold War is, in fact, reduced to the campy imagery and simplistic historical perspective of its favored genre, the spy drama. I realize, of course, that it is not television's job to teach history. Nevertheless, television does teach us about how American culture sees the history and historical fate of socialism: utterly dismissed and rightfully demonized as a political and economic system. It is stripped down to a few cartoonish images unmoored from their historical context, which are as weightless as Coors Light, and propelled by the very force of nostalgia that brought them back to life.[4]

As researchers have lamented across the disciplines, the end of the Cold War in 1989 has not generated increased interest in understanding its history.[5] Instead, the "superpower approach" continues to dominate scholarship. This approach simplifies Cold War relations as an ideological battlefield of confrontations between the Soviet Union and the United States, conducted across a near-impenetrable Iron Curtain. Sari Autio-Sarasmo and Katalin Miklóssy make a case for reassessing this frozen bipolar state of affairs in light of ample evidence of multileveled interactions among a variety of institutions and individuals, rather than just state actors. Their collection, *Reassessing Cold War Europe*, includes case studies of a number of such east-west technological, scientific, economic, and cultural exchanges.[6] It joins several other publications that have explored the everyday life of socialism, inherently defying Cold War stereotypes of a repressive, isolated, joyless gray bloc. This work has been produced mostly by historians and anthropologists who wish to "culturalize" their fields.[7]

Taking television seriously grants access to an image of life under socialism, even a surprisingly good life at times, which the bipolar vision of the Cold War occludes. Television is a better platform for this historical revision than art films and literature, which were the preferred and often the only available sources that informed the world beyond the Iron Curtain about life in really existing socialism. Even in the most sympathetic and discerning hands, much of art film and literature tended to serve up proof that socialism was depressing, doomed, and defunct. As I argue in detail elsewhere, the reason for this was that these high cultural accounts were produced by and for the most part also *for* intellectuals and artists who were already part of a cosmopolitan circulation of talent. To put it simply, Eastern intellectuals used their national informant status to deliver to Western audiences what those audiences wanted to hear about the oppressed, backward, and exotic East of socialism, in a pattern of self-orientalization that is still largely unacknowledged in Europe.[8]

As I show in this book, television has been a more reliable barometer of the political, economic, and cultural life of socialism. In the most obvious sense, it was an institution that lived in the intersection of the public and domestic spheres, between top-down attempts at influencing viewers and bottom-up demands for entertainment. Where much of art and literature informs us of the relationship between the party leadership and the intellectual elite, TV gives us a sense of the real complexity of the relationship between the party leadership and the public. By virtue of its cross-border production, circulation, and consumption, television also challenges the national containment of these exchanges.

In a less obvious way, television also grants us access to subtle but all the more significant divisions within the "public" that both socialist ideology itself and Cold War discourses about socialism have envisioned as homogeneous. Instead of confirming the blanket oppression of the people by authoritarian or dictatorial leaders, the history of television highlights the more fluid workings of micro-oppressions and exclusions: of women, of nonnormative sexualities, of foreigners, of the Roma and other nonwhite populations. These exclusions were and continue to be embedded in the very structure of nationalism that socialist TV adopted from Western public broadcasters. However, thanks to the unpredictable, home-based, entertainment-oriented workings of television, at times they failed to be enforced in a straightforward fashion.

(Post)socialist TV and Television Studies

Given the indispensable role of television in navigating between the official and unofficial spheres throughout and after socialism, one needs to ask why the medium has been ignored by scholars of (post)socialism. Until very recently, it seems that all possible academic fronts have been united in their resistance to taking television seriously. In Slavic and Eastern European studies, where researchers have the necessary linguistic and cultural competence to search the archives and watch programs, television has long been relegated to the status of a "bad" object, following a

Eurocentric hierarchy of high and low culture also embraced by Eastern European intellectual and political elites. Within Europe, much of the postsocialist media region has recently been folded into the European Union's strategy of creating an integrated, competitive European audiovisual arena. At the same time, media expansion and the flow of programming has remained one-directional, west to east. Academic assessments of postsocialist media change, mostly in communication studies, have favored issues of regulation and institutional shifts and have included television only as part of large-scale media transformations rather than as a cultural-political institution. While this kind of work is undoubtedly important, it has maintained a nation-state framework and an exclusive interest in postsocialist developments. For the most part, it has ignored continuities between socialist and postsocialist television, intra-European flows during socialism, and television's role in shaping culture, desires, tastes, identities, and ideologies.

A major purpose of this book is to contribute to laying the foundations of socialist television histories, a vast and necessarily collective project only recently begun by scholars in research centers in Europe and scattered across the globe.[9] There is a reason why, as Daniela Mustata writes, "there is a momentum for television histories from Eastern Europe" right now.[10] Revisiting socialist television also inevitably rewrites European and global TV histories by virtue of questioning television's reigning national logic, as well as the Cold War divisions between East and West and between socialism and postsocialism. What emerges from this history is an alternative narrative of temporal and geographical continuity that validates the "regional" as a category of profound importance. The particular hybridities developed by socialist and postsocialist television outline, above all, a regional pattern, which is itself rooted in the shared imperial histories on which the region's television infrastructures were built and which programming trends, distribution patterns, and reception practices have perpetuated into the present day.

However, the main ambition of *TV Socialism* is neither drawing up a chronological history nor providing geographical coverage. This would be an impossible task for a single book, given the region's cultural and linguistic heterogeneity and the scope of the historical period in question. Rather, the book is organized according to a broadly conceived *generic* logic. Genre is understood here as a transcultural form of expression rather than a set of specific television genres, since socialist genres do not exactly overlap with those derived from Anglo-American television. For instance, as I discuss in chapter 12, while there were very few American-style sitcoms produced during socialism, there was plenty of comedy on TV. In a similar vein, what I call "soap operas" in chapter 9 for lack of a better term were dramatic serials that shared some traits with American and Western European soaps but preferred a humorous, often satirical tone to sentimentality. Genre thus provides a platform of recognition and comparison between the categories of Western television studies and those of socialism while it also helps foreground the regional specificities of socialist TV. The generic grid makes socialist television accessible to readers unfamiliar with local cultures, let alone with specific television programs.

Each of the four parts of *TV Socialism* explores how a certain generic cluster's aesthetic, political, and ideological dimensions functioned within socialist television. Each part concludes with a chapter that discusses how these dimensions have shifted since the end of the Cold War. The four broad generic categories—reality-based educational programming, historical and adventure series, dramatic series, and comedic programs—were selected based on the kinds of ideological and political roles they have performed on socialist and postsocialist television across the region.

The generic lens highlights the cultural-ideological and political-economic significance of the institution of television in a historical and regional perspective that supplements and counterbalances the recent preoccupation with the transformation of postsocialist media systems. However, the very complexity of television as an institution requires mobilizing the full range of possible approaches. Each chapter draws on media industry studies and cultural studies and incorporates available qualitative and quantitative research on socialist and postsocialist media industries and audiences, as well as archival sources. I also draw on extensive interviews I conducted with prominent Hungarian television professionals and archivists.

Every chapter also weaves together large-scale examinations of regional and continental trends within case studies of programs that illustrate these trends and generate surprising historical and theoretical insight. This comparative, genre-based approach reveals that the actual topography of socialist television is vastly different from the uniform propaganda programming into which the Cold War and its enduring legacy have frozen socialist media. Under the loose umbrella of ideological commitment to Soviet principles, one finds a variety of hybrid aesthetic and economic practices. These include frequent exchanges and collaborations within the region and with Western media institutions, a programming flow across borders, a steady production of genre entertainment, borrowings from European public service broadcasting, the development of an underlying, constantly expanding commercial infrastructure, and transcultural, multilingual reception practices along shared broadcast signals in heavily populated border areas. Rather than scarcity, homogeneity, and brainwashing, *TV Socialism* conveys a mixture of recognition and strangeness, which should defamiliarize some of the basic questions and frameworks of television studies as well as our notions of socialism. It is these moments of defamiliarization and surprise around which the chapters are structured.

Surprise 1: Television's Ambivalent Status

Rather than an instrument of propaganda, television was a profoundly ambivalent medium in the hands of party authorities. Sabina Mihelj explains that, through the 1960s, mass, domestic television viewing remained a new phenomenon in Yugoslavia, which neither broadcasters nor politicians had yet learned to master. More centralized attempts at political control over television increased only in the 1970s.[11] Kristin Roth-Ey describes the postwar development of Soviet television as a messy process, which resists straightforward historical periodization and silver-bullet explanations. It proceeded by trial and error and was in no way determined by technological innovation. Its relationship to Soviet political tradition, to other arts, and to modern Soviet life in general, remained unsettled until the 1970s: "Television was in the paradoxical position of being celebrated and denigrated, pampered and ignored in its first formative postwar decades."[12]

As Hungarian media archivist Katalin Palyik succinctly put it, television was a medium without real owners.[13] This echoes a statement by Richárd Nagy, president of Hungarian Television between 1974 and 1983. According to meeting minutes, in his oral report back to Television's leadership about his visit with party secretary János Kádár in 1979, Nagy said, "So I told [Kádár] that Hungary is a country where . . . every institution needs a—what do you call it?—a godfather. You know how it is. The Operetta Theater has someone. If they build a bridge, that has a godfather. If they build new apartments in the capital, those are sure to have someone. But television, and I think poor radio is the same, they don't belong to anyone."[14] Nagy then explained that he had reminded Kádár that television was under the administrative sphere of "culture" in the government, yet it did not get the funding or legitimacy attached to other cultural branches such as the film industry, or to those in the sphere of "communication," despite being a crucial tool of communication and governance for the party:

> We feel that they look down on us, these "kulturniks . . ." And this is why we feel that we don't have a "godfather." There is no one to support the cause of television. . . . We are Hungarian Television and not some private TV company. And there is only one of these in the Hungarian People's Republic. And if there is only one of these, then someone should champion its cause. Because it seems that a canning factory has a minister who lobbies for it, a meat factory has another one, and a chicken factory yet another. But television doesn't belong anywhere.[15]

The Hungarian case was far from unique. Socialist TV caused a great deal of confusion among authorities, professionals, and viewers throughout its history. This was particularly true in its early era. After experimental broadcasts in the interwar period, television was relaunched in most countries after the war in the mid-1950s, in synchronicity with similar developments in Western Europe. While the communist parties of the 1950s technically owned the new institution, its purpose and potential remained something of a mystery to them. Television's technological base as well as its programming was a mix-and-match of ideas imported and borrowed from Western European broadcasters, filtered through Soviet ideological directives. Communist parties tried to mold the new medium to their own purposes: they developed centralized programming to standardize citizens' everyday, domestic life rhythms. But they were also compelled to sever content from the actual experience of socialism, which invariably fell short of the idealistic picture delivered by party propaganda. In the early decades, this contradictory goal yielded cheerleading docufictions, educational programming, uplifting entertainment such as theatrical coverage of Russian and European classics, doctored news, and domestically produced dramatic serials focused firmly on the romanticized historical past rather than the present.[16]

By the late 1960s, when TV sets became the norm in households, socialist authorities had to reckon with television's power as a mass medium. But party officials were never quite sure how to control or appropriate television and were thus relegated to playing catch-up. By the end of its first decade, viewers had already identified television as a medium of leisure. It had irrevocably absorbed elements from radio, which had incorporated the earlier legacy of "bourgeois" stage variety entertainment. This "bourgeois" element, most visible in television comedy (discussed in chapters 11 and 12), only became more pronounced through the 1970s and 1980s as socialism thawed. The gap between the projective ideals and the actual experiential realities of socialism sustained a layer of ironic distance between television and its viewers. This was exacerbated by the increasing leakage of information about capitalist lifestyles and consumer products despite even the most repressive states' efforts to keep it out. By the 1980s of late socialism, television had turned into the primary medium of parodic overidentification with official socialist rhetoric.[17]

Television's lower cultural status often allowed it to go under the radar of censorship. It also kept away writers and actors who were reluctant to be associated with such a light medium and preferred to work in film and literature—something constantly bemoaned by party executives and television's leadership. Despite its nominal centralization, television operated through a range of alternative approaches that were often ad hoc and subject to party functionaries' own peeves and preferences. Longtime party leaders' attitudes toward television best illustrate this pattern.

Leonid Brezhnev had programs made for him and his family by his appointed head of Soviet television, Sergey Lapin. Roth-Ey characterizes television in the Lapin era as a kind of court TV to the Kremlin, with Lapin as chief courtier.[18] Lapin's TV issued a special address to politically important viewers in their homes. Brezhnev's house had two TV sets: a Soviet model for Brezhnev and his wife, and a Japanese model with a VCR for the younger generations.[19] By contrast, as almost all of my interviewees told me, it was common knowledge in Hungarian Television that party secretary János Kádár did not watch TV at all.[20] Given his enormous political clout, Kádár's own cultural snobbery had a trickle-down effect, which allowed the head of television, almost invariably a sophisticated professional rather than an apparatchik, to make important programming and personnel decisions without party involvement.

In yet another telling case, in the 1970s Romanian dictator Nicolae Ceaușescu created a hospitable environment for importing entertaining U.S. series in order to demonstrate his independence from the Soviet Union and to gain favor with the West. In the 1980s, however, as his reign turned increasingly megalomaniac, he reduced television broadcasting to a few hours a week, which were all about himself and his family. This version of court TV was not simply made *for* the royal family; the family was virtually the only content.[21] Erich Honecker, secretary of the East German Socialist United Party (SED), also single-handedly redefined television and redirected its history when he famously diagnosed "a certain boredom" around television and urged its leaders to create "good entertainment" at the Eighth Congress of the SED in 1971. As a result, the SED folded entertainment into its ideology as an important condition for reproducing labor and raising intellectually active individuals.[22]

Far from being just amusing anecdotes, these stories demonstrate the confusion television caused in the attitudes of the highest decision makers. They had to reconcile the political role of TV as a massive potential instrument of centralized control with the private and emotional relationship they themselves had with TV. This dual function had a direct effect on how television operated in socialist countries. Part of the political establishments' and more prestigious cultural institutions' hostility was fear of competition. As early as 1951, the Soviet Ministry of Cinematography lobbied the communist party to ban feature films on TV to prevent the loss of ticket sales at the movies. Theaters also tried to limit broadcast access to performances. Both efforts were unsuccessful, but the hierarchy remained in place.[23]

At the same time, top-down hostility and confusion actually sustained television's bottom-up momentum throughout the socialist period, giving viewers some leverage in defining the medium's development. Television's cultural stigma and subsequent low pay also allowed for laboratories of innovation to be formed, where the first creative professionals could invent television in a trial and error of jobs, technologies, and genres. This environment attracted young people who cared less about prestige than about new challenges. My interviews with Hungarian television professionals resonate with findings in other countries that television was an exciting place to work,[24] fueled by camaraderie, enthusiasm, and a sense of genuine collaboration, which spilled out into lasting friendships outside of work.[25]

Surprise 2: Undiscovered Socialist Audiences

Recovering television from the shadow cast by intellectual snobbery and political confusion throws into question the enduring and near-exclusive attention to (dissident) literature, film, and samizdat journalism that has dominated academic approaches to socialist cultures. Television offers an alternative view, from the vantage point of everyday practices of socialism. These practices were motivated by discourses and desires that considerably muddy the entrenched idea of the binary opposition between official party-led cultures and dissident intellectual cultures. In fact, neither of these camps cared much about audiences. The real target audiences of art films and high literature were other dissident intellectuals and educated, left-leaning Western publics. By contrast, television could not be made to function without actual viewers.

Determining what these viewers wanted or even watched is crucial to understanding socialist television and socialism through the lens of television. It is not an easy task, however. The scarcity and unreliability of both viewing data and viewer memories are obvious obstacles. Most socialist television industries established more or less developed audience research arms by the late 1960s. This was a vast improvement from counting viewer letters, let alone weighing the mailbag, which was the preferred method of measuring audience interest in early Soviet television.[26] But even empirical, survey-based audience research remained somewhat unreliable. In the Soviet Union, the surveys were often face-to-face rather than anonymous and contained leading questions.[27] This was not a Soviet specificity: while Western European public broadcasters were more invested in audience research since they had to justify their public support, their surveys also often created an aspirational, static, and passive national audience.[28]

Another central and often overlooked problem is that the top-down confusion about the function and cultural value of television was also internalized by its viewers. Viewer letters to national broadcasters express a clear preference for entertaining programming such as quiz shows, pop music, comedy, and drama serials from the beginning. At the same time, interviews and personal conversations consistently reveal a gap between what people liked about socialist TV and what they thought they were supposed to like. Let me evoke just one of these conversations to illustrate a recurring pattern. On a recent flight I sat next to an elderly couple, both architects, who had left Hungary and settled in Southern California in the early 1980s. When I asked them about their favorite memories of socialist television (as has become my habit), they eagerly recognized some of the entertaining programs I mentioned but made sure to point out to me how excellent socialist TV's live broadcasts of classical music concerts were. Then, without missing a beat, they proceeded to rave about their current favorites: *Homeland, Shark Tank, Dancing with the Stars*, and *The Bachelor*. While the couple's old Hungarian selves censored their pleasure in popular genres, they had no trouble enjoying a range of popular television programs as Americanized immigrants within the less hierarchical taste culture of the United States. This split consciousness was so naturalized that they were utterly unaware of it—a paradigmatic example of the cultural conditioning of status conferred by television taste.

The experience echoed a familiar contradiction in the insistence of a number of postsocialist viewers that they did not watch television or even that no one watched television during socialism. This of course is squarely contradicted by viewer letters and by socialist television's well-documented struggle to meet viewer demand for popular programming, as I discuss throughout the chapters ahead. It is also undermined by the onslaught of postsocialist nostalgia for socialist popular programming, which I address in chapters 7, 8, and 10.

Surprise 3: Socialist TV's Transnational History

Broadcast television around the world has had an unparalleled capacity to gather the nation-family around the proverbial fireplace. Television under state socialism was no exception. There is no doubt that the only way to do justice to its history is by understanding the intimate cultural clues and affective bonds it wove among national citizens over time. At the same time, one of my missions here is to resist the power of the national to monopolize emerging histories, and to refuse to yield these entirely to the institutional influence of nation-states.[29] As I argued earlier, the momentum around studying television as a way to access real-life socialism is an opportunity to reconsider the Cold War as more than the binary struggle between the two superpowers and the nation-states in their satellite systems. Socialist elite cultures formed around literature, theater, and film have been almost exclusively wrapped up in the bipolar model and adopted its dominant nation-based worldview. This approach internalizes and confirms the assumptions of marginal nationalisms: intellectual leaders rightly speak for and unite the population in opposition to the oppressive political regime. Such a model leaves unrepresentable subnational and transnational affiliations that would disrupt this alignment. It also gravely distorts the histories of socialist television. It ignores the fact that television industries under Soviet influence developed in simultaneity and interaction with those in Western Europe and beyond. Sylwia Szostak shows that socialist TV has followed John Ellis's three-stage chronology, from the postwar era of scarcity through the 1960s-1970s era of availability to the era of plenty since the 1980s, only with a slight delay in the latest phase.[30] Charlotte Brunsdon's adaptation to European broadcast television of Raymond Williams's periodization from emergent through dominant to residual cultures also applies to television in the East.[31]

Television was first introduced in most countries of the region in the prewar period, in step with the United States and Western Europe. Small-scale state television broadcasting began in the interwar years.[32] World War II and its aftermath, involving the political and economic restructuring of the Soviet sphere of influence, interrupted the development of television infrastructures. State broadcasting did not start up again until the 1950s. It began, for the most part, with sporadic broadcasts received by a few thousand subscribers in each country. Regional cooperation began almost immediately. The first program exchange, a 1957 Hungarian initiative named Intervision, included Czechoslovakia, Poland, the German Democratic Republic (GDR), and Hungary.[33] In comparison, postwar British and French television continued prewar experiments and began limited service in 1945–1946. Radiotelevisione Italiana (RAI) began service in 1952, Danish and Belgian broadcasting in 1953, Spain in 1956, Sweden and Portugal in 1957, Finland in 1958, Norway in 1960, Switzerland in 1958, Ireland in 1961, Gibraltar and Malta in 1962, and Greece in 1966.[34]

Much like elsewhere in Europe, by the 1960s the proliferation of television sets in the home and the quality and quantity of programming transformed socialist television into a truly national form of entertainment. In Hungary, where regular broadcasting began in 1957, the number of programming hours a week jumped from twenty-two to forty between 1960 and 1965.[35] The Slovene broadcaster, Television Ljubljana, started transmitting its own television programming in 1958, with seven to eight hundred television sets in Slovenia and about four thousand in all of Yugoslavia, compared with 90 percent of all homes in the United States at the same time.[36] In Czechoslovakia, where the war also interrupted prewar experimental broadcasts, trial public broadcasts began in 1953. The rapid increase in television access in the 1960s played a central role in the liberalization of the country's political climate. This liberalization was arrested following the Prague Spring of 1968, which was brutally crushed by the Soviet Union.[37] Television Romania was established in 1956 and added a second channel in 1968. This was then suspended in 1985 due to dictator Ceaușescu's energy-saving program until after 1989.[38] In most countries, however, the mid-1960s saw the launch of a second channel and the extension of broadcast time to five, then six, and eventually seven days a week.

By the mid-1960s, all Soviet satellite governments faced a pressure to revise their ideological positions and programming policies to adjust to the opportunities and challenges presented by the new home-based mass medium. The launch of communication satellites, beginning with *Sputnik 1* in 1957, the first Earth-orbiting artificial satellite and a key component of the Soviet space and communication strategy, increased the regimes' fear over their populations' access to Western programming. This challenge could only be minimized by rechanneling desires for capitalist lifestyles toward fostering national cohesion on the party leadership's terms. Socialist governments therefore revisited their import policy and began a strategic domestic production of scripted programming in the 1960s. Much like in Western Europe, the first postwar broadcasts produced in socialist Eastern Europe were of live theatrical and sports events, as well as news programming, feature films, and a range of educational cultural programming. As I discuss in chapters 2, 3, and 4, similar to Western European public broadcasting, television's shift to the center of public culture in the 1960s allowed socialist governments to expand and solidify their educational-propaganda directives by wrapping those in increasingly entertaining forms.

The ideological goals behind the new programming policy had to be carefully formulated lest they undermine a regionally coordinated vision of socialist utopia. Media and communication reforms in the 1960s therefore focused on television as the main institution for implanting socialist democratic values within entertainment. Television had to provide carefully selected information. It also had to shape citizens' tastes so they understand and value Eurocentric art and culture and resist what were widely perceived as the detrimental effects of television: reducing appreciation for cultural quality as well as general mental and physical laziness.[39]

The greatest political risk involved in the expansion of television broadcasting was that, unlike feature films or print publications, broadcast signals could not be confined to state borders. Inhabitants of large regions in Yugoslavia, East Germany, Czechoslovakia, Hungary, and Albania received either Austrian, Italian, or West German programming. Shared TV signals had the most profound effect in East Germany, where viewers—with the exception of the "Valley of the Clueless" near Dresden, where foreign signals did not reach—were able to view West German broadcasting in a shared language, often specially directed at East German viewers. But border-crossing signals literally disrupted communism even in the most isolated corners of the communist empire. In Enver Hoxha's Albania, while the communist elite retained the privilege to watch foreign broadcasts in the 1960s, the brief liberal period of the early 1970s removed restrictions on consuming foreign (Italian) TV. By 1973, the party leadership realized that the pleasures of Italian programs enchanted Albanian populations rather than demonized capitalism, so they launched a campaign against foreign liberalism and installed signal jammers. However, much like everywhere else, these proved ineffective, especially in border areas where one did not need antennae to receive signals.[40]

In a similar vein, TV-deprived Romanians took advantage of the overspill of terrestrial broadcast signals to watch more liberalized Hungarian, Bulgarian, and Yugoslav programming in the 1970s and 1980s.[41] This was a means to escape the isolation and deprivation imposed by the Ceaușescu regime. Annemarie Sorescu-Marinkovic's ethnographic research, conducted in the Banat region (bordering Yugoslavia and Hungary), shows that it was not only the significant bilingual and trilingual populations who watched foreign TV. Romanian viewers went through the trouble of learning foreign languages just to access a slice of the outside world. Ironically, the nationalistic restriction on bodily mobility across borders motivated a TV-mediated flow of exchange that re-created, at least virtually, the multilingual, multiethnic culture of the region during the Habsburg Empire and before.[42]

Romanian viewers' reactions to Yugoslav and Hungarian TV echo Annika Lepp and Mervi Pantti's interviews with Estonian viewers, who were fixated on Finnish programming in the 1970s and 1980s, after the Finnish broadcaster YLE built a new TV broadcast transmitter in Espoo, which brought Finnish TV to households in northern Estonia. Even though only two Finnish public broadcast channels existed during this period, these carried American and Western European series. This opportunity even created a weekend "TV tourism" from other parts of Estonia to the northern areas so fans could follow their favorite serials. Many people who lived in the north were also able to learn the Finnish language from TV, which immediately conferred cultural capital that could be converted into economic capital as trade with Finland expanded in the 1980s and 1990s.[43] Television thus facilitated cultural identification with Nordic Europe, reestablishing the Baltic region's older imperial ties with Scandinavia in a quest for independence from the Soviet Empire.

As I discuss in more detail in chapter 8, the commercials Eastern viewers watched on Western TV held a particular attraction and whipped up desire for greener consumer pastures. But state socialist televisions also had their own more or less developed commercial departments. Television advertising in the most liberal socialist economies was embedded in an extensive set of commercial activities. At the most liberal extreme,

Slovenian TV Ljubljana and Croatian TV Zagreb established an official cooperation with the Italian RAI in the early 1960s. This happened despite protests from communist party authorities, who were anxious about the influx of Western news programs and the consumerist values transmitted by fictional programming.[44] Significantly, such unprecedented openness toward Western-type entertainment was finally approved because it strengthened the national leadership's own strategy of championing Slovenian national autonomy against the encroachment of Yugoslavian federalism, which was pushed by the Yugoslav state broadcaster RTV.[45]

Sabina Mihelj even speculates that, in some ways, the televisions of the member states of Yugoslavia, particularly of Slovenia, were more commercially oriented than some Western European public broadcasters.[46] Yugoslavia's relative ideological independence from the Warsaw Pact under Josip Broz Tito's leadership opened up greater financial independence for media elites in exchange for supplementing decreasing state revenue. As early as 1968, 20.8 percent of Slovenian Ljubljana TV's revenue came from advertising. While this represented the most market-oriented variant, supplementing state support with increasing commercial revenue was common practice among socialist broadcasters in the East. Hungarian TV and Radio established its joint marketing department in 1968 and engaged in extensive domestic and international marketing activities, including its participation in the European Group of Television Advertising (EGTA), as I discuss in chapter 8.

The interconnectedness of television systems across the Iron Curtain was not limited to simultaneous development but was also ensured by ongoing exchanges from the start.[47] As Jonathan Bignell and Andreas Fickers write in the introduction to their important edited collection *A European Television History*, international cooperations, while more densely woven among Western countries, also included the East. The cross-border nature of radio waves enabled the launch of international, nongovernmental broadcasting institutions such as the International Broadcasting Union (IBU, founded in 1925), the European Broadcasting Union (EBU, 1950), and the Organisation Internationale de Radiodiffusion et de Télévision (OIRT, 1946), which became the dedicated "eastern" network.[48]

European cooperation was first necessitated by technical issues: before World War II, there were different technical standards for the number of lines and images per second as a way to protect the national industries of TV set makers.[49] The IBU was created to regulate international broadcasting but was broken up after the war due partly to the abuse of its technical facilities by the German army and partly to competition with the OIRT, which was founded by Soviet proposition. The EBU was established in reaction to the OIRT in an effort led by the BBC to form a union for Western European broadcasters. The EBU initially consisted of twenty-three broadcasters but soon expanded to include some Mediterranean and Middle Eastern companies. The OIRT and the EBU finally merged in 1993 under the goal of developing a shared European consciousness.[50]

While the Cold War did split the continent's television industries into two networks, the channels between these remained open to traffic, which was facilitated by television diplomacy conducted by executives and creatives alike. Finland, balanced between Eastern and Western interests, was a member of both the EBU and the OIRT.[51] After Finland (1965), Mongolia joined the OIRT in 1972, Cuba in 1979, and Afghanistan and Vietnam in 1982. Collaboration between the two networks became increasingly active as the Cold War thawed: the first discussion of exchanges happened in 1956; the first Eurovision-Intervision transmission, of the Rome Olympics, in 1960.[52] Program exchanges were particularly extensive in children's television, where Eastern European broadcasters made a very significant although rarely acknowledged contribution.[53] The program exchanges ensured that most of Europe was watching many of the same programs, often simultaneously. The dual system of broadcasting was adopted in most EBU countries by the 1980s. This was not even the case for all capitalist countries. Greece allowed private television to exist only in 1989, the year the Cold War officially ended.[54]

A shared socialist ethos of public service broadcasting (PSB) permeated these exchanges, based on a common European ethical and ideological ground that reaches back to the pre–Cold War era. The main features, successes, and difficulties of PSB have been a common denominator across all of these television cultures: the government-led mission to inform and educate while promoting nationalism, which has always been challenged by the imperative to entertain,[55] as well as the nationalistic cultural hierarchy that assigned low value to television.[56]

As Bignell and Fickers explain, the identity of TV was defined already in the 1930s and crystallized around what was to become a shared European public broadcasting mission at the broadcasting technology exhibits of the 1937 World's Fair in Paris. A clear difference emerged in how American and European televisions marked out their future ethos, however. In the European version, spearheaded by German discourse, nation and education already appeared as key terms, in clear distinction from commercialization and entertainment, which characterized U.S. discourses around television.[57] As Bignell and Fickers sum up, "The dominance of the public service concept of broadcasting in the European context and the commercial patterns in the US shaped hegemonic narrations of television on each side of the Atlantic. The World's Fairs in Paris and New York both created and represented alternative symbolic frameworks in which television as a revolutionary technology and a new mass medium was presented. They were two windows giving a slightly different view of the new electronic 'window on the world.'"[58]

Bignell and Fickers offer a valuable model and methodology to write European TV history comparatively, transnationally, and collaboratively. Yet, even they treat the other Europe as a mere addition, confirming its status as the Cold War mystery land out of sync with European history. Their otherwise very thorough introduction includes only a few paragraphs about Eastern Europe, which reiterate blanket assumptions about the region: TV and other media institutions were closely controlled by Soviet-influenced governments until 1989; regional program exchange remained within and restricted to the COMECON bloc; and the function of television was to publicize decisions made by the ruling party, to educate the population, and to establish a channel of communication between the party and the people.[59] The editors do include a disclaimer for reducing Europe to Western Europe, pointing to the scarcity of TV historians in Eastern Europe. Indeed, of the twenty-nine contributing authors, only two are from and write about the former East.[60]

It is important to ask why the trend continues to reaffirm the essential Cold War difference between East and West. Why is it that even in otherwise progressive and pioneering projects such as *A European Television History*, in which the editors consciously set out to think about European TV transnationally, one comes across statements like this: "In most Western European countries, television developed into a medium for the propagation of consumption, leisure and individualism; in the Eastern countries, it became a medium for the political socialization of the individual and the subtle implementation of ideology and political values."[61] As I show in the following chapters, one could safely switch East and West and the statement would be just as true. There is no evidence to support such a polarized distinction.

Not only did television under socialism generally operate in a liberalized fashion, with little or no censorship—apart from extreme cases and periods of dictatorship, as in Ceaușescu's Romania—tight state control and censorship also characterized periods of Western European broadcasting. As Bignell and Fickers themselves argue, the Nazi government in Germany was interested in the propaganda value of television, partly to compete with large U.S. corporations. The 1936 Berlin Olympics were a stimulus to the development of German TV, with viewing rooms established in cities to hold audiences as large as four hundred.[62] Television was formed under military dictatorship in Greece in 1967, and the second channel remained under direct army control until 1982. Throughout this period, the government censored all programs, particularly news. Key TV personnel were selected based on their ideological conformity. Even the French government monitored and censored TV programs from the 1950s onward. Under Charles de Gaulle, this was direct political control, impacting every type of program, which also provoked direct resistance during the 1968 strikes, when some TV staff resigned rather than agreeing to submit scripts ahead of time.[63]

Using television as an instrument of positive propaganda also united eastern and western broadcasters around educational initiatives—first to promote literacy in rural regions and then to educate the population about a wide range of subjects, as I discuss in chapter 2. Most often, propaganda took very subtle forms in the East, not unlike it did in the West. In the chapters on socialist and postsocialist domestic drama serials (chapters 9 and 10), I explain that, by the 1970s, dramatic programming was recognized as a much more hospitable and effective place for affirming the regimes' cultural and political directives than the news and other factual programming, which were hardly taken seriously by the public. The last two chapters (chapters 11 and 12) show that even humor and comedy, which were ostensibly charged with antiregime criticism, can be seen as a strategically tolerated expression that co-opted both artists and audiences and served the parties' interests.

The Future of Socialist TV Studies

Thankfully, work on socialist TV histories is no longer in short supply. In fact, those of us researching socialism and television now face the opposite problem: there is too much new material to process and incorporate for any single project. This is a delightful problem to have. Instead of gatekeeping and competition, it has given rise to some highly productive collaborations, which unapologetically crisscross Eastern and Western Europe, North America, and other postsocialist locations in an expanding network dedicated to mapping the global history of socialist TV.[64] The emerging work on the history of socialist TV has been effectively removing the Cold War lens that has occluded alternative histories of European television. Instead of a clear-cut East-West divide, we see various local and regional patterns defined by cultural and political-economic similarities and differences. A much more important difference emerges between what Bourdon et al. call the "courteous" European model that reigned through the 1980s and the "competitive" Americanized model that challenged European broadcasters to shift to a dual broadcasting mode in a commercial, multichannel, deregulated global environment.[65] In this alternative historical view, Eastern European broadcasters were simply a little slower to join the competitive model than Western European ones. But competition always underscored their operation, as I explain in chapter 4. During nominal state monopoly, states always had to compete for eyeballs distracted by foreign broadcasts and, from the late 1980s, against satellite programming. In addition, state broadcasters were compelled continually to increase the volume of imports to fill schedules on state channels.[66]

As I emphasize in every chapter that follows, no technical innovation, program, or policy can be isolated from its regional, European, and global context. While national histories do need to be written and remain crucial resources, I focus attention on patterns that stretch across national borders and defy common assumptions about the story and the potential of both socialism and television. This work can only be accomplished collectively. In researching this book, I have relied heavily on the labor of others who have browsed national archives, discovered and commented on old programs, and theorized about socialism and television. The conclusion that jumps out from virtually all this recent work is that the story of blind adherence to ideological dogma has been a Cold War construction from the beginning. Through the window that television opens, we see more or less desperate, often belated attempts at top-down control, constantly tempered by other, often openly unspeakable imperatives that these societies absorbed and negotiated, such as the actual needs of viewers to be entertained, educated, and invited to consume, the role of competition as a sustaining force in socialism, and experiments with various realist aesthetics in an effort to construct and convey authenticity.

But this book is not simply about correcting the record. The suggestion is that the history of existing socialism should not be thrown out with the tepid bathwater left over from the Cold War. Socialism is a globally shared legacy. If we forfeit this story to Cold War stereotypes, we also enable the naturalization of neoliberalism as an economic logic that does not have alternatives. Since the inevitability of this logic tends to be justified in cultural forms, these alternative histories are especially important to revisit, particularly in a crisis-ridden Europe, which has been rearranging itself into a new "Cold War" between the core and periphery of the Eurozone, between "surplus" nations and the perpetually debt-ridden ones. The hybrid formations that socialist TV reveals are worth revisiting because, as Daphne Berdahl argues, socialism continues to have an active social life within postsocialism. Postrevolutionary societies, she suggests, make visible cracks and contradictions within neoliberal capitalism, especially if one "eavesdrops on the anxieties" to be heard in such places. I argue that socialist and postsocialist television magnifies these cracks and anxieties. Berdahl expands on anthropologist Katherine Verdery's idea that postsocialism's emerging forms should be assessed within the international context of global capital flows. Berdahl adds "that it also works the other way around: Postsocialism's 'emerging forms' provide a means of assessing and critiquing global capitalism."[67]

Conceptual Organization

Rather than geographical coverage or chronological ordering, the logic of broadly conceived genres is crossed with the guiding force of key concepts. Like TV genres, these concepts connect the two world systems in surprising ways and offer additional platforms for comparison and historical revision: *competition, consumption, emotion, realism, history, memory, nostalgia, gender and (post)feminism, education, entertainment, humor,* and *satire* were not only compatible with socialism; viewed through the grids of television, they are also able to unhinge and modify our view of socialism. While these notions travel through the chapters, there are also dedicated points where I unwrap their specific historical and theoretical significance in relation to the generic forms discussed.

PART I: GENRES OF REALISM AND REALITY

This bulkiest part is dedicated to examining program types that prioritize *realism* as a representational tool to advance the ideological tenets of socialism in an *educational* fashion, modeled after the European public service broadcasting agenda. It includes an introductory chapter and four others that discuss four different "realistic" program types, all of which developed and functioned in a European and global circulation: straightforward educational programs, public affairs and documentary shows, crime appeal programs, and quiz/game shows. The progression through the chapters is from the most to the least ideologically strict genres, from the tightest centralized control to the most audience involvement.

PART II: GENRES OF HISTORY

The three chapters in part II examine socialist and postsocialist television's intricate relationship to *history, memory,* and *nostalgia*. In chapter 6, this relationship is extracted from the historical drama and adventure series, a staple of the 1950s and 1960s. Chapter 7 explores the postsocialist explosion of nostalgia around television, while chapter 8 takes on the nostalgia around late socialist commercials in particular to shed light on the contradictory temporal relationship between socialism and postsocialism.

PART III: GENRES OF FICTION

These two chapters unfold the connections among *gender, consumerism,* and television. These connections are most explicit in dramatic programming, which had come to occupy increasing airtime by the 1970s. Chapter 9 surveys how women were positioned and positioned themselves as television professionals and viewers, particularly in relation to programs that specifically addressed them. Chapter 10 discusses how late socialist soap operas interpellated women to be superwomen who can do it all with no reward other than pride. The chapter tracks several of these serials through to their postsocialist remakes and reruns to show how they facilitated the spread of normative *postfeminist* ideas.

PART IV: GENRES OF HUMOR

The final two chapters bring to the forefront socialist and postsocialist manifestations of television comedy, particularly satirical political humor. The chapters show that, far from being the grim, allegorical cultural landscape associated with Eastern European art films, television incorporated and cultivated presocialist cabaret, a comic form of performance that developed in fairly specific ways in the region. Cabaret perpetuated not only political humor but also bourgeois entertainment within the socialist mass medium. In the last chapter I explore the analogy between the performative, self-justifying forms and ironic sensibilities of late socialist TV satire and contemporary, late capitalist comedy news.

Disclaimer

This book was not easy to write. My scholarly focus was hijacked over and over again by the affective charge of revisiting Hungarian television from the 1970s and 1980s, which was part and parcel of my upbringing. This emotional recall was different from my relationship to the TV of the 1950s and 1960s, which I inherited, and that of the 1990s and 2000s, which I followed from a distance for the most part. The power of nostalgia took me by surprise. At every turn, I was drawn powerfully to videos posted online by former viewers like myself, which led to other irresistible clips and made me laugh, cry, and, yes, sing out loud. Newspaper articles from the 1970s and 1980s automatically triggered a complex memory of specific programs viscerally embedded in their contexts of watching, the centralized rhythm of the socialist family's dysfunctional life in a tiny apartment, the Russian barracks opposite the standardized yet comforting architecture of the housing complex, the single school and grocery store where the neighborhood converged, and other enfolding environments, which were all linked by the fiber of these programs. It was strange to sift through a random database of digitalized traces of this old world, intimately close but registering with me as if they were someone else's memories in a different life, sandwiched among kitten videos and prefaced by commercials for things strikingly contemporary and American.

The power of nostalgia permeates this book, and without it, the book would be different. It would not be less authentic; but *TV Socialism* bears the mark of having been written by someone who carries the bittersweet burden of the memory of really existing socialism in her very cells. I have decided not to exile the trace of nostalgia into some kind of private realm, since I want to conjure up socialist TV in its effects, interactions, and continued life in people's memories. I do not want to cover up the visceral experience with academic jargon and theory. After all, there is a good reason why, paradoxically, there is so much nostalgia attached to television as the most authentic resource on socialism. Because viewer surveys and official party assessments are not only tucked away in archives but were also doctored to feed the undying spirit of socialist optimism, more "authentic" memories of socialism are paradoxically preserved in the shared *emotions* evoked by socialist TV. This emotional recall opens up a less quantifiable but all the more precious window into the surprising pleasures and contradictions of socialism.

I • GENRES OF REALISM AND REALITY

1 From Socialist Realism to Emotional Realism

Socialist Realism, Socialist Realities

We tend to think about reality-based TV programs as recent phenomena. In the considerable amount of academic writing on the subject, reality TV is generally discussed as the joint result of economic and ideological forces that have become dominant since the late 1980s: the increasing global integration of media, which favors the exchange of cheap television formats that can be customized to suit different national environments; and reality formats' structural and moral alignment with the discourses that underscore neoliberal policies of deregulation, privatization, the weakening of state institutions, and the strengthening of corporations. Makeover and competition formats, in particular, didactically demonstrate how to help oneself in a cutthroat competition for the survival of the fittest, whether the backdrop is an exotic island, the workplace, the bridal salon, the weight room, or the living room. In the process, such formats naturalize the fraying of the social net and point the finger at individuals for their own failure.

Reality series are inexpensive to produce. But "cheap" is also how most of us tend to think about their cultural value, even if we happen to be avid fans. With their predictable narrative script, celebration of middle-class values and mediocrity, and tear-jerking display of sentimentality, they are generally considered the bottom of the television barrel—in contrast with "quality" fictional programs produced by HBO, Showtime, or the BBC.

Of course reality formats did not just burst onto the scene in 1992 following MTV's show *The Real World*. *The Real World* itself, often credited as the first reality program, was inspired by *An American Family*, a 1973 PBS documentary series about the everyday life of the Loud family in Santa Barbara, California. A similar program titled simply *The Family* was produced in twelve parts by BBC One in 1974 and was recently remade for Channel 4. While these predecessors grew out of the very different ethical ground of public service broadcasting, they share with contemporary reality formats a fascination with documenting real life in a fly-on-the-wall, unscripted fashion.

Television under Soviet socialism followed Western European broadcasters' commitment to realism and the ethos of public service. In addition, Soviet and Western European versions of socialism both drew on the values of cultural nationalism and a top-down intention to educate and enlighten all social classes. The differences were less evident in the principles than in the degree of dogmatism with which they were put into televisual practice. More precisely, while the letter of Marxist-Leninist imperatives continued to be rigidly repeated in the Soviet-controlled region into the 1980s, its spirit operated much more closely to the ideological principles of Western European socialist democracies. This discrepancy between letter and spirit enacted an ongoing, performative repetition of the socialist order in the East. In and on television, the discrepancy was particularly striking. The more elitist, austere, realistic, and educational television attempted to be, the more it was mocked and abandoned by viewers, who wanted fiction, humor, and entertainment. In essence, Eastern European socialist TV reproduced in more pure form and preserved well into the 1980s the educational principles and realistic aesthetic that Western European public broadcasters gradually abandoned under pressure from competition with commercial broadcasters.

This is why, in analyzing the popular "ghosts" that have haunted European public service broadcasting, such as game shows, stars, seriality, audience ratings, the influence of U.S. television, and voyeurism, Jerôme Bourdon speculates that much of his analysis can be applied to Eastern Europe—as well as to public service TV in some developing countries.[1] I argue throughout this book that this is the case. But this first part provides the most substantial proof as it takes up the genres most closely associated with public service, which also happened to be in the center of socialist programming. These are genres that valued politically committed documentary realism above fictional representations. The aesthetic of socialist realism they adopted was supposed to support an overarching educational intention to teach viewers how to be good socialist citizens. This pairing of realist aesthetic with pedagogical intent is not unlike the self-professed profile of contemporary reality programs. The difference is that the latter are in the business of neoliberal citizenship education, as the channel brand TLC (formerly The Learning Channel) encapsulates. They teach us how to behave, dress, build, decorate, raise children, lose weight, and gain confidence. Much of postwar European public television was meant to teach its viewers how to read and write; to understand math, physics, and geography; and to appreciate fine national and European literature, film, and music, and Marxist-Leninist philosophical principles. But it also offered a broader educational program in how to raise children and navigate legal issues, in cooking, sewing, gardening, agricultural work, mining, and operating heavy machinery. It was anything but cheap in its intentions. It was driven by noble initiatives to democratize access to education, to create a level playing field among people of different class and educational backgrounds, and to socialize the individual as always primarily a community member. In this regard it was the opposite of contemporary reality shows, which isolate the individual and teach the virtues of self-help. Socialist television's contribution to the prehistory of reality-based programming is not only significant in itself but also offers a critical counterdiscourse to reality TV's ideological presumptions and academic assessments.

The prevalence of such programs on socialist TV is not a surprise: realism was the preferred aesthetic delivery channel of Marxist-Leninist ideologies in the Soviet-controlled region. However, to dismiss socialist TV's realist genres as mere propaganda devices not worthy of serious analysis would be hasty. First of all, as a mass medium charged with fostering national cohesion, much of television is didactic. What distinguished socialist television's approach was that it did not make any secret of its didactic intentions. It was supervised by government departments that had the words "agitation" and "propaganda" in their names, after all, even if these terms did not quite carry the nefarious connotations they have taken on in English.

But television, perhaps more than any other socialist institution, fell short of controlling the relay between the leadership and the citizenry. As I show in the accounts of realist-educational genres that follow in the next four chapters, the relay often worked the other way around: the leadership played catch-up with the citizenry, for whom the logic and capacities of television as a medium were much less mysterious. As a result, the rigid, aspirational aesthetic codes of socialist realism that one associates with giant Lenin statues, public paintings of robust peasant youth, and films about self-righteous factory workers denouncing capitalism never really took root in television. This was partly because television entered the scene in the late 1950s and rose to mass-medium status only in the 1960s. By then the postwar Stalinist purges were over and communism began to mellow into centralized socialism in most countries. The thaw rendered the cheery didacto-fictions of the 1950s laughable. Television, as a home-based medium, provided an outlet for this shared mockery from the start. Its relatively privatized reception greatly contributed to the confusion among socialist party leaders about television's mission, effects, and future directions. While the party leadership made TV an increasingly crucial piece of its cultural policies by the 1970s, once those policies translated into programs that became embedded in citizens' daily lives, their effects and interpretations proved elusive to control. Instead, television turned its antennae toward hybrid influences, including foreign ones, and foregrounded the very internal contradictions of the official ideology and rhetoric.

One of the most confusing points was socialist realism itself. Realism was both an essential principle and a stumbling block for TV. The official Marxist-Leninist worldview presumed and prescribed a clear-cut relationship between what John Corner distinguishes as "thematic realism" and "formal realism." Thematic realism is the relationship between a program's content and reality. Formal realism is the program's way of achieving "real-seemingness" through representation.[2] This mediation is something socialist ideology had to downplay, since Marxist materialism considered reality to be objectively preexistent. Corner introduces this distinction because in British television studies, while realism had come to be regarded as television's central aesthetic and social project, its use has also remained ungrounded and confusing. This is because any notion of realism, whether it is a project of verisimilitude or of reference to the real, is based on a normative construction of "the real," whose existence is "disputable independently of any media representation."[3]

Marxism presumed the existence of material reality and assigned representation a mirroring, rather than performative, re-presenting role. Idealist philosophies, while not banned, were taught to be simply wrong. The system's great seduction lay precisely in holding out the promise that it possessed historical truth and placed everyone on the road to its fulfillment, the perfect society. However, life under socialism was a far cry from this eventual good life. By the 1960s, as the grand promise appeared to be further and further delayed and as communist parties continually redirected and adjusted their truth-seeking ideologies to match the reality of economic lag and deficit of political trust, the gap between public Marxist rhetoric and its private translations grew increasingly wide. This is the gap in which television quietly performed its work of ideological fermentation. By the mid-1960s, socialist parties began to grab onto the new mass medium as a vehicle around which to consolidate their dwindling legitimacy. Because of its ability to link the private and the public spheres, television became an experimental kitchen in which to adjust the recipe for making an ideal, then an adequate, then at least a livable socialist society. The economic contours of this society resembled capitalism more and more with each reform, while holding on to the social protections and nationalistic cultural leanings typical of Western European socialist democracies.

Realism became a flexible ideological and aesthetic instrument in the course of these adjustments. While factual programming that "mirrored" reality such as news shows and documentary programs enjoyed priority and higher cultural value than fiction, most of it also contained an element of utopianism. Instead of depicting life as it was, factual programs shifted the emphasis to teaching citizens how to behave in an ideal socialist society. "Reality" thus functioned in two inseparable dimensions: the present as it looked and as it should look. The two dimensions were inextricably linked by television's educational mission.

Given the fundamental ideological primacy of the alliance among realism, socialism, and education, one could argue that all programming made by socialist state televisions falls under the umbrella of "genres of realism." In chapters 2, 3, and 4, I look at three particularly influential generic constellations around the preference for realism in factual television, all of which anticipate reality television in various ways. Chapter 5 offers a glimpse of the continuities and ruptures between socialist reality-based genres and postsocialist reality formats. I leave aside news reporting, which was most obviously and easily controlled.

"Not Yet": The Time of Educational Realism

In her wonderful history of Soviet television, Kristin Roth-Ey evokes Russian theorist Vladimir Sappak, who, in his book *Television and Us* (1962), argues that television should capture everyday reality in the spirit of Dziga Vertov's *kinopravda*. It should be not so much an instrument for staging reality but, rather, a force of democratization and truth.[4] In a way, television was romanticized and "futured," along with its imagined audience. The operative term about television's temporality was "not yet."

A survey of the rhetoric of periodical assessments of Hungarian television by party officials and television professionals alike foregrounds a common script in these decades. They issue the same wishful-thinking reports year after year, driven by principles that drifted farther and farther into the past of nostalgia as the future drifted into utopia: they take a self-boosting count of the many hours of broadcasting devoted to news, education, factual and current affairs programming, documentaries, theater broadcasts, historical teleplays, adaptations of literary classics, and program exchanges within the Soviet camp. They express some carefully worded reservations about the "tentative" approach to teaching social sciences on TV caused by the many "unresolved" historical questions and the "inadequate courage" of some TV professionals. They also note "divided opinions" about popular entertainment programs, whether imported crime series or home-produced pop music talent shows or humorous programs, which are often deemed to be "in bad taste." Then they propose plans for the future: to increase the level of political awareness and expand political education.[5] For instance, after the Tenth Annual Congress of the Hungarian Socialist Worker's Party, an article in the party newspaper states: "The hardest task for the leaders of our television is to find the right balance between providing cultural service and guiding the audience. Because this right balance has not yet emerged with reassuring certainty."[6] Or, a prominent critic writes in the journal *Rádió és TV Szemle* (Radio and TV Review), "Society does not yet prescribe the mandatory behavioral models and achievement levels in the sphere of entertainment as it does in the sphere of education and the acquisition of higher culture."[7]

The audience imagined by such assessments was always a bit disappointing: never quite sophisticated or enlightened enough, always falling slightly short of the standards marked out by high literature and art films, the true vehicles of aspirational Eastern European cultural nationalisms. The "not yet" paradigm ignored the fact that the majority of viewers preferred fictional and entertaining programming to tele-education according to audience surveys and letters. By the late 1960s, Eastern European socialist television broadcasters were fairly well established, provided at least six days of programming a week, in some countries introduced a second channel, and began to experiment with color. Socialist authorities tried to assert more control over television the more it was slipping away. This control manifested itself in the centralized planning of programming structures, directives for scientific research on television's effects, and efforts to fold television into the foundational mechanisms of a socialist society. The problem was that the ideological foundations were under continual reform along with the economic mechanisms. Particularly in Hungary, Czechoslovakia, Poland, and the rogue socialist country of Yugoslavia, the leadership gradually allowed capitalist features to mix in with centralized planning in the form of owning private property and small businesses, international travel, and competition on the global market.

Film and television were no exceptions to this. Increasingly throughout the 1970s and 1980s, programs were produced with international exhibitions and exports in mind. As media sociologist Tamás Szecskő wrote in 1971, while ideological control was increasingly tightened around the realist-educational television genres that were seen to be in support of socialism, fictional genres were often dismissed altogether as "just entertainment," not even deserving policy. These genres of entertainment were subject to the forces of the market, which increasingly impacted their consumption and distribution. Television was in the force field of conflicting influences from nationalistic policy and transnational markets, and it foregrounded socialist societies' characteristically stark division between mass and elite cultures.[8]

One of the main strategies socialist authorities employed for message control was precisely to insist on a line of separation between fictional and factual programming. While genres in both categories were designed to model socialist citizenship, there was a strict hierarchy between the two. The only exception to the low value assigned to TV fiction was art. But what qualified as art was also determined by ideological principles: although it did not have to be realistic, it was assumed to be educational, contributing to the central mission of "taste training." It had to demonstrate social commitment to the cause of the nation, to European high culture, and to the future of socialism—for instance, in the form of moralizing historical teleplays and theatrical broadcasts of European classics. As vice president of Hungarian TV and Radio Ferenc Pécsi put it in 1969, "TV is a journalistic institution; it is film, theater, and even school."[9]

This value hierarchy was so marked that, if one read television criticism from the 1960s and 1970s, one would hardly know nonfiction and nonartistic programming even existed—except for the occasional short piece lamenting the popularity of imported dramatic serials or expressing hope in the future results of taste education. This was an increasingly schizophrenic situation, where TV as public educational ideal and TV as it actually functioned in the living rooms were segregated.[10]

Educational Realism's Emotional Issue

The hierarchical segregation of factual and fictional programs was a way for socialist ideologues to block questions about the nature of reality's construction and to bracket invention, imagination, and representation as practices legitimate only in art, a privileged realm for artistic creators, distinct from that of television artisans and viewers. The preference for factual realism also implied a suspicion of emotion and performativity. To be sure, in this regard socialist TV was no different from Western European public service broadcasting, particularly after the latter's turn in the 1970s toward "progressive" documentary realism to oppose Hollywood's "regressive" realist pleasures.[11] Where Hollywood's realism represented a negative realism of form, progressive realism was supposed to emphasize realism of theme. As a canonical piece of progressive realism, John Corner mentions the four-part BBC drama *Days of Hope* (1975), which depicted historical and contemporary events within the British working class's politicized experience, a program not unlike many on socialist Eastern TV.

The intention to represent experiences formerly delegitimized or invisible, the concern with the romanticized working class and peasantry in particular, certainly linked Eastern and Western socialisms in the 1970s. This was most evident in the abundant Eastern European documentary film production,[12] much of which made its way across the Iron Curtain and was on regular offer on socialist television. However, this consciousness-raising documentary realism was always in tension with the private pleasures of television's emotional realism. This was a particular dilemma for socialist TV, fearful of uncontrolled, diffusive emotional mobilization. John Corner, looking for a proper way to capture television's relationship to realism, is doubtful that the age-old debate about what realism is or should be, much of which was adapted from cinema and other arts, is any use for television, except for the concept of *emotional realism*. Neither realism of form, attributed negatively to Hollywood, nor realism of theme, taken up by socially committed broadcasters East and West in the 1970s, captures television's relationship with realism nearly as well as the approach that centers on viewers' emotional engagement. Corner points to Ien Ang's study *Watching Dallas* to find at the core of television's address emotional realism, a "deep-level resonance with the emotional organization of the viewer," which connects text and experience.[13]

Socialism had a hard time with television's emotional realism. This is not to say that it neglected emotion. Christine Evans traces TV's reliance on emotional persuasion to early Soviet political and aesthetic theories. Lenin himself famously distinguished between *propaganda*, a way to convince through rational argumentation, and *agitation*, which mobilized affect. Using mass media to shape and monitor popular mood (*nastroenie*) was also crucial for Soviet authorities from 1917 onward. Stalin also attributed great importance to "mood" as a political objective essential to productivity in the short term and to building communism in the long term. Following Stalin's death, television became the primary instrument of perpetuating a cheerful, revolutionary mood.

By the late 1960s and 1970s of the political thaw, Soviet Central Television developed another, more complicated way of engaging emotion, which was in the service of the emerging concept of the "socialist way of life." This concept was defined by Leonid Brezhnev at the Twenty-Fifth Party Congress in 1976 as "an atmosphere of genuine collectivism and comradeship, solidarity, the friendship of all the nations and peoples of our country, which grows stronger from day to day, and moral health, which makes us strong and steadfast."[14] It embodied a new direction in Soviet ideology, away from failing economic competition with the West toward identifying a moral, spiritual, and emotional existence unique to socialism and superior to capitalism. This new form of emotional engagement was to break up the boredom and ineffectuality of formulaic news and documentary programs. It was to serve as a form of passionate counterpropaganda that would bring ordinary people and their stories of everyday heroism to the screen. Evans analyzes the popular Soviet program *Ot vsei dushi* (From the bottom of my heart), launched in 1972 and hosted by legendary female Central Television hostess Valentina Leont'eva, as the most evocative showcase of how television's emotional realism came to be deployed to represent the Soviet socialist way of life as a way of feeling: "The show's central purpose was to evoke emotions, on screen and

Valentina Leont'eva.

among viewers, and, most crucially, link those emotions with state myths and goals. The strategies the show used to accomplish these tasks, including creating a festive atmosphere, subjecting the featured community to intense surveillance both before and during the show, and relying on Leont'eva's own highly emotional performance, create strong continuities between late Soviet and post-Soviet cultural life in Russia."[15]

Ot vsei dushi, Evans adds, foreshadowed the explosion of talk and reality shows on post-Soviet television, several of which continued to feature highly emotional stories of past sacrifice and suffering in order to foster nationalism. The program developed a powerful format for Soviet ideology's "affective turn." It packaged propagandistic messages about the strength of the working class and the peasantry in the form of a live, semireligious traveling celebration, which was complete with sentimental music and imagery (close-ups, candles, pastoral scenes).[16]

While the mode of sentimentality was fairly specific to Soviet culture, this type of emotional variety show also functioned as a regional format

Hans-Georg Ponesky, host of *Mit dem Herzen dabei* (With open hearts).

for creating a new emotional TV realism. For instance, the 1960s East German variety show *Mit dem Herzen dabei* (With open hearts), produced by the Entertainment Desk, was a live, traveling variety show intended to "celebrate socialism" and "honor ordinary East Germans for embodying 'socialist' values such as hard work, devotion to *Heimat* and teaching children the value of *Familientreue*."[17] Like *Ot vsei dushi*, the show solicited audience involvement, from nominating coworkers and neighbors to an abundance of viewer feedback in the form of letters. Both programs relied on hidden cameras to surprise their unsuspecting protagonists, often showering them with prizes such as a new car or a vacation, in a way that was quite lavish for socialism and anticipated the manipulative reveals of reality shows to come. Heather Gumbert calls *Mit dem Herzen dabei* a utopian "spectacle that 'advertised' socialism."[18]

In a similar vein, Paulina Bren describes the post–1968 normalization period's televisual turn in Czechoslovakia in terms of pursuing "a more qualitative socialist lifestyle."[19] But Bren also characterizes this turn as part of a European and even global shift in the 1970s and 1980s toward moving the exercise of politics into the sphere of private relations. In Czechoslovakia, Hungary, Poland, and Yugoslavia, where the opposition to Soviet occupation and cultural colonization was most intense from the start, the affective turn within television's dominant realistic orientation took on less sentimental and more ironic and sarcastic tones. During the thaw, socialist parties in these countries consolidated their leadership on the platform of cultural nationalism, often in subtle opposition to the imperial Soviet regime. Television remained at odds with these nationalisms' inflated, Eurocentric intellectual superego and backward-looking temporal structure. While socialism fixated on the future, nationalism's origin and justification were always in the past: in the glory of national history, and in the undisputed achievements of national literature and other arts. But both nationalism and socialism addressed an allegedly homogeneous public perceived to be in need of high educational and taste standards. And both increasingly relied on emotion, rather than educational realism, in order to reach that public. In the next few chapters, I analyze program types that mobilized affective involvement, often achieved through docufictional dramatizations, competition, and humor.

From Emotional Realism to Reality Programming

The arrival of global reality formats in the late 1990s was at once an organic development, given the prevalence of reality-based programming during socialism, and a shock to postsocialist populations. The shock came from having had to relearn "the correct performance of sincere emotion," which John Ellis calls "the problem for our age."[20] In Britain and the Western television world in general, he explains, TV performance styles gradually evolved to convey sincerity through emotional expression, to develop "a recognizable repertoire of ways of being in public."[21] Ellis's history begins with the first, awkward experiments in expressing public emotion in the ITV game show *Double Your Money* (1955).[22] Postsocialist reality programs had a similar cringe-inducing sense of awkwardness. Much of Eastern European television valued a toned-down delivery even in its fictional programs. Instead, official socialist culture channeled public ways of performing emotion through tendentious celebrations of itself: mass rituals of singing, marching, and reciting poetry. While these collective exercises were not ineffective, particularly since they evoked nationalistic sentiment, by the 1970s and 1980s they were reduced to empty or nostalgic rituals. The only legitimate, "authentic" emotional reaction was distancing from the experience and from its undeniable pleasures through mockery and humor.

After the end of socialism, there was no direct, unmediated way back to sincerity.[23] Ellis writes to conclude his account of how factual television has been gradually overhauled by reality TV on Western European televisions: "Reality TV is part of a general social trend toward the blurring of leisure and information. It looks like entertainment; it is treated like entertainment. But it gives rise to conversations that, while still compelling and enjoyable, have wide implications."[24] Laurie Oullette and James Hay also track reality television's continuity with earlier attempts to educate the public in ways that were "abstract, didactic, unadorned, and dominated by academics, journalists, and other bona fide intellectual authorities."[25] Unlike these earlier educational programs, however, which wished to empower "a gullible mass that needed guidance in the liberal arts to participate in the rituals of public democracy," contemporary reality formats address the individual, "whose most pressing obligation to society is to empower her or himself privately."[26]

In the next four chapters, I follow the socialist history of this transformation, from reality-based forms that turned TV into a school through forms that successfully incorporated emotion, competition, and fiction, to postsocialist reality shows. While the patronizing intention to guide a "gullible population" toward a utopian future undoubtedly prevailed throughout this history, this is not a narrative of failure. It is one of experimentation with creating collective value, with socializing individuals to (self-)educate in ways that were community-oriented. The genres and programs borne out of this experimentation were often playful and creative, deploying ideological and aesthetic devices that were problematic and disruptive for socialism. The number of boring, propagandistic reality-based programs should not overshadow the bright achievements that punctuate this history and resonate even today.

These experiments are especially important to explore now that socialism is universally considered defunct. Contemporary reality programs help people to help themselves. They operate by governing at a distance, by replacing disappearing public welfare with governing technologies of do-it-yourself entrepreneurialism.[27] Socialist educational reality programs supplemented, rather than replaced, existing social work and public welfare, and they did so in a nonexploitative fashion, not beholden to commercial interests. In their best, most subversive moments, when they minimized dogma in favor of audience involvement and emotional engagement, they remain testimonies not only to the enduring need for the ethos of public broadcasting but also to the enduring potential of socialist ideas.

2 Tele-education

TV as a Classroom

Legendary Hungarian comedian Géza Hofi's annual New Year's Eve one-man cabaret act was a much-awaited television event through the 1970s and 1980s. It provided a satirical commentary on the events of the year and a collective release valve for the tension between party leadership and the public. Hofi titled the 1977 edition "Searching Public Opinion"—a pun that referenced the manipulated and unreliable nature of socialist public opinion research. The show was broadcast during the last hour of 1977, the "prime-time" slot of the television year. As he had done in earlier New Year's shows, Hofi recapped some of the year's events by parodying highly watched television programs. In essence, he volunteered to be a translator between official public messages and unofficial interpretations, highlighting television as the primary channel to facilitate this exchange. For instance, he peppered his performance with clips from the popular four-part German adventure miniseries *Michael Strogoff* (ZDF, 1975, based on the novel by Jules Verne), in which he replaced the figure of the protagonist, played by Raimund Harmstorf, with his own. His act was also interspersed with a parody of a long-winded interview with a foreign news correspondent and a talking head program featuring an art critic.

It is remarkable in itself that one of the most trusted voices of a very skeptical population, in what was an annual television event of "truth telling," would announce his diagnosis of the nation's health by examining the nation's TV. Even more telling is that Hofi, the honest mouthpiece of public opinion, singled out as part of the problem the didactic, non-televisual nature of the kinds of factual programs that dominated TV's schedule, something the studio audience rewarded with grateful laughter of recognition. In his commentary, Hofi said that everywhere he turns he feels like he's in school, especially if he turns on the TV. He put this down to the socialist regime's tendency to overreach in its effort to toe the ideological line. "As an important man said a long time ago, 'To study, to study, to study,'" he added, evoking the slogan attributed to Lenin that was so trivial to begin with that it was impossible to separate its incessant vulgar-Marxist deployment from its incessant parody.

As usual, Hofi put his finger on what everyone knew about socialist TV but few criticized in public: that it was meant to function as a massive school for the masses. Every program was imbued with the intention to educate. Tele-education was seen as a key to the citizenry's erudition, from political training through gaining a variety of practical skills to that all-important but most contradictory goal, "taste cultivation"—something rooted in the Kantian idea of aesthetic education. Programs varied as to how explicit this educational intent was. This chapter revolves around factual, reality-based program types that most explicitly identified themselves as educational. I start with School TV, which coordinated subject-specific programming with the centralized school curriculum and gradually encompassed all aspects of citizens' lives. Then I discuss the expansion of tele-education to program types that moved from straightforward instruction to more audience-friendly formats, which allowed for more participation and emotional engagement. These kinds of programs constitute a critical global prehistory to reality television.

Sociologist and later the first postsocialist president of Hungarian Television Elemér Hankiss compared features of Hungarian and American television broadcasting in a 1982 article, following an extended trip to the United States. One of the obvious differences, he points out, is that American television's address is interactive and inviting, whereas Hungarian TV's tone is condescending and pedagogical. "In its overall effect, American TV is more popular and democratic, emphasizing the possibility and fact of social participation; as opposed to Hungarian TV, which conveys information, explains things, teaches, addressing viewers from the inside out, from the top down, in an aristocratic fashion."[1] As an example, he contrasts a typical American morning exercise program in which a goofy fitness expert leads a cheerful crowd of participants outdoors with the slightly absurd nightly "TV Exercise" segment on Hungarian TV, where former gymnasts (and later their families) silently performed exercises in a sterile, dimly lit room. This comparison alone captures the spirit of "education dictatorship"—a term that Heather Gumbert applies to the German Democratic Republic, which can be safely generalized across the socialist region.[2]

Indeed, in the GDR, feature films and TV films made up 22.4 percent of broadcasting time in 1968; news took up 16.9 percent, and sports 14.8 percent. By 1970, the proportion of sports was reduced to 6.6 percent while feature films increased to 26.3 percent, educational programming to 10.2 percent, and informational, news, and current affairs to 17.7 percent. In the early 1970s, the proportion of political documentaries and current affairs continued to increase.[3] A large part of the schedule was occupied by reality-based programs that were only indirectly educational in intention. This was a varied category, which ranged from historical teleplays through various public affairs formats to variety and quiz shows. In 1968, TV separated from radio, which brought more independence to the former. As a result of General Secretary Erich Honecker's famous criticism of television in 1972, reforms were introduced to improve the programming structure and offer better entertainment and more effective journalism.[4]

The Polish broadcaster TVP allocated 45 percent of TV's airtime to current affairs and news programs in 1959.[5] In Hungary, in the 1970s, 25 percent of programming was political and economic in theme, 50 percent was qualified as cultural, art, and entertainment, and 25 percent was dedicated to education, children's and youth programming, and School TV.[6] In 1972, Hungarian TV's total annual programming time (close to 170,000 minutes) broke down like this among the various programming desks: 22.9 percent for the political division, 15.1 percent for School TV, 14.9 percent for the international exchange and film division, 10.4 percent for the youth and educational division, 9.4 percent for the entertainment and music division, 6.9 percent for the literature and drama division, 8.1 percent for the evening news, and 4.2 percent for the public cultural division.[7] It is obvious that the educational intent crossed the divisions and left very little, if any, TV time untouched. It is also telling that, in the same year, according to the data kept by the Hungarian Mass Media Survey Institute, the most watched programs were two foreign and one domestic fictional police series (each earning more than 87 percent of viewer share), a quiz show (88 percent), and, after a large drop in popularity, the first edition of the nightly news (71 percent) and the weekly news program *The Week* (49 percent).[8]

TV in the Classroom

In its most direct educational form, television actually functioned as a people's classroom in the various national manifestations of School TV. Such efforts to turn TV into an extension of formal state education were of course not unique to Eastern European socialist broadcasting. The first television experiments in Europe created classrooms around television sets before corporations began to push for standardizing domestic viewing in the 1930s. In Nazi Germany, television was crucial to the National Socialists' cultural policy after they came to power in 1933.[9] The Berlin Olympics of 1936 stimulated further interest in television as a technology of mass persuasion. Viewing rooms were established in cities to hold audiences as large as four hundred. And even after the war, when interest in television technology picked up again all over Europe, domestic viewing remained a collective experience organized around the first, scattered TV sets.[10]

In Italy, the program *Non é mai troppo tardi* (It's never too late) was financed by the Italian Ministry of Education to promote literacy in rural regions. It was broadcast by Radiotelevisione Italiana (RAI) from 1959 to 1968 for a mostly older audience, who watched it weekly in classrooms or municipal buildings. The French télé-clubs are perhaps the most influential examples of education in the context of collective viewing. They began in 1951 and operated mostly in rural primary schools, where people could attend TV transmissions by the state broadcaster RTF once or twice a week. Screenings were followed by public discussions about the programs. The initiative gained support from UNESCO in 1953, which helped produce a series of theme-based programs. The screenings were studied by sociologist Joffre Dumazedier's team of sociologists, who were affiliated with the French National Centre for Scientific Research (CNRS). Télé-clubs expanded beyond France to Italy and Japan and, by the 1960s and 1970s, to India, Senegal, and Côte d'Ivoire.[11] They drew on antecedents in radio such as the BBC's Listening Groups (1927–1947), which provided early adult education;

farm radio programming based in Canada for adult education produced by the Canadian Broadcasting Corporation; and farm radio produced in cooperation between UNESCO and All India Radio in Poona, which was followed by similar radio experiments in the developing world. Educational radio broadcasting aimed at schoolchildren also preceded public service educational television in Belgium, Switzerland, Germany, Portugal, and other countries throughout the 1920s, 1930s, and 1940s.[12]

In most of the educational programs inspired by the télé-clubs, education was seen as embedded in leisure activities afforded by television.[13] This is a significant difference between how tele-education was viewed in the social democratic systems of Western Europe (and some of their former colonies) and in the highly centralized state socialist systems of Eastern Europe, where social transformation was targeted on a more ambitious, near-utopian scale and wrapped within an all-encompassing, anxious cultural nationalism.

In the socialist region, School TV was launched in the 1960s. In most countries, it complemented and then replaced School Radio. In Hungary, for instance, School Radio began in 1962 and went into decline as TV rose in popularity.[14] Hungarian TV offered its first explicitly educational program as early as 1959. The program, entitled "About Our Children," featured an educational expert giving lectures on issues of child rearing, illustrated by didactic docufictional scenes the expert wrote himself, which were performed by professional actors.[15] The program presumably targeted women, who were understood to be in charge of parenting. Actual School TV began in 1961 with experimental courses in Russian language.[16] These were soon followed by lectures in physics, chemistry, literature, and history, planned in coordination with centrally mandated school curricula. The broadcasts were first shown in fifty to one hundred selected elementary and high schools and continuing education night courses for adult workers.[17]

School TV was extended on a national scale in 1964, along with a campaign to put TV sets into every school. In 1964, there were 700 to 800 sets in schools altogether. By 1965, there were 2,122.[18] In 1970, a newspaper report proudly announced that the "Television for Every School" campaign had been a success: every school that had electric power also had at least one TV set. As elsewhere in Europe, the movement had initially focused on small, sparsely inhabited farmlands. It moved gradually into smaller towns and cities. In 1970, there were still about four hundred schools without electric power. But about a hundred of these had installed a generator just so they could turn on the TV set gifted to the school.[19] According to a survey in 1974, by then 60 percent of all elementary schools were incorporating School TV into instruction.[20] Authorities had hoped television would effect a breakthrough in adult education as well. As late as 1962, almost a third of Hungary's population had not had an eighth-grade education.[21]

The Polish story was similar. School TV (*szkoła telewizyjna*) made its first appearance in 1960, first as an experiment, but with the ultimate purpose to complement the school curriculum in a visually appealing way. Initially, nine hundred schools subscribed, since not many more owned a TV set. The curriculum was divided into thematic blocks, which were hosted by scientists and other academics.[22] As elsewhere, School TV found its real mission outside of the centralized curriculum, in rural areas, in adult and continuing education. In 1970, TVP1 aired 718 hours of educational programs, including 500 hours of "School TV" and "TV Polytechnic" lectures.[23]

In Romania, *Telescoala* was launched in 1968 in a joint effort between Romanian Radiotelevision and the Ministry of Education. It was broadcast from 9:05 to 10:00 AM so as to correspond to the daily school schedule. As elsewhere, it delivered lessons that complemented classroom instruction in particular subjects. Initially, these were constructed as televised lectures for students of all ages. They included *Consultatii pentru elevi* (Tutorials for students), *Telescoala, Universitatea TV* (The TV university), and, in an initiative unique to Romania, foreign language courses in French, English, Spanish, German, and Russian. Within a few years, as in other countries of the region, School TV grew to offer educational programs that taught technical and practical skills, such as *Consultatii tehnice* (Technical consultations) or the children's competition program *Ex-Terra*. These were typically scheduled on the weekends or in the evening broadcast block that began at 6:00 PM following a daily break in broadcasting in the afternoon. As elsewhere, weekend children's magazines combined educational, instructional, and entertaining programs. Romanian Television also offered educational programs focusing on general knowledge (e.g., *Universal Sotron* [Universal hopscotch]) and civic issues (e.g., *Bratara de aur* [The golden profession]).[24]

As in Romania, School TV gradually expanded in other socialist countries to include all school levels and learning areas and to address everyone from those enrolled in formal education to those who just wanted to pick up a bit of quantum physics on a Saturday morning. Much like at the the BBC, it developed into a "free university" by 1975. The curriculum heavily targeted the natural sciences, where unmediated "truth" about objective reality could be delivered by academic experts. Socialist School TV was also linked to similar TV and radio initiatives across Europe. This tele-educational network was prominent at international television festivals and the annual international meeting in Paris, where socialist program makers often received awards for their outstanding products.[25]

It is important to note that, even in the Eastern Bloc, School TV was not seen as simply, or even primarily, a propaganda instrument. Rather, it was considered a tool of social transformation that could bring knowledge and cultural sophistication to the masses by opening a window to the world in tiny schoolhouses, community centers, and eventually family homes. The knowledge disseminated was to be a grand equalizer among different social classes, professions, and educational levels. There was a great deal of enthusiasm about tele-education in the early years, and it was not entirely unfounded. In a speech given in 1966 in the Hungarian Parliament, a representative called School TV, then broadcasting four days a week, a key element of the cultural revolution brought about by television.[26]

TV Education for Everyone

School TV was by no means a universal success, however. By the 1970s, more and more questions arose as to how far it really enhanced public education when it was directly folded into the centralized curriculum. The problem was not just the fact that scientific experts were rarely the most charismatic television personalities; it was also the technical conditions of transmission and reception: small black-and-white sets with frequent signal problems. The exceptions were remote village and farm schools, where School TV was often the primary source of learning given the shortage of educators trained in specialized subjects, and where students were truly cut off from modern technological developments, including electricity in some cases. The majority of appreciative viewer letters about Hungarian School TV came from rural teachers, who explained what a difference it meant for the students to see images of trams and other modern means of transport on TV for the first time or to watch a lesson about hygiene when most of them did not have a bathroom at home.[27]

The two most targeted areas remained science and art. Both were conceived in a top-down fashion as fields where one should aim for finding truth—either scientific truth based in the objectively existing material world or the Kantian aesthetic truth revealed by the canonized creations of

Professor Zin gives architectural lessons on TV "with a pen and charcoal."

the truly talented. In this teleological journey, only expert guidance would suffice. There were countless programs focused on popular science education. Romanian science programs included *Romania la ora atomului* (Romania at the time of the atom), *Panoramic stiintific* (Scientific panoramic) and *Univers XX*.[28] In 1960, Polish TV launched *Wszechnica telewizyjna* (TV academy), a block of programs dedicated to science education. Some of the popular shows this included were *Eureka*, *Spotkania z przyrodą* (Rendezvous with nature), *Magazyn postępu technicznego* (Magazine of technical progress), *Klinika Zdrowego Czlowieka* (The healthy man's clinic), *Klub opowieści z myszką* (Little mouse story club), and, perhaps most popular of all, *Piórkiem i węglem* (With pen and charcoal), hosted by the beloved Professor Wiktor Zin.[29]

The Hungarian series *A fény természete* (The nature of light, 1966) had two academic experts discuss the science of light, which they illustrated with drawings.[30] A more promising approach was taken by *Kronovízió* (Chronovision) in 1970, which adopted the model of a time machine to track the history of research on nuclear energy, a theme central to Cold War geopolitics. Even this more creative framework could not overcome the difficulty of teaching a specialized topic to a broad audience, however. Things were not helped by the fact that the series was hosted by a handful of physicists, who could only hope to appeal to a handful of teenage boys dedicated to physics. *Találkozás az ősemberrel* (Encounter with prehistoric man, 1967) featured another expert giving thirty-minute lectures on the topic and elicited this review in a daily paper: "What makes a good series? When the very first episode amazes and captivates us, making us look forward to the next ones with excitement.... The first episode of István Benedek's new series did not elicit this reaction. Viewers had expected an actual encounter with prehistoric men. However, Benedek restricted the topic to the history of *research* on the topic, which is not conducive to mass education. We expected more visual illustrations. It's a shame lectures are so long, too. Listening to a lecture on TV for thirty minutes is exhausting."[31]

Tele-education found more success with viewers when it moved from teaching school subjects to teaching areas of self-improvement. In Hungary, there was a program for just about anything that can or should be learned in the 1960s and 1970s, from algebra to ballroom dancing. In the least formalized, "lifestyle" areas, television personalities were recruited to replace professors. Youth were especially treasured as an audience to educate. For instance, jovial actor Kamill Feleky, star of old-fashioned film comedies, hosted the etiquette show for young people *Tudni Illik, hogy Mit Illik* (It's proper to know what's proper) in 1962. Several programs were offered about how to use the language properly, most of them led by linguist Lajos Lőrincze, starting in 1963 with *A magyar nyelvről* (About the Hungarian language), which aired a few times a year.[32]

Lucia Scuteri describes the many programs devoted to cultivating the Slovenian language in Yugoslav Slovenia, such as the 1966–1967 series "On Our Speaking." Such linguistic programs took a backseat in the schedules of the 1970s, but they came back with a vengeance in the 1980s, with enticing titles such as "Linguistic Highlights" (1987), "Textual-Linguistic Highlights" (1986), and "Grain to Grain" (1980–1983).[33]

Lifestyle-based tele-education was prominent in other countries of the bloc as well. In the Romania of the 1970s, such programs included *Emisiuni lectie pentru lucratorii din agricultura* (Lessons for agricultural workers), *La volan* (Driving), *Sport si sanatate* (Sports and health), *Caminul* (The household), and *Pentru timpul dumneavoastra liber ... va recomandam* (For your leisure time ... we recommend). Cultural programs dedicated to language and literature, theater, film, or socialist ideology included *Mult e dulce si frumoasa* (The beautiful language), *Istoria filmului* (Film history), *Seara de teatru* (Evening theater), *50 de ani, 50 de evocari* (50 years, 50 evocations), *Carti si idei* (Books and ideas), *Dinamica societatii romanesti* (The dynamics of Romanian society), and *Varstele Peliculei* (The ages of film).[34]

Socialist TV also developed its educational version of niche programming, addressing targeted social classes and groups such as factory workers, agricultural professionals, women, and youth. Some courses offered specialized instruction for young people going into trades or farming rather than university studies. Agricultural programs were in particular abundance. The Romanian program *Viata Satului* (Village life) began on the radio, transitioned to TV in 1957, and has been on the air since then. In its socialist form it was a roughly ninety-minute magazine that focused on agricultural affairs but also on folk culture, traditions, and village life. It also featured letters from viewers. Daniela Mustata writes that the program's success and longevity are due to its segmented address to different rural demographics and a flexible approach that allowed its makers to accommodate changing party lines within the content.[35]

In 1959, Polish Television's rural agricultural program *Niedzielna biesiada* (Sunday feast) was launched. It was a two-hour show for farmers, full of practical tips. It aired despite the fact that the Polish countryside had a very small number of TV sets at the time. The year 1962 saw the beginning of the educational series *Telewizyjny Kurs Rolniczy* (TV course in agriculture).[36] In 1962, Hungarian Television aired a series of seventeen hour-long educational lectures on farming, broadcast on Wednesdays.[37] In 1965, it created a program called *Figyelem, mérnökök technikusok!* (Attention engineers, technicians!) The first episode was a program about "moving material . . ."[38] Many experiments like this stretched the limits of televisuality. Another set of specialized offerings prepared children of workers and peasants for university studies. *Irány az egyetem!* (Off to university!), in 1969, was a twenty-four-lecture open-access course in physics and math.[39]

The default national viewer addressed by socialist television was the white, male, heterosexual citizen, whether a little boy, a male teenager, or a man. This, again, was not a particularly Eastern, Soviet socialist feature. Western European public broadcasters also favored the male citizen in their address; they also idealized the worker, who needed to be shown the way to enlightenment. "Indeed, the figure of the worker—disciplined, eager to be educated even after a full day of work—seemed best to fit the ideal target of public broadcasters. There is a gendered side to the popular here: this ideal viewer was usually male, while other, theoretically more entertainment-prone, less educated characters would be female," explains Jerôme Bourdon, in a description that would fit Eastern socialism just as well.⁴⁰ When it came to differentiating among audiences, despite its avowed coverage of all social groups, socialist TV privileged the categories of social class, profession, age, sex, and geography.

The few programs with a female address explicitly signaled their invitation to a special demographic, which existed somewhere on the margins of citizenship, imagined to be dedicated to special female duties such as mothering and cooking. These were also often the only programs with a majority of female creative personnel.⁴¹ The Hungarian program *Nők fóruma* (Women's forum), for instance, offered an episode on children of divorced parents, taking it for granted that it was women who kept custody of the children after divorce. *Anita, a "tévé-bébi"* (Anita, the "TV baby") made her appearance in Hungary in 1965 as the star of a protoreality series that followed baby Anita and her family from the moment of her birth with the intention to teach mothers (not "parents"!) useful skills when caring for an infant and small child. It was one of many semieducational programs that discussed and illustrated recurring family issues, much like *Csak felnőtteknek* (Only for adults, 1965) and later *Családi kör* (Family circle), a program I discuss in detail at the end of this chapter.

Political Tele-education

The least memorable category of education concerned overtly ideological, agitational-propaganda programming about Marxism, socialism, and the workings of a socialist society. In Romania, the genre included *Cadran. Emisiune de actualitate internationala* (Cadran. A program of international current affairs); economic current affairs programs such as *Cabinetul economic TV* (The economic TV cabinet), *Revista economica TV* (The economic TV magazine), and *Actualitatea in economie* (The economic actuality); and political programs such as *Agenda politica* (The political agenda) and *Cincinalul 1966–1970 in cifre si imagini* (The five-year plan in figures and images).⁴²

In Hungary, the unimaginatively named seven-part series *Politikai tanfolyam a televízióban* (Political course on TV) launched in 1965 on a fortnightly basis. It featured TV education on subjects such as current issues in world politics, the development of the socialist world system, the world economy, and the meaning of work in socialism. As the *Radio and TV Guide* optimistically wrote, it was meant to be watched collectively in offices, factory clubs, and cultural centers.⁴³ To illustrate how out of touch the Socialist Party was with television's working as a medium, in 1969 the Central

Committee's Committee on Agitation and Propaganda decided to broaden the range of themes to be covered by the "course" to include cultural revolution, contemporary issues in science, and the decisions of the Central Committee. To make the program even less watchable, the broadcast time was also increased from thirty to forty minutes, which would include "illustrations" in addition to twenty- to twenty-five-minute lectures.[44]

There were exceptions even within this driest and most shunned tele-educational genre. Socialist parties made more concerted efforts to catch up with television's development by the end of the 1960s. By then it was obvious in much of the region that economic and political thawing had to be accelerated. Television could be used as a forum to inform citizens about these new developments and revise the party's original goals in a careful manner that made the introduction of free-market mechanisms and the expansion of consumerism appear to be an organic stage of socialism's own progress. In Hungary, one of the first programs designed to ease the transition to what the Kádár regime named the New Economic Mechanism was called *Ruble, Forint, Dollar* (Rubel, forint, dollár, 1969). This was an entirely top-controlled, didactic show whose mission was to inform the public about and popularize the Economic Committee's decision to expand the range of products on the domestic market and improve relationships with the world market.

By contrast, in the same year, MTV produced an altogether novel animated propaganda series called *Magyarázom a mechanizmust* (Explaining the mechanism), whose episodes illustrated specific aspects of the new economic policy. The series came to be remembered as "Dr. Brain" after the "host," a bespectacled, by definition male, cartoon professor figure with an oversized head, who faced the TV classroom from behind a desk. The public recognized him as someone modeled after Professor Öveges, the most popular tele-scientist of the socialist period, who was lively enough to get his own show.[45] The counterintuitive idea to explain economic policy through animation proved to be a breakthrough in educational-propaganda programming, due to the tight, humorous format and the character, whose name also called up associations with science fiction. The series literally animated the robotic party representatives who usually populated propaganda programs. The lessons were condensed into ten minutes, replacing the sprawling lecture.

The series was so successful that it continued throughout the seventies in subsequent "I Explain . . ." series: *I Explain the Future, I Explain Ourselves, I Explain the Explanation*, and so forth. The animated teaching format inspired a similar series in 1988: *Párbeszéd* (Dialogue) had popular actor Péter Haumann and a devil-like figure discuss a planned tax reform during the twilight of socialism. It was even resurrected as part of the postsocialist *Modern Képmesék* (Modern picture stories) series produced by the public broadcaster. "Dr. Brain" united an evil but comical scientist from a Cold War sci-fi movie with the know-it-all but benevolent real-life professors who were fixtures of educational TV. It allowed for gently mocking Big Brother, who put its own cartoon parody forward to mock itself. This gesture was not unlike Hofi's earlier and bolder New Year's parody of relentless tele-education.

Taste Education

When it came to the other major area of tele-education, art and culture, countless programs took on the cause of "taste education" by introducing citizens to classical music, art, literature, and cinema. Theatrical broadcasts and concerts remained on the agenda throughout the period along with art films and quality serials exchanged among socialist countries and imported from Western Europe. Hungarian TV had its own classical music department, which, just in the year 1969, offered four educational series aimed at "the broadest audiences": a program featuring Leonard Bernstein; another named *Legyen a zene mindenkié* (Music should belong to everyone); *Tévé bérlet* (TV season's ticket), a concert series that had been put together based on viewer requests; and *A szereposztástól a premierig* (From casting to premiere), which offered behind-the-scenes looks at opera productions and was hosted by famous conductors.[46] A similar, long-running program on Polish Television, specializing in popularizing classical music, was called *Słuchamy i patrzymy* (We listen and we watch). The program ran in prime time and featured an orchestra performing live in the studio.[47] The twenty episodes of *Po prostu muzyka* (Simply the music), created by Polish Television's Dział szkolny or School Department in 1982–1983, were meant to educate first and second graders about music. *Pegaz*, Polish TV's high-profile magazine for cultural and art education, first aired in 1959 and continued to earn its prime-time 8:00 PM slot on Saturdays. It consisted of film, book, and art reviews, which were taken very seriously by the audience and culture critics. Its creators came up with a clever solution to attract a younger audience as well. The last few minutes of the show were devoted to contemporary Western media stars who were visiting Poland. In this way younger members of the audience—while waiting to hear a few words about the Rolling Stones or Marlene Dietrich—learned about sculpture, architecture, or cinema.[48] A peculiarity of socialist art-educational broadcasting was the abundant airtime allotted to poetry. Polish and Hungarian television regularly included actors reciting poems for the TV audience.

A typical visual arts program on Hungarian television was *A Tévé Galériája* (TV gallery, 1965), in which an art expert gave a guided tour of a selected artist's work, offering lengthy explanations and taking questions from the group. One brave critic of the program suggested finding someone who could establish a less condescending connection with his audience even if they ask apparently naive questions.[49] *Irodalmi Klub* (Literary club), launched in 1967, featured a group of experts analyzing a "classic" piece of national or European literature on each broadcast. As a true educational program, it concluded with a quiz to test what studio audiences had learned.[50]

Clearly, the normative moral universe and condescending address of some of these programs were at odds with the overall goal of democratizing education. One telltale sign of this friction is how many of these shows were actually titled "club" of some kind or another. Soviet television's most watched program, a quiz and game show I discuss in chapter 4, was called *The Club of Merry and the Quick-Witted* (known as KVN for short). The Soviet series *Film Travel Club* educated viewers about films and travel. As Kristin Roth-Ey dryly notes, it was host Vladimir Schneiderov's own club, in which he was the only traveler. Other programs also issued a selective address to a supposedly undifferentiated national audience. Even variety shows such as the Soviet *Stories of Heroism* (about World War II heroes), which were conversational and introduced interesting people to the audience, functioned like clubs driven by leading personalities. Schneiderov's club featured young, well-spoken men as role models.[51]

A critic sums up the ambivalence of tele-educational clubs in reflecting on an edition of the Hungarian discussion program *Tudósklub* (Scholars' club), dedicated to the "problems of youth," in 1969:

> Scholars' Club about youth? But for whom? I could not have been the only one to ask this question on Wednesday night. I had expected a lot from this program and, I confess, got very little out of it. The topic is extraordinarily exciting and of great interest to many. It is definitely worthy of TV viewers' attention. But this way? I had hoped to find out something about youth—especially today's youth—from our

scholars. I had had every reason to hope that I would be a partner in the conversation as the highly educated experts analyze the situation of youth. There was a special phone line set up for this purpose. But what happened? Our scholars discussed "youth" in a specialized language completely incomprehensible and alien to the television viewer. To the nonexpert, this hour-long conversation took place in the most rarefied dimensions. Summa summarum: this was an academic dialogue.[52]

Educational TV as Democratic Forum

By the 1970s, more and more educational programs began to solicit viewers' emotional engagement and participation, hitting playful and humorous tones like "Dr. Brain," and employing well-liked, entertaining personalities as guides instead of scholars. In the long run, these proved to be the most enduring shows. Many of them survived socialism.

Such was the Romanian *Teleenciclopedia*, a general interest magazine, which mixed fiction films with short documentaries featuring the voices of popular actors, singers, and other celebrities as narrators. It took a thematic approach to topics of general knowledge. Because it was neither elitist nor exclusivist, *Teleenciclopedia* actually popularized scientific knowledge in Romania. The balance it found between informative, educational programming and popular, general topics of interest guaranteed its survival through the 1980s, when programming was reduced to two hours a day.[53]

The Hungarian program most similar to *Teleenciclopedia* was called *Delta*. It was a long-running popular TV magazine that covered mostly scientific and technological topics of popular interest, launched in 1964. One key to its success was its charming hostess Júlia Kudlik, one of the most universally liked announcers and celebrities of the entire period. While viewers responded very positively to *Delta*, critics voiced what was an evident conflict between the serious, masculine nature of positivist science espoused by the program's short documentary segments and the blonde female host associated with the maternal, decorative position of the program announcer. One critic wrote this barely coded, condescending assessment in a national paper in 1972:

> Júlia Kudlik's lovely smile is legendary among the audience and in the press. Her charming personality seduces even those who are less interested in the program. However, she's entrapped by *Delta*, which is on every Sunday. She is expected to make science popular; she is expected

Júlia Kudlik hosting the popular science magazine *Delta*.

to talk about subjects she obviously doesn't know much about. So she has no choice but to stick to the script. This script is nothing more than the routine text that accompanies short science news documentaries. Therefore, she and *Delta* are not in harmony. She should save that lovely smile for topics closer to her personality.[54]

Polish TV launched its first current affairs program, *Tele-Echo*, in 1956. It remained on the air until 1981. Like *Delta*, it featured a charming hostess, Irena Dziedzic, who was also the creator and writer of the program. *Tele-Echo* covered current affairs, arts, and culture in an interview format. During its twenty-five-year history, *Tele-Echo* invited more than twelve hundred guests. While Dziedzic—much like Kudlik—was often and rightly accused of political conformism, Tadeusz Pikulski calls her a phenomenal example of a TV personality, who was able to stir up intense emotional reactions.[55] Her role was somewhat similar to that of legendary Soviet Central Television hostess Valentina Leont'eva, who helmed the melodramatic talk show *Ot vsei dushi* (From the bottom of our hearts) between 1972 and 1987, a program that, Christine Evans argues, played a central role in visualizing a "Soviet way of life" through the emotional display of a "Soviet way of feeling."[56]

Programs dispensing legal advice formed a distinct subgenre. The East German series *Das Fernsehgericht tagt* was launched in 1961 on ARD and ran for seventy-four episodes until 1978. It featured trial scenes dramatized by actors playing plaintiffs and defendants. The judges and state attorneys on the show were actual legal professionals. Since the trials' results were open, all participants had to improvise without a script. The format drew on American legal television shows, which had been on the air since the 1950s. Each trial lasted two days, broadcast as ninety-minute episodes in prime time, on consecutive weekdays. This was followed by a hiatus of several weeks. The sitting judge, Dr. August Detleve Sommerkamp, affectionately nicknamed "Papa Lenient" by the audience, had been an active judge for thirty-six years before he began his television career. During breaks in the trial, reporter Giselher Schaar asked people in the studio audience about their opinions on the case. In its first nine years, the program worked exclusively with professional actors. In 1970 it began to include nonprofessionals.[57] Other courtroom shows followed *Das Fernsehgericht Tagt*, including one that allowed the audience to act as judges, and others that specialized in marriage problems or traffic cases. Greta Olson argues that the post-Wall German reality judge show *Richterin Barbara Salesch* (Judge Barbara Salesch, 1999–2012), allegedly modeled after *Judge Judy* (1996–present), also draws on the rich legacy of Cold War courtroom shows, particularly *Das Fernsehgericht Tagt*.[58]

The most memorable Polish educational courtroom shows were *16-tu przekupnych* (The corruptible sixteen) and *Wszyscy jestesmy sedziami* (We are all judges). The latter was an educational program about the judiciary system, which involved prosecutors, judges, witnesses, and the public. The Hungarian socialist protoreality program *Jogi esetek* (Legal cases) also featured common legal issues for the purpose of education. It employed actors who dramatized these cases, and a popular legal expert, attorney Pál Erőss, who had a flair for translating legal quandaries for the public in simple but lively language.

Many of these programs increasingly mixed documentary realism with fiction and also reached into viewers' actual lives, making television the most vivid and organic platform for public engagement. Once again, the same program types could be found throughout the region, many of them also variants of Western European PSB programs. While the resistance to finding any redeeming value in television remained steadfast throughout the period, it was also increasingly recognized among TV professionals and critics that television viewing was not simply a passive state unworthy of the active socialist citizen. Rather, it was interwoven with other activities socialist ideology deemed educational, such as reading, listening to classical music, or learning about the natural world. Thus television's function was seen as a spark that would ignite further inquiries, preferably pursued in a collective fashion, enhanced by playful and emotional engagement. Self-directed, lifelong learning is a very contemporary idea, as is the notion that competitive play increases interest and participation. György Sándor, programming director for Hungarian Television, in an interview for the journal *Rádió és Tévé Szemle* (Radio and TV Review), said that television is a central "force of organization." Hundreds of groups were formed to create local versions of the popular quiz show *Ki Mit Tud* (Who knows what) and organize folk music circles inspired by the popular competition show *Röpülj páva* (Fly peacock).[59] By the 1970s television was seen not simply as a school house but also as a public forum.

The tellingly titled Hungarian program *Fórum* (1969) bypassed lectures and propaganda and invited artists, intellectuals, and politicians to a live town hall meeting held in various locations. It put party leaders in front of the cameras and connected them with actual viewers, who asked questions about the economy and its reforms, political issues, and foreign relations. On the September 15, 1972, broadcast, for instance, Péter Vályi, vice president of the Council of Ministers, answered questions about foreign economic relations from the workers in the meeting room of the electric factory Egyesült Izzó and from viewers who called in. In this experimental format, "forum" meant an actual public forum, where party officials took a considerable risk: they realized they could not hide behind official releases any longer in the age of television, but once on TV, they were unprepared for the visibility it afforded.[60] In this 1972 edition, Vályi is obviously uncomfortable. If anything, his answers foreground the effort with which he is trying to avoid straight answers, falling back on clichéd phrases that evidently fail to convince the audience. The camera intentionally pans around the room to show knowing smirks or explicit skepticism. When Vályi is faced with actual questions from actual citizens, on live television, his canned phrases throw open the gap between the leaders' performance of the principles of socialism and the actual direction that existing socialism was taking. In 1969, a critic commented in the party's daily print organ, *Népszabadság*, on *Fórum*'s increasing reliance on viewer questions: "What we saw on Thursday night's edition of *Fórum* was superior to the usual public affairs programs.... There is more at stake here than discussing economic matters in a popular format. If we consider antecedents such as the interview János Kádár gave last summer or the conversation with Jenő Fock, or the television interview given by Zoltán Komócsin about foreign affairs, or the answers leaders in the capital gave to viewers' questions, we see a definite effort to make matters of governance more transparent."[61]

Another commentator went so far as to sneak some criticism of the program's transparency within the obligatory praise. In *Népszabadság*, he wrote about a 1969 *Fórum* edition that dealt with "socialist law and legislature":

> The legal edition of *Fórum* was the most exciting public affairs program of the week and perhaps the most successful edition of this question-and-answer program so far. Gradually, everyone is beginning to figure out how the program works, viewers and participants alike. The questions are direct, the answers are open. It'll bring further progress if we hear less of the phrase "We'll examine the question" and if the respondent offers his personal opinion about the problem at hand. Statesmen are allowed to indicate if the opinion is theirs alone and not an official statement.[62]

Fórum even went international. In 1971, it featured representatives from Soviet Television and the space program as well as the editor of *Literaturnaya Gazeta* and a science writer for *Pravda*, who had agreed to participate after a set of negotiations and conditions approved in the highest echelons. The critical echoes were positive, praising the educational value of the debate.[63]

The desire to use television as a public forum brought forth a region-wide format. The program *Current Debates* in Yugoslavia (TV Belgrade, 1965–1969) was very similar to *Fórum*. It was a participatory discussion program that revolved around current issues based on audience suggestions, including unemployment, living standards, and political reforms. The East German *Prisma* ran from 1963 to 1991. As Heather Gumbert explains, it was one of the most tangible outcomes of the Agitation Commission's appeal to television producers to create popular programming that would uncover and find solutions to the contradictions of socialism.[64] The ultimate goal, of course, was to teach viewers to see themselves as part of a functioning socialist collective. Gerhard Scheumann, creator and first host of the show, modeled *Prisma* after the West German current affairs magazine *Panorama*. Unlike *Panorama*, however, which focused on large-scale political issues, *Prisma* was positioned as a liaison between the party leadership and ordinary citizens, inviting viewers to contribute questions, comments, and complaints about a variety of issues that affected everyday socialist lives.[65] Like *Fórum*, *Prisma* performed a delicate dance. On the one hand, it offered critical, participatory journalism that invited viewers to feel like they had a voice in shaping the system, and that the SED (Socialist United Party) was on their side. On the other hand, *Prisma* embraced the leeway to be critical of the party and did allow a range of previously unheard voices to be part of the national conversation. In one of the most influential cases, *Prisma* successfully intervened on behalf of a young woman who was disqualified from attending teachers' training college because she refused to swim due to a water-related childhood trauma and subsequently failed gym class.[66]

Programs like *Prisma*, *Current Debates*, and *Fórum* opened the door to wider audience involvement than ever before. Television had begun to take advantage of its unique ability to let people watch and vicariously participate in others' lives. Propelled by the socialist ethos of collectivity, such programs directed the attention to collective memory and systemic inequality rather than to displaying others' misery for voyeurs. For instance, the popular Hungarian series *Ebédszünet* (Lunch break), launched in 1971 and hosted by Mária Balogh, followed up on viewer letters that called attention to systemic problems. One of the broadcasts in 1971 explored the inhuman conditions of a provincial industrial area, where factory leaders had refused to make even the slightest improvements for the previous twenty years. *Lunch Break*'s crew traveled to the location and interviewed the workers. As a critic wrote, "Television's principle on *Lunch Break* is not cheap sensationalism. Rather, it uses the force of the public forum to press those in charge to make progressive decisions."[67] The same year also saw the beginning of another long-running program, *Nyitott boríték*) (Open envelope), on which hostess Margit Molnár set out to solve problems raised by viewer letters. As the *TV Guide* explained, the program was prompted by the fact that viewers saw television as an institution that can bring remote locations and issues into public visibility. It is this collective responsibility that the show's creators took up and put into practice.[68]

Some programs incorporated playful and entertaining elements that successfully tapped into the intimacy created by television at the intersection of private and public lives. The Hungarian *Belépés csak tévénézőknek!* (Entry only to TV viewers!, 1963) invited viewers to behind-the-scenes locations of socialist institutions such as the police, the state water company, Hunnia Film Studio, the National Manuscript Archives, and MTV itself. The creators of another participatory program that directly anticipated reality subgenres, *Ki tud róla?* (Who knows about them?, 1970), published in the *Radio and TV Guide* photos taken in the immediate postwar years of 1945–1949, soliciting responses from people who recognized themselves or others. One hundred applicants were then selected for interviews, and the postwar lives of twenty of those in the images were portrayed in the series. Cocreator Dezső Radványi said in an interview, "[We wanted to] meet the generation who undertook the socialist revolution, for whom the issue of our nation and people was a personal issue."[69]

This opening toward socially committed participatory TV was accompanied by television's increasing reliance on mixing realist and fictional genres as a way to reach viewers and loosen the definition of tele-education. It would deserve more than a note here that socialist television was always a welcoming home for prolific documentary production and exhibition. In Hungary alone, a documentary department was set up in 1972, borne of the realization that television was well suited to ethnographic portraits that also critically analyzed social problems. The department produced forty films a year in a studio that operated separately from MAFILM, the state film production company, where most documentary production had previously taken place, although collaborations continued.[70]

Documentary work also involved contributions from amateur filmmakers, a tradition that goes back to the beginnings of television. In 1972, a new series was dedicated to their work, entitled *Pergő képek* (Spinning images), to complement the annual amateur documentary film festival. Some of the most outstanding and enduring achievements of documentary-making were also created by women, who thus expanded their reach into television beyond the pretty face and reassuring voice of the program continuity announcer. It is also likely that television as a whole provided more space for women directors, since male filmmakers were disdainful of television and reluctant to associate with it, with few exceptions. In Hungary, women reinvigorated television documentary in the 1960s and brought home international prizes from film festivals.

On Hungarian TV alone, fiction and documentary mingled in hybrid genres that favored realistic representation and often found ways to probe tough questions disguised within the Trojan horse of party-approved themes such as World War II and the communist period. These were often allegorical works, such as director Éva Zsurzs's documentary trilogy

Példázat (Parabol, 1964). Márta Kende's ethnographic documentary *Bognár Anna világa* (The world of Anna Bognár, 1963) was a pioneering work, which brought to the viewers the fate of people living in deep poverty in small provincial communities and farms through the life of a fifty-two-year-old blind woman who can see for the first time after having eye surgery. Several TV documentaries set out to bring visibility to the lives of Roma populations, who have been subjected to both institutionalized and unofficial discrimination. The film *Cigány Zsuzsó* aired in May 1971, about Zsuzsanna Bacsi, a forty-four-year-old Gypsy woman living in the village of Monok.[71]

Family Circle

As a mature and enduring program that had incorporated the lessons of more than a decade of tele-education, the Hungarian *Family Circle* gives us a case study of socialist educational TV at its best. The show invited participation through the force of its emotional realism. It delivered a collective public address with a personal touch. It was one of the outstanding successes produced by the School TV Department. Its most direct antecedent was a roundtable conversation program called *Szülők nevelők egymás közt* (Parents and teachers among themselves), which ran for 67 episodes in the late 1960s and early 1970s. The connection between the two shows was so organic that *Family Circle*'s long-term host, Endre Kelemen, referred to his own program as the 68th episode of *Parents and Teachers*.[72] *Family Circle* produced about 215 episodes, not all of which were archived. As a sign of its popularity, it survived the Cold War. It was on the air for a full twenty years, from 1974 to 1994. It was conceived as a TV magazine, following Western European initiatives that began to fold dramatized segments into educational programs. It included practical parenting advice, miniplays written by well-known playwrights, and, most important of all, dramatic enactments of situations that crystallized around the thematic core of each episode: divorce, drugs, taking care of aging relatives, raising teens, teenage pregnancy, single motherhood, raising an independent child, loss and mourning, and even otherwise taboo topics such as unemployment (officially nonexistent in socialism) and male impotence among seniors (a topic that warranted a rare call on the legendary and feared "K phone" from the Ministry of Culture).[73]

What was the recipe for success? First of all, unlike many of the other tele-education programs, *Family Circle* did not try to impose ideologically correct lessons on viewers. Rather, the creators responded to what they perceived as a bottom-up need for practical parenting guidelines. The increasing divorce rate, the struggles of families with two working parents, the lack of advice on raising emotionally secure children were all indications of this need. As Kelemen put it, the creators of the show "reached their hands out to families."[74]

The second ingredient of the recipe was a perfect collaborative team for such a program. The original idea came from a woman, Margit László, who also directed the first episode and stayed on throughout as a member of the creative team. The show's brand, however, came to be associated with its longtime host, Endre Kelemen, whose benevolent, mild-mannered, paternalistic persona was closest to that of a father-teacher. Another key contributor was psychologist Jenő Ranschburg, who analyzed dramatized situations for viewers and helped them draw lessons for themselves—often in conversation with Kelemen. For instance, an episode that addressed allowing children in the family bed began with a ten-minute dramatized scene where the child has a bad dream and wants to crawl in between the parents. The father gets up, carries the child around, and tells him a story. The mother also gets up and makes some tea; soon everybody is wide awake. At this point, the scene freezes, and Ranschburg appears in front of the bed. He identifies what we have seen as one possible, albeit rather permissive, model to respond to children who wander into their parents' beds at night. Ranschburg then introduces two other models: the strict, disciplinary parents who shame and punish the child; and what he calls the liberal model, where the parents soothingly respond to the child's emotional needs, but the ultimate goal is to allow each family member to go back to sleep as soon as possible. After this interruption, Ranschburg releases us to these other two skits.

While Ranschburg made it clear that the last, liberal model was the most effective, he was careful not to issue judgment on the other options either. As Margit László explained at a recent event to commemorate *Family Circle* and its creators, the show's goal was to get people to think about their own parental strategies rather than to force cookie-cutter solutions on them. László compared these dramatized vignettes to contemporary soap operas, which are much more didactic, whereas the scenes from *Family Circle* left problems open-ended.

As someone who has been a fan of both *Family Circle* and soap operas, I was particularly struck by this comparison. Growing up with the program, I enjoyed *Family Circle* precisely because it was a rare, albeit controlled, window into the thrill that soap operas and soap-like "women's" programs later opened wide. I could not care less about Ranschburg's lengthy lectures about family models or the social problems addressed by the show. Even when rewatching episodes today, I tune out quickly, wondering instead how a person of Ranschburg's appearance, so much better suited for radio, was selected for and could survive on TV for so long. I only perk up when he introduces the next dramatized segment. I am still taken by these skits. It was easy to get lost in them because they were so engagingly written and acted. Indeed, they were star-studded affairs, which showcased the best acting talent in the country for twenty years. Kelemen revealed that, although generally it was hard to get A-list actors to work in television because of the medium's cultural value, they were eager to work on *Family Circle* because it was in prime time, the scripts were prepared by well-respected writers, and its viewership often reached five million, which was half the total population.[75]

The consensus among the creators of the show is that the episodes worked because they were so realistic. However, my 1970s and 2010s selves are in consensus that they are realistic precisely the way a well-written "quality" drama is, rather than like a reality show: they create the illusion of realism thanks to smooth dialogue and celebrity actors, whom the audience no doubt enjoyed recognizing. László acknowledged, in a humorous anecdote, that viewers kept confusing reality and fiction. For instance, when a handsome actor played a father who was obligated to pay 40 percent of his salary in child support, female viewers offered him donations to help him out.

More precisely, the program combined the scripted pleasures of a soap opera with the voyeurism of a reality program by peeking into what seemed like slices of ordinary families' daily lives. It authorized such pleasures by framing them with the approval of male authorities. László's comments echo those of the other people who worked on the show and other programs produced by School TV. She firmly erects what is in fact a much more elusive boundary between fictional soap opera and reality-based educational program. The unspoken gendered value of this division is especially significant. At the commemoration event in December 2013, all the official speakers were men, whose recollections were valued because of the show's cultural prestige. The below-the-line team members present were also eager to recall—sometimes raunchy—details of production. With the exception of creator-director László, these were all men. The female contributors remained silent. One editor was so uncomfortable she said

Kelemen and Ranschburg discuss parenting philosophies in a 1981 episode of *Family Circle*.

she had nothing to contribute even when the moderator directly asked her a question. While László had come up with the idea for the program and spoke very thoughtfully about it at the event, much of her effort went into affirming Kelemen's and Ranschburg's crucial impact on the "values" transmitted by the show.

The final ingredient of the program's success was that it actively solicited viewer ideas and feedback on the episodes. László said the letters poured in after each broadcast. Viewers responded most positively to the dramatized segments, which made the creators gradually shift more emphasis to these and make them more engaging. The creators drew on viewer suggestions, sociological research, and their own experiences to create a list of themes for each broadcast year. Moreover, the program mobilized a kind of public family therapy by encouraging local discussions to process the lessons of each episode. As a result, more than three hundred *Family Circle* clubs were formed throughout the country, where viewers watched the program on TV or video and then shared their thoughts.[76]

Thankfully, and in a way that was typical of much of Hungarian TV, particularly in the 1970s and 1980s, party authorities almost never interfered with the program. In December 2013, it was rebroadcast in its entirety as part of the inaugural programming for the new Hungarian public TV channel M3, dedicated entirely to nostalgic reruns. It is ironic that the ruling right-wing, ostensibly anticommunist FIDESZ Party embraced this quintessential socialist program because it focused on the family, which is central to FIDESZ's religious-nationalistic platform. In fact, the values espoused by *Family Circle* in late socialism are far more liberal than the retrograde, disciplinary, pseudoreligious attitudes to education espoused by the current government.

From clumsy and technologically burdened ambitions of mass tele-education through a variety of hybrid docufictional experiments, socialist TV reached its most effective educational formula in programs such as *Family Circle*. The program illustrates how the tension inherent in expert-led, top-down democratization was managed by drawing on previous successes with emotional mobilization and viewer participation, deploying a mixed aesthetic of educational realism and dramatic fiction, led by paternal masculine figureheads but infused with the sensitivities of behind-the-scenes female labor. The program highlights that, in their most mature forms, socialist educational "reality programs" were far from ideological mouthpieces for the party. At their best, they were more loyal to the stated goals of public service broadcasting than the original Western European programs that may have inspired them: they supported self-improvement and lifelong learning as goals always embedded in the collective interest rather than isolated as individual problems. They encouraged learning through participation and mobilized affective engagement without yielding to voyeurism or self-serving emotional display.

3 Crime Appeal

The "crime appeal" or "reality crime" genre is an especially revealing part of reality television's prehistory because of its deep historical roots, consistent intermedial quality, and horizontal global connections. Its most familiar products are *Crimewatch UK* (BBC, 1984–present) and *America's Most Wanted* (Fox, 1988–2011). However, it is only by extricating these programs from the transnational history of television that one can call them "early 'real crime' programming."[1] In fact, these English-speaking series were late additions to a format that had thrived and circulated in Europe since the very beginning of television. Nazi Germany had a short-lived crime appeal program in 1938 called *Die Kriminalpolizei Warnt!* It had little impact given the lack of mass penetration and the scarcity of public viewing spaces.[2] Bourdon et al. tie the beginning of mass crime appeal TV to the West German program *Aktenzeichen XY . . . ungelöst* (Case XY . . . unsolved), which began on ZDF in 1967 and inspired both *Crimewatch* and *America's Most Wanted*. Its format was quickly adopted in Austria (1968–2003), in Switzerland (1969–2003), and later by the Dutch AVRO (1982–present), the BBC (1985–present), and the French TFI (1993–1996).[3] Spain, Italy, Sweden, Israel, New Zealand, and Australia developed similar programs in a subsequent wave, as part of an international boom in reality TV.[4]

While Bourdon et al. are right that the early public service broadcasting programs were "key forerunners" of the subsequent reality boom,[5] that history omits socialist programs, some of which were not only a significant part of the original wave but actually preceded *Aktenzeichen XY*.... The Hungarian program *Kékfény* (Blue light, named for the flashing lights on top of police cars), my main case study in this chapter, began in December 1965. It started out as a public affairs series that focused on real-life crime cases that had been solved, using dramatic reenactments as well as interviews with criminals, law enforcement, and other professionals. In 1969, it began to solicit the public's help with solving unresolved cases. *Blue Light* and other socialist crime appeal series shared the goal of fostering viewer participation with their European counterparts. These shows were also embedded in an obsession with spy and crime dramas nurtured by the spirit of the Cold War. However, they were unique in their political approach, since under state socialism all crime was considered to be against collective property and values. In addition, similar to Western European crime appeal programs, they displayed a significantly more critical attitude toward voyeurism than later series, particularly the U.S. formats. At the same time, they authorized a more accepting attitude toward state surveillance. Because of their fairly uncontrolled flow and unanimous popularity across borders, crime appeal programs require a transnational comparative historical examination, to which socialist formats made a significant, so far unacknowledged, contribution.

Cold War Reality Fiction

Crime appeal programs existed at the borders of reality and fiction, where television does its most effective work. Fictional series that revolved around crime and detective work were a universally loved genre of the Cold War, from detective and spy dramas to historical adventure shows. In fact, as Jonathan Bignell shows, they produced transnational formats before formats were officially codified as such. Bignell examines the interchange between Hollywood and the British Elstree Studios, which swapped a number of long-running detective and adventure drama serials in the 1960s and 1970s, including *Rawhide* and *Gunsmoke*; crime dramas such as *77 Sunset Strip* and *M Squad*; and spy series such as *The Man from UNCLE*, *I Spy*, and *Mission Impossible*. British companies ABC and ITC sold series back to the United States. The most memorable of these was *The Avengers*, which used British vocabulary, costume and decor, and story lines similar to those in *The Man from* UNCLE, *The Prisoner, The Champions*, and *The Saint*, the first one-hour British series to accommodate the U.S. market. Historical series like *The Adventures of Robin Hood* were structured as similar to U.S. Westerns but with the addition of more complex narratives than the conventional good versus evil scheme and the regular chase and fight scenes.[6]

This international genre family blended elements of crime, espionage, and costume adventure. The programs developed a "distinctive spatial aesthetic that is a national and international hybrid."[7] Bignell calls the generic style such shows shared "telefantasy." Narratively, the British programs tended to feature international adventurers and spies who traverse, police, and manage space. Politically, they were about a world system that needed to be stabilized and managed by elite nations and their institutional representatives from Britain and other major European countries, working together with the United States. This hybrid genre also prefigured a cross-fertilization between TV and film technology that is now a routine aspect of media convergence.

While the crime appeal series were an organic crop in the socialist Eastern European TV soil, we cannot ignore the fact that this soil had already cultivated many of the "telefantasy" hits. These translated well into the dualistic worldview of socialism, which allowed little ambivalence between (male) heroism and cowardice. *The Saint* was a wildly popular event on socialist screens.[8] Socialist countries also imported *The Adventures of Robin Hood* and produced their own homegrown adventure shows based on the same narrative and aesthetic models. *Columbo* (1971–2003) swept Eastern European nations in the 1970s and 1980s, when the atmosphere became more welcoming to American imports in the east and west of Europe. German police dramas also remained popular in Eastern Europe throughout the socialist period. *Derrick, Tatort*, and their kin were a good fit for the authoritative ethos of socialist TV by virtue of their older, more respectable, statesmanlike detectives and their more subdued, dialogue-based styles.

East German television was under particular pressure to confront the competition presented by West German police and crime series, which most households of the GDR were able to receive. One of the GDR's most successful responses was *Polizeiruf 110*, a detective show launched in 1971 as a rival to *Tatort*.[9] It was later picked up by ARD and was so popular that it survived the GDR's demise. Its longevity is likely due to the balance it struck between telefantasy, or the fictionalization and dramatization of crimes, and the pedagogical drive and reality-based aesthetic of socialist

TV. Unlike *Tatort*, which focused on the protagonists' private lives, *Polizeiruf* foregrounded and exalted the shared public investment in police activities involved in frequent crimes such as fraud, theft, juvenile delinquency, alcoholism, child abuse, rape, and domestic violence. The scripts were keen to model appropriate socialist behavior and dismiss inappropriate conduct. As the socialist order declined, *Polizeiruf* also shifted toward more serious crimes, the psychological motivations of the people involved, and a more sensationalized presentation—essentially replicating the aesthetic and moral universe of *Tatort*. Postunification episodes differ from *Tatort* only in their preference for former East German settings. *Polizeiruf 110* was a prime example of how socialist television tried to navigate between the educational imperative that it had to privilege, the ideological expectation to support the authority of socialist parties, and viewers' yearning for telefantasy.

A 1985 preview of Hungarian TV's upcoming offerings promised to please the "populous camp of crime-drama lovers," the most popular genre on television, with new episodes of *Derrick*, *Tatort*, *Starsky and Hutch*, *Agatha Christie*, a Soviet series about Sherlock Holmes, and the Czech program *The 30 Cases of Major Zeman* (1976–1980).[10] The latter was an especially high-profile production, originally planned as a tribute to the thirty-year anniversary of the Czechoslovak National Security Police in 1975, produced by Czechoslovak Television's Army and Security Department rather than the Department of Entertainment, which was in charge of other serials, and sponsored by the Czechoslovak Ministry of the Interior, whose officials closely supervised the production. Each of the thirty episodes (as opposed to the standard seven to ten) cost a million and a half Czechoslovak crowns, almost as much as a feature film.[11] The show follows young communist Jan Zeman for thirty years of his life, from joining the police force until his retirement. Each episode is dedicated to one year of socialist history from 1945 onward. Petr Bílek calls the serial "propagandistic entertainment," which blended the detective or crime genre with features of the adventure drama and spy thriller.[12] While Zeman was responsible for solving criminal cases, the episodes also emphasized his harmonious collaboration with the secret police. Although it was never officially acknowledged, his character was conceived as a kind of socialist James Bond. Bílek claims that this influence was mediated by other socialist serials that carried the impact of James Bond more explicitly, such as the Polish serial *Stawka większa niż życie* (More than a life at stake, 1967–1968.) The "Polish James Bond" of that show, Hans Kloss, is a double agent during the war, a Pole captured by Soviet intelligence, who impersonates a German spy and pretends to work for the Nazi Abwehr. It was left obscure whom Kloss ultimately worked for other than that he was serving a socialist cause.[13]

Kloss's persona also closely resembles that of Max Otto von Stierlitz, the spy hero of the Soviet serial *Seventeen Moments of Spring* (1973), another important influence on *Major Zeman*. Stierlitz is actually Maxim Maximovich Isaev, a Soviet spy who operates in Nazi Germany to gather intelligence on secret negotiations between Nazi leaders and Western allies.[14] This twelve-episode drama, created by Tatiana Lioznova at Gorky Studio for Children's and Youth Films, was one of the first attempts by Soviet Central Television to use the miniserial format to relieve documentary and news programming of their burden to disseminate ideological content but without yielding to the serial form's addictive "Western" pleasures. Christine Evans notes the similarity between *Seventeen Moments* and Czechoslovak serials such as *Zeman* in their purpose to "reforge the relationship between state authority and the public."[15]

Besides the ideological gains, Soviet television also embraced the miniserial for its economic benefits. As Evans notes, Soviet cultural producers were quite willing to compromise their ideological principles to get access to foreign markets.[16] *Seventeen Moments* proved to be an effective vehicle to reach audiences within and beyond the bloc. Like *Zeman* and similar serials that circulated within Europe in the 1960s and 1970s, *Seventeen Moments* mixed crime and detective drama with the spy and adventure series and partisan films set in wartime. It was based on a spy novel by Iulian Semenov, which was turned into a "genuine political film" promoted "from above," mixing in the features and goals of a serious documentary. The show was popular not simply for its fictional pleasures but also for the jokes it generated due to its extreme long takes, nostalgic, slow movements, and relentless seriousness. Indeed, Stirlitz barely cracks a smile throughout the episodes.[17]

The hybrid global spy genre epitomized by James Bond not only linked up the Soviet-controlled world with a European television market but also shifted socialist televisions' didactic thrust from straightforward news and educational programming to more enjoyable, fictional formats. The way socialist televisions filled the Bond template varied in significant ways, however. While Major Zeman solved his thirty cases with the help of a national and international collective, showcasing the principle of collaboration, Stierlitz acted as a lone wolf, who had a firm command over

Vladimír Brabec as Major Zeman.

his helpers. While Zeman was a dedicated family man, Stierlitz only managed to cobble together a temporary, symbolic family during one of his missions. Otherwise, *Seventeen Moments* "entirely excludes everyday life, romantic love, and family dynamics," the essential ingredients of Czechoslovak serials, and revolves around "a kind of sexless, imperial nuclear family."[18] The Soviet serial, Evans argues, had a goal distinct from those of Eastern European serials: to cultivate and embrace a superior, imperial identity.

Like Bond, both Zeman and Stierlitz continue to thrive in reruns and nostalgic recollections as regenerative figures of countless intertextual references, parodies, and political discussions. They continue to bind together the politics of everyday life and the politics of the state.[19]

Socialist Crime Appeal

The iconic West German crime appeal program *Aktenzeichen XY . . . ungelöst* was the first reality crime show to present reconstructed real crimes as short filmic narratives. It asked the audience to call in live and turned the TV studio into an extended police department. An hour-long program, it was broadcast once a month in Friday prime time. It presented three to five cases per episode, interspersed with interviews with senior detectives following the dramatic reconstructions. The program caused much controversy when it was first launched. It was accused of blurring the boundaries between fact and fiction and between information and entertainment. It was also seen to violate journalistic conventions. Host Eduard Zimmermann became a controversial representative of West German conservatives' call for law and order in reaction to the student protest movements of the late 1960s and early 1970s.[20] The program engaged in prosecuting members of the Red Army Faction (the Baader-Meinhof Gang) in the late 1960s. *Aktenzeichen* was also obsessed with rape and openly discriminated against women. It was accused of yielding editorial authority to the police and the state, undermining the principle of public service broadcasting, disseminating fear and anxiety about crime, profiting from voyeuristic pleasures, and interpellating the national audience as police informers.[21] But the show also became a catalyst for a more widespread discussion about democracy and the cultural effects of TV.

Aktenzeichen XY was never copyrighted as a format, so national channels were free to create their own adaptations. In 1982, twenty years after German-speaking countries launched their versions, the Dutch AVRO made *Opsoring Verzocht* (Detection requested), which dealt with low-level crime and used a neutral style of representation. It did not include dramatized reconstructions. Despite being dull, it had a 25 percent audience share in the 1980s and 10 percent still in the 1990s.[22] *Aktenzeichen* is still on the air, now under its third host.

The British *Crimewatch UK* also collaborated with police authorities in 1984. The program was created after a freelance researcher more or less accidentally came across *Aktenzeichen XY*. In Thatcher's Britain, *Crimewatch*

Eduard Zimmermann, host and heart of *Aktenzeichen XY . . . ungelöst*.

was in accord with the government's policy of reinforcing law and order, with the focus on detecting and convicting criminals instead of exploring social backgrounds or delinquency. It contained interviews with victims and their relatives. It was also *Crimewatch* that made crime appeal shows accessible to the international TV market. In Southern European countries, the format was less successful and was dropped shortly after it was introduced. In France, it ran into popular opposition to the culture of informing and its association with trash TV and Americanization.

Eastern European televisions also produced similar programs. Czechoslovak TV's criminal investigation program, launched in 1973, had the long and unappealing name *Federální kriminální ústředna pátrá, radí informuje* (The federal criminal bureau investigates, helps and informs). The title was so unfortunate that people still refer to it in jokes.[23] The Romanian program that comes closest to the genre was called *Reflector*. It dealt mostly with minor crimes such as theft, corruption (including political corruption in the 1960s and early 1970s), and other forms of social misdemeanor. Reporters would investigate cases brought to them by viewer letters. Romanian TV minimized the presence of serious crime on TV because it undermined the regime's idealized image of itself. News about serial killer Ion Rimaru in the early 1970s, for instance, never made it to TV because it would have reflected badly on the regime.[24]

Polish Television's most popular crime appeal program was *Magazyn Kryminalny 997*.[25] Although it was modeled on *Aktenzeichen*, it began only in 1986, nineteen years after the German program started. The show aired on TVP2, the second public channel, in thirty-minute episodes. Its format resembled that of *Aktenzeichen*, including crime reconstructions and appeals to viewers to help with solving cases. The episodes began with freeze photos of criminals flanked by the 977 emergency number, while a droning male voice read out their alleged crimes. This was immediately followed by scenes of crime reconstruction, in realistic black-and-white footage that could be mistaken for surveillance videos used in reality programs today. Between 1986 and 1996, each episode attracted almost fifteen million viewers, rivaled in popularity only by the Brazilian telenovela *Isaura*, a massive success everywhere in Eastern Europe.[26] Even the producers were surprised by the enthusiastic response. Initially the program was hosted by police colonel Jan Plocienniczak, replaced by Michal Fajbusiewicz in 1990. The Polish police had some discomfort with the program's potential to showcase police inadequacy in solving crimes. However, the show quickly proved that it could facilitate collaboration between the police and the public. Like *Aktenzeichen*, *Magazyn Kryminalny 997* survived socialism and has continued with some interruptions (1993–1995 and 2010–2013) into the present day. In 2013, its name was changed to *997 Fajbusiewicz na Tropie*. Its nostalgic value is indicated by the fact that the theme music has remained the same: part of the song "Cronus" (Saturn) by the American band Chase.[27]

Blue Light

The Hungarian *Blue Light* (*Kékfény*) was launched in December 1964 with the goal to revisit some of the most famous crimes committed in the postwar period. Its less explicit but equally important intention was to improve the image of the police. It was produced by an all-male team of journalists in cooperation with the Ministry of the Interior, which provided the criminal material for the program. It absorbed the lessons, experiences, and themes of other established nonfiction programs about law and order such as *Visszapillantó tükör* (Reverse-view mirror) and *Tárgyalás után* (After the trial), which had already built an audience. The *Radio and TV Guide* announced *Blue Light* in this way: "The flashing blue sirens of police cars will move into the TV studio. From December 12 on, the new program *Blue Light* will be broadcast monthly. One of the interesting features of the program is that it will finalize its contents at the last minute, incorporating the events of the past week, up to the day of the broadcast.

Reporters will take turns contributing stories from various parts of the country. We can already reveal that the show will include fascinating footage captured by hidden cameras."[28]

The thirty-minute show was an instant success. In its first few years, it revolved around closed cases, alternating dramatic reenactments, interviews with criminals sentenced to prison, and commentary by reporters. An article in a 1965 daily described the fledgling series as a "criminal museum."[29] To fulfill the program's social mission, its creators took an explicitly educational, moralizing perspective. The July 28, 1966, episode titled "Villas at Balatoni Street," for instance, sought to expose not only the criminals who broke into the villas in question but also "human indifference and carelessness, which [enable] the proliferation of crimes against collective property and violate us all."[30]

In 1969, the creators began to solicit viewers' help with solving ongoing cases. According to László Szabó, who hosted the program for its entire duration under socialism (1964–1989), the change was inspired by foreign versions of the format, particularly ZDF's *Aktenzeichen*. *The Radio and TV Guide* issued this call to viewers before the first participatory broadcast in 1969:

> Real crime is always different from crime borne out of someone's imagination. We, the creators of *Blue Light*, are convinced that there is nothing more exciting and fantasy-filled than real life, even if that life takes place in the underworld. There are crimes that never get resolved, even very serious ones. It's like that all around the world, including our country—although even the Scotland Yard or the West German police, known for its precision, could learn a thing or two from the efficiency of Hungarian police units, especially when it comes to solving crime against property and persons. Can one improve on this success? . . . Yes. With your help, dear viewer. We make a persuasive case: a person can hide from the police for a while—but not from society. When a crime is committed, the police have to arrange many little pieces into a mosaic, which is a lot of exhausting work. Some of you, however—one, or ten, or a hundred viewers, who knows how many ahead of time—can help us find shortcuts![31]

Viewers responded with great enthusiasm. The police caught a wanted criminal in mere minutes after the first participatory broadcast: "Escaped criminal Sándor Görög . . . evidently thought that Budapest's 2-million-strong population is the thickest forest to hide in. How could this wanted and dangerous criminal have known that, while he was hanging around the Hotel Metropol, perhaps plotting his next crime, the country would break out in detective fever? Hundreds of thousands are watching their neighbors and passersby with suspicion. Imagine the criminal's surprise when the detectives surrounded him and the handcuffs closed around his wrists."[32]

Following the shift to viewer involvement, the show settled into the one-hour format it would follow until the end of the Cold War. It was broadcast once a month, in prime time, followed by a rerun on the Saturday after the main broadcast. In its first fifteen minutes, the program showed photos and other relevant information about violent offenders sought by the police. Similar to *Aktenzeichen*, sharing pictures of alleged criminals who were not actually convicted raised serious ethical questions about the program's practices and tight collaboration with the police. Viewers were able to call the show during the broadcast and write or call in for five days after it. Viewer comments were delivered to Szabó on pieces of paper by an assistant during the broadcast. Each program also contained a "thematic block." The themes—alcohol-related crimes, crimes against public property, violence within the family, infant murders, and so forth—were chosen by Szabó; and the police helped locate cases that fit the theme.[33]

Each episode featured regular police and legal experts, also chosen by Szabó, who would answer his and viewers' questions on the show. What these officials contributed was the stamp of seriousness and the reassurance that authorities were fighting crime and keeping the population safe. In effect, most of their responses were variants of "It's all good" and "We'll look into it." Their participation in this televised democratic exchange was as symbolic as that of the audience: Szabó comments that following up on citizens' tips often simply gave the police extra work, which rarely paid off in terms of closing cases. Another fixture of the show was the popular Judge Aranka Gróf, whose job was to read the list of crimes to be investigated at the beginning of the broadcast. Szabó picked a woman for this job because, in his words, "bad things are made more pleasant by the presence of women."[34]

Blue Light remained a hit throughout its long run. According to a large-scale audience survey conducted in 1972, it was watched each week by an average of 5.9 million viewers, about 60 percent of the total population, which is no small feat even in an age of broadcasting monopoly.[35] In a system that attributed crime to capitalism and only allowed it to be represented in campy fictional form in detective and spy dramas, *Blue Light*

Szabó at the helm of *Blue Light*.

offered a glimpse into the unspoken parts of socialist reality, no matter how moralizing, didactic, and controlled its perspective was.

One of the key factors in the show's success in navigating between the prohibited and the tolerated, between the official take on crime and its everyday reality, was the figure of the host, László Szabó. He had started out as a crime reporter for the daily *Népszabadság*. Even though he continued to produce investigative journalism for various print outlets and television programs, and also served as a host for the Sunday night television newsmagazine *The Week*, *Blue Light* was such a recognizable and popular brand that his own image became inseparable from it. Put in his own characteristically down-to-earth style, "*Blue Light* stuck to me like bugs to a dog."[36] His twenty-five-year career at the helm of the program exemplifies the surprising amount of freedom and power afforded to leading television personalities and the corresponding role these people had in shaping television's direction. At a time of very limited travel opportunities for ordinary citizens, Szabó visited the Scotland Yard six times for professional exchanges. He published a series of newspaper reports about these visits and wrote about them in his many books. He also visited the New York Police Department and the FBI. He kept a correspondence with Eduard Zimmermann, the infamous host of *Aktenzeichen*, at Zimmermann's initiation. They mutually visited and observed each other's programs, and they each wrote two books about their experience with hosting their own shows. While *Blue Light* adopted from *Aktenzeichen* the practice of processing open cases and soliciting viewer help with solving these, the West German show had actors dramatize scenes, whereas on the Hungarian show "everything was original," as Szabó put it.[37]

Szabó insists that the only restriction on what kinds of cases could be featured on the show was his own internal self-censorship. This in itself is not specific to the socialist regime. What is specific is the nature of the issues that had to be avoided. Szabó says, and many of my other interviewees confirm, that because party secretary János Kádár had no interest in and did not watch television, internal control was usually set by the president of Television and Radio, with minimal and random interference from party authorities. Nevertheless, everyone in television knew that the one taboo topic for Kádár was the Soviet Union. Therefore, Szabó recalls he knew he would not be able to discuss on the show the case of the Soviet soldier who shot at random cars with a machine gun and killed seventeen people. This was an event everyone in Budapest heard about but that never existed as far as the official news media was concerned. However, in all other matters, Szabó says, "No one ever told me to do or not to do anything. There was one case when they pushed me to do a story on a case but I resisted, only because it was a petty little case, not interesting enough."[38]

Szabó was able to keep his privileged position as the host of this politically important and sensitive program because he believed in socialist ideology and was committed to the system and its legitimacy. While he says he recognized the socialist system's mistakes and limitations, he trusted, like many others, that these could be corrected.[39] However, even though everyone in a leadership position, particularly in the news and current affairs division, had to demonstrate some understanding of where the official line was drawn, television also "had some air to breathe." For instance, Szabó recalls that the long-term head of the news division, Mrs. Matúz, otherwise widely held to be a loyal socialist, forbade the use of the word "comrade" on the news. Szabó got in trouble with her when he once accidentally said it on the air. Someone from the party center also noticed this inconsistency, since party leaders were aware of and turned a blind eye to the "anticomrade" policy. Characteristically, at that point Mrs. Matúz came to Szabó's defense and told the party functionary to leave him alone. Szabó himself had so much political clout that he took the liberty to hang up the phone on party functionaries when they tried to interfere with his work on the show. He had personal access to Kádár, who backed him up against such interferences on several occasions.[40]

Because his political image as a journalist was so deeply intertwined with the socialist government's crime-fighting machinery, Szabó clearly saw that his TV career could not be prolonged past the life of the system. In 1989, he took an early retirement. Two weeks later, he opened the first postsocialist private detective agency in Budapest, which he successfully led for twenty-five years—as long as he had hosted *Blue Light*. While this may seem like a remarkable career change, it makes perfect sense: he was not only able to capitalize on his existing connections with politicians and law enforcement but could also indulge his lifelong fascination with crime and detective work. Szabó is an avid consumer of detective novels, police dramas, and legal procedurals and wrote several detective novels himself. His career is emblematic of the mutual imbrication of popular fiction and Cold War politics and lends a socialist color to crime-based "telefantasy."

Regrettably, Szabó rarely grants interviews even though he is obviously an experienced and amusing storyteller. What is even more regrettable is that much of *Blue Light* is lost. The early episodes were mostly broadcast live, and the taped segments have either disappeared from the archives or are impossible to access.

But this is not the end of the story of *Blue Light*.

Postsocialist Crime Appeal

Szabó registered the name "Blue Light" as a trademark when the program ended in 1989. About ten years later, the public broadcaster MTV approached him for permission to use the name for a program it wanted to launch. He agreed, on the condition that the show's producers would continue to work in collaboration with the police. The new *Blue Light* borrowed the old one's name but was in fact the third postsocialist crime appeal program to continue the old format. The first two, *Kriminális* and *112*, both begun in the 1990s, were reluctant to evoke associations with *Blue Light*, which was seen as inextricable from the tattered legacy of socialism. While these first two postsocialist attempts at the crime appeal genre were fairly successful, MTV finally decided that the associations with the original *Blue Light* might actually add more nostalgic value to the show and increase, rather than decrease, ratings. This is when they asked Szabó to grant use of the title. They were right. The new show began under the old name in 2002.

Gergő Olajos, one of the hosts and producers who took over the postsocialist *Blue Light* in 2006, explains that they deliberately evoked much of the original program's aesthetic and structure precisely to trigger recognition. They kept the memorable opening sequence featuring the flashing blue lights and the theme music, which recalled the joint memory of 1960s crime series and the crime appeal program. They also had a policewoman read crime reports to evoke Aranka Gróf's fondly remembered role in the original series. This format lasted until 2011, when the current right-wing government had them do away with the music and the policewoman, presumably to distance the public broadcaster from the socialist legacy once again. While the government radically revised the entire programming and personnel of Hungarian Television, interestingly, they allowed *Blue Light* to continue because it guaranteed a certain level of viewership they did not want to lose: an older demographic, who may remember the original *Blue Light* and deliver conservative votes to the ruling FIDESZ party. According to Olajos: "*Blue Light* is an untouchable brand. The old *Blue Light* was a heavily watched, successful program. Even as a monthly show, it was shorter than our current monthly magazine. But at the time that was the only place where people could hear about crime because the news did not deal with it. They also interviewed a lot of criminals. That's what people remember."[41]

Of course, the new *Blue Light* has had to survive in a very different, much less hospitable environment. Olajos explains that the old program thrived not the least because socialist governments censored crime, since "crime itself did not fit the socialist worldview. It was a feature of the West. This is why they had determined what fit the program and what didn't, and who could be interviewed and who couldn't. Criminals were made to confess their crimes with a great deal of contrition. And of course the program had a monopoly."[42]

The current *Blue Light* needs to make it in an environment where regular news mostly revolves about violent crime and public broadcasters cannot compete with commercial channels when it comes to the money, personnel, technology, and willingness it takes to display blood and generate fear. Therefore, Olajos and his team created a profile for the show that, as he puts it, is actually closer to fulfilling the public service goals of the original show than the original had been. And thus *Blue Light* continues to be politicized. Olajos, who had worked for TV2, one of the two largest commercial broadcasters in Hungary until 2006, explains that both TV2 and its rival RTL Klub have entire divisions specialized in covering crime. The new *Blue Light* therefore found a niche in something the commercial broadcasters do not cover: exploring cases that happened sometime in the past. It became a program that analyzes rather than wallows in crime, focusing on the psychology of criminals and the social context of certain types of offenses. This deep coverage, a strategy of "going behind" crime, as Olajos puts it, while borne out of the realization that they are not competitive for all eyeballs in an environment of high thresholds of impressionability, guarantees a reliable rate of viewership and is more in line with the public service broadcasting remit. The new *Blue Light* has settled into a program for older, more educated viewers with sensibilities trained in the old system, who are more resistant to spectacle and sensationalism.[43]

Crime Appeal as Early Transnational Reality Format

Crime appeal shows open up unexpected windows into actually existing socialism and its afterlife. They place socialist televisions firmly in the prehistory of reality television, as institutions participating in European and transatlantic program flows that mixed crime and spy fiction with real-life crime reporting, rendering these genres mutually permeable within a shared Cold War culture. Socialist crime appeal programs were some of the earliest experiments in reality-based programming that balanced an educational intent to demonstrate the operation of state institutions with a sensationalized look at private lives. Their crucial distinction was that they made their propaganda intent quite transparent, in line with an official ideology of privileging collective values and property. The story of the long-running program *Blue Light* also reveals the special role powerful personalities played in manipulating the letter of the law by relying on personal connections with party leaders and with foreign institutions. Such a story goes against the typical assumption that an all-powerful party monitored and controlled the media. The high level of viewer participation also, and perhaps positively, distinguished these programs as forerunners of reality formats. No wonder *Blue Light* migrated so smoothly to the postsocialist public broadcaster, fulfilling a service remit in opposition to the commercial channels.

Deborah Jermyn, in her book-length discussion of *Crimewatch UK*, notes that the emergence of reality-based programming raises new challenges for TV and cultural studies, particularly due to such programs' often uncomfortable blurring of the boundaries between documentary and fiction. "Real crime" programs cause particular discomfort because they may confuse the ethical borders between real and fictional crime—as evidenced by the number of documentary-style reality spin-offs inspired by fictional crime dramas.[44] I argue that this blurring is not new but has a significant history in socialist protoreality programs. Tracking this history sheds light on television's role in the negotiations across reality and fiction that sustained socialism.

The Great Socialist Game (Show) 4

The Socialist Game Show

The fact that game and quiz shows were present and popular throughout the history of socialist TV is at least somewhat counterintuitive. After all, the genre has been one of the "ghosts" of public service broadcasting even in Western Europe, where it was nevertheless no less popular. It was often considered a "bad genre," "a damning synecdoche for the whole of the medium."[1] It was repeatedly accused of turning knowledge into trivia; its history is blemished by cases of corruption; it pitted participants against one another for financial or other material gain; it created television celebrities; and it thrived on humiliating candidates for viewers' voyeuristic pleasure. In these regards, it built a slippery historical slope toward the murky flood of reality programming.[2]

In Eastern Europe, these formats bring up even more fundamental contradictions embedded in the structure of socialism. In the first place, since they were not domestically developed for the most part, they reveal socialism's intricate international connections with capitalism. They were often formats more or less directly borrowed from Western European public service broadcasters and, like those broadcasters, also incorporated elements of American commercial variants. The generic boundaries among game, quiz, and variety shows tended to be unclear everywhere. While they changed over the decades to register the political and economic shifts in national or regional socialist cultures, we can also see the same types crop up everywhere. Some were coordinated with the help of Intervision, a regional cooperative network of program exchanges that begun in 1957 and involved Czechoslovakia, Poland, the German Democratic Republic (GDR), and Hungary. Such was a 1963 quiz show about space travel, which included local broadcasts from member countries; or *Fly By*, the 1967 international competition among flight attendants organized by eleven international airlines, which also included live local broadcasts from socialist capitals.[3] Others, such as musical talent shows, were seen by governments as prime export products. Despite their ambiguous moral status, game and quiz shows remained staples of socialist programming. They contribute to an alternative prehistory of reality-based programs and of the entire bipolar Cold War world order.

Furthermore, while socialist television programs participated in the circulation of European and American game show formats, for the most part they adapted these formats to the stricter moral codes of socialist citizen training. With the genre, socialist TV found a balance between educational content and entertaining format. As I show, this balance was elusive to begin with. But when commercial television broke up Western European public broadcasters' monopoly in the 1970s, the ensuing dual-system broadcasting also pushed socialist game shows to become less educational and more commercialized. The 1970s and 1980s brought about what popular "quizmaster" István Vágó, creator and host of numerous quiz and game shows for Hungarian TV, called the golden age of the genre.[4] The golden age issued a threat to the equilibrium between the official ideologies of state socialism and the "capitalist" properties of most game show formats. After all, these programs whipped up competition, fostered a desire for consumer goods, and revolved around individual talents rather than democratic participation.

At first sight, the role of competition appears to be one of the clearest divides between the two world systems. At the heart of socialism is a collaborative, collective ethos, routinely set in contrast with the competitive and individualistic forces that drive capitalism. How is it that the competitive nature of these programs was embraced by socialist populations and authorities alike without causing significant ideological friction? Does the popularity of televisual competition undermine our received notions about socialism? Or, to take the implications a step further, what does the popularity of game shows explain to us about the fact that socialism raised several individualistic, ambitious, competitive generations, evident not only in socialist countries' achievements in sports, the arts, and the sciences but also in the ease with which a large number of citizens and institutions adjusted to the demands of cutthroat individual competition in the early 1990s?

An obvious answer would be that socialist ideals of collectivity and democratic collaboration fizzled out by the late 1960s of the ideological thaw. Game shows, which became staples of socialist entertainment by this time, nurtured cynicism toward socialist ideals and a corresponding longing for the consumer comforts of capitalism. While there is certainly some truth to this, the situation is far more complicated. What the seamless embrace of the genre reveals is the existence of an inherently competitive structure within everyday socialist societies. This is a historically layered framework, whose roots reach back to pre–Cold War Europe and whose traces show their most visible patterns in popular culture. In other words, quiz and game shows are much more than instruments of entertainment and education; they are sedimented historical and ideological practices. In this chapter, I examine the layers of competition as they crystallize within game and quiz show formats in relation to Cold War international relations and nationalism, in relation to consumption, and in relation to the Romantic notion of talent. I conclude with a glimpse at post–Cold War changes in quiz and game shows following the arrival of codified formats.

TV Competition and the Cold War

Kennedy and Khrushchev agree that they will have a car race to decide which world system has technological superiority. Kennedy wins. The respective countries' presses announce the results: According to the *New York Times*, "Kennedy came in first and Khrushchev second in the car race to decide which world system is technologically superior." *Pravda* writes, "Yesterday, in the car race to decide whether socialism or capitalism is superior, Comrade Khrushchev managed to nab the prestigious second place. Mr. Kennedy was only able to finish as the one before last."
—HUNGARIAN JOKE FROM THE 1980S (AUTHOR'S TRANSLATION).
"PESTI VICCEK A SZOCIALIZMUS IDEJÉN" WEBSITE

In the broadest sense, all socialist institutions were implicated in the Cold War competition between the two superpowers. But beyond constant reminders of the arms race and the importance of diplomacy, even friendly encounters that showed no obvious traces of contest were underscored by a competitive spirit. Some of these encounters disclosed lines of alliance that ran contrary to the competition between the two superpowers. As Katalin Miklóssy writes, the entire period was overdetermined by the narrative of an almost supernatural battle between superpowers, confirmed by the winner's story after 1989. However, the story of bilateralism is repeatedly subverted by alternative paradigms. There was, in fact, a dense network of interactions involving a variety of institutional and individual players, often built by the superpowers themselves. Sari Autio-Sarasmo and Katalin Miklóssy posit that "Europe is an interesting research subject because of the fact that, although its space was divided most transparently by the Iron Curtain, this continent still bore strong evidence of a shared cultural hemisphere, in addition to vivid memories of traditional networks, trade relations and political alliances."[5] Some of these networks continued pre-1945 alliances and traditions. Some were intra-Soviet camp alliances among nations, others were intranational among classes or groups of people within nations.

As a result, competitions of all kinds were part and parcel of Soviet and Eastern European national cultures and daily lives. According to Christine Evans, "There were sports, from soccer and hockey to figure skating and everything in between, at levels ranging from young children to Olympians. There were local, regional, national, and international competitions in music, mathematics, and chess; 'socialist competitions' pitting everyone from grade schoolers to factory workers against their peers; examinations, dissertation defenses, and so much more."[6]

As economic, diplomatic, and military competition had proven to be a losing battle for the Soviet Union, culture became the preferred battlefield. From as early as the 1930s, the Soviet Union pursued a policy of cultural dominance, declaring itself to be a true guardian of European classical heritage, as opposed to the corrupt and commercialized culture of the West. This rhetoric of cultural warfare intensified in the entire region during the Cold War.[7] However, Eastern European nation-states also mobilized nationalism to claim their own cultural superiority to the Soviet Union, which was widely seen in the satellite states as a backward, uncultivated colonizer rather than the benevolent leader official rhetoric had to insist on. By contrast, Poland, Czechoslovakia, Hungary, Yugoslavia, Romania, and the Baltic Republics in particular defined themselves as culturally Western, only forced by the Soviet occupation onto an inferior economic track. Popular television, under the radar of official state culture, was a major facilitator of this anticolonial cultural nationalism and competition against the Soviet Union.

By the late 1950s and early 1960s, precisely during the ascendance of TV as a mass medium, Khrushchev shortened work hours and expanded leisure time for Soviet citizens. Competition with the West in industrial and agricultural production gave way to competition based on technological advances and consumer lifestyles, holding out the promise of daily comforts after decades of strife and hardship in the Soviet Union.[8] Television was not just a conduit in this shift but literally the centerpiece of the domestic sphere, bringing the promise of rest and relaxation into the flats of mass housing estates. Television represented the epitome of the comforts of panel living,[9] paralleling the way it came to occupy the center in Kennedy's domestic America during the space war. But of course leisure had to be kept within the appropriate guidelines of cultural training and lifelong education—an area where the Soviet and other socialist regimes claimed superiority over the "corrupt" West.

In the Soviet Union of Khrushchev's thaw, television played a major role in shifting the emphasis to leisure and a particular way of life as the areas where socialism was to prevail over capitalism. Soviet Central Television's musical and youth programming underwent a significant procedural transformation after 1968 to lead this charge. For instance, it began producing popular musical competition programs such as the *Song of the Year* contest.[10] Television was the primary medium to coordinate Cold War competition in the form of various contests referred to as cultural Olympics.[11] The largest international televised events of these cultural Olympics were the World Youth Festivals. But while the ostensible role of the festivals was to foster collaboration and cultural exchange among the Soviet Bloc countries and foreground the cultural superiority of the socialist camp, this most normative of socialist television events was fraught with contradictions that revolved around national competition, tension within the Soviet bloc, and leaks within the bipolar paradigm.

Pia Koivunen explains that the festival offered contests and exhibitions in all fields of arts and culture, from Olympic sports to classical music and ballet, film and theater, fine arts and photography, folk art, political education, and even mass demonstration. It displayed the concept of "socialist competition" in all its glory and contradictions. Competition had to be downplayed in the rhetoric, which instead highlighted other notions such as talent search, enrichment, and general education. Moreover, the rhetoric of universal brotherhood was constantly undermined by the domination of Big Brother. The festivals were restricted to socialist satellite states, with the rare appearance of Third World delegations and voluntary, ad hoc groups of Western participants. Most of the winners came from the Soviet Union because juries were pressured by Soviet authorities to prove Moscow's supremacy.[12] The festival displayed on TV one of the suppressed aspects of ubiquitous competition: the intra-bloc contest between the Soviet Union and its rebellious vassals.

The German Democratic Republic was another major laboratory of socialist competition. The entire history of GDR TV can be seen in terms of increasing competition for its own audiences against the lure of West German TV.[13] This is why TV historians have argued that German TV history can only be written as a combined and comparative account of Eastern and Western developments.[14] The demand for entertaining content presented itself earlier and more urgently for GDR television than elsewhere in the Soviet camp. In 1967, GDR TV's Department of Entertainment issued guidelines that aesthetic experiments that were too intellectually demanding were to be avoided.[15] At the Eighth Congress of the GDR Socialist United Party (SED) in 1971, party secretary Erich Honecker famously diagnosed "a certain boredom" around television and urged that TV should create "good entertainment." The SED thus folded entertainment into its ideology as an important condition for reproducing labor and raising intellectually active individuals. This form of entertainment was still to be distinctly socialist, unlike the "pseudo entertaining measures" employed by capitalist media, which lacked a "positive, character-forming and culturally educating component."[16] Heinz Adameck, chairman of GDR TV, put these new guidelines into practice, phrasing the initiative in the language of competition and even war: the task was to keep people in the line of fire in order to increase their socialist awareness and prevent them from turning to West German channels.[17]

The most notorious results of ongoing competition were news programs that took clips from the other side and rebroadcast them out of context, with commentary. The GDR's *Der schwarze Kanal* (The black channel, 1960–1989) was modeled on the West German *Die rote Optik* (The red optic, 1958–1960), which used East German clips for its own anti-Soviet agitation.[18] The Federal Republic of Germany (FRG) hit hardest by showing off its superior lifestyle, implying that the GDR was economically lagging behind. East German propaganda zeroed in on the misled, isolated individual of capitalism and the FRG's lenience toward Nazi nationalist ideology.[19] Broadcast signals from the FRG reached all territories in the GDR except for the "Valley of the Clueless" near Dresden. On the Western side, only 4 to 5 percent of viewers could receive GDR programs. East German viewers living close to FRG transmitters had the most variety: even back in the late 1960s, they had at least five channels to choose from, including ZDF's first and second, the regional affiliates of ARD, and the second GDR network. The ZDF magazine show *Drueben* was produced in 1966 specifically for Eastern audiences. Morning programming on ARD was scheduled against the GDR morning show. Rather than opting to watch only the Western broadcast, however, GDR viewers watched the two systems in parallel fashion, making constant choices.[20]

The GDR tried to incorporate West German TV into its own programming and pitted popular Western shows against its own most successful products. This was especially important in high viewing times of the week.[21] In Friday prime time, the beginning of the weekend, GDR TV showed thrillers, as well as popular clips from old movies, as part of the variety show *Rumpelkammer*. Saturday night was reserved for variety shows (such as *Ein Kessel Buntes*), against ZDF's and ARD's programming. Sunday night was important in influencing the following week's mood, so GDR TV broadcast the thriller serial *Polizeiruf 110*, dramas and feature films, variety shows, and game shows such as *Schaetzen Sie mal* (Take a guess).[22]

East German quiz and game shows were strategically important in this relationship of competitive codependence. East German TV began broadcasting game shows within the first years of its existence, which often served as traveling formats that inspired similar programs in other countries. Much like on Western European public service television, quiz shows were some of the earliest genres on socialist TV everywhere, introduced as part of live broadcasting in the late 1950s. If we trace their history, we see a transformation from the early, open-ended formats of the 1950s to more or less centralized attempts at instituting more rules and controls, which were to adjust the genre to serving the mass-educational policies of the 1960s. The earliest formats arose in an era of fairly low regulation and high confusion among socialist parties as to the purposes, potentials, and dangers of the new medium. This uncertainty gave TV professionals some leeway to experiment with the genre, which was cheap to produce. Similar to Western European public service television,[23] the distinction between variety and game shows remained blurry. As entertainment increasingly came to define television in the 1970s and 1980s, quiz and game formats bore more and more of the pressure from capitalist competition and viewer demand. Direct, codified format borrowings began on a large scale in the 1990s.[24]

In the GDR, there were themed programs with specific demographics in mind such as *Glück auf!* (Good luck!, 1957–1968) about workers; *Das Grosse Spiel!* (The great game, 1963) about sports; and *Die Augen—links!* (Eyes left!, 1967–1969) about the army. *Wer rät mit—wer gewinnt* (Who guesses—who wins?, 1952–1954) and *Sehen-Raten-Lachen* (Seeing, guessing, laughing, 1955–1957) were some of the first live shows with a studio audience. *Da Lacht Der Bär* ("What makes the bear laugh," 1955–1965), *Amiga-Cocktail* (1958–1964), and *Zwischen Frühstück und Gänsebraten* (Between breakfast and roast goose, 1959–1991) were also popular live variety-game shows. Several of these developed from radio programs. *Da Lacht der Bär* featured a host trio from Berlin, Saxony, and Rhineland, respectively. Their jokes wove together popular tunes (*Schlager*), comedy, acrobatics, and operettas. The variety show *Jetzt schlägt Dreizehn* (That's the last straw, 1961) celebrated the building of the Berlin Wall and included live conversations with border guards.[25]

By the 1980s, the switch to dual broadcasting in Western Europe had further diluted the public service content within game, quiz, and variety shows.[26] In anticipation of the advent of commercial networks, first allowed in West Germany in 1984, ARD and ZDF reformed their programming to include even more entertainment. This was the beginning of the end for GDR TV, which had lost its identity in the increased competition.[27]

At the other end of the spectrum, we find Romanian television, where the oppressive Ceaușescu regime reversed 1960s policies of relative openness and eliminated most programming in the 1970s and 1980s that was not direct propaganda. This is why the two most popular new genres of post-Ceaușescu Romanian television were the quiz show and the political talk show, created as a sort of belated public service forum to make up for their absence during communism. As Daniela Mustata writes, the quiz show *Robingo*, a Sunday prime-time program under a UK license, was the first general knowledge quiz show in Romania.[28]

Most other socialist televisions were situated in between the two poles of the openly competitive GDR and isolated, entertainment-deprived Romania. Their programming and operations display constant awareness of competition with the West, even if in a less pressing race for eyeballs and emotions than was the case in the GDR. But the comparisons with the West were so common in the print and electronic media that Cold War competition registered as a neutral state of affairs, rather than as a constitutive condition of everyday socialism. A closer look at the main types of quiz and game shows throughout the region helps to make visible the historical layers and political structures of the competitive fabric of socialism.

Music Competition

Popular music competitions, the predecessors of the *Idol* format, were especially dangerous terrain for socialist parties. In Hungary, the first *Pop Music Festival* (*Táncdalfesztivál*), held in the summer of 1966, had 464 entries written by three hundred composers. The work of fifty-two songwriters was selected into the three televised preliminaries that preceded the prime-time final. It is telling of the normative value system of these programs that, while it was technically songwriters whose work was entered and who received the prizes, naturally, all eyes and emotions were trained on the performers, whose careers grew out of these first televised exposures and who popularized and legitimized contemporaneous Western musical styles.[29] The process of celebrity-making that ordinarily propels such talent competition programs was a somewhat unexpected byproduct of these pioneering socialist formats.

Despite its capitalist characteristics, the program was accepted by party authorities not only because of its enormous success with audiences but also because it made pop music television an exportable product that would create a good reputation for Hungarian culture. The presence of Western experts in the festival's international jury was also to facilitate international exchanges.[30] In addition, party leaders argued that popularizing local pop music makes it less likely that younger people would be seduced by Western music and thus reduces the dangerous attraction of capitalist lifestyles in general. Despite the official justification, *Pop Music Festival* was such a radical departure from the demure educational tone of Hungarian TV that it provoked letters of protest from die-hard socialist viewers, especially from rural areas. János Gulyás, party secretary for the Red Star tractor factory brigade in the city of Eger, objected to the long hair, clothing, and Western tunes of one of the festival winners and the British performing contracts earned by others, which he thought was an altogether dangerous thing to allow.[31] Ferenc Gódor from the party's Agitational and Propaganda Division wrote back: "The letter writer only sees the negative aspects of the festival. He ignores the fact that, with the creation of a new type of native music, Hungarian beat, we have managed to shut out Western songs and have satisfied young people prone to admiring the West by offering them the work of Hungarian songwriters, which have become professional hits. The fact that we even manage to export some of these songs is evidence of Hungarian artists' talent."[32]

These calculations proved correct, since the second round of *Pop Music Festival* in 1967 garnered 1,378 entries. The three preliminaries alone attracted 649,008 audience votes, as opposed to the first year's 140,000. Eleven foreign stations ordered the final's broadcast copy, which aired live from a Budapest theater.[33]

In Romania, the five-day televised Golden Stag Festival ran annually between 1968 and 1971, during Romania's brief period of opening toward the West and simultaneous distancing from the Soviet Union. It invited major European stars and awarded significant cash prizes. In the 1969 edition of the festival, about twenty national television companies announced their participation. The festival's broadcast included advertisements for consumer products and was accompanied by foreign language lessons on TV. The National Lottery offered prizes in the form of trips to Paris and Rome. Ceaușescu put a stop to the festival in 1971 in the name of a cultural nationalization program under the leadership of the newly appointed National Council for Radio and Television helmed by Secretary of Culture Dumitru Popescu. Although the Golden Stag Festival was not renewed under the Ceaușescu regime, several other televised music festivals carried the torch of liberalization and international broadcast cooperation in Eastern Europe. These included Poland's Sopot Festival, an alternative to the Western European *Eurovision* song contest (1977–1980). The *Golden Orchid*, held in Varna, Bulgaria, was charged with revitalizing tourism; and the *Golden Lyre* was held in Czechoslovakia up to the 1968 Soviet invasion.[34]

Soviet musical competition shows were a staple of Central Television. They were part of the Soviet leadership's effort to redirect competition with the West from factory production to lifestyle and consumption under Khrushchev. Of course these competitions also carried increasing potential for undermining Soviet ideological directives and for delivering stars, entertainment, and choices to viewers. *Pesnia goda* (Song of the year) began in 1971 and has continued into postsocialism. It was broadcast every year on New Year's Eve, marking the socialist ritual holiday calendar. Much like contemporary music competition formats, it encouraged audience participation and voting.[35]

Hello! We're Looking for Talents (1965–1972) had participants compete for a recording contract with the Soviet label Melodia. As with the Hungarian *Pop Music Festival*, one of the purposes of offering professional music careers with Melodia was to develop a Soviet alternative to seductive Western music. The talent show consisted of an annual tournament with auditions in multiple cities and allowed a significant role for viewer feedback, especially after its 1969 retooling. In the 1970s, the show introduced viewer surveys to complement the elite jury's judgment, but it was unclear how and to what extent these surveys really counted as their purpose was to produce the most "objective" evaluation, which seemed to coincide with that of the professional jury made up of famous musicians and representatives of Melodia and of Central TV. In 1971, the show began to use audience votes to replace the jury altogether. Ironically, this provoked outrage from many viewers, who protested against this overreach of democracy at the expense of professional taste and expertise.[36]

Game Shows as Cold War Olympics

The purest form of showcasing the human resources of socialism was of course sports. Every successful athlete from the Eastern Bloc carried the double burden of proving the competitiveness of their nations and the viability of socialism at once.[37] Broadcasts of international competitions such as European, world, and Olympic championships were cult events. The structure of sports competition was often directly projected onto quiz and game show formats, which helped downplay the genre's ideological disagreement with the spirit of socialist collectivity. In other words, the competitive structure of quiz and game shows was ideologically neutralized by the association with the purity of sports. Many of these programs actively cultivated this association, registering their work as an extension of sports, a form of cultural or intellectual Olympics.

For instance, Soviet television's most successful game show of all time, *Klub veselykh I nakhodchivykh*, or *KVN* (Club of the merry and quick-witted, 1961–), was described by its cocreator Sergei Muratov as "intellectual soccer."[38] The program continued the format developed by its predecessor, *Vecher veselykh voprosov*, or *VVV* (Evening of merry questions, 1957). Both shows borrowed from similar programs produced in Czechoslovakia, the United States, Poland, and the GDR.[39] The show *VVV*, which was modeled after the most popular 1950s Czechoslovak program at the time, *Gadai, Gadai, Gadalshchik*, or *GGG* (Guess, guess, you guessers),[40] was created in 1957 as part of the activities that led up to the Moscow International Youth Festival. It was thus integrated into a quintessential socialist international event. It took place in front of a live audience. Random participants answered random questions for funny, token prizes. Its open-ended format and open-door policy made it a remarkably liberal phenomenon on 1950s Soviet TV. The producers assumed little control over who or what appeared on stage.[41]

VVV came to a screeching halt after a poorly conceived call for participants, which brought an uncontrollable, sweaty mass of people storming into the studio. The producers were fired immediately. This incident confronted the messy reality of Soviet socialism with the staged world of Soviet media space, something that could not be risked again. It visualized the number one threat posed by the new medium: its own unpredictable audiences. This would prove to be a recurring problem with socialist game shows, something authorities had to learn to anticipate and navigate. Investigations following *VVV*'s failure condemned its bourgeois vulgarity, lack of ideological principle, and mockery of Soviet citizenry.[42]

These charges haunted the socialist game show throughout its existence, particularly in the Soviet Union. Four years later, the successor program *KVN* was more overtly guided by socialist principles of democratic education. At the same time, it was enabled by a web of pro-competition ideologies that underscored the working of Soviet society: the pre-Soviet, nationalistic, Romantic elitism of a creative class; the cultivation of work and the Stalinist legacy of competitive labor within factory and agricultural production; and the competition against the seductions of capitalist media. *KVN* was launched in 1961 as a monthly broadcast. It inspired regional competitions among *KVN* teams in factories, schools, agricultural collectives, the armed forces, and many other groups. Thus it significantly fostered youth mobilization and mass recreation. Some *KVN* stars became celebrities. The program was discontinued in 1972 but was resurrected during glasnost and is still broadcast in Russia. It followed a format similar to *VVV* but with more centralized control over the rules: the participants, all students and almost all men, engaged in a contest of wit and satire, including plenty of improvisation. The format also lent itself to political satire, although it was heavily censored on the spot.[43] The competition was organized by leagues, with early matches leading to playoffs, culminating in the annual championship round.[44] Teams were led by a captain, with each member specializing in tasks that best matched their talents.[45] *KVN* offered a microcosm of the hierarchical, militaristic, and sports-like organization of the socialist public sphere, led by male heroes. This was not so much because girls could not be leaders but because they were not thought of as funny or witty. As Kristin Roth-Ey sums it up, "KVN delivered a neat and useful package by design: 'the thinking person on the screen' (a male figure marked universal) as a model for Soviet viewers."[46]

This gendered hierarchy was also mirrored in the two-tier production structure: members of the creative team, whose imaginative capacity was highly valued, all shared the roles of writer, director, and editor. They spent much of their time together in a group, drinking and discussing their work, in self-isolation from the "below the line" crews.[47] At the same time, when it came to viewer mobilization, the show was more inclusive and democratic than the earlier VVV. From about 1968, Central Television's game shows systematically reached out to nonelite participants, mostly working-class men and women, who engaged in competitions that showcased idealized roles in Soviet life such as factory worker, housewife, consumer, or defender of the Fatherland. The competition was no longer live after 1968, which made it more controllable, but it involved more active viewer participation and used viewer votes in addition to professional juries.[48] Nevertheless, as more and more cities and institutions got involved, the competition got increasingly intense and professionalized. Its legacy of amateur theater gave way to the structure of a sporting event. Teams were trained to win,[49] past captains were rehired for money, comedy writers were paid, and improvisation was replaced by a scripted format.[50] The program also began to hand out prizes to winners, and its identity as an amateur game show everyone can enter for fun was eroded as it began to resemble capitalist game shows. This is likely to have made authorities cancel KVN in 1972. Another probable reason was its satirical aim at political issues such as bureaucracy and the quality of Soviet products.[51] It was also well known that Sergei Lapin, chairman of the State Committee for Television and Radio Broadcasting until his retirement in 1985 and member of the Central Committee, hated the show because it had a large number of Jewish players.

Ultimately, KVN fell victim to the contradictory imperatives that underscored socialist competition: Christine Evans writes that Soviet Central Television's staff in the 1960s was tasked with engineering a renewed Soviet personhood, to be developed through more playful, interactive, and entertaining forms of mass culture. While play and competition became key vehicles of this mass culture, they were also in conflict with the overarching top-down, didactic remit of Soviet TV.[52] Even the most trivial televised competitions had to have demonstrably higher stakes than "fun" or play. Rather than a profit motive for television companies, which fuels contemporary reality competition programs, socialist TV contests were to prove the strength of the entire system by showing off socialist societies' only competitive resources: people, their bodies, and their talents.

Similar to the Soviet KVN's concept of "intellectual soccer," the structure of sports was often superimposed on competition programs throughout the region. At times this relay between sports and game shows was quite direct: in the summer of 1964, for instance, Hungarian TV broadcast the program *Szellemi olimpia* (Intellectual Olympics) parallel with the coverage of the Tokyo Olympic Games. It included separate broadcasts that tested contestants' general knowledge of literature, fine arts, and music. It was a participatory program that asked viewers to mail in responses to questions. More than four hundred responses were mailed in after each broadcast. Sixty made it into the preliminary round and twenty into the televised final, to be led by star reporter Tamás Vitray.[53]

The figure of Vitray himself is emblematic of the ideological ties that connected sports and game shows on TV. He made a successful transition from sport reporter to quiz and game show host, and his contributions to both genres are equally significant.[54] Under Vitray's leadership, Hungarian Television developed a sports-quiz show called *Pre-Olympics* (Elő-olimpia) leading up to the Munich Olympics in 1971. The program featured athletes and was hosted by János Egri, a former Olympic hockey player turned quiz show host.[55] The entire spectrum of quiz and game shows in Hungary was covered by just four celebrity hosts: Egri, Vitray, György Rózsa, and István Vágó, who each hosted numerous memorable and successful formats in the 1970s, 1980s, and, in some cases, beyond.

The metaphor and structure of sports helped reconcile two contradictory principles of socialism within these competitive programs: hard work and talent. While sports exalted natural talent, they also required discipline and dedication. Hard work was the backbone of early communism, where factory brigades and agricultural collectives engaged in Stakhanovist competition for higher production levels, to prove the viability of the collectivist system. This kind of competition was based on the principle of equal opportunity, to offset the class distinctions that plagued the capitalist system. However, this heroic enthusiasm had lost its momentum by the time television became a mass medium. Nationalism prevailed over socialist internationalism, and consumerism and lifestyle became the new platforms for international contest. As an ideal, however, Stakhanovist heroism remained present in competitive structures that recalled sports' reliance on achievement that can be numerically measured and compared. A Hungarian program called *Csak egy kicsit jobban* (Just a little bit better, 1965) covered a competition among factories for the number and quality of their innovations. Another program from the same year, *Versengő városok* (Competing towns), set towns in competition with one another. The show *Forog az idegen* (Spinning visitors, 1966) staged a contest about tourism among nine regions. The 1970s *Fekete fehér, igen, nem* (Black and white, yes and no) was a fifteen-month, twenty-two-part competition in prime time among Budapest's districts. The winner, District XI, was awarded a fully equipped preschool. As a commentator enthused after the final, "Along the way, the noble goal ceased to be the 5-million-forint preschool; that became only a symbolic prize compared to a mass collaboration of historic significance."[56]

However, the most successful and memorable formats were talent shows that offered the suspense of a game, the promise of overnight celebrity, and valuable prizes. Such was the GDR's long-running talent show *Herzklopfen kostenlos* (A bounding heart for free, 1959–1973), hosted by different towns each time. Many amateur artists launched by the show became celebrities.[57] In Hungary, the long-lasting talent show *Ki mit tud* (Who knows what), first broadcast in 1962, followed a similar participatory format. It proved to be a recipe for sweeping success. It began with local and then regional competitions to select finalists. The risk of an open-call, open-genre competition was tempered by setting proper socialist frameworks of conduct and evaluation. The *Radio and TV Guide* wrote cautiously prior to the first edition, "When the jury, made up of young artists, begins to vote, they won't just be watching the performances. The performers should be examined on their taste, versatility, and talent; but also on their character."[58]

To further legitimize the competition as a proper socialist event, the winner and two runners-up of the six-month process were awarded a trip to the International Youth Festival, held in Helsinki that year. But despite all the careful control mechanisms, the show was so popular that viewers forced the jury to modify its final decision. People felt so strongly about the fourth-place finisher, teenage whistling virtuoso Tamás Hacki, that the organizers decided to send him to Helsinki as a fourth participant under pressure from an onslaught of viewer letters.

Although the program was a success, it also provoked concern among party cadres for encouraging a kind of urban intellectual elitism. One

Whistling virtuoso Tamás Hacki.

official release of a county-level party committee's opinion about the program, then in its second year, exemplifies the ideological puzzlement about democratic equal opportunity's conflict with the cultivation of individual talent: "*Who Knows What* has lost some quality [over the past year]. The main reason for this is that original, natural talents are overshadowed by those who perform at a high artistic level. What is ignored is that the latter have access to good training while rural talents have to resort to self-training."[59] This reaction recalls Soviet concerns about KVN's increasing professionalization. Hungarian television producers tried to perfect the *Who Knows What* formula and reassert the principles of education and democratization in a whole family of spin-offs. Some dealt with specific institutions. A 1965 edition took place among the armed forces, broadcast from a military location. *Who Suggests What?*, in the same year, solicited participation and ideas from youth about "socialist production and their own lives in society."[60] *Ki minek mestere?* (Who is a master of which trade?), in 1966, also tried to steer the popular talent show back to safe ideological waters when it set out to "show what young people do in factory production." This was code for highly unspectacular competitions where young apprentices in various trades worked on machines for hours on end. The program, which was directly supported by the party and its youth organization, and cosponsored by ministries and associations representing the mining, coal, and metal industries, awarded enticing prizes to the winners, including a motorcycle and a television set.[61]

Journalists had a hard time evaluating these shows without hints of a backhanded compliment. A typical reaction sounded like this: "A competition based on the heavy industry appears to be anti-televisual at first sight. Creating a mold and finishing a product takes a longer time than viewers can bear. There was only one way to handle this: To check in repeatedly during the two-day competition, highlighting phases in the development of the final product. It helps in rendering the program more interesting that they not only conduct hands-on competitions in the Lenin Coal Factory but that the participants also compete in their knowledge of workplace safety and political issues, which should be of interest to many more viewers."[62] Another commentator was more blunt: "Let this be a lesson for the new game shows that have been announced: factory competitions among youth, while of course they require technological authenticity, also need some fun.[63]

Although the themes and execution of these "workplace competitions" did not make for good television, the idea was no different from contemporary cooking, building, or clothes-making reality contests. Adjusting the formula to better suit domestic interests was the next inevitable step for socialist TV as well. As Christine Evans writes, in the 1970s Soviet Television's Youth Department did just that: They created game shows modeled after auctions, talent searches, beauty contests, and casinos.[64] KVN, already in the business of taste education, paled in comparison with *Auction* (1969–1970), created by the Soviet Ministry of Trade in order to advertise products that had failed to move from store shelves. Using game shows this way was an idea borrowed from Eastern European precedent, particularly in the GDR, where advertising was employed in game shows as far back as the 1950s.[65] The ostensible goal of *Auction* was to teach Soviet citizens to get to know certain products and use them to better organize people's everyday lives. It tested contestants on their knowledge of and taste in consumer products and had studio audiences vote (by shout) on their favorite items. It also offered a contest to TV viewers, who could answer consumer expertise questions by telegram the next day. The winners were rewarded with valuable prizes. A program so obviously at odds with socialist principles was bound to irk authorities and was eventually canceled.[66]

Let's Go Girls, a similar talent competition, also brought up contentious issues about Soviet ideology. It was a Soviet take on the beauty contest in that it emphasized intellect, professionalism, and modern homemaking skills rather than beauty.[67] Each broadcast featured contestants who worked in a selected profession or excelled at a homemaking skill (e.g., baking, cleaning or home decoration, salad making, dance). In the first half of the show, participants competed on location in professional contests for the right to represent their brigade or factory. In the second half, semifinalists competed in a range of housekeeping skills. The program got progressively more elaborate, complete with spectacular costumes and sets. Three finalists were selected by the jury, and viewer votes by mail allegedly determined the winner. The program was followed by *Let's Go Guys* in 1972, prompted by viewer requests. This was a game that tested sports and military skills and was judged by rather stiff elites from those professions. Due to the jury's lack of charisma, the program was canceled after two years.[68]

Perhaps the most popular socialist game show in Poland, *Małżeństwo doskonałe* (Perfect marriage) also combined the key ingredients of the format: sports, wit, domesticity, entertainment, participation, and prizes. It started out in 1967 as a live show broadcast from a small theater. The groups of three who competed against one another included a married or engaged couple, who had to pantomime key terms selected by the show host, which the third member had to guess within four minutes. The competition was interspersed with variety numbers, mostly singing and dancing. Winners were determined by four judges and were awarded prizes, some of which were humorous. Theater audiences were invited to join the fun and predict the winners for small prizes. After the first episode, which featured friends of the show's creators, teams were assembled from among viewers who applied to the broadcaster TVP to participate.[69] The five episodes of the first season were followed by twelve in the second, in which a sports-based format dubbed "marital track and field" replaced the pantomime. The challenges tested the couple's knowledge about each other. In 1968, the show's formula changed once again, and it was renamed *Kariera* (Career).[70] This time, teams of three competed in the hope of embarking on dream careers such as sailor, flight attendant, or chef.[71]

Both *Let's Go Girls* and *Perfect Marriage* indicate the strategic importance of the socialist game show as a flexible format that was able to accommodate aspects of everyday life that sat uneasily with Soviet ideology—individual competition, lifestyle, and consumer choices—in a playful, make-believe performance. While game shows officially served as instruments of mass education and participation, they also supplied a battlefield for a tug-of-war between the official intent to inject facts and values into entertainment and viewer desires generated by the thrill of the game.

Art, Talent, and Nationalism

This top-down intent to educate incorporated an elitism deeply ingrained in European cultural nationalism. Elitism also plagued Western European televisions, particularly when they were faced with the more populist fare introduced by commercial broadcasters. This was particularly true in France, where, in 1961, after a period of attacks on trivia-based quiz shows, the emphasis shifted to general knowledge starting with the long-running *L'homme du XXe siècle* (Man of the twentieth century) and continued with *Le mot le plus long* (The longest word, 1965), later renamed *Des chiffres et des lettres* (Figures and letters, 1972), based on math and science. *Monsieur Cinéma*, which ran from 1966 to 1985 under changing titles, tested participants' knowledge of cinema.[72]

Quiz and game shows in much of Eastern Europe were also dominated by an educational, taste-forming intention. The very first Hungarian quiz show on record, in 1959, tested contestants' familiarity with the classic Hungarian novel *Úri muri* by Zsigmond Móricz and was broadcast live from a theater named Literary Stage. Many competition formats that showcased expertise in various fields of knowledge followed. *Szójátékklub* (Word game club) in 1971 was one of several quiz shows intended to teach Hungarians proper use of and appreciation for their language. The host, linguist László Grétsy, wished to use the power of broadcasting to expand on a national scale the classroom-based Language Game Club initiative he had helmed. This program involved viewers and offered prizes (including money) for winners.[73] *Zenélő órák* (Musical hours, 1962) was about classical music, and *Rajzolimpia* (Drawing Olympics, 1963) measured participants' knowledge about fine arts. Some of these brainy quiz shows were aligned with the centralized educational curriculum. As early as 1961, *Próbaérettségi* (Trial high school graduation exam) staged a competition among students of six high schools in front of "exam committees" of academic experts, mimicking the format of the oral exam for high school graduation. The series *Ki miben tudós?* (Who is an expert?) was launched in 1963 to set in competition young people in various academic subjects. In its second year, the Ministry of Education decided that the winners and first runners-up in each field gained automatic admission to the university of their choice. The first cohort of admits were all men. Later, other prizes were added, such as trips abroad.

The antidemocratic implications of quiz shows that disseminated academic knowledge were especially hard to reconcile with the socialist ethos in television's most popular genre. This did not escape critics and viewers. For instance, *Földön járó csillagok* (Stars on earth, 1964), a competition show about world literature, provoked this criticism:

> A world literature quiz at an academic level—this is how we could characterize the new series, which demands high and specialized standards from its contestants. The participants of the final were the best experts on Greek drama, since they had already made it through the arduous tests of the preliminaries and semifinals. In the final, they had to have an almost perfect knowledge of the subject. This led to a contradiction between the goal and actual effect of the program. This competition could only be enjoyed by viewers who possessed a literary erudition several times the average; those who know not only what *deus ex machina* and *hubris* mean but also feel at home in the worlds of Aiskhylos, Sophocles, and Euripides. . . . This goes for Gábor Devecseri's introductory lecture, too, which even the initiated could barely follow. . . . Television didn't hide the fact that *Stars on Earth* is not intended for a broad audience, that it wants to go deeper than *TV Reading Room*. But there is a limit that you can't cross on the screen: aesthetic analysis has to be done in an enjoyable form in order to keep the connection with the viewer. If this is not the case—and this is the situation with two of the three episodes so far—good intentions backfire and the program puts off rather than stimulates.[74]

Literature-based quiz shows nevertheless continued throughout the period despite their modest popularity. Poetry in particular, which is at the affective core of cultural nationalism, was a permanent ingredient of the socialist TV menu. It also made for some of the least dynamic programming and most counterintuitive platform for TV competition.

Socialist TV featured regular recitations of classic poems performed by celebrity actors, poetry recitation competitions, and aesthetic experiments with "televisual poetry." The latter resembled avant-garde films. *Pictures of the Night*, a "television poem," was broadcast on Hungarian TV in December 1966. Its director, András Rajnai, explained in the *Radio and TV Guide*: "Television addresses us in our dimly lit homes directly and individually. This is why TV is a giant propagandist and a vehicle for the poetry of the past, present and future. The difficulty is to find pictorial forms for thoughts. But it's possible to do so and important to try. Television's youth studio, KISZ's [the Young Communists' Alliance] own creative group, took on this difficult task. In his symphonic poem, Ferenc Juhász writes the unimaginable and speaks the unspeakable. This televisual poem wants to make the unspeakable visible and wants to take it to the many."[75] The creators pieced together three hundred meters of used footage out of thirty thousand meters' worth of hybrid film material. They only filmed a single new segment, essentially creating a kind of early televisual remix for conveying poetry.[76] According to a postbroadcast assessment, which underscores the unreliability of such surveys, 89 percent of "poetry lovers" liked the program, and 34 percent of "non-poetry-lovers" (a demographic category that would only make sense under socialism) said that the program made the poem easier to understand.[77]

TV poetry contests were another form of cultural sport, which centralized poetry recitation competitions occurring at all levels, from schools through cities and counties to the national stage. These contests often focused on the work of a single classical national poet. Contemporaneous reviewers evidently felt compelled to praise these competitions, recognizing their nationalistic value. It is noticeable that critics tended to locate this value in the inherent qualities of the poems, which were understood to manifest their authors' genius. Poetry was—and to some extent continues to be—the most sacred part of the shared national cultural heritage, somehow conceived to exist in a sphere independent of changing political regimes. Only rarely, and even then heavily cloaked in layers of praise, do the reviews note the fundamentally antitelevisual character of such competitions. Critic Ádám Niklai, himself a poet, was one of these exceptions in his notes on the televised competition arranged on the national holiday of March 15, 1971, to commemorate the anniversary of revered nineteenth-century national poet Sándor Petőfi's birth. In his article "Screen and Poetry," Niklai objects to the unwatchable aesthetic of such programs. "What if we weren't forced to stare at the reciter's face, more or less appealing teeth, or worse, at the sweat gliding down his face? The point of television is the image. In a way, poetry works with images, too. It's hardly an unrealistic, unachievable goal to produce images appropriate to the poem. Can we follow Apollinaire and others and edit together images made of art, photography, hidden camera footage (and I could go on)—even experimentally?"[78] Note that even Niklai questioned only the mechanical nature of these competitions, not the rightful place of poetry on the nation's TV.

Art appreciation programs like this tried to integrate a Kantian, Romantic sense of artistic imagination that only a select few are able to access with the more inclusive creativity activated by the quiz and game show. Television had a difficult relationship with high art to begin with due to TV's suspicious status as a medium of mass entertainment. It was a constant struggle to recruit the creatives of high culture, cinematic auteurs and literary writers, who often deigned to be associated with TV. Nevertheless, socialist TV tried to bridge the inherent elitism of national culture and socialism's democratizing ethos by hosting programs for art education. This mission required bringing art appreciation to the untalented; but it was also a way to discover and nurture artistic talent. The latter was a goal much better suited for game shows, many of which doubled as talent searches.

In Hungary, several of the first popular TV announcers emerged from winning televised poetry competitions, for instance. Other game shows were more specific in their purposes. In 1964, the first season of the talent show *Riporter kerestetik* (Searching for reporters) yielded two winners, János Horvát and Ákos Moldoványi, both of whom went on to have long-lasting and successful TV careers. *Pályabelépő* (Field pass, 1970) recruited aspiring sports reporters. Of the more than five thousand applicants, thirteen made it into the final.[79]

Nationalism in these small, peripheral nations has always overvalued talent as an almost metaphysical property. Game shows allowed for some shining talents to break into the national spotlight. While economic mobility was limited, talent-based class mobility was possible. But the exaltation of talent as the contradiction within and limit to democratic education erected a solid division between the intellectual elites and the masses. Television, the medium ostensibly best suited for evening the playing field, also made this division deeper. Celebrated quiz and game show host István Vágó commented in my interview with him that during socialism, viewers wanted to watch people who were smarter than themselves. Following socialism, with commercial TV and reality programs well established, viewers wanted to watch people who are less smart than themselves. Unlike many other television professionals and viewers, however, who tend to look back on the old times of normative, educational TV with some longing, Vágó is critical of that mission: "We thought that TV was a tool to inform, elevate and teach people. Bullshit. I think that back then TV was dysfunctional. It's finally in its rightful place. It was a beautiful idea, a beautiful intention, but TV was not used for what it's supposed to be used for. Now it is."[80]

The hierarchical structure of cultural nationalism remained in tension with socialist institutions' democratizing educational mandate. This mandate got redirected and reshaped within the received hierarchy that assigned cultural capital to creative elite groups and relegated all others to the ranks of passive pupils who needed to endure teaching. The glass ceiling that separated the two spheres was considered to exist outside of social categories and ideology, something to be determined by natural selection. In turn, the natural properties of talent were essential to naturalizing nationalism. The deeply ingrained circular logic of the cultural nationalism of small nations implies that extraordinary talent is literally the offspring of the collective blood of the national family. If the offspring is of such outstanding quality, this validates the gene pool itself as one of extraordinary potential. To place the emphasis on the potential is especially important in the absence of collective economic and political strength as a nation, where the few must act as conduits for the many. Eastern European nationalisms thus have a curious schizophrenic psychological effect on their subjects: they interpellate the national citizen to identify aspirationally with the talented upper crust and, by exclusion, to detest the unworthy masses as the reason for the actual, peripheral condition of the nation. There is not much room for identification and a healthy sense of self to develop between the two choices. Eastern European identities balance the self-hate assigned to the talentless with aspirational basking in the collective brightness radiated by the talented.

A Postsocialist Look at the Socialist Game Show

Cultural critic László Halász ponders the popularity of game shows with European audiences in a 1971 issue of the Hungarian journal *Radio and TV Review*. The attraction of these programs, he argues, is not simply that they provide an outlet for the homo ludens in all of us, who is looking for a release in the imaginative activities of play. For the participants, it is more akin to competitive sports, since preparation for and contribution to the program are hard work. For the viewers, the identification with the player-athletes is similar to the way in which one identifies with a film's or novel's heroes. Indeed, the winners are lifted by TV into the pantheon of superheroes, much like widely celebrated Olympic athletes.[81]

István Vágó hosts a postsocialist game show of his own creation.

The champions of TV competition emerged as the celebrity role models of socialism. They represented socialist societies, since theoretically anyone could compete; but they also exempted the 99 percent from having to do the work. Halász also speculates that the educational content might be an impediment to measuring and discovering what really matters: outstanding intellectual faculties and true talent.[82] Quiz and game shows thus resolved the contradiction between two ethical legacies. One was the value of hard work, which meshed together a presocialist, bourgeois, Protestant work ethic and early socialism's emphasis on competitive, numerically measurable production. The other legacy was nationalism's idolization of the Romantic notion of talent. This nationalistic ethos silently despised and chastised the "masses" it overtly legitimized: the "worker," who continually needed to be agitated away from his couch, whose consciousness and intellectual standards were in permanent danger of slacking. The entire idea of socialist education implied a paradoxical contempt for the talentless and the mediocre.

While some late socialist quiz and game show formats incorporated entertaining elements and mobilized bottom-up, inclusive off-the-air competitions, they were relentlessly wedded to the idea that TV should feature people who are better, smarter, and more competitive than viewers. István Vágó, the quizmaster who facilitated such a value scheme during socialism and went on to host *Who Wants to Be a Millionaire* and other global formats after socialism, offers this assessment: "Wheather we like it or not, television is the most global medium of all. People react the same way everywhere. It may boost our national pride to think that we are different than the rest. The lesson is: we're not different. . . . I had believed that the [countries of] the Carpathian Basin worked differently from the Philippines or Argentina. But this is not true. Really good game shows work well everywhere, regardless of the place."[83]

Vágó says he experienced the shift from the ethos of socialist quiz and game shows to that of global formats most directly in his own persona as host. Under socialism, his inclination was to help contestants, to be their benevolent, if condescending, coach and teacher. Postsocialist, global formats required that he learn to be the contestants' enemy, rooting against their success.[84]

Perhaps it is this transformation that best captures the distinctive quality and ideological work performed by the socialist game show in retrospect. Many of these programs were truly democratic, giving everyone a chance to participate in a way that was not tied to TV stardom. But the condition for the existence of this democratic ethos was the heightened national intimacy created under the unique conditions of socialism during the Cold War. State TV was a monopolistic institution of subtle resistance to Soviet imperialism. It positioned itself as an extension of the family, an institution within the home. As such, it did spread knowledge and gave viewers a very real sense of belonging even if this sense was often constructed out of the shared mockery of aggressively educational programs. Vágó as game show host rightly registers the post-1989 turn as one in the status of nationalism under globalizing conditions. Postsocialist televisual competition no longer implicates the entire nation the way the struggle between the superpowers interpellated viewers as national subjects. The warmth of a taken-for-granted national community suddenly disappeared, competition became refocused on the individual, Eurocentric high art and academic knowledge became delegitimated, and nationalism as TV's core value became overshadowed by entertainment.

5 Postsocialist Ethno-Racial Reality TV

Television Entertainment and Eastern European Racial Exceptionalism

By virtue of being hybrid platforms with a globally shared blueprint formula available for local appropriation, reality formats have been argued to facilitate a rearticulation of national identities worldwide.[1] John Ellis writes, "Factual television has been overhauled by the emergence of 'reality TV,' which provides an arena for the examination of the emotions. Reality TV effectively fuses the forms of game show with those of the documentary."[2] Both game shows and documentaries occupied a central place on socialist television—the latter cherished mostly by cultural authorities, the former by audiences. While documentary paired a centrally approved realist aesthetic with socialist ideology, the game show found a way to educate socialist citizens in an entertaining format. Yet, when global reality TV formats finally arrived in the postsocialist marketplace in the late 1990s, instead of triggering a sense of recognition and continuity, they provoked outrage. Reality TV was seen as an inorganic cultural intrusion.

Of course there are very good reasons why contemporary reality formats strike one as radically different from socialist reality-based programs. During state socialism, much of TV was subjected to a central educational drive. After the market broke the state's monopoly over broadcasting, it forced broadcasters to compete for producing the cheapest possible programming for the largest possible audience segments. Instead of university professors explaining to viewers the wonders of the universe, ordinary people and overnight celebrities suddenly flooded the screen. Formerly unseen populations that did not fit the nation's idealized self-image became stars in reality shows.

Programs about the Roma and other racialized groups have ignited particularly heated public discussion about the transformation of the postsocialist nation. This outburst of interest is all the more surprising since socialism left behind a large number of investigative documentaries specifically about the Roma, many of which were shown on television. However, postsocialist reality programs forced into articulation the unspoken racial and class boundaries that have sustained national narratives of cultural and ethnic coherence. This is why the love-hate relationship of the public with reality television—secret love and overt hatred—often crystallizes around programs about Roma and other racialized celebrities. I argue that the aversion to the cultural quality represented by reality TV and the aversion to the ethno-racial quality represented by the Roma and other minorities are thoroughly intertwined. This mutual determination has come into view in the course of radical shifts in the class structures of postsocialist societies. The majority of the Roma population, hard hit by the collapse of socialist industries and subjected to racial discrimination, have slid into an underclass position since the end of socialism. The formation of this racialized underclass has been complemented by the rise into the middle class of some upwardly mobile Roma, many of them entertainers and media stars.[3] Roma celebrities on reality docushows have visualized and brought into question the normalized whiteness of the postsocialist nation.

Eastern European nationalisms have had a paradoxical relationship with race. While the Ottoman and Habsburg Empires ruled over a melting pot of ethnicities across shifting national borders, the role that racial distinctions have played in national identification has been downplayed by historians much as it has been rendered irrelevant in national narratives themselves. In these narratives, "race" is generally occluded by "ethnicity," a term used almost synonymously with "nationality," with reference to linguistic and cultural identity markers. While these identity markers are understood to be as powerful as genetic codes, "race" itself is not part of the vocabulary of nationalism. It has a hidden trajectory in Eastern Europe because the region's nations see themselves as outside of colonial processes and thus exempt from postdecolonization struggles with racial mixing and prejudice. As a result, Eastern Europe may be the only, or last, region on earth where whiteness is seen as morally transparent, its alleged innocence preserved by a claim of exception to the history of imperialism.[4]

This racial exceptionalism, the East's function as an unapologetic reserve for unbridled, because mostly unrecognized, white supremacism, serves as a proof of Europeanness, a way to disavow the colonial hierarchy between Western and Eastern Europe and to make up for the region's long-standing economic and political inferiority. While the kinship ties that guarantee national bonds in the East are officially understood to be the result of shared languages and cultures, the implied cohesiveness and hegemony of these cultural nationalisms in fact rest on a racial agenda shrouded in the invisibility of whiteness. The perceived organic quality and ethical transparency of shared "cultural" values is guaranteed by the unspoken but taken-for-granted superiority of whiteness. The result is the contradiction that whiteness as a moral category, itself a product of imperialism and racism, provides immunity to charges of imperialism and racism. Until recently even the Roma, the largest visible minority, have been persistently categorized in ethnic rather than racial terms. In socialist states' strategies, this was clearly not to foreground the constructedness of ethnicity and the hybridity of the Roma but to disavow the violence of racism.[5]

The postsocialist opening of national borders and media to the flow of diverse images, ideas, and people has begun to burst the bubble of racial exceptionalism. The illusion of white nationhood has been under attack by migration from Asia, Africa, and the Middle East, as well as tourism, business, and media flows from all directions. The post-Wall opening of the borders and the staggered inclusion of the majority of postsocialist states in the European Union starting in 2004 contributed to increased migration flows within Europe as well. The core EU countries' retreat behind the walls of Fortress Europe from the flood of labor seekers, migrants, and exiles from the East confronted Easterners with their own effective second-class status and racialization—the realization that in the eyes of the West, they have never been better than, or even different from, the Roma.

Reality television, in particular, has disclosed the unspoken role assigned to the Roma to mark the whiteness of nations from the inside and the role assigned to "foreign" racial minorities to safeguard it from the outside. In the following, I show how celebrity reality TV has exploded these national racial regimes. I begin with the methodological difficulties that confront a joint discussion of race and popular postsocialist reality TV. Then I contextualize the racial and class discourses that circulate within and around the rise of Roma celebrity through an analysis of the wildly popular Hungarian *Győzike* show and its national reception. Finally, I discuss the recent appearance of black African celebrities on reality television and the distinct racial positions they occupy in relation to the Roma and to the white moral majority.

How to Study Postsocialist Reality TV?

As a major arena of television's globalization, reality programming is particularly conducive to making intercultural connections. Its worldwide proliferation in the 1990s followed large-scale technological shifts and a changing regulatory environment, which favored "cheap, common and entertaining" programming disseminated around the world.[6] Reality programs have also come under scrutiny in discussions across media, cultural, and communication studies in relation to the shifting spaces and meanings of the public sphere, democracy, and citizenship in a neoliberal era of technological and economic convergence and increasing state and corporate surveillance.

Notwithstanding the analytical merits and theoretical insight of such research, and despite calls for understanding how reality formats can be both "culturally specific and globally relevant,"[7] there remains a disconnect between reality TV's spectacular success around the world and the extent to which discussions about neoliberal responsibilization, governmentality, class, gender, and emotional labor are specific to "post-welfare" states.[8] While these issues are not irrelevant to postsocialist cultures, they are inevitably filtered and refracted through the national, which remains the primary reference point. Even though reality programs' relevance to national self-recognition has been noted in the literature, the specific difficulties of studying television in Eastern European nations have not been addressed.

To argue for taking reality television seriously in Eastern Europe presents unique methodological, disciplinary, and ethical challenges. One reason for this is the radical and swift media transformation, which has been characterized by a negotiation between the state and commercial broadcasters over what remain primarily national markets despite increasing segmentation. State televisions first had to compete with and then give up their hegemony of four decades to commercial broadcasters in the years following the fall of socialism. In Hungary, RTL Klub and TV2, the two most successful commercial broadcasters, quickly colonized the landscape with their production and importation of entertainment programming since they were launched in 1997. When finally given the choice, viewers turned away from state TV's serious news shows, political discussions, talking heads, art films, and other national "quality" programs and favored talk shows, competitive reality programs, and locally produced soap operas.

In response, commercial programming across the region has been universally dismissed by critics for lowering cultural standards and corrupting national citizenship.[9] Postsocialist institutions of cultural criticism generally despise commercial television for its affective appeal, its perceived reduction of a literature-based national culture and democratic citizenship to distracting audiovisual infotainment, and its derivative, American genres and ideologies. Reality programs are identified as the trashiest form of television entertainment. But the refusal to take such programs seriously makes them all the more raw and unabashed outlets for a variety of views that were formerly subject to denial and (self-)censorship. Shows about nonwhite celebrities constitute a synergy between the objectionable racial quality of their protagonists and the objectionable cultural quality of reality TV. The moral outrage against such shows is due to the fact that they visualize the intimate connection between these two converging kinds of illegitimacy within the national public sphere. They make it difficult to couch nationalism's racist dynamic within the universalistic European humanism of high-quality national culture.

Győzike: Roma Celebrity and Reality TV

As the poorest and most deprived European minority, the Roma are the subjects of countless European Union, state, and local policy regulations, as well as ethnographic studies and documentary films. The majority of the Roma have clearly been the losers of the post–Cold War transformations, caught in a vicious cycle of poor educational and job opportunities and violent social exclusion.[10] The economic crisis has increased far-right nationalism and raised explicit racism and anti-Semitism to a level unprecedented since World War II. Perpetual scapegoats for the region's marginality within Europe and for its recurring crises of national sovereignty, the Roma have only been tolerated as musical entertainers for centuries. At the same time, as I discuss elsewhere, the globalization and commercialization of Eastern European media cultures have also enhanced the appeal of Roma popular entertainment and created Roma pop stars.[11]

Celebrity docusoaps about Roma musicians have earned a mixed reception. Vali Vijeile (the Stormy Man) or, by his actual name, Valentin Rusu, is a popular Romanian *manele* (urbanized Gypsy pop-folk style) singer. His prime-time docusoap, *Aventurile familiei Vijelie* (The adventures of the Vijelie family, 2005–), was produced by Prima TV, one of the first commercial channels in Romania. The *Győzike* show (2005–2010) aired in prime time on Hungary's most successful commercial channel, RTL Klub, and revolved around Roma pop singer Győző Gáspár, affectionately called Győzike, and his family. Modeled after *The Osbournes* (MTV, 2002–2005), both programs were massive audience successes and universally ridiculed targets of criticism at the same time. From overtly racist rants to highbrow disdain, the emotions that have poured into public discussion in response to these shows reveal profound anxieties about what constitute the racial and class boundaries of the national family and its allegorical extension, the postsocialist nation. Roma celebrity introduces a collective cognitive dissonance. It visualizes intolerable hybridity, which in turn threatens the racial hierarchy that props up distinctions between high and popular culture.

Győző Gáspár rose to fame in 1999 as the front man of the pop group Romantic, which mixed Roma melodies with rap. He subsequently appeared as a celebrity contestant on the Hungarian version of *Big Brother*, *Nagy Testvér* (TV2, 2003). Already established in public as a likable character, Győzike's Roma identity was played up on the program. He also took a cameo role in the satirical comedy show *Bazi Nagy Roma Lagzi* (My big fat Roma wedding, TV2, 2003). This program provoked much controversy for its crude Roma stereotypes and resulted in sanctions against TV2, RTL Klub's rival commercial broadcaster, by the state media regulation agency, ORTT.[12] The show placed Győzike in an ambiguous political position as someone willing to compromise the cause of the minority for national media fame.

The advertising for the new reality show *Győzike* used this history as an enticement.[13] The weekly ninety-minute prime-time program aired on RTL Klub in February 2005.[14] It promised a series with eight episodes that follow the family's everyday lives. Five years later, in June 2010, the show finished its last season. It appeared nine times in the top twenty most popular programs in Hungary in 2005,[15] and achieved an audience share average rating of 46.1 percent among adults aged eighteen to forty-nine.[16] It reached the peak of its popularity in week 20 of the eighth season, in May 2009, when it had an audience share of 50.2 percent, beating the popular domestic soap opera *Barátok közt* (Between friends) out of its longtime leading spot.[17]

Each episode opens with a slow pan over snow-covered hills with a panpipe background music, echoing a romantic documentary style. The gray communist blocks of a town appear, identified in an intertitle as "Salgótarján 2005," home to Győzike and his family. The dissonance between the upbeat music and the dreary landscape evokes a sense of parody. This is amplified as the camera tilts down to a large, new mustard-colored house and then suddenly cuts to a close-up of Győzike's face as he is staring in the distance, apparently lost in thought. The music speeds up and turns into a fast Gypsy tune. A shot of Győzike's legs reveals that he is sitting on the toilet, with his signature zebra-striped pajamas around his ankles and bare toes tapping to the rhythm of the music. The show's main title appears over the pajamas as if it were a clothing brand, in a cunning marketing strategy that anticipates RTL Klub's consistent branding of the show and its ancillary merchandise as "ethnic kitsch."

Győzike's wife, Bea, is then shown in a shiny red-and-black kitchen marked by its expensive but tasteless decor as "nouveau riche." She is wearing a fashionable off-the-shoulder top, stirring a cup of coffee, and shouting to her husband to come downstairs. Győzike yells back that he is "thinking." The camera returns to Győzike's yawning face in several close-up shots. A cut to their eldest daughter, Evelyn, displays her lying on a zebra-striped bedspread as she is threatening to kick the door down if her father doesn't hurry up. To complete the family portrait, the younger daughter, Virág, appears wearing a cowboy hat, rocking back and forth on a rocking horse and waving an American flag. Each of these shots is freeze-framed, with the respective family members' names flashed across the screen. This introduction highlights the show's status as popular entertainment and as a mockery of the traditional, grim style of Roma documentaries about suffering, poor Gypsies. The images—zebra stripes, shiny lacquered kitchen, American flag, cowboy hat, the shouting wife's fashionable dress, and blank-faced Győzike contemplating life on the toilet—all point to something other than the "cultural" or "poverty-stricken" Roma familiar from documentaries and anthropological texts.

Similar to the early MTV celebrity docusoap *The Osbournes*, the *Győzike* show features an "extraordinarily ordinary" family,[18] whose activities are at once banal and excessive. They perform their life on the show in an extravagantly decorated house, which bears testimony to Győzike's well-promoted obsession with zebra stripes and gold. While the program generally avoids attaching price tags to the family's consumption habits, it presents an upper-class family with a lower-class, ethnic taste. Not unlike Ozzy Osbourne, in this domestic setting, Győzike is reduced to a bumbling, often sentimental and childish character, whose repeated failures and "ignominious body" both humanize him and provide many comic moments.[19] His blunt and practical wife, Bea, has also received much media and fan attention. Many of the episodes focus on the couple's marital tension. This tension gets even more explosive than that between Ozzy and his wife, Sharon, and is only occasionally and temporarily resolved. The emotional display that characterizes reality shows is generously exploited and clearly racialized here.[20] It is a major source of public critical aversion and, it is safe to speculate, of private viewer fascination. The two Gáspár daughters, teenage Evelyn and grade-schooler Virág, are often brought out as comic relief or as buffers when the couple's confrontations become especially dramatic. Extreme public displays of emotion are still new and rare on Eastern European television, which has inherited a tame, restrained code of conduct from the era of socialist state control. However, their Roma identity provides Győzike and Bea with a license as well as an expectation to perform the Roma stereotype of the irrational, corporeally driven racial minority.

Besides domestic affairs that, as John Corner describes, ambivalently hover between the fictional and the real in reality programming[21]—such as Bea's pregnancy scare; Győzike's infidelity; generational conflicts among family members; disagreements about buying, cooking, and decorating, and money matters—the show features two other kinds of prominent story lines: one follows trips abroad taken by Győzike and other family members to locations that range from Istanbul through Paris to Florida, highlighting the family's role in representing the Hungarian nation. The other narrative line depicts events in Győzike's public, professional life as a singer or aspiring politician, such as negotiations over performance gigs and his bid for Roma community leadership. Both kinds of stories abound in reflections on the couple's Roma identity and on the family's relationship to both the Roma community and the Hungarian national family, even if such reflections are not always explicit or even intentional.

In its preoccupation with national family values and in addressing a specific national family rather than a niche audience, the show resembles

European celebrity docusoaps more than *The Osbournes*. In Europe, the docusoap tends to solicit viewer affinities along national cultural differences, despite the global mobility and adaptability of the format.[22] For instance, the popular Flemish celebrity reality show *De Pfaffs* (The Pfaffs), broadcast on the national public service channel VTM, featured former Belgian soccer goalie Jean-Marie Pfaff and his populous family. Similar to Ozzy Osbourne's, the tough public image of the head of household was replaced by that of a domestic softy with a pot belly, gently mocked by his wife, who really runs the family. But the importance of authentic Flemish family values was consistently underscored, rather than ridiculed, on the program. The Pfaffs may be a well-to-do celebrity family, but they also upheld the ideal of a decent, middle-class simplicity at the heart of Flemish nationalism.[23]

Such differences among variations of the format also have to do with the national and regional trajectory of stardom. But while Ozzy's domestic persona is contrasted with his earlier, defiant rock idol image, Győzike as a musician has only a local reputation, and not a very wholesome one at that. Furthermore, Győzike's regional accent, frequent use of Roma dialect, and references to his family's membership in a wider Roma community repeatedly undermine their appropriateness as the national celebrity family. Győzike is an antistar, a resented and annoying celebrity, whom many consider a mere media creation.

Győzike and his wife, Bea, were voted both favorite and least liked TV personalities in 2008 by the readers of the Hungarian celebrity gossip magazine *Hot*.[24] Hungarian cultural critics and Roma intellectuals widely condemn the show.[25] Prominent Roma activist János Daróczi said that Győzike's media celebrity brought "severe disadvantage to the Hungarian Roma."[26] "I must send a message to everybody: we, the Roma, are not like that."[27] The media storm around the show raises the question why the reality television format suddenly politicizes Roma representation as an issue of national self-identification after decades of ethnographic documentary film production about Gypsies failed to do so. Much as in other Eastern and Southern European countries, there are scant Roma characters on Hungarian soap operas or dramas,[28] while news and documentary programming tend to focus on the criminality and social exclusion of certain Roma communities.[29]

Official socialist ideology suppressed conspicuous class differences and condemned Western media's consumerist, pop cultural seductions and constructions. Instead, in the absence of commercial media, celebrity was based mostly on merit and achievement.[30] When the postsocialist commercial media began to promote stars on television and in an increasingly tabloidized print press, the celebrity continued to be figured as "one of us"—one simply recognized by many. The editor of the popular tabloid magazines *Story* and *Best*, Miklós Ómolnár, comments on the intimate and locally specific operation of stardom:

> In Hungary, the star is the boy next door, who looks like someone we could pat on the shoulder when we see him on the street. He shops at the same vegetable stand and gets his groceries at the same TESCO as the rest of us do. [He] . . . gets caught by an internet magazine at TESCO as he is buying a television set with his pregnant girlfriend. It is unimaginable that an American or British star would go to TESCO to buy a TV on a Sunday afternoon. . . . The Hungarian star is a lower-middle-class petit-bourgeois, to use a vulgar-Marxist term."[31]

As he points out, communication research shows that stars in Hungary tend to be made on prime-time TV. Viewers consider them as extended family members, virtual dinner guests at the table, or people with whom one can strike up a conversation on the street. Stardom operates in a "virtual family environment," according to a more "provincial, intimate, national logic" than it does in the West.[32]

Given that Győzike does not look or sound like the Hungarian boy next door,[33] a popular prime-time reality show about a wealthy Roma family of media stars on RTL Klub sets off a great deal of anxiety about what constitutes the national family and, by extension, national culture. This anxiety becomes most pronounced when Győzike and his family travel on the show: in foreign countries, the family's local Roma distinction is all but erased, and their identity is reduced to the main point of identification for the foreigners they encounter: the language they speak. The family simply represents Hungarians abroad. Their performance as tourists is familiar to Hungarians, who have long been represented as so many Eastern European Borats, who do not know how to behave, have poor language skills, and have internalized their relative inferiority as the country bumpkins—the Gypsies of Europe.

When Győzike's rental car bumps into a redneck's pickup truck during the family's visit to Florida, the American man's expletive-filled frustration over their mutual failure to communicate is matched by Győzike's colorful Hungarian swearing. Finally, a policeman arrives to discipline the unruly, uneducated foreigner. For most Hungarian viewers, presumably, such a scene evokes an unsettling mix of identifications, in which shared national shame over Győzike's inability to communicate is offset by laughing with him in an imagined, intimate community of Hungarian speakers. Unlike in the domestic episodes, however, it is not so easy to defer the humiliation to the Gypsy minority or to TV celebrities. In a later scene from the same Florida trip, Győzike and his family are resting on the beach. They are approached by a young American woman who had heard that Győzike was a Hungarian pop star. While the communication is still limited by the language barrier, it is now easier to laugh *with* Győzike: this time, he is positioned against a bikini-clad woman, who appears much less authoritative than the American men in the earlier scene and rather naive in her giddy effort to meet an exotic Eastern European star. The gendered register of national identification is underscored by the implication that the United States is represented here by a silly beach girl.

Viewer Responses

The most obvious explanation for the show's popularity is that it is branded as a familiar "Gypsy circus,"[34] reproducing racist stereotypes[35] and inviting viewers to laugh at the family.[36] However, based on critical and popular reactions, I propose a more subtle understanding of the ways in which reality television mediates racialized national identifications in postsocialist Hungary. The first register of responses I consider are online reactions in the form of blogs, discussion lists, and other informal and mostly anonymous commentary. The second set are critical comments that serve a normative purpose in Hungary: reviews and reflections published by critics in established newspapers, magazines, and journals. The third source is ethnographic surveys and a set of ethnographic interviews conducted among children (both Roma and non-Roma), some of the most avid audiences of the show.

> This [Győzike] is a stupid, primitive animal, who parades around on TV at our expense and all those idiotic Hungarians stare at him with their mouths open. Young people today need normal examples to follow, not a monkey-like freak dancing on stage like him. That stupid RTL suggests that the dumber you are the more famous they'll make you.

> The fact is that the majority of Gypsies live off of crime (committed against Hungarians). They know how to make everyone feel sorry for them, but working hard stinks. All they know is how to crank out all

those little mongrels at 14 and then make them do the dirty work of stealing and then collect welfare for them. I did some research about these things even though, believe me, I really don't care, and I still believe that Gypsies are worse than anything else, they are the "black" plague of the world, the last filth, rotten rats, who spread stealing, cheating, lying . . . etc. . . . around the world.

They are not humans. . . . They stink up the whole country. Why don't they get the hell out of here at last? I'd like to drown all the black kids and sterilize all the women to stop them from reproducing. They are like cockroaches. Even their names are disgusting. . . . I wish they were all killed by cancer, from the smallest newborn to the oldest stinking Gypsy. Death to them!!!!!!!!

This is a typical selection from the postings on one of the show's largest fan discussion sites. There are about thirty-five hundred posts altogether.[37] For a program that was so eagerly and universally watched, it appears to have hardly any fans, or at least very few who would defend it in public. Even the self-identified Roma posters tend to dismiss it as a program about "show Roma" (*divatcigány*), who give the entire minority a bad name. The few positive comments one finds appreciate the show's amusement value, the fact that it allows viewers to laugh at Győzike's bumbling performance. The degree of hatred and fear revealed by many of the posts, replicated by thousands of other reactions in similar online discussions, is rightly shocking to Western liberal ears. The comments almost parodically reproduce patterns of ethnonationalism that have been successfully erased from the Western vocabulary of politically correct talk about minorities: the Roma are lazy and repugnant parasites who shun work and drain collective resources. Their excessive procreation contaminates the pristine national body and threatens the survival of the rightful majority.[38]

It is remarkable that a commercial television show's online discussion forum provides such a release for frustrations directed against the Roma. Whereas fan communities have been argued to become spaces of mobilization for political participation, and even alternative, affective public spheres,[39] such arguments always face two substantial objections: the mobilization built around fandom hardly ever transgresses the narrative and ideological boundaries of a television series, actor, or auteur, and it is compromised by the politics of consumerism. The outpouring of opinions around *Győzike* does the opposite: the comments tend to ignore what actually happens on the show and focus instead on the program's political and ethical significance for the national community, in which commentators are profoundly implicated.

Ironically, online reactions constitute precisely the kinds of mediated, affective public spaces suppressed in the Habermasian (ideal of the) national and rational public sphere. Even though they could be dismissed as racist rants by ignorant viewers, most such reflections nevertheless argue for the need for a racialized boundary between national shame and pride, and they comment on the uneasy relations between national and global affiliations mobilized by the television show. In this sense, they manifest what Appadurai calls the "predatory identities" unleashed by globalization, whose construction is not adequately theorized by traditional social sciences. Appadurai defines predatory identities as "those identities whose social construction and mobilization require the extinction of other, proximate social categories, defined as threats to the very existence of some group, defined as a we."[40] He writes: "Predatory identities emerge, periodically, out of pairs of identities, sometimes sets that are larger than two, which have long histories of close contact, mixture, and some degree of mutual stereotyping. Occasional violence may or may not be part of these histories, but some degree of contrastive identification is always involved. One of these pairs or sets of identities often turns predatory by mobilizing an understanding of itself as a threatened majority."[41]

Appadurai's argument aptly explains the excessive resentment toward celebrity TV Roma in terms of the narcissism of minor differences. He takes up this Freudian concept to argue that globalization induces a deep anxiety about the national project and turns nationalistic identities predatory. These predatory identities adopt the cause of defending the majority against perceived threats from minorities, or "small numbers." Minorities' mixed status, languages, and ambiguity in relation to national citizenship, their movement across borders, and their financial transactions (real or imagined) all blur the borders of the nation and make minorities serve as flash points where social tensions about globalization are released. When minorities are wealthy, they evoke the threat of elite globalization. When they are poor, they are seen as symbols of failed forms of development and welfare. Because ideas of nationhood tend to rely on ethnic purity and suppress collective memories and experiences of plurality, ethnic minorities obscure the idealized boundaries of the national community. They are easily scapegoated for the failure of many states to achieve economic sovereignty under the circumstances of neoliberal globalization, which puts considerable strain on states to protect the interests of territorially defined majorities.[42]

The anxiety displayed by the online responses is due to the fact that Győzike and his family evoke in the same national televised space, in the same national identities, both the poor, welfare-bound ghost of the enemy within and the wealthy, transnational threat. He is a celebrity television Roma in a region under continual colonization, where national sovereignty has never truly been more than an unfulfilled promise. As a racially hybrid figure in the increasingly hybrid space of national television, he is a glaring reminder of the permanent inaccessibility of the classical—white and high cultural—European national project. The ethnocidal vehemence of viewer comments and their call for racial purification, quite out of proportion with the spirit of light entertainment associated with a television show, reveal the majority's profound dependence on maintaining the illusion of the "white" nation's ethnic homogeneity.

Győzike must be one of the few television programs in the world where the "press" section of the show's own website, normally a vehicle of promotion, consists entirely of negative reviews. Reflections in print and online critical journals are invariably outraged by the show's "quality" and "values." However, while online responses by ordinary viewers target the ethnic minority with which Győzike and his family are identified, professional critics tend to tone down the racist edge of the criticism and focus instead on the show itself as the flagship of an alarming downward trend in national culture in general and television in particular.

While the worries about commercializing the public sphere are legitimate, and the lifestyle and emotional intelligence models displayed on the show are hardly wholesome by any standards, a number of assumptions remain unreflected in critics' assessment of the show—assumptions that bind together critical and ordinary audience responses much more intimately than it would seem. In fact, the anti-Roma racism of predatory identities and intellectuals' worry about the decline of print-based national culture are two sides of the same coin, which share more in their nationalistic anxiety over hybridity and ethnic mixing than they differ in tact, style, and perceived distance from the issues at stake. Overtly racist comments tend to equate Győzike with "real Gypsies" and personalize their attacks through their own "experiences" with the Roma. More sophisticated, critical comments by liberal intellectuals, who would be abhorred by charges of latent racism or discrimination against minorities, tend to interpret and abstract, while effacing their own personal investment and positioning themselves as the guardians of collective cultural standards. They defer their indignation from the protagonist and the minority he represents to the medium and the genre. However, the threat of ethnic hybridity posed by the suspect transnational ethnic minority and the threat of cultural hybridity presented by transnational commercial television converge in their perceived attack on national culture, understood as the joint product of ethnonational family ties and Eurocentric cultural values.[43]

Critics' unanimous dismissal of commercial television derives from the special rights and responsibilities historically bestowed upon intellectuals in small Eastern European nations. This special class status only strengthened during decades of intellectual-led opposition to the Soviet-controlled communist regime. However, it has become tenuous in the course of the postsocialist transformations. The globalization of state-controlled media, in particular, undermined the ideal of a homogeneous national public and initiated a subsequent crisis of authority for cultural and political leaders. While intellectuals have been traditionally expected to speak for a national public, that public is now being directly addressed by ratings-driven media. Hungarian media sociologist Lajos Császi calls the top-down intellectual tradition of judgment exercised by teachers, politicians, and cultural experts profoundly paternalistic.[44] One critic displays this paternalism blatantly: "With the appearance of commercial television, it has become clear what the Hungarian television viewer needs." He continues, "You cannot expect quality from commercial television stations. I don't even think that a critic who writes for intellectual journals should write about the horrific programs of commercial television. . . . The interests of those who read criticism—or those who read at all—and the interests of TV viewers don't coincide. . . . I'd like to believe that we are not quite the way we think of ourselves based on all this: indifferent, poor and subsequently cynical; and shockingly tasteless. I'd like to believe."[45]

Such a position may be animated by a true sense of responsibility for national culture, but it is also a way of "reclaiming authority in the re-drawing of class relations," to borrow Beverly Skeggs's words.[46] The disgust with low-class celebrity culture is "simultaneously about desire and revulsion," an inextricable blend of cultural pride and racialized shame. It forfeits the possibility of building pedagogical bridges between "high" and "popular" cultural forms.[47]

The liberal sympathy that public intellectuals have long displayed for the single visible racial minority has helped efface the racialized quality of this one-directional, hierarchical relationship. The repressed returns in *Győzike*'s frequent, unfavorable comparisons in the reviews with "proper" ways of representing Gypsies: filmic documentaries about victimized, poor Roma.[48] The implication is that the true Roma is a victim, whose social position is fixed and can only be sympathetically revealed through the hard work of those who are able to see, understand, and show. Gypsies are tolerable on reality shows as long as they are passive victims. The difference from overtly racist views is that those blame the Roma themselves, rather than the exploitative medium.[49]

As Skeggs, Thumim, and Wood have shown, it is difficult to study reality television audiences even in contexts where television ethnography does enjoy some legitimacy.[50] The difficulties multiply when it comes to studying postsocialist television audiences, particularly of a contested program such as *Győzike*. I have argued that responses to the show tend to be channeled through feelings of national shame and (self-)hate over enjoying a cultural text that is so universally deplored by leading critics, and whose pleasures derive from identifying with a Roma family. Emerging studies of celebrity and fandom in Eastern Europe have revealed a range of reactions from skepticism to explicit hatred.[51] The only alternative results specific to the *Győzike* show come from ethnographic interviews with a group of preteen children conducted by Annabel Tremlett.[52] It is relevant to turn to a younger audience not only because they are not likely to have fully internalized proper normative national reactions but also because they have been some of the most devoted fans of the show. Tremlett suggests that this is due to the cartoonish fashion in which the Gáspár family perform their everyday lives. While the transgressions of younger daughter Virág often take center stage, Győzike himself also has an "infantile" appeal due to the gags and verbal comedy he regularly produces.[53] Rather than re-creating the disgust/desire dialectic of adult reactions, the children, from both Roma and non-Roma backgrounds, embraced Győzike and his family as fun characters without positioning them as an ethnic "other." For the children, the main attraction of the program was its ability to make them laugh. Furthermore, when asked whether they would liken their families to Győzike's, the majority of them said yes. This suggests a sense of shared ordinariness within the national family, along with a sense of shared (childlike) humor in transgressing "accepted" behavior.

Tremlett's ethnographic study confirms not only that the show is watched in the context of family viewing but also that Győzike's family could very well represent the national family—a possibility the adult responses, both the overtly racist and the intellectual-liberal types, simply cannot contemplate.

One pitfall of research such as this is to romanticize children's responses by rendering their imaginations unfettered by politics. As we know from David Buckingham, interpreting children's talk in the course of ethnographic research presents its own special caveats. The influence of the researcher, the group setting, and the inconsistencies of individual responses create so many contingencies that any meaningful generalization may seem untenable.[54] But even as we take extreme care not to assume that children's words are windows into their minds, the difference from the "adult" responses to the show is striking: the children watch the program primarily as a TV show. The anxieties about shifting national identities set off by *Győzike* are so overwhelming that the adult responses simply ignore the show's status as a television text that moves between fiction and reality. The children, however, whose memories are not overdetermined by a small nation's social, economic, and political transition, pick up on the most immediate effect of the program: its constructed, performative, playful dimension.

These three audience registers considered together show that the program's intense love-hate appeal goes far beyond the familiar opportunity to laugh at the Roma circus or voyeuristic recoil at the ways of rich Gypsies. It is rooted in the intimate fabric of nationalism within Eastern European cultures, a high degree of *national intimacy*: the kind of affective power that reduces the metaphorical distance between the national and the nuclear family and converts a shared sense of shame over inferiority within Europe into a sense of national belonging and pride.[55] Racialized stardom uneasily blends pride and shame, white superego and Roma unconscious. It reveals an act of collective self-recognition, the implication that a Roma family can quite palatably represent the national family. In turn, this unacknowledged identification with the Roma national self calls for a violent rewhitening, an expulsion of shame by projecting it onto the racialized figure of the undeserving celebrity. National pride and shame, whose usual dynamic is to masquerade as mutually exclusive, are thus called into simultaneous presence by the Roma media star.

African Celebrities: The National Family's New Frontier

The Roma function as flexible ethnic boundary markers, which is essential for the constitution of "white" nations. The Roma minority's ambiguous national status and hybridity have made it possible for viewers to exercise and disavow racism at the same time, to feel national shame through identification and disavow it through falling back on the nation's normative, violent whiteness. The increasing presence of visible racial differences in the streets and on the screens of Eastern Europe, however, has exposed the tenuousness of ethno-racial national boundaries and called for renewed efforts to fix them. Reality TV has at times quite blatantly staged the rewhitening of postsocialist nations, as on the Romanian version of *Extreme Makeover*, *Frumusete pe muchie de cutit*, where a middle-aged Roma woman was turned surgically white so that her half-Roma children would not be ashamed of her. The makeover was so successful that the woman's own mother did not recognize her in the end.[56] In postsocialist states, the makeover, which is central to the dispersed practices of governmentality that reality TV performs in the United States or Britain, is not so much to render the individual a more responsible middle-class subject but to clean up the nation's collective image by removing the taint caused by racial hybridity.

Another recent strategy to keep in check the Roma's ambiguity and secure the borders of whiteness is juxtaposing Roma participants with black African "celebrities." The Romanian show *Satra* (Gypsy camp), most closely related to Fox's *The Simple Life* (2003–2007), began in 2009 at 10:00 PM Monday through Thursday on Kanal D, a broadcaster owned by the Turkish Dogan Media Group. It sent a small group of Romanian celebrities to live with a Gypsy family for twenty-four hours at a time. Their job was ostensibly to experience the hardships and quirks of Gypsy life, carrying out tasks that Gypsies supposedly do, such as selling aluminum boxes or clothes from door to door. Instead of learning from the Roma, however, the guests invariably ended up "teaching" them how to adopt a civilized lifestyle. They staged various makeover fantasies that show their hosts, especially Roma women, how to dress, walk, and even dance properly.[57]

This script is only interrupted by the appearance on the show of a black African man from the Republic of Congo. Victor Yila is an engineer, athlete, and musician, a well-known media personality, who has long established himself in Romania and speaks the language proficiently. On the show, however, his function is to embody a racial category that is even lower on the national scale than that of Gypsies, by virtue of having a darker complexion and a foreign accent. He performs, with apparent willingness, the stereotype of the "native" familiar from imperial adventure tales. He endures various indignities even the Roma are spared, such as cleaning up after everyone and performing a tribal dance around the fire. His participation visually and metaphorically whitens the Roma. To articulate this new, more definitive degree of whiteness even more explicitly, the Roma engage in the colonial mimicry performed by all Eastern European subjects toward Europe. They display the "proper" white national behaviors toward the exotic, "tribal" African subject that the white celebrity guests display toward them: they show disgust when Yila touches them and horrified curiosity at his appearance and speech.

Yila's role is matched by that of Lapite Oludayo, a black Nigerian singer-celebrity, known as "Fekete Pákó" (Black Pákó) in Hungary. Oludayo moved to Budapest in 1994 as a law student and has since become known as a musician and a media personality. His role is to act as Hungary's "village idiot," as an English-language Budapest daily starkly sums it up.[58] Despite repeated media attempts to mock and humiliate him, Pákó always comes back for more. In a 2006 interview that immediately went viral, the reporter intentionally posed an ungrammatical question to confuse him.[59] When Pákó, who speaks near-flawless Hungarian, tried to save face and make sense of the question, the reporter walked off in feigned upset, throwing his hands up at Pákó's hopeless inability to comprehend Hungarian. On another occasion, in 2008, the right-wing radio station Bombagyár (Bomb factory) staged an interview with Pákó, in which he was set up to make pro-Nazi, anti-Semitic, and Gypsy-bashing comments and gestures. After the interview created a national uproar, Pákó explained that he had been intimidated by the hosts into saying what they wanted, including citing names of Nazi leaders he had not even heard of. The hosts acknowledged this was true but still sued Pákó for slander, who was subsequently banned from appearing on the popular TV channels RTL Klub and TV2.[60]

The ban was lifted the same year, when Pákó participated in the national version of *I'm a Celebrity . . . Get Me Out of Here*, a *Survivor*-like reality game format originally developed by Granada Television for Britain's ITV in 2002. The two back-to-back seasons of the Hungarian version, *Celeb vagyok . . . ments ki innen*, were set on a private reserve in the Argentinean rain forest and aired on RTL Klub in the fall of 2008, to high ratings. Pákó's function, once again, was to be humiliated and ridiculed. After he was introduced in the show's promotional clip as the son of the jungle, an African naturally at home among creatures of the wild, it transpired that he was afraid of snakes. He was then forced to feel around for hidden objects among slimy creatures in a dark cave. The more desperate his panic became, the more wholeheartedly the two moderators laughed outside. Győzike was also among the celebrity participants of the show. Even though he and Pákó appeared in two different seasons, as the only two racialized minority competitors, the comparison was inevitable. Similar to that of the Roma in *Gypsy Camp*, Győzike's difference was all but erased and his Hungarian-speaking whiteness all but normalized in light of Pákó's foreign blackness.

Postsocialist Ethno-National TV Realism

While reality formats are disseminated across televisual markets, their success is ultimately determined by their ability to engage audiences who share local histories and interpretive contexts. *Győzike* might be entirely comparable to *The Osbournes* or *The Pfaffs* in its narrative organization, its display of ignominious bodies, its televisual aesthetic of realism, and even its production values. However, the intensity and ambivalence of its local reception are specific to the anxiety about nationhood and nationalism under the conditions of postsocialist economic and cultural globalization. I have focused on how these differences are articulated in shows about racialized celebrities, which foreground the disavowed but essential role played by race and racism in constituting cultural-linguistic nationalisms in the region.

Whereas in the West middle-class viewers addressed by reality shows are able to distance themselves from the abject spectacle of individuals in need of televisual charity and self-help, in the close national intimacy of Eastern European cultures, the distance between viewer and spectacle is reduced and occluded. It needs to be recrystallized in racial terms, by foregrounding Győzike's Roma difference or, if that is not clear enough, Yila's and Pákó's black African difference.

In the case of *Győzike*, such efforts at distancing are undermined by the Roma star's demonstrated class success. *Győzike* is a threat to national culture because it represents an emerging middle-class cultural and economic value that is racially mixed. The economic middle class has long been a missing element in Soviet-controlled, allegedly egalitarian societies. Intellectuals constituted a class charged with the cultural leadership of the nation during socialism, often in unspoken complicity with party leadership. This class leadership has considerably weakened in the postsocialist period. *Győzike* threatens to expose the implicit racial and gendered parameters of intellectual exceptionalism. Eastern European nations and nationalisms are continually confirmed as truly European by placing inordinate value on a natural cultural affinity with (Western) Europe. The naturalization of high culture is "biologically" confirmed by the respective nations' racial bonds. The absence of direct participation in imperial histories that would make the racial underpinning of national high cultural values conspicuous, Eastern European nationalisms have preserved populations in a state of naive gullibility about racial assumptions. Brought together in the hybrid media space created by *Győzike*, the normative responses of public intellectuals and the anonymous comments of ordinary viewers reveal the interdependency between race and cultural value in defining the Eastern European nation as a family. *Győzike* performs and thus renders performative both Gypsiness and national whiteness, to all constituencies' great unease, suspicion, and fascination.

There is very little collective historical awareness of racism, let alone white guilt, to expose this split identification. It seems that white guilt might be a luxury in itself in a transnational network of neoliberal capital, where citizens of more powerful states are expected to pay a premium for their economic superiority, achieved via violent imperialism, by performing charity and white middle-class self-blame. Conversely, small nation-states that have been historically positioned at the bottom of a global system of nested inferiorities are able to justify nationalism as a force that necessarily subordinates all alternative affiliations and sentiments, including guilt, to the needs of a culturally unified white nation.

Győzike and other reality programs about racialized celebrities also expose the lasting effects and limitations of reality-based socialist educational programs discussed in the previous four chapters. One of these effects is a naturalized, nationalistic value scheme that rests on an internalized racial hierarchy. Only children's responses to the program proved somewhat immune to this inherited value scheme. And only one of the prominent former and current television professionals I interviewed offered an opinion contrary to the consensus that socialist educational programming was far superior to the commercial trash that has plugged up postsocialist television channels, with *Győzike* as exhibit one. "Quizmaster" and star TV personality István Vágó told me that, while he was committed to socialist TV's public service mission, he has recently reevaluated his earlier position. He now thinks that it is *Győzike* that finally fulfilled television's true mission. Although socialist TV's pedagogical commitment was admirable, he says, television was never meant to be a teaching tool. Those who despise *Győzike* are jealous of Győzike's success at best and are liars at worst. The fact that someone utterly different from the cast of characters on socialist TV could reach so many people and stir up so much passion is proof for Vágó that people like to watch people who are different from them.[61] The fact that viewers feign outrage over Győzike's antics simply shows that they internalized the paternalistic and white essence of socialist educational television, which tolerated very little deviance from the high cultural ideals of nationalism.

II • GENRES OF HISTORY

The Historical Adventure Drama 6

Socialist Television and Entertainment

By virtue of television's being a home-based medium whose appeal is affective and intimate, its emergence into a mass medium presented party authorities with both a challenge and an opportunity. Television posed a danger as an instrument of quiet subversion in the domestic sphere, which slipped past the surveillance to which other public institutions were subjected. At the same time, its attraction as a medium of entertainment could be harnessed to forge a unity within the larger national family around shared identifications and pleasures, which could in turn fortify the frayed bond between state authorities and the broader population.

Most state socialist regimes recognized early on that, in order to capitalize on the propaganda potential of television, they had to do more than prohibit and censor foreign program flows. To retain some control over the medium that John Ellis called "the private life of the nation state,"[1] they had to get in on the game and provide their populations with indigenous, party-approved entertainment. Nationalism became the cornerstone of socialist governments' media policies across the region; and television was the key instrument of nationalistic edutainment. By the 1960s, Stalinist principles of forced Marxist-Leninist internationalism had lost their credibility in most countries along with the communist utopia of a classless, egalitarian international brotherhood. This created an opening for national regimes to adjust the central Soviet rhetoric in order to consolidate their own domestic powers. The dispersion of television broadcasting allowed for the subtle and measured deployment of entertainment in the domestic sphere. This was to alleviate widespread disappointment with the realities of socialism and strengthen patriotic identification with the cause of the nation. Patriotic television fiction was to help create a common ground between citizens and state governments in an unstated opposition to the Soviet occupier.

In this chapter I focus on what we may consider the quintessential genre of popular fictional television in its first two formative decades: the historical adventure series. Sitcoms, soap operas, and dramatic serials produced in the United States in the postwar years became synonymous with commercial, scripted TV entertainment worldwide. In comparison, when television became a household fixture in socialist countries in the 1960s, national broadcasters modeled their first domestically produced serials after a narrow selection of foreign entertainment fictions focused on the past and turned sharply away from the present.

This generic preference had several advantages. Importing historical drama serials reduced the likelihood that Western products and lifestyles, and with them the contagious ideology of consumer capitalism, would seep in. Furthermore, from the late 1960s through the 1970s, during their heyday, domestically produced historical adventure serials allowed socialist regimes to teach selective history lessons and foster national identifications that also appeared to conform to ideological prescriptions demanded by the Soviet occupiers. These serials often ostentatiously demonstrated adherence to Soviet socialist dogma in formal matters such as the glorification of folk culture or plotlines that rewarded peasant characters at the expense of the wealthy and powerful. Although such elements appear campy today, they were subtle enough not to undermine the shows' power of identification with the real emotional draw, the nationalistic narratives and spectacle. In the most liberal socialist countries, the programs' propagandistic excess was released in another register of entertainment, political cabaret, inspiring hilarious ironic send-offs, as I demonstrate in a discussion of the Hungarian genre parody *Gyula Vitéz* (Gyula the brave) later in the chapter.[2] The nationalistic lessons of these programs were borne out of the powerful convergence between folk mythology and high cultural legitimation. Historical adventure serials glorified masculine national heroism in the face of political oppression, a traveling metaphor that could be applied to any threat to national sovereignty, with little regard for the historical accuracy of such depictions. The serials situated these heroic struggles in the national past, but the dominant allegorical framework remained national resistance against Soviet domination.

The offerings of socialist television broadened considerably in the 1980s with the introduction of color sets and the addition of second and, in some cases, third state broadcast channels, followed by the arrival of cable and satellite programming. However, the emotional impact of the early adventure serials, grounded as it was in the well-timed confluence of nationalistic identification and entertainment value, has left a profound nostalgic residue that has endured into postsocialist times. As I discuss in the next chapter, viewer nostalgia has also turned these series into platforms for political legitimation and touristic self-branding.

I elicit my argument from two popular serials: *A Tenkes kapitánya* (The captain of the Tenkes, Hungarian Television, 1964) and *Janosik* (Polish Television, 1974). These two programs are exemplary of broader aesthetic, social, and media policy trends of the 1960s and 1970s. Their success with audiences and the effectiveness of their political messages are rooted in three interrelated factors, all of which identify television entertainment as a key terrain for sustaining nationalisms and for visualizing the contradictions at their core at the same time.

The first aspect is the socialist historical adventure serial's loose treatment of historical facts, places, and people. Paradoxically, this mythical quality proved essential to consolidating a spatiotemporally bound, linear national history around prominent historical actors. Both shows feature semifictional characters against a vague historical backdrop. As I show, the genealogy of the Janosik story that informed the TV series is particularly informative, since the historical Janosik actually lived and moved across multilingual and multicultural territories well before the nineteenth-century struggles for national sovereignty began and before twentieth-century national borders were drawn.

Second, the nationalistic projects at the heart of these adventure serials are supported by a contradictory double cultural legitimation. They borrow from the alleged authenticity of folk culture, also fulfilling Marxist-Leninist expectations. However, this folk authenticity is invariably established through the mediation of national poets and writers, who have assumed ideological leadership roles in the cause of national independence since the late eighteenth century. The Janosik myth illustrates well how transnational figures became appropriated from folk mythology to spearhead singular national narratives in nineteenth-century literature. This, in turn, legitimized their readaptation into nationalistic popular cultures in film and television in the twentieth century. Regional and continental program exchanges and shared broadcast signals then released these figures into international television flows again. However, the fact that their narrative patterns were recognizable across national borders, thanks to shared regional histories and patterns of nationalism, has not deprived these serials of their primary function as anchors of popular nationalisms.

Third, the historical figures after whom the protagonists were modeled were far from heroic. They were social bandits, local Robin Hoods, who embody a wish-fulfilling, contradictory collective belonging to a European cultural sphere and a voluntary submission to exoticizing Western European images of the periphery. The prevalence of such outlaw heroes lends a regional specificity to the development of nationalisms and nation-states in Eastern and Southern Europe.

European Connections

Socialist historical drama serials participated in a European circulation that reached across the Iron Curtain. From the beginning, most Eastern European viewers were exposed to a number of successful Western historical European serials, which were safe to import for socialist TV, from the German *Heimat* cycle (1984–2000), the British *Forsyte Saga* (1967), and *The Onedin Line* (1971–80) to *Brideshead Revisited* (1981). Many were literary adaptations with strong cultural pedigrees, telling stories about the nation, often dealing with the cultural roots and formative moments of history. They tended to have high production values to match their cultural quality.[3] The profile of historical drama in smaller Western European countries with less abundant resources for television production is quite similar to that of Eastern European historical serials. For instance, on Flemish TV, driven by the cultural nationalism of the Flemish community in Belgium, the majority of output consisted of literary and theatrical adaptations in the 1960s. These serials followed the same script: they drew on literary sources and re-created rural life in Flanders in the first half of the twentieth century; this gave them the name "peasant drama."[4] The prototypical Flemish period serial, *Wij, heren van Zichem* (We, the lords of Zichem, BRT, 1969), was set in the 1920s. It was adapted from the novels of

Ernest Claes, which were part of the broader *Heimatkunst* (homeland art) that inspired much TV and film drama in the 1960s through 1980s in Belgium and Germany. It had a popular cast, a light tone accessible to everyone, and everyday situations that crystallized around conflicts between the village people and the francophone village baron, and between Catholics and the freethinking blacksmith. The show was set against the rise of socialism and liberalism and the struggle for the emancipation of the Flemish language against French. It built on the mythology of suppressed and resistant Flemish folk and took a nostalgic look at the harsh but pure life in the idyllic countryside.[5]

Alexander Dhoest writes that the show reached a viewership of 78 percent in March 1969 and remains one of the most popular Flemish serials. The Flemish resistance to the French influence within Belgium found an outlet in a popular drama that incorporated both high literary and popular folk culture. Similar to Eastern European historical serials of the period, it was a vehicle of cultural nationalism, or "the endeavor to culturally emancipate the nation as opposed to political nationalism striving for independence."[6] The structure of this cultural nationalism betrays an inferiority complex similar to what motivated Hungarian, Polish, or Czechoslovak serials of the time, a complex offset by the cultural credit drawn from literary classics on the one hand and the mythology of an authentic, idealized folk culture on the other.[7]

Outlaws of Old Empires and the Socialist Adventure Series

Socialist entertainment occupied a precarious place: it had to be democratic, addressing all citizens of the state, but it also had to adhere to the standards and values of Eurocentric taste education. In both imported and domestically produced programs, it had to avoid genres that would create too much excitement about the West or were perceived to be low taste. Nationalistic historical adventure series were an ideal genre to cater to these contradictory demands. They seamlessly transferred to the new medium the project of an already established nationalistic literary culture focused on battles between good and evil, where the good side was embodied by masculine allegorical figures who defended the nation and resisted the evil intruder or oppressor. Such depictions ranged from nineteenth-century epic poetry that immortalized earlier nationalistic movements and antiestablishment rebellions to the tales of partisan resistance and World War II heroism particularly favored by Moscow.

The allegorical structures and gender schemes of these narratives were also easily mapped onto a number of existing literary and film genres: popular boys' adventure stories by valued national and regional authors (e.g., Ferenc Molnár's *Pál Street Boys*, first published in 1907, an international favorite among boy-bonding stories); adolescent adventure tales about boys conquering nature; overtly propagandistic novels and films about heroic boy groups, often in wartime contexts (e.g., Arkady Gaidar's *Timur i evo komanda* [Timur and his platoon, 1940]); an abundance of war films and partisan films (e.g., the Yugoslav epic *Walter Defends Sarajevo*, dir. Hajrudin Krvavac, 1972); male-bonding TV series set in wartime (e.g., the Polish favorite *Czterej Pancerni i Pies* [The tank crew of four and a dog, 1966]); and historical novels and film epics that evoked selected and glorified events from the national and European past. Feature films such as the Polish *Colonel Wolodyjowski* (dir. Jerzy Hoffman, 1969), the Bulgarian *Measure for Measure* (dir. Georgi Dyulgerov, 1981), the Romanian *Mihai Viteazul* (dir. Sergiu Nicolaescu, 1970), the Albanian *The Great Warrior Sandberg* (dir. Sergei Yutkevich, 1953), the Yugoslav *Battle of Kosovo* (dir. Zdravko Sotra, 1989), and the Hungarian *The Stars of Eger* (dir. Zoltán Várkonyi, 1968), for instance, are all set during the region's Ottoman occupation and provide memorable lessons in patriotic male heroism. American Western films were also seamlessly incorporated into this loose genre of historical family edutainment.[8]

An entire subset of literary works, films, and television programs about larger-than-life men fighting enemies of the nation revolve around outlaws. The television serials of the 1960s and 1970s with outlaw protagonists often drew on national writers' reworking of the unruly, often scant sources, which were at times embellished by folk songs and stories and were often almost entirely reinvented in subsequent literary treatments. The seven-part Hungarian series *Sándor Rózsa* (1971), about the eponymous nineteenth-century outlaw, was adapted from novels by the early twentieth-century writer Zsigmond Móricz. The Lithuanian *Tadas Blinda* series (1972), featuring popular actor Vytautas Tomkus, was named after an outlaw hero whose story had been center stage within national literature. In Bulgaria, the series *Kapetan Petko Voyvoda* (1974) celebrated nineteenth-century insurgent Petko Kiryakov Kaloyanov, who had joined forces with Garibaldi around 1866 to fight Ottoman Turks in Crete. The Romanian state commissioned a number of adventure films and television serials, including the feature film *Haiducii* (The outlaws, 1966), followed by six other films about outlaws, such as *Iancu Jianu, the Tax Collector* (1980) and *Iancu Jianu, the Haiduc* (1981). They were directed by Diny Cocea and scripted by party-favored writer Eugen Barbuthe.⁹

The early eighteenth century yielded an especially rich and ideologically profitable historical background against which to develop domestic historical adventure series about mythical outlaws-turned-national-heroes. In the territory of the Habsburg Empire stretching across present-day Hungary, the Czech Republic, Slovakia, Poland, the Ukraine, Romania, Serbia, Croatia, and Slovenia, the late seventeenth century and early eighteenth century were a time of peasant uprisings against the Habsburgs. The most memorable and successful of these was led by Hungarian magnate Ferenc Rákóczi II, prince of Transylvania, the richest landlord in the Kingdom of Hungary. His military operations were mostly conducted in the borderland area between the Habsburg and the Ottoman Empires. Rákóczi, also funded by the French crown looking to overthrow Habsburg domination in Europe, recruited the emancipated peasant soldiers of northeastern Hungary called *hajdus* or *haiducs*. With their help, he seized control of much of Hungary by 1703. After several battles and much negotiation, the uprising failed, and the prince was forced into exile first in Poland and then, for the last eighteen years of his life, in Turkey. The subsequent return of Habsburg domination turned him and his fighters almost instantly into folk heroes. Some of Rákóczi's men went into hiding in inscrutable border areas and sustained themselves by highway robbery. Although these outlaws were not discriminating as to whom they robbed—or murdered, in many cases—folk stories, songs, and later nationalist writers elevated them to the status of justice warriors who carried the legacy of the uprising by protecting the poor against the rich, many of whom were German-speaking foreigners.

Rákóczi and his outlaw followers were further revived and embraced in the region during the national revolutions of the 1840s. They were also appropriated by socialist party authorities after the 1950s, when nationalism made its way back into the official rhetoric. For the socialist regimes of the 1960s, the Rákóczi uprising and the outlaw resistance in its aftermath were appropriately heroic, safely removed from the present in history, and not associated with bloody revolts, unlike nineteenth-century national revolutions, which were feared to ignite street demonstrations. The uprising's benefits also included a narrative of unity and cooperation between peasants and the highest nobility. It was ideal for fortifying national consciousness. At the same time, it provided a contained affective outlet through television entertainment, restricted to a kind of national fandom and intimacy that fused the national and the nuclear family.¹⁰

Not the least important, unlike feature films or literature, the historical adventure series often slipped under the radar of party attention because it qualified as family or youth entertainment, aligning such shows with a flourishing animation and children's film production. By contrast, art films of the time that took up the resistant hero theme fell into two different categories, both under heavier censorship. Some were produced as propaganda material by official party culture, such as the Romanian *Mihai Viteazul* (*Michael The Brave*, Sergiu Nicolaescu, 1971), the spectacular national epic production commissioned by Ceaușescu to boost national pride. Others expressed subtle allegorical opposition to the regime. Miklós Jancsó's stark black-and-white feature *Szegénylegények* (*Round-Up*, 1966) depicts the Austro-Hungarian monarchy's revenge on outlaws who had gone into hiding in the aftermath of the 1848 revolutions. It features blatant historical anachronisms and a modernist aesthetic, which invited comparison with the ideological purges conducted by communist governments in the 1950s.

The TV series were instrumental in fostering national unity not despite but *because of* the fact that they were mostly made up. In other words, their affective power and longevity within national memory derive precisely from folk culture's and high literature's mutual validation of nationalism's loose treatment of historical fact. These series are, for the most part, also transregional and often trans-European in their construction. The nationalism they weave around improper outlaw heroes implies an unacknowledged embrace of colonial, Western European constructions of the Eastern peripheries as rebellious, a kind of permanent Wild East where the laws of civil nation-states are subordinated to popular justice. The mythology they created around local Robin Hoods also subtly justified the violence involved in socialist redistribution.

Nationalistic TV Entertainment: *Tenkes* and *Janosik*

A Tenkes kapitánya (The captain of the Tenkes, 1964) was the very first drama series produced by the Hungarian state broadcaster Magyar Televízió, in thirteen twenty-five-minute parts in 1964. It is also one of the most memorable series of all time. It is set in the early 1800s, during the Rákóczi uprising. Peasant *kuruc* rebel leader Máté Eke and his handful of freedom fighters hide out in the hills of western Hungary to protect the poor against the occupying Habsburg army, which is headquartered in the castle of Siklós.[11] In each episode, the outlaws circumvent or overcome the well-armed Habsburg soldiers with cunning, an intimate knowledge of the local environment, and the help of local villagers.

The series began broadcasting in January 1964, on a Saturday. The episodes were repeated over the course of the next day. The entire series was repeated in the second half of 1964, followed by more than ten subsequent reruns so far. Almost immediately, the episodes were molded together into a feature film, which was released in 1965.[12] Writer Ferenc Örsi turned his script into a juvenile adventure novel in 1967, to be reprinted six more times just during the socialist period. Thanks to regular reruns, the theme song is recognized by virtually everyone in Hungary to this day. The show even inspired a popular song, which topped the Hungarian charts shortly after the series was launched. A stage musical adaptation has also been produced, performed annually against the backdrop of Siklós Castle, the location for both the series and the actual historical events on which it is loosely based.

The Polish *Janosik* (1974), directed by Jerzy Passendorfer, has also enjoyed uninterrupted, cult popularity since its release. It is about a Slovak outlaw with a Hungarian name, who operated across several fluid borders during his short life in the eighteenth century. Poems and novels written about Janosik's life are required reading in Slovak and Polish schools. Altogether, his story inspired ten films and TV series in the Czech, Slovak, and Polish territories between 1929 and 2009.

Janosik and *Tenkes* are remarkably similar in their aesthetic and narrative features, their educational intent to reinforce a Marxist-socialist version of national history, and their postsocialist cult endurance. Their construction is virtually identical: a memorable title sequence shows the heroes, in folk period costumes, riding on horseback in a wide shot that evokes Westerns, to a dynamic "adventure" tune. In both cases, the theme music took on a life of its own by mobilizing affective associations with freedom and social justice. The music itself generated a kind of socialist television fandom at the interface of folk motifs and state-sanctioned high culture. In *Janosik*'s case, the theme was composed by Jerzy Matuszkiewicz, a widely celebrated jazz musician and composer, who had also established himself in the Polish film industry, something that lent instant prestige to the production. At the same time, the theme evokes Polish highland folk songs, with flutes, trumpet, and guitar sounds, infusing the folk tunes with the sense of adventure and romance. *Tenkes*'s theme was written by venerable composer (of Serbian origin) Tihamér Vujicsics. The instrumental melody resonates with the "Rákóczi March," which is considered an unofficial Hungarian anthem. It is likely that the march itself was actually written in the aftermath of the uprising, in the 1730s, and existed in several versions. But the popular tune had also been lifted into classical music by Hector Berlioz in his *La damnation de Faust* (1846) and by Franz Liszt, who drew on the theme in his Hungarian Rhapsody no. 15. The music thus instantly carried a subtle set of connotations in which folk culture, national history, and national art were validated by the music's previous career in European high culture.

Both series consist of self-contained adventures with predictable outcomes, with plots that have the heroes get out of a hopelessly tight spot, set against the larger collective story arc of historical events. The adventures take place in a dialectically conceived nationalistic universe where the honest underdog fights the good fight against the evil but not too smart oppressor. The episodes often introduce a humorous tone, mostly due to the failed intrigues of the ridiculous Count Horvath in *Janosik* and the bumbling Baron Eberstein in *Tenkes*, as well as comic sidekick characters such as the scheming innkeeper Dudva in *Tenkes*. Both shows obey the rules of tame socialist representational decorum and stay away from depictions of sex and blood—often cited by fans as the main positive distinction of this native entertainment format from most of American film and television. Sword fights, chases, and modest battle sequences provide low-budget but effective spectacle. The shows' heteronormative gender regime is fundamental to the central socialist regulation of nationalistic pleasures. The inevitable romantic element involves broadly drawn female characters whose main contribution is to pine after the heroes. The heroes then appropriately resist these temptations and demonstrate loyalty to a single special, clean, and handsome peasant girl (Maryna and Veronika, respectively). The romance is already established at the beginning of *Tenkes* and develops only slightly across the episodes, mostly due to outside intrigue, which only serves to reinforce socialist family values.

Although the series are unwatchable by today's standards of nimble cinematography, special effects, fast-paced, clever dialogue, and naturalistic acting, they delighted socialist audiences at the time. By the 1960s, the historical adventure genre had been well recognized by Polish and Hungarian audiences, who were familiar with Zorro movies, Douglas Fairbanks films, and other Western costume adventure dramas, such as the French-Italian production *Fanfan la tulip* (1952, dir. Christian-Jacque). The nationalistic fandom that the serials ignited was also tied to the actors who played the leads. Marek Pepereczko, widely considered a "hunk," de-

The Captain of the Tenkes (Gyula Szabó) and his wholesome bride.

Marek Pepereczko as Janosik.

livered many viewers in Poland as well as the GDR to *Janosik*. His role was similar to those of other television and movie actors who gained transnational fandom within the socialist bloc. The best known of these is probably Gojko Mitic, the Serbian-born movie and television star, who played the lead Indian characters in the famed GDR Westerns, or *Indianerfilme*. Gyula Szabó, who played Eke Máté, the captain of the Tenkes, was less young, less tall, and less dashing but well liked and credible as the heroic paternal protector and freedom fighter. Both serials enlisted the best and most popular acting talent of the time.

The oddest aspect of these shows to the contemporary viewer is probably the ethnographic sequences that interrupt the narrative's unfolding to feature folk dance and music. These apparently unmotivated inserts were meant to authenticate the historical events and characters on which the programs are loosely based, showcasing "organic" elements of national culture. The folk elements often clash with the other, high cultural mandate, which requires teaching European erudition. The two purposes conflict most jarringly in the serials' use of language: while the Eurocentric education of the masses necessitates using the most normative, literary register of language, the desire to create folk authenticity produces a forced provincial dialect. The dialect used in *Tenkes* is a geographically unspecific mix of rural accents, that is, the "folk" accent imagined by actors trained in prestigious drama schools. Janosik and his band use the Polish Górale highlander dialect, for reasons I explain in the next section. What is missing from both shows is precisely the daily language that most viewers spoke. This schizophrenic situation, in which catering to the regular viewer was undermined by efforts to educate the ideal viewer, characterized socialist media culture as a whole and left a lasting effect on postsocialist media.

Scriptwriter Ferenc Örsi said in his memoir that he had written *Tenkes* at the request of his children, who were disappointed when imported serials such as *Robin Hood* and *Zorro* ended in the early 1960s.[13] This is a charming anecdote that covers up what were no doubt a range of ideological considerations behind launching the first domestic dramatic series. It also inadvertently points out the intention behind such a serial: to address what was perceived as a childlike populace's legitimate yearning for entertainment. This entertainment was in step with European trends but also reinforced nationalism as a glue between party-led government and anticommunist viewers in their homes, while flashing its Soviet-approved educational intention. The series was recognizable to viewers for its folktale resonances with youth and children's fiction, most notably *Ludas Matyi* (Matt the goose boy), an epic poem written by Mihály Fazekas in 1804, first published in 1817. *Ludas Matyi* has its origins in folktales that go back to the sixteenth century, about a poor boy who takes cunning revenge on a greedy feudal overlord who stole the boy's goose. The story, embraced by the socialist regime as a parable about the superiority of peasant intelligence over capitalist greed, inspired a number of filmic adaptations, most famously Attila Dargay's 1977 animated tale of the same title. *Ludas Matyi* was also the name of the Hungarian socialist government's own satirical newspaper (1945–1992), which published officially approved humor that also allowed mockery of socialism.

Apart from the episodic structure, there is nothing particularly televisual about either series. The historical adventure cycle encompassed and easily crossed between film and television at this experimental time when socialist regimes were trying to figure out what to do with an emerging mass medium, and when—in the absence of commercial television—film, TV, and radio were under the same state control and budget. This is why both series were easily condensed into feature films, which further elevated their prestige.

From Cross-Border Social Bandit to Socialist National Hero

Both series solicited nationalistic identification right from the credit sequence by the joint effects of music, heroic action, and spectacular landscape. The introductory themes evoked and encapsulated the oppressed poor's rightful fight against the rich and, in the case of *Tenkes*, against foreign overlords. The backdrops were different: in *Tenkes*, it was the rolling hills of western Hungary near Siklós Castle; in *Janosik*, the high mountains of the Tatras. However, both are open outdoor landscapes that provide the perfect hiding spots and battlegrounds for manly men, much as in Westerns; neither was a historically accurate site of the Rákóczi uprising and its aftermath. Siklós Castle simply provided an appropriately scenic location, irrespective of the fact that most of the actual military operations and brigand activities took place in northeastern Hungary and present-day Ukraine and Slovakia. Such inaccuracy was minimized by referencing some of the historical figures and events of the uprising in selected episodes, including Rákóczi himself.

In a similar vein, the Polish serial moved the historical Janosik from his actual place of birth and life in the Slovak-Hungarian lower Tatras to the Polish highlands. This area had been previously embraced by Polish intellectuals of the 1830s and then again after the failure of the anti-Russian Polish uprising in 1864 as the mythical birthplace of ancestral Polish culture. Nationalist writers were fascinated with the local ethnic group called Górale, a shepherd community whose members spoke their own Polish-Slovak dialect and originally migrated to this border area from the Romanian region of the Carpathians. The Górale were "discovered" and romanticized in nationalistic accounts as a group unspoiled by civilization and foreign influence. Literary accounts of outlaw heroes, including Janosik, were associated with the Górale long before the TV series, which gives its protagonist a highland accent that instantly evokes a long history of popular nationalism located in the Górale highlands.[14]

The same liberal treatment of history applies to the main characters in both shows. Although the protagonist of *Tenkes*, Máté Eke, is not based on a single historical person, the character and the plots are familiar from the large folk and literary production around the Rákóczi uprising, the majority of which was generated in the nineteenth century. When it comes to *Janosik*, the actual life of the outlaw Juraj Janosik is dwarfed by the complexity of the mythic afterlife in which he became a national legend in Slovak, Polish, and Czech cultures alike. Even his name has multiplied in the course of its various appearances, oscillating among Johannes, Georg, Janko, Janik, Janicek, Jasiek, Janosz, Janos, Juro, and Durko.[15] "Janosik" is a derivation from the Hungarian "János" (John) with the Czech/Slovak "-ik" suffix attached.[16] A Slovak-Hungarian borderland figure, his legend only entered Czech culture in the late nineteenth century, after he had been established as a Slovak folk hero. In his work on social bandits, Eric Hobsbawm saw him as a noble robber, while others considered him a rebel against feudal exploitation. A measure of historic ethnic and religious hybridity in the Carpathian region, Janosik's story was shaped by market songs, fairy tales, brigand stories, shepherd myth, nativity plays, the literatures of national revival, and across various media during socialism and thereafter.[17]

To add another layer of complexity, Janosik only became nationalized during the nineteenth-century national revivals once Western European literary Romantics became interested in the exotic peripheries and their outlaws. His legend fit the European outlaw model, which was greatly influenced by Friedrich Schiller's drama *The Robbers*. Schiller was a professor of history at the University of Jena in Saxony, where many Slovak intellectuals took his courses and absorbed a fervent German ethnic activism. Cultural nationalism was thus first channeled back to Central and Eastern Europe through German high cultural mediation. On a European scale, Janosik's nationalistic-romantic appropriation was further facilitated by Romantic poets such as Lord Byron and Alexander Pushkin. Byron became available in Polish in the 1830s and in Hungarian in the 1840s.[18] From Schiller to Dumas, from Scott to Mérimée, from Pushkin to Verga, European high Romanticism rendered the old outlaw-bandit figure palatable, honorable, and at times misanthropic in stories set in the European peripheries, which were associated with passion, desire, pride, revenge, and lack of concern for the rule of law and convention. At the same time, this Western European projection created a wider exposure for Eastern European literatures and cultures. Eastern European folk poetry collected by writers was translated into French and German and was then plagiarized and pastiched, embellished by colorful haiducs and vampires.[19] Unlike folk songs, which rarely celebrate the brigand, high cultural works paint the image of an ethnic rebel against Hungarian oppression. Jan Botto's poem *The Death of Janosik* is one of the most memorable records of the legend's high literary nationalization and a staple in the Czech and Slovak educational curricula.[20]

Under twentieth-century authoritarian regimes, two kinds of Janosik myths were taken up: in the pro-Nazi Slovak Republic and postwar Czechoslovakia, Janosik was deployed variously as both representative of and resistant to the ruling regimes. During the war years, communist artists evoked Janosik subversively. In 1941, the illegal Slovak Communist Party initiated "Janosik Combat Units" to carry out antigovernmental agitation. Underground agit-prop literature of the time reactivated Janosik's rebellious Hungarian kuruc imagery. After the communist takeover of 1948, the new rulers decided to convert the subversive Carpathian highwayman into a patriotic icon of the socialist state. The Czechoslovak national opera embarked on a giant production of Jan Botto's *Death of Janosik*, and the state sponsored several patriotic films about him. The most successful of these was the two-part *Janosik* (1962–1963), directed by Pal'o Bielik, featuring battle scenes with thousands of extras. The film fuses the myth of a noble robber with a socialist-realist interpretation of class struggle. It is comparable in its parameters and effort to build a shared national ground to Passendorfer's Polish film version of *Janosik* (1974), which followed the 1973 TV series. The film and the series established Janosik as a Polish national hero, subtly repositioning him in Polish history through the location, costumes, and set design, which were suggestive of the late eighteenth and early nineteenth centuries as much as the early eighteenth century. The new ethnic contours of the noble robber in the Polish versions are evident in the choice of his antagonist Bartos, a sneaky killer who is identified as a Slovak-Hungarian.[21]

Socialist governments eagerly capitalized on the accumulated cultural appeal of outlaw historical figures when they deployed television as a nationalistic edutainment platform. The shared recognition of the underlying propaganda intent did not necessarily undermine the affective bonding within national fandom. On the contrary, it added a layer of ironic awareness, which was articulated in cautious jokes and political parodies of the time. For instance, while the Janosik myth was embraced by the Czechoslovak state, it was also often parodied or rendered fantastic, as in *Zbojnik Jurko* (Robber Jurko, 1976), Viktor Kubal's animated feature. From the 1970s on, political cabaret provided an outlet for a growing number of satires. The film *Paco, the Brigand of Hybe* (1975, dir. Martin Tapak, based on a novel by Peter Jaros) is a parody of Bielik's sweeping nationalistic movie *Janosik*. In the 1970s, Stanislav Stepka's Radosina Naïve Theater performed the parodic play *Jaááánosííík* in student bars and other places of alternative culture, connecting political cabaret with the avant-garde as well as jazz, rock, beat, and amateur theater. Such performances demystified not only the Janosik tradition but also the institution of academic theater, along with official socialist state culture and its fabricated national identity, conveyed through the convoluted language of official socialism.[22] Political cabaret thrived in Hungary as well. The fandom around *Tenkes* and the historical outlaw adventure genre was no doubt boosted by comedian Géza Hofi's legendary parody of the tendentious acting and contrived speech in the outlaw series *Sándor Rózsa*. Such parodies only fomented a kind of oppositional nationalist unity over the shared sensitivity to double-talk and solidarity in laughter.

Gyula the Brave: The Making of a Historical Series

The mock versions of historical adventure dramas speak to a cultural context that makes socialist television irreducible to propaganda. Perhaps the most persuasive case in point is the remarkable film comedy *Gyula Vitéz télen-nyáron* (Gyula the brave all year round), a hilarious and incisive early mockumentary about the making of a historical adventure series. It was made by the Hungarian state film production company MAFILM in 1970, at the peak of the genre, anticipating the first signs of its fatigue.

The year 1970 was also when the lavish Romanian historical epic *Michael the Brave* was released. The most popular Romanian film of all time, *Michael the Brave* is one of the major reference points of the genre. Commissioned by Ceaușescu, the film remains a memorable achievement of nationalistic propaganda entertainment and was Romania's official Oscar entry for Best Foreign Language Film in 1971. The two-part epic loosely follows events between 1595 and 1601. The historical Mihai was a medieval prince who managed to unite the three principalities of Wallachia, Moldavia, and Transylvania for a few months in 1600. The film adheres to the spirit of history rather than to the facts, as the real Mihai was far from the brave liberator he is in the film.[23] The film was part of a concerted effort to build retroactive nationalistic legitimacy around Ceaușescu's government and to forge national unity among the majority of Romanians.[24] It is one of several movies that dramatize the importance of the eastern borderlands in stopping the barbaric Ottoman invasion and thus upholding Western Christianity and civilization.[25] The internalized role of defender against barbarian eastern forces inevitably represents national sovereignty as something caught up in an unacknowledged colonial identification with the West. This dual dynamic—a sense of explicit superiority to the East and implicit inferiority to the West—was recognizable in the socialist epic across the specific historical narratives depicted.

It is more than likely that *Gyula the Brave* references *Michael the Brave* in its title and critique of region-wide efforts to inscribe nationalistic mythologies into popular film and television productions.[26] The Ottoman Turks occupy the place of the enemy in *Gyula the Brave* as well. The film's main source of humor is the behind-the-scenes look at the various political and industrial mechanisms that shape the genre. The absurdities start with the precredit scene, where the director of the planned TV series within the film, played by Lajos Őze, and his assistant sidekick are scouting for an amateur actor to play the lead role. They are looking for a real man of the people who can represent the heroism of the socialist citizen. The real men who appear in the screen tests at the market and the meat-processing plant, however, deliver their lines in a wooden, lifeless fashion, if they can read them at all. Finally, they hit the jackpot in an accidental encounter with passionate beer factory worker Ferenc Prohászka, played by the dashing Gábor Koncz, who went on to star in a host of historical TV series and films after *Gyula the Brave*. Once "Gyula" is thus identified, the credits flash over cartoon images of folk-patriotic clichés complete with images of national colors, maps, and flags. György Vukán's music, which plays under the credits, is a hybrid of folk tunes and revolutionary marching songs, subtly making fun of both.

The preference for documentary realism casts a mocking shadow over the grand costumed spectacle of "real" historical epics such as *Michael the Brave*. The plot twist of the making of accidental celebrity obviously resonates with Hollywood rags-to-riches stories while it also conforms to the socialist state's idealization of the worker-hero. The film is full of contemporaneous Western popular cultural references, which undermine any Cold War stereotypes about everyday life in the socialist city. In the first scene, Prohászka, wearing a Rolling Stones T-shirt, heads to the pub to watch a soccer game with his buddies on a TV set placed in the window facing out toward the street. In the next scene, two girls discuss their crush on Roger Moore, star of the British spy thriller series *The Saint*. There is obviously a thriving fan culture that is not that different from its Western counterpart in structure and content.

Once the first episodes of the new series are shown on TV, Prohászka becomes an overnight celebrity. He even acquires an agent, a taxi driver who lives in his apartment complex, and who sees a business opportunity in his client's popularity. He arranges an impromptu photo shoot, instructing Prohászka to show his teeth "like foreign actors" when he smiles. Later on, when Prohászka receives 640 fan letters from girls, his chauffer-manager takes him to visit a woman who had sent a particularly explicit invitation. They end up at the address of the wrong woman, who turns out to ask no questions and issues no complaints after Prohászka visits. Prohászka even begins to act in commercials. The prominent display of Kinizsi beer throughout the film, named after a real-life medieval hero who fought the Turks, makes one wonder if we are witnessing a cunning instance of socialist product placement—a practice technically banned during the period. The TV-series-within-the-film is repeatedly interrupted by commercials in which Prohászka promotes products and services in full medieval costume.

The self-reflective concept where the making of a TV show and the film in which it is embedded are tied together by a commercial flow clearly suggests a sense of simultaneity with Western industrial and aesthetic practices. The film constantly confuses character and actor, reality and fiction. It revolves around people making and consuming TV. Throughout, we watch episodes of the TV series along with the characters in the film, in

Gábor Koncz as Ferenc Prohászka as Gyula the Brave.

their homes, or in communal places, often with Prohászka watching himself on TV, or in the production offices along with the director or other production personnel. Real celebrities appear as themselves in various scenes, such as popular announcer Mari Takács, who introduces the new show and subsequent episodes. Once the series is established, it also warrants a serious talking heads discussion on the contemporaneous, real-life current affairs magazine *Társalgó* (The chat room). The program is presented in an unmistakably sarcastic light as boring intellectual nonsense alienated from the real excitement that viewers feel about the drama series.

Lajos Őze, who plays director Lukács, and Ferenc Kállai, who plays producer Bodó, also carry inferences from their previous roles in the film *The Witness* (Péter Bacsó, 1969), which revolved around the political compromises required to survive in socialism. The title sequence of the series within the film is eerily similar to that of *Tenkes*, which was no doubt another point of recognition for contemporary viewers. *Gyula the Brave* gives a rare, stunningly candid glimpse into the fabric of cultural intertextuality created by television. It confirms the consensus expressed by virtually every television professional of the socialist era whom I interviewed that Hungarian television, at least, was an institution with an unusual amount of freedom. It operated without any direct party control, let alone censorship, where authorities rarely got involved with internal decisions made at the institutional level.

Throughout the film, party functionaries' interferences with the series appear panicked and ridiculous. At the very beginning, Bodó advises

Lukács that they should change the original enemy from Czech to Turk, "just to be careful" in light of tense cross-border diplomatic relations with Czechoslovakia. Bodó frets repeatedly about too much eroticism on screen, which would not suit the aesthetic of a "patriotic adventure film." As the show takes off and viewers get increasingly caught up in the story, Bodó and his team worry that the series incites anti-Turkish sentiments, evidenced by an attack on a Turkish runner at an athletic event. Eventually, the decision is made to abort the series for diplomatic reasons. In the last episode, Prohászka is hit in the head in a particularly vigorous fight against the Turkish antagonist and passes out. Immediately after this, the end credits appear, followed by Mari Takács announcing the conclusion of the series. Viewers are so upset, however, that Bodó gets a call on the special "K-line" reserved for direct calls "from above" to do something to calm down the crowds. The producers decide to dedicate an episode of a contemporaneous call-in talk show, led by legendary reporter Tamás Vitray, to airing public sentiments about *Gyula the Brave*. Lukács, the director, is the studio guest answering questions from viewers, who are gathered at two different locations. The fans are not to be pacified by lies, however, and demand Prohászka's "rehabilitation"—a politically charged term in 1970, when the memory of fake trials and executions, most notably that of Imre Nagy, spearheaded by long-term party leader János Kádár, was quite vivid. Vitray responds with an inadvertent sigh, which implies that he is well aware of the double meaning of "rehabilitation" but recognizes the limits of political action under an authoritarian regime. Director Lukács, however, joins in with the crowds, who are demanding to vote (another loaded verb) on the fate of the series. Bodó, the spineless bureaucrat, swears as he watches this rebellion unfold on TV, until he gets another call on the K-line telling him that the people should be allowed to vote.

The vote turns out to be as pointless as actual voting is in a one-party system. In the film, all viewers are asked to turn all electric appliances on at the same time to affirm their support for continuing the series so that a central electric measuring unit can measure the electricity. This was an actual practice of gauging audience ratings in Hungary in the 1970s. The viewers win, but electricity is knocked out right in the middle of Prohászka's brain operation, which leaves him in a coma and confines him to a hospital bed forever. At the film's conclusion, Lukács is shooting a new science fiction series set in space. As they are watching the first episode, Prohászka's pub buddies rate the new show as "totally idiotic." However, suddenly they recognize their old pal Prohászka on the screen, with a

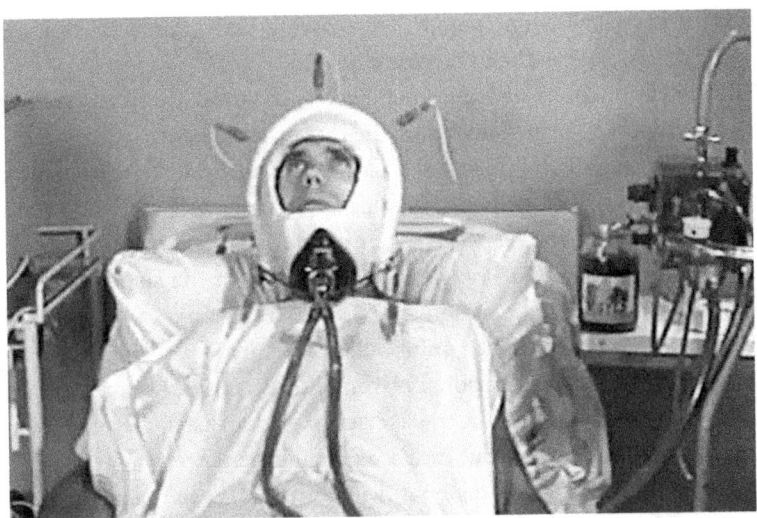

Gyula the Brave in the hospital.

giant bandage on his head, passing for a cosmonaut. Unfortunately, as they also note, the shot accidentally includes the pickle jar that sits on the dresser by his hospital bed.

The Afterlife of Socialist Bandits

In the decades since the end of state socialism, the popular nationalism associated with the early adventure series has been deployed by various corporate and state players to build political legitimacy and consumer brands. Right-wing nationalist factions have drawn on the early eighteenth century for validation, as is indicated in the very name of the most prominent Hungarian ultranationalist website, kurucinfo.hu. In 2008, on the fifteenth anniversary of Slovakia's founding, Prime Minister Robert Fico called Janosik "the greatest role model for [his] government."[27] *Tenkes* has been embraced for destination branding by the city of Siklós, where the series was shot. The local government, eagerly supported by citizens nostalgic for the memories of the early 1960s when TV cameras and stars swirled around the small town, built a wax museum that features the main characters. In addition, since 2009, the Year of Cultural Tourism in Europe, Siklós has been home to a folk festival in the form of a historical tableau based on the TV show, complete with women in folk costumes baking bread, an equestrian parade, wine tasting, crafts, and a musical set against Siklós Castle as the background.

The transition from national mobilization to touristic city branding has been rendered fairly seamless by the blatant inauthenticity of the national myth generated by the TV serial. Early historical adventure dramas provided a database of elements that are interchangeable among the national narratives of the respective countries of the region, and to some extent within Europe as a whole, precisely because of the shared cultural memories, which singular national histories have disavowed. Historical adventure series thus produce unintended accounts of a regional culture arching over the singular national histories. This cross-border relevance, itself building on the common trajectories of nationalism emerging from common imperial cultures, outlines a regional experience, way of expression, and identification. This regional vision contests the national fragmentation to which academic research in the social sciences and Slavic studies often subjects these cultures, and to which they subject themselves for economic and political reasons.

Postsocialist Nostalgia and European Historical Drama

The European Revival of Historical Drama

Much of television programming is attached to the present and the everyday. At times, the medium has been accused of undermining memory and perpetuating a sense of ephemerality and transience.[1] Despite its amnesiac qualities, however, television is also a powerful mnemonic tool. This is not a contradiction: it is precisely TV's propensity to resonate in different temporalities at once that has lent it a sense of living connections among the past, present, and future. As John Ellis puts it, television brings history alive because it is a constituent part of the everyday lives of citizens; it is a vehicle for the transformation of and a source of information about the quotidian.[2] Gary Edgerton goes so far as to claim that "television is the principal means by which most people learn about history today."[3] It is a primary generator of collective memory, where popular and professional histories inevitably mingle.[4] This is why, matching the rise of interest in history among the general population, historical drama is in high currency on North American and Western European television in the twenty-first century across genres such as biography, pseudodocumentary, and period drama series.[5] Historical television drama provides viewers with a "usable past" that is always related and relevant to the concerns of the present.[6]

However, there is a sharp difference between the ways history has been claimed by drama production in the two Europes since the end of the Cold War. In Western Europe, historical television drama is experiencing a revival. It is engaged in the work of revisiting sore spots of national and European history, which is particularly pressing at this time of European identity crisis when the future of the European Union is in question. Historical drama is also good business, especially when it is exportable. In the East, where issues of national and regional self-examination are equally timely, fictional drama production has not gotten off the ground because of the scarcity of resources and the relative economic weakness of public broadcasters against commercial competition. Instead of facing their historical baggage, the region's nations are often accused of wallowing in nostalgia for the lukewarm comforts of state socialism. I argue for suspicion about efforts to reconstitute the East-West divide as something that pivots around nostalgia and showcase evidence of a continued, messy interdependence between East and West.

Ironically, as I explained in the last chapter, during the heyday of historical drama in the 1960s and 1970s, the two Europes on the opposite sides of the Iron Curtain were largely in sync. Because socialist televisions modeled themselves after Western European public broadcasters to a great extent, they also adopted the educational profiles and high cultural programming preferences of those to promote the project of cultural nationalism. After the early years of live broadcasts, some of the first imported fictional dramas were historical adventure programs, followed by a decade of steady domestic historical drama production. Historical drama went into decline in the late 1970s throughout Europe. Although historical teleplays continued to be produced in Eastern Europe, these were much less popular than the earlier adventure series.[7] The decline of the genre was due to what Bourdon calls the shift from a "courteous" to a "competitive" model of broadcasting. By the 1980s, a global, multichannel landscape was forming, where satellite technology made it cheaper to import entertaining American drama and made it harder for European public broadcasters to compete.[8]

In the 1990s, however, European domestic production bounced back. In Italy, Germany, and Britain in particular, public channels increased their programming of homegrown fiction. Even though public broadcasters remain the principle commissioners of domestic drama in Europe, the balance has shifted slightly toward the private channels since 2000.[9] Unsurprisingly, the largest European economies have been best positioned to provide large volumes of national works. In France, this proportion was 28.2 percent in 2004; in the United Kingdom, 19.4 percent; in Spain, 18.3 percent; in Italy, 14.9 percent; and in Germany, 13.4 percent. The smaller countries usually broadcast European works from other countries, including coproductions. These constituted 41.6 percent of fictional programming in Switzerland, 41 percent in Finland, 38.4 percent in Belgium's French community, 33.4 percent in Ireland, and 32.2 percent in Austria.[10] The data about "European" TV only occasionally include any postsocialist countries.

Most remarkable has been the resurgence of the period historical drama on Western European public broadcasters and commercial channels alike. Between 2001 and 2012, about sixty programs of historical fiction were produced in Spain and about forty in Portugal. More than half of Spanish and two-thirds of Portuguese productions were made by public broadcasters, which gained strength in the new millennium, not the least by drawing on these national broadcasters' rich archives. Spanish and Portuguese historical fiction includes a variety of formats from telefilms, TV movies, and miniseries to serials and telenovelas. They encompass all periods from ancient to modern times, although the nineteenth century has been favored in Portugal and the twentieth century in Spain. The Franco and Salazar periods, respectively, particularly the private lives of the two dictators, have been especially popular topics. Perhaps the most beloved of these serials, *Cuéntame cómo pasó* (Tell me what happened, TVE, 2001–), reconstructs daily life during the Franco regime. These programs also show a marked shift from the adaptation of classic national authors to original scripts.[11]

Another large proportion of recent Western European historical drama is set in the interwar or the World War II period. In Germany, the attempted assassination of Adolf Hitler and the biography of Albert Speer inspired drama series along with mythological tales about the Nibelungen.[12] In France, colonial history also made it to TV, particularly that of the Algerian war.[13] Nowhere has the revival of historical telefiction been as extensive as in Italy, where 112 prime-time domestic dramas have been made since 2000. As Milly Buonanno notes, the "period of obsessive return" is no longer the nineteenth century, as it was in the early years of TV, but the twentieth, particularly the Fascist regime, World War II, and its aftermath.[14]

The third public channel in Italy, Rai3, began to broadcast docudrama in prime time in the late 1990s, mostly targeting an older, male, educated demographic. Private networks adopted this programming choice shortly after.[15] Most of these serials reach back to the early 1940s. *Perlasca un eroe italiano* (Perlasca an Italian hero, Raiuno, 2002) tells the story of the "Italian Schindler," Perlasca, a Fascist businessman who went on to save thousands of Jews during the Nazi occupation of Budapest in 1944. *Il cuore nel pozzo* (The heart in the pit, Raiuno, 2005) is set on the eastern border and is focused on the *foibe*, a massacre of thousands of Italians by Yugoslav partisans at end of World War II. This remains a controversial event that was consistently denied by the Yugoslavian government.[16] Such series are involved in a nationalistic historical revision that has been criticized for absolving Italy of its Fascist past. They mobilize the character of the "good Italian," who is well-meaning albeit easily swayed, but ultimately able to correct his path.[17] There is no clear divide in such series between historical and popular representations of the past.[18] They depict historical events through the lens and concerns of the present, often foregrounding anachronistic body language, sensibilities, and acting.[19] Historical series such as these can also be seen as a response to the domination of reality programs and their preoccupation with the present. Ultimately, especially in the miniseries format, they capitalize on the thriving business of quality television costume drama.[20]

The increase in domestic European drama production has no doubt been facilitated by the European Union's Audiovisual Media Services Directive, formerly called the Television without Frontiers Directive. The directive was supposed to help offset the trade imbalance between the United States and (Western) Europe by requiring EU member states to reserve a majority percentage of their broadcast time for works of European origin.[21] However, data analyzed by Havens et al. suggest that the directive is likely to have had a one-directional effect: it favored the rich, core EU countries that are able to produce drama by obligating poorer postsocialist countries to import a higher proportion of Western European products—effectively to replace some of their American imports. Moreover, an important consequence of the directive has been a significant decrease in program imports from other nations in the Central and Eastern European region. Ironically, while the directive was designed to strengthen European cultural heritage, it has done so in a lopsided fashion, actually undermining cultural diversity in the postsocialist region.[22]

The only postsocialist economy robust enough to sustain domestic drama production seems to be Poland's. Poland followed the lead of Western European companies to import less and produce more, although with a ten-year delay, in the first decade of the millenium.[23] The directive does not play a coercive role in Poland because the European fiction quota can be fulfilled mostly by domestic drama.[24] But even in Poland, the main dramatic fictional serials tend not to be expensive costume dramas. In Czechoslovakia, Hungary, and other postsocialist countries, drama production is typically restricted to inexpensive soap operas set in the present, mostly made by commercial broadcasters.

In the absence of resources to produce domestic historical series, most Eastern European television systems are relegated to competing for below-the-line services to large European or global productions. This emerging East-West distribution of labor may be captured by the case of *The Borgias* (Showtime, 2011–), a lavishly cinematic, English-speaking historical television serial. Created by Irish film director Neil Jordan and featuring English actor Jeremy Irons as Rodrigo Borgia, or Pope Alexander VI, *The Borgias* is set in late fifteenth-century Italy and centers on the dangerous and seductive lives of the infamous papal family of Spanish origin. The serial was coproduced among four production companies and is distributed globally, most prominently by Showtime Networks. *The Borgias* was shot in Budapest and employs an almost all-Hungarian below-the-line crew. It represents one of Hungary's victories in the competition among former socialist states for a slice of the global entertainment market, mostly in the form of temporary jobs created by media conglomerates. This victory was scored by offering the producers an unbeatably cheap and experienced workforce and generous tax credits, which cover up to 25 percent of foreign investors' production costs according to a 2004 law. Thanks to these incentives, Budapest has recently become the most desirable postsocialist destination for outsourcing Hollywood-based film and television production, overtaking the formerly favored Prague and standing in for other, less affordable European locations such as London, Berlin, Paris, or Rome. *The Borgias* was shot in the recently built Korda Film Studio, named after Sir Alexander Korda, a Hungarian refugee turned celebrated director of historical films such as *Bonnie Prince Charlie* (1948) and the Oscar-nominated *Private Life of Henry VII* (1933). There is an almost ironic postcolonial logic to claiming Korda's legacy in a country where state financing for filmmaking is currently helmed by Hungarian-born Hollywood producer Andrew Vajna, whose name is attached to the *Rambo* and *Terminator* franchises.[25] In the latest development to make Budapest look even more seductive to international producers, the old state film studio MAFILM and its associated lab facilities were transferred to new ownership under the country's recently established Film Fund. The fund, headed by Vajna, took control of $27 million worth of property previously run by the defunct Motion Picture Public Foundation in 2012.[26]

Jack Rapke, who produced *The Borgias*, said he had long planned to write the script as a feature film with Oscar aspirations but eventually decided to transform it into the next best thing, a quality costume drama series directed by one of Europe's preeminent auteurs and starring one of its most reputed actors. The success of *The Tudors* (2007–2010), another spectacular costume drama series with high production values and elevated by its European, historical subject matter and talent, was a reassuring economic trial run for Rapke and Showtime.[27] While the story of the Borgia family has been a source of intrigue, power, violence, and romance for fictional treatments, it has also been popularized by the *Assassin's Creed* videogame franchise, a series of three historical games in which one plays as an assassin in Rodrigo Borgia's court. Gaming blogs and discussion sites were animated with comparisons between the game and the TV show and speculations about mutual influences even before the series was launched. After the first episodes were aired, gamers immediately commented on the "CGI" quality of some of the crowd scenes, which showed a remarkable similarity to the highly realistic video game. None of these discussions ever mentioned the actual location of the shooting. Eastern Europe, and the entire below-the-line context of production that made possible this spectacular, gamelike, cinematic illusion of European history, stays invisible as the other, submerged side of global convergence.

The Borgias was not designed to offend anybody. This was all history to entertain, says Jack Rapke, confirming the notion that history on TV is big global business.[28] The blurring of the division between high and popular culture, or more specifically between art film and quality television, speaks to a global leveling out of geographical and cultural sensibilities in the cheery melting pot of Hollywood production values and European historical heritage and artistic prestige. In the post–Cold War media world, global consumer sensibilities crystallize around brand preferences and economic class. From the ruins of state-run film industries, cash-strapped Eastern Europe has emerged as an indispensable site for this transnational rearrangement: a cheap resource of production and a new consumer market, which offers to the cosmopolitan consumer eye an affordable, generic template for virtual historical tourism.

Postsocialist TV and Nostalgia

In Eastern Europe, the past has especially sensitive nerve endings in the present. Virtually any instance of communication, public or private, is saturated with historical reflection. This near-obsessive concern with history has been consistently identified as one of the core features of film, literature, and other arts produced during the Cold War period. However, it has taken on even greater urgency after the collapse of socialism as national regimes and individual citizens alike have tried to revive usable paradigms of identity from past periods to clear away or at least cover up the historical debris left behind by socialism.

"History" and "memory" are two of the key terms that have channeled and framed academic research on the Soviet Empire's transition to a postsocialist form of capitalism. It is common to see the two words juxtaposed in the titles of publications, courses, and conferences to distinguish between two different modes of remembering: "history" calls up official, public, and professional modes such as commemoration and musealization, while "memory" implies unofficial, popular, and private modes frequently associated with nostalgia and consumerism. Television's fabric of everyday socialism weaves together both history and memory. It productively muddles the differences between the two kinds of practices and corresponding research approaches lined up behind "memory" and "history." Precisely because television as a medium has resisted the binary schemes of political control and the disciplinary divides that continue to parcel out "proper" research areas on (post)socialism, its potential contribution to the study of history and memory is immense. The groundwork for this research has only begun to be laid by scholars such as Irena Reifová, Daniela Mustata, Zala Volčič, Sabina Mihelj, Lars Lundgren, and a handful of others. Building on this groundwork, here I connect the dots between television's relevance to postsocialist collective memory and the much-discussed phenomenon of postsocialist nostalgia.

Nostalgia has continued to flourish throughout the former socialist region since it erupted in the early 1990s following the Soviet Empire's disintegration. An entire field of scholarly and popular analysis has sprung up around it. I see nostalgia as far more complicated than a near-visceral yearning for the false sense of safety derived from the memory of socialism, fetishistically attached to public personas or consumer products of the past. Instead, I agree with those who tie nostalgia to the disruption of a sense of intimate sociality caused by the collapse of a centralized system of governance and the influx of globalization. I also understand nostalgia as something that is by definition national at its core, which can be easily appropriated in the service of nationalistic party politics as well as commercial gain. Postsocialist nostalgia, however, is not simply an alternative expression of nationalism, which merges with consumerism.[29]

Rather, postsocialist nostalgia foregrounds the coexistence of different temporalities, or living socialisms in the present. Postsocialist nostalgia also implies the overlap and interaction of different geopolitical vectors across space: while it has identifiable regional features, the temporalities of the national histories concerned do not necessarily align within the region. For instance, as Zsuzsa Gille notes, postsocialist nostalgia in Romania is similar in structure to late socialist nostalgia of the 1980s in Hungary.[30] Furthermore, expressions of postsocialist nostalgia are embedded in and respond to discourses that are European or global in scale. Postsocialist nostalgia sets in conversation a variety of expressions that process the end of the Cold War and the alleged demise of socialism as a viable political and economic form of governance. Describing nostalgia as something that originates in or is immanent to a particular Eastern European state of mind is itself a politicized assumption that falsely implies a clear and final break between socialism and its superior "posts."

In other words, more than a certain way or content of longing, postsocialist nostalgia is an interpretive framework for understanding post–Cold War Europe's living relationship with its socialist history. This interpretive framework is in synergy with cultural practices around television, a medium whose chief mode of operation is in reruns, recombinations, circulating formats, and generic adaptations that constantly interlace national, regional, and global scales.

In the post-Soviet region, as elsewhere, nostalgia almost invariably finds expression in TV memories shared within—and often across—national communities. As Dominic Boyer explains, nostalgia and nationalism have common roots in the history of Central and Eastern Europe. The term "nostalgia" was coined by German medical university student Johannes Hofer in his 1688 dissertation.[31] Hofer diagnosed the "condition" of students and other intellectuals who were studying away from their homes in German-speaking towns of Eastern and Central Europe. These intellectuals organized themselves into so-called *natios* in order to manage feelings of dislocation.[32] The university, the main site of reproduction for the educated middle classes, also became an institutional site of germinating nationalisms, where, by the late seventeenth century, the natios turned into sites of zealous patriotic competition. For Hofer and his contemporaries, nostalgia was an early expression of longing for what began to be identified at the same time as national homes. Hofer identified nationalism as a physiological state, one that has turned out to have "widespread consequences for European nationalism."[33]

This history highlights an enduring component of Eastern European nationalisms: that the nations were first construed by and continued to be shaped by the ideas of intellectuals and the educated middle classes.[34] One of the consequences is the consistent preference for literature and high art as expressions of *cultural nationalism*.[35] The inherent conservatism of high culture was concealed by the allegedly rebellious, "dissident" status of intellectuals during socialism, a status contingent on Western approval of their cause as "good nationalism." This explains why a large number of formerly dissident Eastern European intellectuals turned explicitly nationalistic in the 1990s and took a nostalgic stand in favor of the "national tradition" of high art. As I argued in chapter 5 on Roma and black reality TV stars, after 1989, this nationalistic conservatism has exposed its racialized and gendered foundations.[36] Television has also posed a threat to a predominantly male intelligentsia, whose investment in the class power nationalism conferred on them has been duly threatened by a medium associated with femininity and mass culture.[37] While socialist television addressed its viewers as masculinized national citizens in the first place, it was also *the* mass medium of the period, through which desire for entertainment and consumer products most commonly seeped into socialist lives. As such, TV constantly posed a danger of the passive, mindless consumption of formulaic narratives—a danger that has been ascribed to women's inferior psychosocial needs and tastes as opposed to the cerebral modernist masculinity of art.

It is no wonder that the first attempts to recover the displaced memories of socialism in the 1990s took place "in the demiworld of popular culture," below the radar of official state politics and elite intellectual culture, as Irena Reifová, Kateřina Gillárová, and Radim Hladík explain in one of the very few empirical audience studies of television-mediated postsocialist nostalgia.³⁸ Popular culture, and television in particular, remain the principal sites where people can experience the continuing intimacy of the socialist past without having to face public reproach.³⁹

Equally important, the way cultural nationalism repudiates television as an instrument of history also has a European dimension. Postsocialist nostalgia as an epistemological grid helps uncover a haunting postcolonial dynamic within European cultural nationalisms. Although unique in many respects, the relationship between the two Germanys that generated "Ostalgie" has served as the default paradigm of the postcolonial dynamic within post–Cold War nostalgia. Many of reunification's lessons can thus be extended to describe a broader European pattern. According to the common understanding of Ostalgie, it is a natural by-product of the backward-looking former East's inadequate preparation for the transition to democratic capitalism. Some scholars suggest, however, that Ostalgie is largely a West German projection of a sense of disappointment onto East Germans. The notion of an inherently nostalgic and premodern postsocialist population, by implication, props up Western Europe as the epicenter of progressive, scientific modernity.

Rather than a longing for the GDR by naive East Germans going through the shock of transition and a way to monetize socialist memorabilia on the postunification market, Dominic Boyer argues that Ostalgie is the symptom of a historical blaming game between the two Germanys over who is responsible for nationalism, *die Deutsche Krankheit* (the German illness) that had led to Fascism. As long as there were two Germanys, they could each defer the guilt over Nazism to the other and suppress it at home. However, after reunification, the finger came to be pointed firmly by the more powerful and richer Germany to the one on the losing end of the Cold War. Ostalgie is thus a result of West Germany's blaming of bad nationalism on the East. In Boyer's analysis of the film *Good-Bye Lenin* and the nostalgic magazine *Super Illu*, both produced by West Germans, Ostalgie confers a split temporality on postunification Germany: easterners are naturally affiliated with the past while westerners are affiliated with the future, which makes the latter the proper representatives of a unified Germany.⁴⁰

Extending this dynamic onto a European scale, Boyer calls the West's fanning of Eastern European nostalgia a "post-imperial symptom."⁴¹ It is an expression of a growing Western European awareness that modernity is plurinodal rather than centered in European metropolitan headquarters. Boyer writes, "In this postimperial environment, the need for

Eastern Europe as a *still lesser* node, a space that Western Europe can still suppose itself to dominate, has been vital. Indeed, the post-1989 Western European obsession with Eastern Europe's obsession with the past must be understood as an anxious lateral signal that the pastness of Eastern Europe can no longer be taken for granted."[42]

Gerd Gemünden gives a perfect example of how cultural nationalism and nostalgia are intertwined to support a defensive, elitist European revisionism. In Germany, some of the most prominent (West German) intellectuals, including directors Wim Wenders and Jans Jürgen Syberberg and playwright Botho Strauss, have famously revised their formerly cosmopolitan positions and outlined what are utopian national rebirth scenarios for a united Germany. In the wake of reunification, all three published controversial essays that consider the suppression of German nationalism after World War II harmful because it opened the gate to the influx of American audiovisual culture, which must be resisted in order to preserve and nourish German culture in its purest, literary manifestation. These intellectuals look nostalgically to the former GDR as an authentic resource for reinvigorating true German culture, something that had been ostensibly frozen and preserved in the East during the Cold War.[43] According to Gemünden, this logocentric return to the ethos of German Romanticism is linked to a new nationalism that wants to do away with Western integration and democracy over the last forty years. He writes, "The eighteenth-century notion of *Kulturnation* (that is, the idea of a shared literature, music, art, philosophy and so forth) that provides a certain cultural identity in lieu of nationhood is invoked with all its cliché-ridden, elitist and racist implications."[44]

This postimperial European dimension considerably complicates the cultural politics of postsocialist nostalgia in Eastern Europe. On the one hand, postsocialist nostalgia is a response to and repudiation of Westerners' own projection of nostalgia onto socialism, which is represented as a culture of scarcity and naïveté where people long for Western goods and toppled statues. The repudiation of this notion tends to find its expression precisely in television and other popular venues nervously excluded from official discourses of cultural nationalism. On the other hand, postsocialist nostalgia also includes elements of acquiescence to the Western projection that is fascinated by the supposedly naive gaze of the East staring back at the West. This acquiescence is a price the East is willing to pay for inclusion in the European Union and for assimilation to Europe.[45] This sentiment renders the nostalgia released by television and popular culture in general too muddy and uncontrollable. Television threatens to trouble the aspirational narrative of the Eurocentric postsocialist nation that has now fully returned to the Europe of high culture to which it has always already belonged.

Unwrapping the layers of postsocialist nostalgia provides further proof that the study of Eastern European TV is not a simple extension of Western media studies to uncharted territory. It also involves acknowledging and confronting a postimperial power dynamic that presents Western and Eastern researchers with very different stakes. While the former possess the necessary political capital to afford studying popular media, the latter have to insist first on faithfully fulfilling the role assigned to them, which is to represent their national cultures in terms of their elite achievements lest they risk feminization and racialization by association with popular culture.

Jérôme Bourdon et al. ask two important questions in their chapter in the book *A European Television History*. First, "What do Europeans have in common?" Their response is that the most obvious commonality is a focus on high culture. Their second question is whether there is a specificity to European cultures of popular television. In my view, this question can only be properly answered if one takes into account the different investments in cultural nationalism on the two sides formerly divided by the Iron Curtain. In the absence of such a postimperial perspective, the answer will continue to fall back on centralizing the West and forgetting about the East or treating the latter as a nostalgic extension in a continual state of catch-up.[46]

In the introduction to the collection *Post-Communist Nostalgia*, coeditor Maria Todorova asks: "Can we offer a typology of post-Communist nostalgia, one that is also sufficiently discriminating between regional and national differences?"[47] In response, she lists the "spheres of life or genres" in which postsocialist nostalgia is expressed: "Here we have everything in the oral domain from casual conversations to scholarly interviews, and genres from song and literature to film."[48] It is telling that television does not qualify as a "sphere of life or genre" of nostalgia. Indeed, none of the fifteen essays in this substantial collection deal with television.

In the final section of this chapter, I look at postsocialist nostalgia by taking television into serious account. I follow up on the question of the specificity of European popular television by identifying certain national and regional patterns of television-mediated postsocialist nostalgia. Television historians have repeatedly reminded us of the importance of considering the national features of memory systems developed around television.[49] It is equally important to stress, however, that this requires more than adding to the repertoire of examples within an existing paradigm. Rather, it takes an intervention, based on the recognition that the paradigms of popular media studies have developed within and continue to neutralize a postimperial hierarchy within Europe, and that this hierarchy has been internalized in the very research paradigms influenced by Eastern European cultural nationalisms.

Modes of Postsocialist TV Nostalgia

If we want to analyze postsocialist televisual nostalgia, we will quickly notice a variety of relations between socialist histories and postsocialist developments across the region. One consistent feature across these varieties is that television has been a melting pot where different modes of nostalgia inevitably mix. In every country, state and private actors have engaged in a tug-of-war over the political and financial profits to be gained from deploying the socialist TV heritage.

In Russia, state-sponsored nostalgia has become the dominant mode of television, the result of the Putin government's attempts at recentralization. Because the leading channels in Russia are owned either by the government or by media groups loyal to the government, the Kremlin retains a significant influence over television. This situation has favored programming that selectively reinvents Soviet television tradition in the shape of programs of high cultural quality saturated by a Russian postimperial discourse of cultural superiority. In terms of content, literary adaptations by Russian classics have been revived, along with Soviet films and historical series such as the World War II drama *Seventeen Moments of Spring* (1973). Even adaptations of global reality formats have tended to feature old Soviet stars. Kateryna Khinkulova contrasts this self-aggrandizing nationalistic "quality" brand with the brand-new television system of the Ukraine, which has been eager to shed Soviet control after the country's independence from the Soviet Union and has embraced investment by global corporations and welcomed program imports. In place of nostalgia for the television of the Soviet past, the dominant mode is a desire for a Western (European) future.[50]

State nationalism is not the only brand of TV nostalgia in Russia. Private cable channels have also attempted to cash in on television nostalgia. Retro Channel and Channel Nostalgia both broadcast reruns of socialist programs. Channel Nostalgia reproduces the schedule of the typical socialist day followed in prime time by studio conversations with invited guests, who analyze and discuss the past. Ekaterina Kalinina argues that the talk show segments frame the actual reruns as "jokes," effectively creating a temporal hybrid that marries selective programming from the past with contemporary satirical attitudes. Rather than re-creating socialist programming to offset the loss of the good old days, "nostalgia" here delivers an aspirational TV socialism that viewers of the past may have actually liked, according to producers of the present.[51] Most recently, the channel CCCP-TV.ru has taken the nostalgia business online. It is a partnership between the private company Uravo and the State Television and Radio Fund, whose vast archives provide the content uploaded on the site. The venture is also supported by ads, which link to online auctions for communist memorabilia. Similar to the retro cable channels, the site features communist propaganda as a joke; but it also showcases less politicized content such as comedy, ballet, and sports, which have proven to be its most popular offerings.[52]

In the past decade virtually all postsocialist governments have moved toward recentralizing control over television, particularly over public broadcasters. However, there is variation as to what kinds of television memories are strategically selected—and erased—to generate nostalgic nationalism. The current Hungarian administration, led by the two-thirds majority party FIDESZ, has resuscitated populist programming from socialist television to seek support for its conservative policies. The four public broadcasters are essentially under party control. While the first channel, M1, closely resembles the centralized party device it was under socialism, M2 has been recently reconfigured as a nostalgia machine (after a previously announced and then abandoned plan to turn it into a children's channel that would show mostly old socialist children's programs). Since 2010, several nostalgia programs have been launched on M2. *2-es retro* (Retro on the 2) began in April 2012 as a late night variety show where contemporary actors and actresses perform the quaint role of the program announcer to introduce musical programs, cabaret shows, and biographies that showcase the work of popular performers from the past. These depoliticized reminiscences generate a sense of late socialist sociality as a natural connecting glue among citizens gathered around the warm glow of their favorite singers and comedians. It exploits the entrenched view of TV as "just entertainment" and erases the institution's history of constant negotiation with ideological interference, in order to naturalize in the present precisely such interference.

The third public broadcaster, Duna TV, began in 1992 as the first Hungarian-language channel broadcast over satellite, with a remit to serve a broader language community that includes the diasporas. The main studio is in Budapest but there are regional stations in Romania, Slovakia, Serbia, and Ukraine, as well as North and South America and Australia. As a channel dedicated to nurturing a Hungarian audiovisual heritage, it is profoundly nostalgic and nationalistic. It specializes in rerunning vintage content: old films, television series, and documentaries. Under FIDESZ guardianship, it has added to its repertoire a series of socialist program "remakes": the folk music talent competition show *Fölszállott a páva* (The peacock has taken off) resurrects the long-running program *Röpülj páva!* (Fly, peacock!), broadcast on M1 between 1969 and 1981. Most recently, in December 2014, the FIDESZ government launched yet another public channel tellingly named "M3 Anno." This cable venture seems to have been modeled after similar Russian enterprises as its programming consists entirely of depoliticized socialist favorites. While technically this is a public broadcasting channel fed by the state television archives, it is only available through subscription cable.

Public radio also launched a new channel in December 2012, which carries a genre of "light" folk music especially popular among rural listeners—FIDESZ's largest voting base. The current regime's cynicism manifests itself in the fact that it named the new station Radio Dankó after Pista Dankó, a popular Roma musician, whose career success is meant to prove that "you can work your way up to the top" if you're "hard-working, talented and dedicated," according to the official rationale.[53] This message comes from the regime that has fostered an atmosphere of rising racism and anti-Semitism and whose drastic neoliberal economic restructuring has pulled much of the remaining social safety net from under the poor, which has disproportionately affected the Roma.

At the same time, the FIDESZ government eliminated the five provincial public service radio channels created under socialism and concentrated Hungarian Radio's operations in Budapest in order to control all news programs—undermining its stated intention to cater to rural listeners. The ironies do not stop here. Concentrating the media under state control is eerily similar to the very state socialist initiatives that FIDESZ has actively repudiated. Despite its stated ideological opposition to socialism, the government borrows selectively from the cultural forms of socialist media to reignite a sense of nationalistic bonding cultivated by János Kádár's regime of goulash socialism. Kádár's government, however, at least preserved some of the original socialist ideals, even if in a watered-down version. It promoted programming that reached the widest possible audiences, particularly across class and geography, and decentralized broadcasting by launching the local radio and TV stations that FIDESZ has now eliminated.

Another important difference from the Kádár era is that public broadcasters, much like elsewhere in the postsocialist region, have slipped far below the major commercial broadcasters in ratings and popularity—a far cry from the total national coverage their predecessors enjoyed during socialism. In 2011, M1 had a 7.9 percent audience share across the population overall, trailing by a large margin the two leading commercial broadcasters, RTL KLUB (20.3 percent) and TV2 (18.6 percent). M2 came in ninth overall at 1.9 percent, and Duna TV at 1.8 percent. Among viewers aged eighteen to forty-nine, M1 scored only 3.8 percent of viewer ratings, while M2 came in at a minuscule 1.2 percent, and Duna TV at fifteenth place with 1.1 percent.[54] Public broadcasters operate on a terrain that is infinitely more dispersed and varied than that of the two government-controlled channels that had enjoyed a monopoly up to the mid-1980s. As a result, they essentially function like niche channels that cater to the government's right-leaning, older, mostly rural base.

Popular music's capacity to call up depoliticized memories that can be retooled to serve party politics has also been amply deployed on public television. In the former Yugoslavia, turbo-folk was instrumental in whipping up militaristic nationalism during the 1990s,[55] epitomized by the wedding of Serbian warlord Arkan to turbo-folk singer Ceca in 1995 in a lavish media event.[56] Zala Volčič writes that national television stations in all the former republics have invited their viewers to become part of an ethnically pure national family imagined as superior to the other post-Yugoslav states. As elsewhere, television works at the interface of official state nationalism and a commercial "nostalgia industry." A number of Yugoslav-themed TV shows, pop-music compilation albums, and films have turned Yugo-nostalgia into mainstream entertainment. For example, the popular Serbian radio station Radio Nostalgia plays only the songs of the Yugoslav era.[57]

Television nostalgia has paid off most handsomely in the case of socialist drama reruns and remakes. These are a ubiquitous fixture of the regional landscape on public and commercial broadcasters alike. In the Czech Republic, in particular, socialist drama serials from the post-1968 "normalization" period have been rerun in unprecedented numbers. This is only surprising because, as I discuss in more detail in chapter 10, TV drama production in the 1970s and 1980s was part of the party's propaganda mission. Between 1959 and 1989, Czechoslovak TV aired drama serials 283 times: 54 percent first runs and 46 percent reruns; 139 of the total of 151 drama serials produced were made during normalization. Since 1990, 89 new series have been produced and 311 reruns broadcast, or a proportion of 22/88 percent.[58] The political content of socialist serials has only occasionally caused friction. Most memorably, a debate erupted in 1999 around the first postsocialist rebroadcast of the serial *Thirty Cases of Major Zeman* (1975), which revolved around a loyal communist detective. One side argued that the rerun offended political prisoners, trivialized violence under communism, and distorted history. In response, the public broadcaster launched a website for comments and organized a TV roundtable to discuss each episode. But when the commercial Prima TV rebroadcast the serial in 2004, it entirely depoliticized the show through whimsical music and other features that anachronistically referenced other entertainment programs, including the ABC sitcom *Friends* and the East German Western *Winnetou*. As Irena Reifová sums it up, Prima reduced socialist memory to socialist kitsch.[59]

Socialist kitsch is also back on German TV. Uwe Breitenborn notes that even major German commercial networks such as RTL and Sat1 have dug up old GDR shows from the archives and recycled them in a "hackneyed," depoliticized way that makes these shows more compatible with global pop culture and appealing to younger audiences. For instance, RTL's *GDR Show* (2003), presented by Katarina Witt and Oliver Geissen, drew on socialist film material in a "relaxed" manner to conjure up the "faded" everyday life of the old GDR.[60]

Television's Split Screen of European History

When it comes to television's role in processing national and regional histories, there are marked differences between East and West. The large Western European economies have revived costume drama since the end of the Cold War. However, unlike during the genre's heroic period, this time TV history is borne out of private-public partnerships and yields large profits on the national and international markets. It also allows wealthier nations to revisit and even correct dark spots of history such as the Nazi period or the Franco and Salazar dictatorships. In the East, struggling economies have been relegated to supplying runaway industries with facilities, tax incentives, cheap labor, and markets for Western productions. This discrepancy confirms the East's economic belatedness and dependency despite nominal inclusion in EU directives that create a common labor, production, and distribution market. In the absence of large-scale domestic production, Eastern European televisions, often under semiauthoritarian party control, have been recycling the contents of socialist archives on dedicated public channels, online, and on public and on private broadcasters alike. This picture cannot be reduced to inferior Easterners wallowing in nostalgia for socialism. Television nostalgia has catered to a range of desires and motivations, from evoking shared experiences otherwise erased from public representation through cynically whipping up populist, nationalist sentiment, to producing revenue.

Television's engagement with socialist history and memory proves that postsocialist nostalgia is not a sole product of Eastern European populations' disappointment with and inability to deal with the advent of market democracy. Rather, it is a relational expression of heterogeneous desires that operate in an intercultural network. Televisual nostalgia implicates Western Europe and makes explicit the Western investments in the divided Europe of the Cold War and its continued legacy of economic and cultural hierarchy. Television's role at the pressure points of postsocialist institutional and economic policy, consumption, and aesthetic concerns makes it an indispensable window into the intertwined workings of nostalgia and nationalism in Europe. Amy Holdsworth writes that television's current memory boom is an expression of present anxieties about history and memory in general, which run parallel with television and television studies.[61] Research on postsocialist nostalgia has a special relevance for understanding these anxieties. Televisual nostalgia bears out Daphne Berdahl's claim that socialism continues to have an active social life.[62] Examining the role of television in relation to postsocialist nostalgia therefore has great potential to revise not just the relationship between memory and history but also the relationship between European socialism and its pasts.

Commercials as Time-Space Machines 8

Television advertising allows us a unique glimpse into the surprising complexity of socialist cultures and European cultures' relationship to the socialist past. Socialist commercials were ideological and economic anomalies that defied the regimes' official images of themselves and retroactively upset any easy Cold War stereotypes about socialism. They reveal the existence of an underlying commercial infrastructure within state socialism, which developed into a semiofficial matrix by the 1970s and 1980s. Television literally broadcast the contradictions that party leadership constantly tried to negotiate away, attempting to absorb market-based operations into its rhetoric. In this chapter I discuss advertisements' officially downplayed but all the more significant role as a challenge to socialist principles and a symptom of leaks in nationalistic containment and isolation.

First, I examine the place media marketing occupied within two of the most developed and commercialized countries, Yugoslavia and Hungary. Then I look at how commercials' out-of-place quality in the socialist landscape triggered and spread identification with consumer lifestyles across the region due to cross-border watching. Commercials helped even out the time differences that existed among countries of the region and within Europe in an experience of virtual simultaneity. Television advertising did not simply encourage identification with other places; it also conveyed a complex temporality that inscribed longing for a more colorful future within the present, an alternative timescape to be found mostly across the borders of other countries. Commercials have also served as vehicles of nostalgic travel across time, from postsocialism back to late socialism, the preferred period of postsocialist nostalgia. The complexity of postsocialist nostalgia cannot be understood without grasping how commercials embodied longing for alternative times and places within late socialism.

Socialist TV's Commercial Production: "We Already Had Everything on a Small Scale"

All socialist countries engaged in some form of television advertising. This in itself is not that surprising given that, as Heather Gumbert succinctly put it, "the entire system was geared toward advertising itself."[1] As I discussed in chapter 4, competition was inherent to the structure of Soviet-type socialism, since the system was built on utopian principles that needed constant fortification, justification, and adjustment on the domestic front, particularly in light of ongoing competition and comparisons with Western European socialist democracies.

Commercials bore the trace of these ideological negotiations in a range of aesthetic forms that would be characterized as awkward, funny, or campy today. Much of earlier television advertising resembled public service announcements. These were often fairly lengthy and tedious short films about products or services or informational videos about the dangers of smoking or littering. The East German film studios, DEFA, began to make TV commercials in the 1960s but ended their production in the 1970s because there simply was not enough stuff to advertise. Like other socialist countries, the GDR continued to produce informational public service announcements. Television also assisted in inserting overt product placements that helped manage the inadequacies of socialist economic planning such as featuring herring recipes on cooking shows in order to move excess herring out of the warehouses.[2]

The largest supplier of ads for Soviet TV was Eesti Reklaamfilm (Estonian Commercial Film Company), which began making TV commercials in 1967 and produced more than five thousand TV commercials advertising a variety of organizations, services, and products over the company's twenty-four-year run. The company was headed by Eedu Ojamaa, a documentary filmmaker.[3] Soviet ads were broadcast in five-minute advertising blocks that aired three times a day to minimize interruption. They became one of the highlights of the TV day, televisual events that gathered a massive cult following. As elsewhere, they displayed symptoms of central economic planning's weaknesses. Often they advertised products that were in short supply or nonexistent by the time the ad aired, or they were aired preemptively, in the hope that the product would be available in time. In a way that was true all through the region, what these ads lacked in production values and marketing savvy, they often made up for in creativity.[4]

Polish ads, in particular, were often abstract and even absurd, especially when they promoted products that were not available in stores. A good example is poet and songwriter Agnieszka Osiecka's ad that read, "Alligator—super coats for supermen."[5] In Poland, TV advertising began as early as 1956. At first it was limited to fifteen minutes a week. The earliest ads were modeled after promotional segments developed for Polish Radio.[6] The very first ad was for the detergent Kokosal. It was not until the early 1980s, however, that an advertising market developed.

Television advertising in the most liberalized socialist economies was embedded in an extensive set of commercial features. In fact, Sabina Mihelj argues that, in some ways, the televisions of the Yugoslavian member states were more commercially oriented than some Western European public broadcasters. Yugoslavia's relative ideological independence from the Warsaw Pact under Tito's leadership also opened up greater financial independence for media elites in exchange for supplementing decreasing state revenue. Advertising on Yugoslav TV grew from 4.2 percent to 6.2 percent between 1968 and 1971. First this meant advertising blocks; later commercials began to interrupt programs, which provoked some backlash from viewers. Commercially funded programming also existed in Yugoslavia, in the form of sports and entertainment sponsorship. As early as 1968, 20.8 percent of Ljubljana TV's revenue came from advertising. A Slovenian radio station even advertised in Italian to Italian audiences across the border, attracting major revenue.

Typical products advertised were food, cosmetics, chemical products, and services. In 1968–1969, the Yugoslav Telecommunications Commission approved and gave frequency to a fully commercial music radio station broadcasting to Italian audiences. The plan was canceled only because the army raised alarm over security issues. There was also some concern about the probable loss of revenue for Yugoslav broadcasters. These objections were couched in ideological form. In Yugoslavia, we see the most developed form of a consumer culture under state socialism. The appearance of advertising to harness market competition went hand in hand with the emergence of niche markets and audience research. The first studies of commercials' audience ratings were conducted in the 1960s, with the purpose of making commercials more effective.[7]

The situation was similar in Hungary. Hungarian TV and Radio established its marketing department in 1968. This created an institutional framework around the commercial activities that had been features of Hungarian broadcasting from the start, what the institution's longtime commercial director Ilona Pócsik calls a "manager" type of thinking. The first advertisements appeared in the late 1950s, just a few years after television's launch in 1956. These first ads came out of an agreement between Hungarian Television and the advertising agency Magyar Hirdető (Hungarian advertiser), which had been in the business of movie advertising since the 1940s. In the beginning, TV ads were run as text columns interspersed with pictures. Television's marketing arm also produced ads for a set of other large state institutions such as unions. The foreign trade agency HUNGEXPO advertised products for foreign trade exhibitions.[8]

Television's own marketing activities went well beyond the production of commercials. They encompassed a wide range of activities that yielded commercial profit: concert organization; film, video, and record production and distribution; book publishing; and trading film rights. As in the case of Yugoslavian TV, Pócsik and her team placed significant emphasis on contact with viewers. They established a public information department for this purpose in the 1970s, which was in charge of organizing public access across the country and responding to viewer letters and calls. Even though such outreach continued to run under the label of "propaganda," it more closely resembled public relations. Such activities required the creation of hybrid categories such as "socially oriented propaganda," which referred to providing free or inexpensive informational outlets for socialist institutions that catered to public health or education. From the 1970s, the sponsorship of programs was allowed, although it remained wrapped in ideological discomfort on the regime's part.[9]

The Marketing Department had its own budget, which was independent from Television and Radio's central budget. While the department paid taxes on its profits, the majority of the money it made with commercial activities was invested back into Television. As was true for the rest of Hungarian Television's operations, party authorities rarely interfered. When they did, they often did so mistakenly, hearing political resonances where there were none. Pócsik's example is the advertising slogan for the coffee brand Idea: "Odaát és ideát kedvelik az Ideát" (Over there and over here, Idea is liked everywhere). A party apparatchik was convinced that "over there" referred to the West and had the ad canceled. Other former TV professionals I have interviewed also frequently recall such misunderstandings. These illustrate well the ideological confusions in which the system increasingly entangled itself, and which wove a particularly dense web around television.

While its extensive marketing activity sat uncomfortably with socialist ideology, it was also clear that Television and Radio were greatly invested in the profits thus produced. As Pócsik put it, "We looked for every possible commercial revenue. We took advantage of every opportunity that produced profits." According to a summary of Hungarian Radio and Television's marketing activities, produced in 1988 for the twentieth anniversary of the Marketing Department, in their twenty years of existence they increased their annual revenue forty-fold, from 3.9 million to 200 million, and their staff from five to eighty people.[10]

Television and radio marketing was modeled after foreign, mostly Western European examples and continued to function as a bloodline between Hungarian socialism and market-oriented European socialist democracies. In the early 1980s, Hungary was the first socialist country to join the European Group of Television Advertising (EGTA). Founded in 1974, EGTA was a nonprofit group that included virtually all Western European broadcasters. This membership opened the door to more frequent East-West professional exchanges. In the 1980s, Hungarian TV's marketing department rapidly built up an institutional infrastructure from ethical codes, contract conditions, research frameworks, and other elements adapted from Western examples. As a result, by 1989, "everything already existed on a small scale," as Pócsik put it, which prepared the ground for a smooth transition to television's postsocialist, market-based operations. Professional travel and exchanges also meant that marketing professionals such as Pócsik lived schizophrenic lives. Their actual daily jobs, while they were creative and essential to the socialist economy, were looked down upon and officially only "tolerated." Pócsik says she was occasionally handed lists of actors who were not allowed to appear in commercials for fear that it would compromise their cultural capital. At the same time, at international exhibitions and festivals in London or Cannes, Pócsik was able to glimpse the creativity and excitement within her own profession, on which she periodically charged up to be able to carry on among the relatively restrictive conditions of late socialism.

To illustrate the limitations of working in media marketing in a socialist country, rules of EGTA membership meant that Hungarian TV was not allowed to deny advertising for foreign products. Because most of these were not actually available or permitted in Hungary, the Marketing Department had to find bogus reasons for refusing these ads. Through the mid-1980s, most television advertising revolved around domestic or Warsaw Pact agencies or services: appliance repair, dry cleaning, car insurance, or various department stores. Most ads were rather general, since the ordering agencies did not have long-term marketing plans. Therefore, their commercials served as templates that could be repurposed with minor editing. There were no lavish ads for cars, which were an item of scarcity on the socialist common market, and for which people had to wait for years. Ads for medications were also prohibited, as was political advertising.

"The weak economy was mirrored in the quality of commercials," says Pócsik. In fact, the broadcasting fee was higher than the cost of production—a proportion that was flipped after 1989. The exceptions to the poor quality were ads made by MAFILM, the state film studios, rather than by Television. These had higher production budgets and more professional production facilities and they more commonly advertised products and brands. These late socialist, flashier commercials tend to stand for all "socialist commercials" in nostalgic remembrances.

Cross-Border Time Shifts, Consumption across Borders

Annemarie Sorescu-Marinković describes how TV-deprived Romanians took advantage of the overspill of terrestrial broadcast signals across borders to watch Hungarian, Bulgarian, and Yugoslav television in the 1970s and 1980s. This was a means to escape the isolation and deprivation imposed by the Ceaușescu regime. Marinković's ethnographic research conducted in the Banat region (bordering Yugoslavia and Hungary) shows that it was not only the bilingual and trilingual populations who watched foreign TV. Romanian viewers took the trouble to learn foreign languages just to access a slice of the outside world. Ironically, the prohibition on actual mobility across national borders motivated a flow of televised exchange and re-created, at least virtually, the multilingual, multiethnic coexistence that characterized this region during the Habsburg Empire. One of the recurring memories Marinković's interviewees describe is the excitement they felt as they tuned into Yugoslavian TV and watched the iconic clock tick down to the beginning of daily broadcast time.

This image of the ticking clock struck a chord with me. It brought back memories of the clock I used to watch on Hungarian television during the 1970s and early 1980s of television scarcity, well before the advent of twenty-four-hour programming. I suppose this visceral recognition of the TV clock that promises the beginning of broadcasting could be described as nostalgic. However, I do not associate the countdown with excitement, like the Romanian viewers remembering to watch Serbian-language TV. Instead, my memory is tainted with preemptive disappointment about the tedious programming that I knew would follow the countdown (especially on weekday afternoons, leading up to prime time) and indignation that I was reduced to watching the clock tick instead of being able to count on my favorite series whenever I was ready to watch them.

While this comparison is merely anecdotal on my end, I am certain that the very symbol of the TV clock as an affective regulator of socialist citizens' days identifies television as a key institution in understanding how people experienced different socialist spaces as different time scales. Whereas in the Romania of the late 1970s to early 1980s broadcasting was reduced to a few hours a day (along with access to electricity) and was almost exclusively about the dictator and his family, in Hungary television was loosely regulated and virtually uncensored. Viewers had access to a variety of entertainment, both domestically produced and imported. Television created expectations it simply did not have the infrastructure to satisfy, which resulted in frustrations about broadcasting breaks in the middle of the day and on Mondays, when there was no programming until well into the 1980s. The TV clock is at once a symbol of the time lags among different countries in Europe and within the Soviet bloc and of television's capacity to time-shift across borders, its role in mediating temporal differences caused by developmental unevenness.

Marinković notes that Romanian viewers' favorite programs on Yugoslav and Hungarian TV were American serials, sports, and commercials: "Many participants even remember the text, music and images from the television commercials they saw, despite not knowing what was being advertised."[11] Commercials delivered a more colorful, melodious, boisterous universe from a different place that felt like the future. Romanian viewers' reactions to Yugoslav and Hungarian commercials echo Annika Lepp and Mervi Pantti's interviews with Estonian viewers who were fixated on Finnish programming in the 1970s and 1980s, after the Finnish broadcaster YLE built a new TV broadcast transmitter in Espoo, which brought Finnish TV to viewers in northern Estonia. Even though only two Finnish public broadcast channels existed during this period, these carried American and Western European series. Their availability placed in great demand antennae that were able to catch the signal, and even induced a weekend "TV tourism" of viewers to the northern parts of Estonia, where they could watch their favorite serials. People who lived in the north were able to pick up Finnish from TV, which conferred cultural capital that could be converted into economic capital as trade with Finland expanded.

Lepp and Pantti's interview subjects describe watching commercials especially fondly. They remember the bright colors these ads brought into their daily lives, which made Estonian and Russian Central TV look monochromatic in comparison. A viewer named one of these colors "the Finnish green," which represented the greener, cleaner, fresher pastures of an attractive alternative world. Much like Romanians remembering Yugoslav ads, Estonian viewers recollect specific commercials for food, fashion accessories, clothes, interior decor, and other consumer items. They "remember singing the tunes of Finnish commercials and dreaming of the advertised products."[12]

In the best-known case of cross-border (and, literally, cross-Wall) watching, East Germans had good access to West German programming. As I explained in earlier chapters, even the two governments closely followed and often coordinated their schedules and programs in constant competition for eyeballs and ideological advantages. The GDR was clearly on the losing end of this race to begin with. This was particularly true for consumer products and lifestyles, which were visible in their full seductive color on West German broadcasters.[13]

Postsocialist Nostalgia Is a Longing for Late Socialism

Socialist commercials are favorite triggers of postsocialist nostalgia. The key to their appeal is precisely that socialist advertising is an oxymoron. Socialist commercials always contain an element of awkwardness because they advertised products and services that had limited or no competition in the absence of a real market and because they were situated at contradictory ideological crossings. They were elements of a market-based economy operating within the matrix of centralized planning. They sold services that had no competition, or sold products that were often scarce, nonexistent, or redundant. As one of the many articles that responded to the boom in TV ads in 1970s Hungary cautions: "We need strictly to adhere to the codes of socialist advertising ethics. Advertising, a tool of market competition, cannot lead to actions that hurt the interests of workers and companies. It's not allowed to mislead consumers and it's not allowed to favor or disfavor companies."[14]

Ads for the central state-owned bank, insurance company, or supermarket thus evoke the contradictions of an era in a subtle way, which lends authenticity to remembering and mutual recognition among members of the nostalgic community. Neither official history and its opportunistic, nationalistic deployment on public service TV, nor common notions of nostalgia imposed from the outside are able to capture these contradictions. It is no coincidence that the most "authentic" manifestation of nostalgia is attached to a contradictory genre of a contradictory medium that has itself caused so much puzzlement and confusion among politicians and historians alike that they had to erase it from legitimate consideration altogether. It is also little surprise that the nostalgic gathering around commercials takes place almost exclusively in virtual space, in the vast fan collections on YouTube and other file-sharing and social networking sites, or offline in casual settings.[15]

It is not simply that socialist commercials have been some of the most dependable vehicles of popular nostalgia in the region. Contemporary commercials also often use nostalgic elements. Perhaps most jarring among these is the appearance of the figures of totalitarian leaders. In the post-Yugoslav republics, Josip Broz Tito is alive and well as the hero of not just films and television shows but also TV ads for a variety of products. Zala Volčič notes the irony that, as a socialist party leader, Tito embodied anticapitalism and anticommercialism.[16] Even dictator Nicolae Ceaușescu has surfaced in commercials in Romania, where he and his wife Elena were brutally executed by insurgents in the anticommunist revolution of 1989. A series of commercials and public service announcements featuring Ceaușescu now advertise cell phones and car tires and advocate for the adoption of stray dogs. These ads use previously suppressed images of the dictator walking his dog or being flustered during a speech. These are instances in which top-down history lessons profoundly mingle with the work of popular memory. They punctuate continuities with the communist regime that are taboo in official narratives but prevalent in popular perceptions of history. No wonder this mixing has caused upset in Romania: the fact that Ceaușescu's ghost appears in a humorous, commercial context is seen by some as trivializing the horror of the dictatorship. However, Diana Georgescu argues, such hybrid representations assist, rather than obstruct, coming to terms with the past. They provide a mode of popular countermemory that may challenge what is congealing into a master narrative of dominant interpretations issued by politicians and intellectuals. These practices use Ceaușescu's figure as a release valve to start processing the paralyzing past and the humiliating present of renewed state control and continuing marginalization within Europe.[17]

The postsocialist nostalgia that has been triggered by TV commercials is a defiant longing for a bond specific to an elusive era—that of late socialism of the 1970s and 1980s. This period unraveled Cold War scripts of a stark opposition between communism and capitalism. Television was a vehicle for this unraveling, where the softening and feminizing of socialism within popular culture first began—unlike in high culture, whose products had to sustain the illusion of dissidence in opposition to the regime. By implication, then, postsocialist nostalgia is a fairly narrow generational phenomenon, shared among those born in the 1960s and 1970s. One hardly hears members of older generations wax nostalgic about the 1950s or earlier decades. Nostalgia for late socialism is an indispensable, popular gesture to compensate for the loss of specific, contradictory temporality. But it is also, and perhaps more important, a mode of continuity with an era that was *already nostalgic* for "real" socialism. As Maya Nadkarni observes, the nostalgic consumption of the detritus of official state culture began before socialism ended.[18] She writes, "The ... enthusiasm for consumer luxuries and weekend houses (as well as the second jobs necessary to acquire them) ... meant that it was the regime's own policies that produced the modern consumer subjectivity that made possible the fantasies of Western consumption."[19]

The 1980s of late socialism had a suspended temporality, when everyday life was permeated by a sense of being stuck between a past of (longing for) heroic communism, forever out of reach, and a future without hope, since no one expected socialism to fall. Alexei Yurchak talks about late socialism as a time of frozen present.[20] Frozen present is the time of nostalgia. It is because late socialist culture itself lived in a nostalgic mode, at a certain ironic, knowing distance from what it was supposed to be according to the memories of the heroic 1940s and 1950s and the remnants of socialist propaganda, that it has been so seamlessly and eagerly adopted even by generations who never experienced socialism. It is a familiar mode of experiencing history and temporality vicariously, ironically. In her ethnographic study of postsocialist audiences' recollections of late socialist Czech serials, Irena Reifová evokes Susan Stewart, who associates nostalgia with repetition. As Stewart writes, nostalgia "is the repetition that mourns the inauthenticity in all repetition."[21] Late socialism introduced and prefigured an affect and epistemology that can only access the "authentic" through repetitions of contradiction, ambivalence, and self-reflective irony.

Late socialist commercials thus constitute a genre of continuity between late socialism and postsocialist capitalism. For viewers who remember late socialism, they represent an emotional anchor in the sea of commercials that flooded the region after socialism officially ended. Their awkwardness and imperfection provide a platform for bonding, which is manifest in the ironic winks over the low-quality products that the commercials advertised, and which everyone shared and used. Compared with the perfect veneer of contemporary commercials and the terror of endless choices provided by corporations, state socialism seems like a navigable, manageable state of affairs.

III • GENRES OF FICTION

Women and TV   9

In America, television as a medium, industry, and object of study has been profoundly gendered from the start. Lynn Spigel's work gives us perhaps the most extensive account of the role that television played in perpetuating the nineteenth-century "doctrine of separate spheres," defining the postwar American household as a feminine realm, in contrast with the masculine public sphere. This division applied most rigidly to white propertied classes.[1] The networks' special attention to women also implied a coordination between program scheduling and household routines to maximize viewership. This lent women some agency even though it was based solely on their consumer power.[2]

The special connection between women and TV was also registered in what Lynne Joyrich calls a gendered synergy between commercial television's economic imperative and its melodramatic aesthetic. Melodrama, which permeates most American television programming, targets the emotionally available consumer within the home. Melodramatic TV is part and parcel of a never-ending cycle of consumerism within an eternal postmodern present. "Melodrama, television and postmodernism, which all share [a] particular construction of flattened space and weightless time, have been linked to the dissolution of a stable site of mastery, the ideal of masculinity."³ The femininity associated with melodrama and consumerism undermines classical reason and a unified sense of identity grounded in oppositions such as active and passive, subject and object, masculine gaze and feminine spectacle. It "threatens to draw all viewer-consumers into the vacuum of mass culture—the irrational and diffuse space coded as feminine."⁴

Elihu Katz and Rowan Howard-Williams ask if there is something inherent to the medium, the technological form itself, that is gendered—something beyond TV's feminized content and position in a feminized space. If so, the authors speculate, 1950s television may have contributed to the "empowerment" of women. "Empowerment" is a difficult term, they admit, as it is usually measured in the degree of political participation, whose relationship with television has been tenuous at best.⁵ The authors draw on studies that suggest that early television may have helped democratize the domestic sphere in "developing countries" such as India, giving women a perspective on the world outside and prompting men to do more household chores.⁶ At the same time, however, Katz and Howard-Williams agree with feminist media scholars such as Lynn Spigel, Tasha Oren, and Janet Thumim that in "developed" countries like the United States television reinforced the doctrine of separate spheres as a response to popular postwar paranoia about the disruption of traditional gendered divisions in family life, to fears that TV turned men passive and made women neglect their household duties. This paranoia was fueled by mass culture's older association with corruption and feminization as opposed to high culture's supposedly authentic, masculine status.⁷ Katz and Howard-Williams also evoke Beverle Houston's psychoanalytic theory that TV puts all audiences in feminine positions because it addresses viewers as passive audiences who are subjected to constant deferral, waiting, and delay as they switch among programs and identifications.⁸ Katz and Howard-Williams find the most persuasive argument in favor of TV's "empowering" impact in dramatic content: representations in 1950s popular drama that blurred the lines between domestic and public, work and home. Along the same lines, Helen Thumim argues that television's blurring effect fed into the women's liberation movements of the 1960s.⁹ Katz and Howard-Williams also find evidence that women's power as content producers also steadily increased at this time, most obvious in figures such as Lucille Ball and Ida Lupino—although the authors note that television has remained a male-dominated industry on the whole.¹⁰

Television's gendered dimension, in turn, has inspired scholarship that distinguished itself precisely by acknowledging and analyzing viewers' feminine pleasures and practices. Michael Kackman claims that television studies owes its current prestige to feminist television theorists, who turned the medium's low cultural value and disdained pleasures into a positive ground for serious criticism.[11] Television studies is inextricable from its feminist context, no matter how hard certain strands of aesthetic and industrial scholarship have downplayed the field's feminist origins.

This sophisticated feminist context has been absent in research about socialist and postsocialist television cultures. Any serious attention to television already needs to justify itself against a nationalistic, Eurocentric dismissal of television as a low-quality medium within cultures of a defensive patriarchal bent, which have long nurtured a hostility toward feminism. Television has been a bad object in academic fields focused on Soviet and Eastern European cultures as well. Slavic studies has traditionally been anchored in the study of literature and other established arts, while history and the social sciences have concerned themselves with large-scale issues of sociopolitical change. A branch of anthropological research has recently begun to incorporate cultural studies in its inquiries and explore aspects of everyday life under and after socialism.[12] However, even such work has stayed clear of television's dangerously feminizing vortex.

Even more recently, the first extensive studies of socialist television have been produced by pioneering historians such as Paulina Bren, Kristin Roth-Ey, and Heather Gumbert.[13] These otherwise pathbreaking, meticulously researched and lively books still tread cautiously around issues of gender. When they do engage with such issues, they tend to adopt a sociological lens to look at the ways in which changing political-economic circumstances forced socialist regimes to adjust their policy and attitudes toward women and how these changes were reflected by the institution of television. While these studies at least acknowledge the elephant in the room, they remain within the confines of liberal feminism, assuming an essentialist division between the sexes, which is overdetermined by singular national contexts. This is also the direction that dominates gender studies in the region. Gender studies scholars, however, tend to omit television from their concerns altogether.[14] Finally, for the most part, media and communication studies have limited their attention to issues of policy and regulation in the course of the postsocialist transition, and have had very little interest in either television or its history.[15] The "F-word" rarely occurs in any of these approaches.

My goal in the two chapters within this part is to build on the work produced in these fields but channel my analysis through the feminist orientation borrowed from television studies. This integrated approach helps unearth the gendered aspects of television outlined earlier and the gendered story of socialist and postsocialist TV. Where nationalism, state socialism, and the Cold War paradigm worked together to construct the appearance of seamless, homogeneous socialist populations, a feminist lens reveals a variety of different, often conflicting, affiliations. In this chapter, I consider socialist TV's gendered address in terms of scheduling and content, and in terms of women's participation as TV professionals and viewers. Chapter 10 lingers on the genre I call the late socialist soap opera, a regionally specific formation that manifested itself across national varieties. I follow the story of this transitional genre into postsocialism, when foreign drama inundated the market along with postfeminist ideas, which have hindered as much as stimulated feminisms in the region.

Socialist Television's Men and Women

The socialist period interrupted the prewar trajectory of academic and activist feminism and filtered most gender-related politics and research through the communist concern with the "woman question," as defined by Engels, Bebel, Lenin, Luxembourg, Stalin, and other major ideologues.[16] In effect, socialist state feminism meant policies that segregated women into a homogenized social group identified with special needs and tasks (reproduction, family care, and emotional labor) and with inferior skills for political participation (prone to emotional identification, insufficient ability to reason). The flip side of this homogenization was reflected in policies of "positive discrimination" in the form of generous maternity leaves, free child care centers, and reduced-price meals. Following the end of state socialism in the 1990s, such policies were radically reduced if not entirely removed.[17]

Socialist TV issued a decidedly masculine address to its citizens, especially compared with American postwar programming. After the first years of scrambling, while it was maturing technologically, television became a medium dedicated to education in the broadest sense, working in a socialist-realist mode, as I discuss in the first part of this book. Women were not absent as TV professionals, screen characters, or consumers. However, all these positions were configured as masculine, were dominated by men, and assigned specialized, narrow roles to women.

Hungarian television's very first postwar experimental broadcast illustrates this well: on December 16, 1954, three years before the beginning of regular programming, a portrait of engineer Éva Láng was successfully broadcast within a four-kilometer radius.[18] The broadcast glorified postwar policies that actively denounced the private sphere and domestic duties as irrelevant to the cause of socialism and that ejected women from the kitchen into the workforce.[19] Láng was not singled out to embody the power of women, like a socialist Rosie the Riveter. Rather, her sex was relevant only to the extent that it exemplified the universal, absolute nature of the category of "socialist worker," to which *even* inferior characters such as women can strive to adapt. In effect, it confirmed masculinity as the default, morally transparent mode of socialist citizenship.

By the mid-1960s, socialist parties caught up to the ideological potential of television and were busy shaping its profile as a public institution. Unlike TV in the United States, which explicitly favored the housewife in the postwar home who may be receptive to advertising, socialist TV targeted the man or masculine worker, who plops down on the sofa after a long day at the factory. Surveys in the Soviet Union and Eastern Europe showed over and over that men spent more time watching TV than women.[20] Kristin Roth-Ey notes that cartoonists in Soviet magazines and newspapers often made fun of the isolated and obsessed TV viewer—almost always a man.[21] In 1976, Hungarian men spent an average of ninety-five minutes a day watching TV, while women spent eighty-four. This difference persisted into the 1980s. A 1986 analysis explains, "There is no doubt that one of the reasons for this difference is that the world of Hungarian telecommunications is populated by educated men over 30 in leadership positions."[22]

An equally, if not more, important factor was the well-documented disparity between women and men when it came to spare time. Women were encouraged to take an equal part in the workforce. In addition, however, they continued to shoulder the full range of household and family duties without help, since "work" meant only paid work outside the home.[23] This effectively imposed a double or often triple shift on women, which left little time to enjoy television. As Hungarian viewer Mrs. Miklós captures in a rhyming poem she sent to the *Radio and TV Guide* in 1959 to address how difficult it is for women to catch any TV: "Always on the alert, the iron is burning the shirt, warming the milk, making dinner. TV is a great invention. The problem is, it needs attention!"[24]

When women were addressed by television as an audience at all, they were considered a special demographic who needed targeted political-educational programs, much like factory workers, college students, or the elderly. This niche address invariably revolved around the family and the household and focused on issues of caretaking, lifestyle, and education. In Romania, public service magazines for women bore titles such as *Emisiune pentru femei* (Program for women) and *Caminul* (The home) in the 1960s, *Clubul Femina* (Feminine club) in the 1970s, *Noi, femeile* (Us, women), and *Universul Femeilor* (Women's universe) in the 1980s. The Romanian TV Guide previewed the following segments to be covered in the October 21, 1967, edition of *Emisiune pentru femei*: a women's clothes department; the leather trench coat; the leather clothing factory; exhibition of culinary products; master chefs; the woman at home and at work; fashion show; dining at Dunarea restaurant; painting and sculpture; practical tips; and cosmetic treatments with modern technology. In the 1980s, such programs developed a stronger propaganda agenda to promote the ideal socialist woman, modeled by Elena Ceaușescu. *Noi, Femeile* and *Universul Femeior* discussed agricultural work, the working woman, women leaders in different professions, the revolutionary woman, and the many virtues of Elena. The May 27, 1984, broadcast of *Almanahul familiei* (Family almanac) included the following topics, according to the TV Guide: school for mothers; food for newborn babies; how to harvest bee venom in your own garden; how to raise silkworms; quitting work for pregnant women or stay-at-home mothers; the home pharmacy; culinary recipes; and healthy lifestyles.[25]

A similar shift toward more explicit propaganda content occurred in Hungarian "women's programs" of the 1960s. The Hungarian Central Committee's Agitational and Propaganda Department's evaluation of public interest magazine programs for women such as *Lányok, asszonyok* (Girls and women) reads: "[Such programs] help the educational work of the Youth Communist organization, schools and the family in diverse ways. It is commendable that Television offers specialized programs to address women. These kinds of programs were rather apolitical at first; today, however, they are more politicized and pay more attention to the issues of working women and girls."[26]

In the Soviet Union, the long-running game/talent show *A nu-ka devuskhi!* (Let's go girls!, 1970–1985) was developed specifically as a form of Soviet "niche outreach." It was supposed to expand the narrow participant range of earlier quiz shows like *KVN* (discussed in chapter 4) to include demographics other than male intellectuals and to demonstrate the versatility of Soviet youth in terms of professions, talents, and, yes, gender. As Christine Evans writes, *Let's Go Girls!* featured young women from female-dominated professions, such as tram drivers, bakers, and telephone operators.[27] To reinforce the legitimacy of Soviet women's double burden, the first half of each program was a contest among participants from a single profession, often shot in a factory. This was followed by the same women competing in homemaking skills. The eight semifinalists who survived the first half then competed in housekeeping and consumer skills. The organizers tried to downplay physical characteristics of beauty and emphasize professional qualities and brains as well as taste in clothing and personal maintenance. *Let's Go Girls!* was supposed to showcase all the ingredients of the ideal modern 1970s Soviet woman, who is superior in every way to the Western beauty contestant.[28]

Women in TV Production

Television's denigrated and feminized cultural status also made it a more accommodating place for female professionals than either film or other institutions of cultural production. Even so, women in TV typically worked below the line, except as actresses and program announcers. Most announcers were women. Their job was to let viewers know about upcoming programs on the broadcast menu in a pleasant monotone, with a reassuring smile. And reassure they did. They were reliable, attractive presences operating in a modest, nonflirtatious socialist mode, mothers of the national family that television re-created every night. Their role magnified women's roles in general: to look good, follow instructions without having an opinion, and occasionally model a fashionable hairstyle or blouse. Above all, their presence ensured an intimacy between the home and the nation by marking the dependable, repetitive rhythm of the socialist day, week, and year in a pleasant manner. Viewers referred to announcers by first names as if they were family members. According to Russian critic Anri Vartanov, announcers were custodians of the TV hearth and priestesses of the cathedral of television, embraced by viewers as representatives of ideal womanhood.[29]

At the same time, the overwhelming majority of above-the-line personnel, including most of the creatives—writers, directors, reporters—were men. The memorable exceptions only proved the rule. In chapter 1, I mention Valentina Leont'eva, longtime hostess of the Soviet program *Ot vsei*

Irena Dziedzic, hostess of *Tele-Echo*, in 1965.

dushi (From the bottom of my heart), launched in 1972. As Christine Evans argues, it was crucial to have a woman host a program charged with giving an emotional boost to the party's emphasis on socialist lifestyle and nationalist mythology.[30]

Leont'eva's legacy is similar to that of Irena Dziedzic, hostess of the first Polish cultural current affairs/cultural magazine *Tele-Echo* (1956–1981). While Dziedzic's TV manner was much less sentimental than Leont'eva's, both were accused of political conformism, particularly after 1989. Polish sociologist Paweł Śpiewak writes that Dziedzic tried very hard to "create an atmosphere of charming conversation, during which no one said anything interesting or important. As if it were embarrassing to mention important or—God forbid—painful things in such good company."[31] Others call Dziedzic a phenomenal TV personality because of her ability to stir up intense emotions.[32] In chapter 11, I discuss Olga Lipinska, a legendary Polish satirical artist, talk show host, writer, and director, a key figure of TV cabaret in Poland.

For the most part, however, when women received a creative assignment, this was typically bracketed as women's issues and social issues—a nice addition to the TV lineup, but marginal to the concerns of national citizenship. The occasional powerful woman in television often did everything to efface herself and masquerade as one of the boys. When Hungarian director of photography (DP) Marietta Vecsei, who worked for the nightly TV news program, received a festival award in 1969, she was reluctant to be interviewed on TV. In the print interview with her published in TV Guide, most questions revolved around what it is like to be such a curiosity—a woman DP. How can a woman perform such a physically demanding job? To the question whether she had met other female DPs, Vecsei responded, "Here in Hungary I'm the only one. But once in a Moscow newsreel I saw another girl. It would be nice to find out who she is and meet her."[33]

To take an even more illustrative example, virtually the entire socialist history of Hungarian TV news centered around the work of one woman. Matúz Józsefné (Mrs. Joseph Matúz) or just Matúzné (Mrs. Matúz), as she was known, was tasked to create the first independent news program in the institution's first year, 1957, and remained news director in charge of successive versions of the prime-time news broadcast Híradó throughout the socialist period, for an unprecedented twenty-nine years. She navigated this most important ship of socialist mass communication and propaganda with great skill and precision. For her entire career she went by her husband's name and consistently stayed out of the spotlight. While all the television professionals I talked to had many stories to tell about her, I have been hard-pressed to find any interviews with her.

Television compelled but also allowed women to assert themselves in the available forms of masquerade—genres whose formal conformity to the regime's ideological preferences was beyond scrutiny. In Hungary, documentary or docufictional forms that foregrounded a socialist realist aesthetic and social commitment experienced a golden age beginning in the 1960s thanks to the work of some outstanding women directors. The 1962 teleplay Menekülés a börtönbe (Escape to prison, 1962), written by the female duo Ágnes Fedor and Judit Kovács, takes place in 1944 and revolves around a woman who is hiding out with fake papers. It received an award at the 1962 Cannes Film Festival. Another realistic teleplay set during the war, Nő a barakkban (Woman in the barracks), was also created by two women, director Éva Zsurzs and writer Boris Palotai. It won a series of surprise international recognitions for Hungarian television in the early 1960s, including the Golden Nymph Award at the second annual Monte Carlo TV Festival in 1962. As recounted in an interview with director Zsurzs in the journal *Radio and TV Review*, which followed the story for three consecutive weeks, it turns out that the members of the festival jury could not believe that the teleplay was written by a woman, since there is not a single female character. The play is about an international group of prisoners in a Nazi concentration camp toward the end of the war, and the title character is an imaginary woman. Zsurzs recalls that Marchel Archard, the festival jury chair, noted after the ceremony, "It's too bad they did not show [the protagonist] at least for a moment. She probably would've received the award for best female lead as she seemed so present to us." Zsurzs adds, "I feel like a director's work could not receive a larger praise than that."[34] In this early 1960s all-female production, a woman's role is literally rendered imaginary, buried in the story of anti-Nazi struggle endured and remembered exclusively by men.

Stories that related to World War II and the Holocaust were a fairly safe shield for female writers and directors to contribute to television as they were favored by the ruling party, which had built its legitimacy on postwar regime change, liberation, and peace. Such historical narratives also came with an instant interpretive fodder that related their significance to universal, human issues. These factors muted the gendered undertones of the production and reception no matter how significant these were.

Nevertheless, women in the forefront of television documentary production often came out with highly gendered topics and treatments. But instead of taking on politics directly, women did better with the politics of empathy, calling public attention to the plight of neglected groups that needed care, such as children, the elderly, ethnic minorities, isolated rural populations, and the sick. In Hungarian TV, these productions included *Bognár Anna világa* (The world of Anna Bognár) in 1963, directed by Márta Kende, a moving documentary film that had a decisive impact on the emerging genre of TV sociography. The film, which received a special recognition award from the BBC, portrayed a fifty-two-year-old blind woman living on a farm, who gets her vision back due to a successful eye surgery.[35] Margit Molnár's documentary *Leányanyák* (Teen mothers, 1970) created a stir when it explored the plight of pregnant teenagers. In the same year, Molnár also hosted a public affairs program called *Nők fóruma* (Women's forum). Unlike the previous socialist educational "niche" program, *Lányok, asszonyok* (Women and girls, 1964), each episode of Molnár's show was dedicated to specific areas where public culture blatantly discriminated against women and families: how children of divorced parents coped; or the effects of inflexible work schedules on the lives of mothers who had to get their children to child care at dawn to make it to work.

Women and Late Socialist Lifestyle TV

Of course, no matter how incisive TV sociographies were, their audiences remained limited mostly to urban, educated viewers. Programs that blurred the boundaries between fiction and documentary fared better, as I explain with reference to the Hungarian public interest program *Családi kör* (Family circle) in chapter 2. The thaw period, beginning in the late 1960s, brought political and economic changes that required socialist parties to readjust their gender policies. As Soviet-controlled countries fell behind in production and imported more and more Western programming, the competition with the West shifted to the sphere of consumer ideology and leisure, bundled under the term "socialist lifestyle." By the 1970s, the penetration of TV sets in most countries of the region caught up with Western levels.[36] At the same time, most domestic programs were found too didactic and tedious, while Western programming could not be shut out thanks to shared broadcast signals along borders and the appearance of recording technologies, cable, and satellite in the 1980s. Rather than raising ideal socialist citizens, the dullness and overt political bias of programming threatened to drive an irreparable wedge between party authorities and the population.

Christine Evans explains that, in the Soviet Union, by the late 1950s and early 1960s, precisely during the ascendance of TV as a mass medium, Nikita Khrushchev shortened work hours and expanded leisure time for Soviet citizens. Competition with the West in industrial and agricultural production gave way to competition based on technological advances and consumer lifestyles, holding out the promise of daily comforts after decades of strife and hardship.[37] Television was not just a conduit in this shift but literally the centerpiece of the domestic sphere, bringing the promise of rest and relaxation into flats in mass housing estates.[38]

This shift in competition with the West from production to consumption and "lifestyle" redirected the spotlight onto women as key agents of socialist citizenship. Éva Fodor writes that, in Hungary, the "woman question" had been considered "resolved" by the end of the 1960s but was reopened following a 1970 party decree that put women's role in society back on the agenda. In the decade the followed, a variety of state institutions produced 110 reports on women's roles in society.[39] The single party-controlled women's organization, the Women's Council, published about forty books that, for the most part, focused on lifestyle and consumption, such as skin care, self-help, child rearing, divorce, and cooking.[40]

Susan Zimmermann captures the peculiarity of socialist gender policies in the following contradiction: socialist states made extraordinary efforts to include women in the workforce and to ensure (heterosexual, white) women's equality with men in terms of civil and family rights. These efforts "constituted a spectacular intervention into the traditional relationship between the sexes and hierarchical family structures." They questioned women's dependence on men and the family.[41] At the same time, socialist governments consistently and anxiously limited women's equality by maintaining a wage gap between the sexes, ignoring or minimizing women's unpaid domestic labor, and insisting on women's biological roles as mothers and caretakers. This contradiction resulted in "practices and attitudes that conflicted directly with official policy and efforts at creating equality, or activities that undermined official policy at unnoticed, disregarded or hard-to-influence levels."[42]

While sociologists and historians have abundantly explored official and unofficial policies toward women, the crucial role that socialist, particularly late socialist, popular media culture played in processing these contradictory attitudes has escaped attention. In the next chapter, I zoom in on the late socialist dramatic serial or socialist "soap opera" as a juncture where official policy and everyday attitudes inevitably met, clashed, and ultimately compromised to pave the way for a postsocialist version of postfeminism.

Socialist Soaps 10

The 1970s and 1980s Turn to Dramatic Fiction

The late socialist Eastern European domestic drama serials I call "soap operas" were developed in an atmosphere of increased attention to women, consumerism, and the ideological power of emotional engagement. They continued the earlier project of political education in less didactic, more entertaining ways.[1] They also took for granted viewers' familiarity with and yearning for imported drama serials. While most domestic scripted dramas of the early socialist period revolved around men doing manly things in the public sphere, from war drama through adventure drama to historical miniseries, the post-1960s period variously called the "thaw," "consolidation," or "normalization" era turned the spotlight on the family as the microcosm of the socialist nation.

In some ways, the "socialist soap opera" returned television to its gendered roots. Much like Western soap opera, it showcased communities that were metaphors for modern society, offering fictional, "feminine" pleasures of identification.[2] In other ways, however, the socialist soap was a peculiar hybrid specific to the conditions of late socialism. Rather than addressing women only as consumers, it addressed them first and foremost as citizens, whose biological features simply assigned them to unique roles within the socialist collective. It was also distinct in tone and aesthetic as it absorbed the influence of other socialist TV genres, most prominently the didacticism of public affairs programs and the satirical tone of comedy shows.

While socialist soaps were not overtly politicized, they all modeled ideal socialist lifestyles in ensemble dramas that encompassed the workplace and the family. Unlike historical dramas, which removed the narrative into the past and revolved around heroic male figures in the public arena, these domestic serials took place in the present and featured central female characters who acted as problem solvers, linchpins between the public and private worlds. I am most interested in how this regional genre put women center stage to emphasize the shift from production to consumption and lifestyle in the competition with the West and in how they processed the feminization of late socialist cultures without allowing any feminist politics to seep in. I conclude that they prepared a smooth transition to a postfeminist, postsocialist landscape, where feminism ostensibly never existed and is not necessary.

The TV world of the 1970s and 1980s probably would not have resembled anything one would expect from a socialist country. In essence, it was no different from the transitional terrain of Western European broadcasters. In fact, much of Europe enjoyed the same or the same types of popular programs in the 1980s. These ranged from German crime dramas such as *Tatort* through popular American drama and soap serials such as *Colombo, Star Trek, The Fugitive, Kojak, Charlie's Angels, Starsky and Hutch, Roots, Isaura, Dynasty,* and *Dallas* to more highbrow fictions such as the German *Heimat*. In most Eastern and Western European countries, the gap between domestic supply and audience thirst for American-style drama caused a great deal of consternation about U.S. media imperialism's threat to national cultures and to public broadcasting. The exception was Britain, where a cross-pollination of imports and format exchanges with the United States had been ingrained in television from the beginning.[3]

As Sabina Mihelj shows, as early as the 1960s, the proportion of foreign programs in Eastern Europe (excluding the Soviet Union) ranged from 17 percent in Poland to 45 percent in Bulgaria. In the early 1970s, 12 percent of all imported programming on Hungarian television came from the United Kingdom, 10 percent from France, and 10 percent from Western Germany. In nonaligned Yugoslavia, a full 80 percent of all imported programs came from outside of the socialist bloc and 40 percent from the United States alone. In the early 1980s, an average of 43 percent of imported programming in Eastern Europe came from Western Europe, almost equaling the 45 percent from the Soviet Union and other Eastern European countries.[4] Even in Albania, perhaps the most isolated country during the Cold War, a period of relative liberalization began in the 1970s. While Enver Hoxha's dictatorship tried to keep the consumption of foreign media in control, broadcast signals from Italy could not be successfully blocked.[5] In Romania, where television experienced a regression under dictatorial control, selected U.S. content and genre models were nevertheless welcome—not the least due to Ceaușescu's attempt to demonstrate his Western orientation and independence from Russia.[6] It was only in the mid-1980s, as the regime became especially isolated and paranoid, that the temporary second channel set up in 1968 ceased to operate (in 1985) and broadcasting hours were reduced from ten to eleven hours to only four to five hours a day on weekends and to two hours on weekdays. *Dallas* was one of the last programs to go. It was broadcast on Saturdays into in the early 1980s, severely censored and shortened.[7]

In a scenario that was more typical, in Hungary the rate of imported programs was 40 percent, 80 percent of which came from the United States in 1985. A sixty-minute imported drama episode cost an average of $1,000, or 60,000 Hungarian forints, while it would have cost 4 to 5 million forints to produce domestically. About a quarter of the population had a choice of programming beyond Hungarian TV's offerings through access either to a VCR or to foreign channels. By the mid-1980s, the estimated number of VHS machines was 100,000—that is, one attached to about every fifth TV set.[8] When browsing the Hungarian popular press and specialized media journals from the 1980s, one can immediately see an obsession with the idea of entertainment, the realization that television is inevitably transforming into a mass medium devoted to relaxation and fun. The debates are routinely configured in terms of the choice or, rather, the clash between the "value-transmitting" and "audience-focused" functions of television, with a clear transition from the former to the latter.[9] Surveys show, as elsewhere in the Soviet camp, that people rejected the educational programs that had overwhelmed socialist television.[10] They chose foreign drama series, talent shows, and sports programs or tuned into better programming in neighboring countries. In the late 1980s, Hungarian TV was woefully unequipped to meet the demand for TV entertainment. Its technical facilities did not allow for more than ninety-five to one hundred hours of programming a week between the two channels.¹¹ In 1986, the first satellite channel, Sky Channel, launched in 1982 as a holding of Rupert Murdoch's News International, premiered at the Budapest Hilton before it was made available to households. At this time, 7.1 million Western European households were able to access Sky Channel.¹²

Print publications about television's transformation repeatedly struck a resigned tone about the force of the market, which small media economies were powerless to resist. They noted that television was in a bind between its commitment to national programming and viewers' increasingly differentiated needs. One compromise was to air in prime time imported drama serials that cut across various niche desires, such as the West German crime series *Derrick*, the British family saga *The Onedin Line*, or the Czech soap opera *Women Behind the Counter*.¹³

Popular socialist serials presented far less ideological risk in prime time than the ever-popular American serials, which were feared to lead to ambiguous or subversive interpretations.¹⁴ From the beginning, the East German broadcaster DFF was never able to fill its schedule with original programming.¹⁵ In the GDR, competition for eyeballs was especially intense because of the ready availability of West German programs.¹⁶ In 1968, a new cultural policy was launched under the name "Range and Diversity."¹⁷ The new policy pushed television drama to the forefront as the privileged vehicle for reaching viewers, replacing more didactic genres that had failed to create a socialist consciousness. The newly favored genres included live studio films, made-for-TV movies, and dramatic series. Ratings became a much more important indicator than before to decide which shows should be kept on the air—although, much like elsewhere in the bloc, domestic production still lagged behind the increasing broadcast time.¹⁸

The turn toward entertainment gained momentum after head of state Erich Honecker famously declared at the Eighth SED Congress in 1972 that television needed to "overcome a certain type of tedium" and "take the desire for good entertainment into account."¹⁹ The programming reform in the wake of this criticism brought an increase in programming hours. As for content, while news and current affairs continued to be privileged on both channels, on DFF 2 the proportion of feature films, TV films (*Fernsehspiele*), and dramatic series rose by almost 10 percent to a total of 38.2 percent; as opposed to the 20.3 percent of news and information programs and 10.9 percent of musical programs. 6.3 percent of airtime was dedicated to special events designated as "ceremonies and parades."[20] As elsewhere, the new direction manifested itself in a more humorous tone, an increased concern with contemporary topics rather than classical stage plays or historical drama, and reasonably well-rounded characters who also carried the collective mission of modeling the "socialist lifestyle."[21] In other words, the protagonists still needed to be exemplary socialist workers, but their breadth and depth increased. As Beutelschmidt and Wrage write, "The inclusion of psychological, social, and even gender-specific conflicts can be considered the most important reform in this time period."[22]

In most cases, socialist domestic serials addressed an audience that had grown up on radio soaps. Radio and TV lived in symbiosis in each country, sharing centralized control, institutional resources, and creative personnel to varying extents. One of the longest-running radio soaps in the world, the Hungarian program *A Szabó család* (The Szabó family), for instance, was a multigenerational story of the everyday Hungarian socialist family. It was broadcast from 1959 till 2007, for forty-eight years and twenty-five hundred episodes, employing about a thousand actors altogether, essentially encompassing the entirety of the Hungarian acting scene for generations. The serial reached its heyday and highest viewership in the 1970s and 1980s.[23] *The Szabó Family* inspired a Yugoslav version called *The Jovanovic Family* and also a Polish version.[24]

While *The Szabó Family* was undoubtedly a didactic allegory for the socialist family, it was neither unprecedented nor peculiar to socialism. It was not unlike the American radio soap the *American Family Robinson*, a daily fifteen-minute program that started in 1935, starring Luke and Myra Robinson and their children, Bob and Betty, of Centerville. The program was produced by the National Association of Manufacturers and broadcast to radio stations for free. It was at times highly propagandistic, intended to combat Roosevelt's New Deal on the heels of the Depression and on the brink of World War II. The first BBC radio serial drama, *Front Line Family*, also began as a propaganda vehicle in 1941, broadcast on the BBC's North American shortwave service, and was modeled after American and French Canadian radio soaps. It became one of the most popular programs, later retitled *The Robinsons* and inspiring soaps such as *Mrs. Dale's Diary* and *The Archers* and long-running TV soaps such as *Coronation Street* and *EastEnders*. These radio soaps marked broadcasting's attention to women as a special audience on both sides of the Atlantic.[25]

Socialist Soaps and Socialist Women

I take a closer look at some of the most popular late socialist domestic serials to highlight the narrative and ideological features that constitute a historically and geopolitically specific cycle that resembles the soap opera. At the same time, the case studies allow for identifying local differences within the cycle. While Czech soaps were the most successful in terms of ratings and geographical reach, the genre was also popular in Poland, Hungary, Bulgaria, and the GDR. Soap-like dramas were also produced in the Baltic republics of the Soviet Union, but Soviet Central Television never warmed up to the genre.[26] The most popular Estonian show was called *What's New in the Koosta Family?*, while a Lithuanian version was called *The Petraitisov Family*. Both were long-running soap-like serials that began in 1965.[27]

Socialist soaps were character-driven dramas with basic plotlines. It was the characters who carried didactic messages in a more or less successfully fictionalized form. The protagonists were ordinary people in situations recognizable to viewers—a winning strategy to create the appearance of bottom-up design and thus inspire trust and loyalty. It clearly worked. Unlike the majority of programming in earlier decades, these serials consolidated national audiences. According to a 1988 Czechoslovak TV survey, 82 percent of viewers watched domestic serials, and some episodes reached more than 90 percent of viewers.[28] Even in the era of broadcast monopoly, this is an impressive feat.

Such serials were carefully planned to strike a desirable balance between demonstrating political conformity to socialist ideals and gently mocking the realities of those ideals. They relied on the fictionalized, serialized format to influence public opinion and model proper socialist behavior. However, this residue of propaganda was balanced by social satire and humor. The serials were set in the present and wove together family and public dynamics. The conduits were almost invariably women, who were able to navigate both spheres with success. Children were often smarter than the parents, used as mouthpieces to state the evident truth. Many of the shows were set in housing blocks or workplaces, where a cross section of society could be displayed and a desirable balance between critique and conformity could be demonstrated. Despite their evident mass appeal, political value to the party, and enduring popularity into the present, they were shunned by national critics and have just recently been discovered by cultural and media studies scholars.

Perhaps the most beloved Polish serial of all time, *Czterdziestolatek* (The forty-year-old, 1974–1978), was created by prolific writer-director Jerzy Gurza. The serial revolves around a "typical" Polish middle-class family ensconced in their housing development and workplace environments. The title character is engineer Stefan Karwowski, married to Magda, who works for the city's waterworks. They are parents to school-age Jagoda and Marek, who regularly prove to be much more insightful than their parents. While the serial was meant to foreground the security and comfort of Edward Gierek's socialism,[29] there is also a satirical subterfuge about living conditions in housing blocks and other absurdities of the era.[30] A typical product of Poland's economic and political thaw, *Czterdziestolatek* was one of several comic versions of the socialist "Neighbors" produced around the region, set in a panel dwelling of interconnected families, whose class and professional diversity was meant to represent socialist society. The extreme popularity of the show has to do with the fact that it only brushes with political issues lightly and humorously. Instead, the main story lines concern personal problems viewers could identify with: midlife crisis, extramarital affairs, quitting smoking, hair loss, exercise, professional life, social activities, and so forth. As a mark of its popularity, it was adapted into a feature film in 1976.[31]

The most distinctive character of the serial is Kobieta Pracująca, or "Working Woman," the Polish version of Rosie the Riveter, played by star Irena Kwiatkowska. Working Woman is an allegorical character who shows up and knocks on the door whenever the Karwowski family faces a problem. She changes character and profession in each episode. She is a milkwoman and a postwoman; she sells veal to her neighbors; she sweeps chimneys; she becomes a flight attendant and an excavator operator. Meanwhile, her motto remains the same: "I'm a working woman and I'm not afraid of any kind of work." She's street-smart and savvy, ironic and funny. She's a self-taught character, who is able to absorb any knowledge and learn any new skills.

As an allegory in a decidedly female form, she invites interpretation at various levels: she embodies socialist parties' rediscovery of women as crucial resources for shoring up the regimes' legitimacy and ensuring their continuity into the future. Unlike Stefan's wife, Magda, a typical "Matka Polka," the Polish Mother who is visibly suffering under the double burden of domestic and paid work, the Working Woman makes the best of her situation. She models pride in being able to do it all, exhibiting a kind of late feminist postfeminism. She is also an early manifestation of a feminized,

The family in *Czterdziestolatek*.

flexible workforce willingly engaged in lifelong training. While she is a tool of Gierek's modernization and Westernization project, her likable and unthreatening persona dispels charges of didacticism.[32]

Television in Yugoslavia produced remarkably similar serials in the same period. *Spavajte mirno* (Sleep peacefully), produced by TV Belgrade in Serbia in 1968, and *Naše malo misto* (Our small town), made by TV Zagreb in Croatia in 1970–1971, both used humor as a means of eliciting identification with socialist ideological principles. The eight episodes of *Sleep Peacefully* address major social problems, including unemployment, income disparities, social solidarity, and corruption, in a way that lays blame at the feet of bad, corrupt individuals who try to undermine an otherwise perfectly good system that is always open to improvement. *Our Small Town* is rather more depoliticized. It is set in a picturesque little town on the Adriatic coast and follows the life of local inhabitants from 1936 to 1970. The sociopolitical context is reduced to a backdrop to the important narrative events, which have to do with personal relationships, leisure activities, and shopping trips to Trieste. Such events demonstrate the safety and security of the late socialist lifestyle, deemed superior to the hectic Western pace. Sabina Mihelj explains that the humorous treatment, combined with the migration of important issues from the public into the private sphere, made these programs particularly popular—a tendency already visible in *Our Small Town* and most clearly exemplified in TV Belgrade's popular comedic serial *Pozorište u kući* (Theater in the home, 1973–1984).[33]

The "Working Woman," played by Irena Kwiatkowska.

The comic soap opera *Theater in the Home* ran for four nonconsecutive seasons, in 1972, 1973, 1975, and 1984. It is no surprise that it was also remade in 2007, adapted to a postsocialist context. A comic soap based around a family who lived in a housing development, it belongs to the cycle of "housing block" drama serials along with the Polish *The Forty-Year-Old* and the Hungarian *District 78* and *Neighbors*. Within its long span, the serial chronicled the expansion of consumer society in Yugoslavia. Products such as the Yugoslav car Zastava 750 and fashion items are frequently foregrounded in the episodes; while comic situations often arise from the systemic deficiencies of socialism, which are treated with light satire.[34]

The Hungarian comical-satirical serial *A 78-as körzet* (District 78, 1982) offers few surprises after even this brief introduction to similar Polish and Yugoslav programs. One difference is that, instead of the multistory housing development, the narrative setting is a district of Budapest that consists mostly of single-family homes. Although most of the episodes revolve around the dilapidated conditions of the district (unpaved roads, outdoor toilets, a divorced couple having to share a divided space), this is still a fairly idealized setting in itself given severe housing shortages under socialism. The most utopian feature of the serial, however, is the protagonist:

Ilus, a middle-class housewife, who does not work outside the home—a condition almost unheard of in socialist Hungary.[35]

The importance of a female protagonist is made abundantly clear in the very first of the six episodes, written by a woman, Ilona Dávid. A bumbling but well-intentioned apparatchik who works for the city council ambushes Ilus as she is walking home from the store. The comrade explains that the council would like her to run for district representative, since the position has been recently vacated. To Ilus's question "Why me?," he responds, "Because you don't have a job." "How do you mean that?" Ilus asks with an indignation that intimates that rendering domestic work invisible is no longer fully acceptable in the 1980s. The comrade quickly corrects himself, "Only the household. Also because you're a woman. And you're young." When Ilus still resists, he adds: "I imagined you, comrade, to be more enthusiastic. Like someone who believes that things can change."

This exchange not only sets up the central situation from which all subsequent events derive but also displays the program's twofold rhetorical strategy, typical for late socialism. It conveys a didactic message: socialist citizens should take care of each other and, at least at the local level where face-to-face interaction is most crucial, this duty should fall to women, who are already natural caretakers. At the same time, the dialogue acknowledges the difficulty of such a proposition in the circumstances of goulash communism, where the default is for people to be cynical about socialist principles.

The main representative of such a default attitude is none other than Ilus's husband, Dezső. When Ilus first presents the idea of running for the council to him ("I felt so sorry for the poor man they had sent out to agitate. . . . And, well, I've got big plans"), he responds with anger: "That's what I'm most afraid of. What difference can a district representative possibly make?" Dezső's other objection is that his own needs will be neglected by his wife, who should be ready to serve him when he comes home from work. The serial walks a fine line here between rendering Dezső ridiculous in his retrograde neediness and eliciting sympathy for him. There is a great deal of meaningful ambiguity about shifting gender roles within a family, which the serial broached in the open while the official party line remained conservative and public opinion continued to demonize feminism. On the one hand, while Dezső's recurring temper tantrums over the empty soda bottle and over having to heat up his own dinner are hard to watch, they are set up as innocent comedic gags, which continue to be a source of nostalgia for the show to this day. On the other hand, as Ilus's community activism begins to flourish, Dezső becomes increasingly isolated, even from his own teenage children, who act as spokespersons of a different generation, taking a stand against their father's conservative attitudes. Dezső goes from trying to sabotage his wife's public service by filing an anonymous report against her in the second episode to grudgingly helping her out in the last one.

Similar to contemporaneous drama serials elsewhere in the region, *District 78* typifies socialist parties' ambivalent outreach to women in the 1970s and 1980s. In a country where the "thaw" began relatively early on, the Politburo spent a decade or so after 1956 rethinking women's roles in society. This involved reinstalling and solidifying the main institution of state-led feminism, the Women's Council. The latter also functioned as an ideological gatekeeper: it had its own publishing house and controlled research on women and feminism. Its weekly publication, *Nők lapja* (Women's magazine), was the only periodical aimed at a female audience between 1949 and 1989.[36] The Women's Council also reaffirmed a liberal abortion policy and women's position as a permanent workforce. This involved forms of both positive and negative discrimination. First Secretary Kádár famously advocated a hiring policy that preferred women over men among equally qualified candidates. However, positive discrimination was supposedly necessitated by women's inherent weaknesses: their political unreliability and emotionality. This deep-seated suspicion toward women explains why the Politburo intentionally set limits on women's political participation and designated local, rather than national, politics as their proper sphere. Éva Fodor quotes Politburo member György Marosán, who declared after 1956: "Local politics is women's task. They should visit the hospital, check if there is a good road in the village, if they have child care centers, what the schools are like, how well the food store is supplied."[37] The policy of positive discrimination also incited a private backlash: according to party documents, husbands regularly hindered their wives' promotions.[38]

The party's increased concern with women is exemplified by a 1970 decree discussing women's role in society, which generated about 110 official documents across various institutions between 1970 and 1980.[39] Nevertheless, after 1970, women were considered generally caught up and the "woman's problem" largely solved. Much as in Poland, socialism thus ushered in a period of pre-post-feminism, when women were assumed to be equal and feminism redundant. Only in the mid-1980s did concerns rise again, in the wake of population decline.[40]

This background renders both Ilus's and Dezső's figures in *District 78* recognizable allegories, who translate party policy into narrative form. However, the TV serial format also aired the ambiguity around party intentions. The show takes an experimental stab at the genre, to begin with. The six episodes of *District 78* vary in length between twenty-five and forty-four minutes, similar to Czech drama serials. All of them feature a hybrid mix of music within the episodes, from communist marching songs through music associated with classical melodrama and the spy thriller to avant-garde noises. Often, the editing also provides ironic countercommentary on the events. Every episode revolves around Ilus facing seemingly insurmountable problems in the community and at home, which compel her to demonstrate a socialist woman's combination of multitasking skills, perseverance, empathy, and cunning. The show at once celebrates and pokes gentle fun at socialist institutions and rituals. In the first episode, a public council meeting is held in the local elementary school to vote in Ilus as the district representative. This scene is a parody of socialist elections in general. As the officials are introduced, they take their place on the podium one by one. At last, Ilus is the only one left sitting in the benches. Even though she is the only nominee, they need actual humans to do the voting. In a comic turn, Ilus makes a deal with the council: if it promises to fix the pavement in the district, she will fill the benches in fifteen minutes. She manages to deliver the neighborhood on time by telling everyone that the pavement will only be repaired across the street from them.

The second episode veers toward socialist utopia: Ilus goes around the neighborhood to find out which families are expecting babies so she can alert them to take advantage of a certain government family policy. This turns out to be a narrative device to get her inside the secret life of a couple. Thanks to what appears to be her insistent nosiness, Ilus learns that the wife, a devout Catholic, is unable to have children. The husband is pathologically jealous and refuses to discuss their infertility issues. Ilus springs into action despite Dezső's warnings not to insert herself. She takes the wife to a gynecologist, who establishes that she is in perfect reproductive health. The husband thinks his wife had gone to see a lover and, in a fit of jealous rage, moves back in with his mother. Ilus tracks him down to explain the situation, just to find out from the husband's mother that he is the one who cannot have children. The so-called happy ending here does not leave much room for feminist empowerment: the couple is reunited, and Dezső's usual nagging supplies reliable comic closure: "I hope you know I haven't even had dinner!"

The third episode features a more confident Ilus, who secured approval from the council to repaint the neighborhood school. Unfortunately, and as a send-up of socialist irrationality, the council decides to do this in the middle of the school year. Ilus's proposed solution is to empty half the building at a time so that instruction can continue in the other half. For this she needs to organize families to temporarily store various school supplies in their homes. This process allows the show to foreground the nagging shortage of housing space in late socialism. It also gives Ilus the opportunity to solve more family problems in the neighboorhood: a divorced couple who had been forced to continue living in a divided house move back into a shared room to free up space for school supplies. We leave them at the end of the episode sipping tea together. Ilus also inadvertently opens an elderly couple's eyes to their married son's deceit when it turns out he had secretly bought a car (a fancy Volkswagen Beatle at that, rather than a socialist make) instead of saving money for his own place while living with the parents for free. Ilus demonstrates how a woman can get things done by deploying a range of emotional strategies: she performs a meek, girly masquerade with a county official but takes a firm stand with a lazy painter sent by the state building and maintenance company. After she talks to the painter's boss on the phone, the boss tells him "not to mess with her." Her work comes across as a triumph of feminine will and strategy, which overcomes all obstacles put up by male functionaries, workers, and family members.

The fourth episode, only twenty-five minutes long, is an odd one out. It abandons Ilus's management of the district altogether and features only her and her husband, Dezső. The two are caught up in a series of tragicomic misunderstandings around a suitcase that Ilus finds in the street and insists on returning to its owner. Dezső reluctantly helps her track down the owner, only to realize that the two of them accidentally left the suitcase on the tram. As it turns out, the (now missing) suitcase has led Ilus into the middle of another explosive domestic drama. The suitcase's owner is a chronic gambler, who left the suitcase in the street to pretend that it had been stolen from him, along with his salary. In turn, his wife accuses Ilus and Dezső of taking the money that was supposed to be in the case. The wife finally rushes out of the apartment, upset. The husband follows her, accidentally locking Ilus and Dezső inside. When the two descend from the window on a makeshift rope ladder, a policeman is waiting for them, confirming the failure of Ilus's adventure and justifying Dezső's view that her zeal to help others is inappropriate and unproductive. One wonders what the ideological intention of this brief and ambiguous episode was. To keep in check Ilus's increasing empowerment and give Dezső more authority as the moral center of the serial? To reestablish the sense of the dangerously frayed marital bond between the two through the shared adventure?

Episode 5 amplifies the moral ambiguity and campy irony of the serial and reinforces its experimental feel. The problem in the center is that Annuska, a lonely old lady usually seen gossiping in the street, breaks her leg while using her outhouse. While she is in the hospital, Ilus rallies the neighbors to build a bathroom for Annuska so she will not risk slipping and falling again. The narrative crescendos to the big reveal when Annuska finally comes home from the hospital and sees her remodeled house for the first time. However, socialist reality intrudes on our well-deserved catharsis when Annuska announces she is planning to rent out part of her house with the new bathroom to the state tourist agency. She will continue to use the outhouse and make a financial profit off the voluntary labor of the collective. The moral is as mixed here as in the previous episode: the spirit of socialist collectivism is noble, but it can't compete with the natural drive of individual entrepreneurialism.

It was in the final, sixth episode, aptly titled "The Victory," that the show finally found its magic formula of success—combining the best features of all the other episodes and settling into the comic-realistic-soap form that best suited its late socialist historical milieu. It is the most utopian and wish-fulfilling story line of all, which takes us nostalgically into a lost future of socialism, resigned to the fact that this possibility remains firmly buried in the past. Much as in the case of the late socialist commercials I discussed in chapter 8, it is this temporal-emotional journey that gives the episode its authentic feel. The main conflict here is between the district's citizens and the city council. The council wants to cut down the old trees in the district and plant new, decorative ones that will lend the neighborhood a positive image when observed by people in cars zooming by on the new freeway of the near future. The entire concern with the infrastructure of the future, increased mobility, and community branding blows with the winds of a transforming political-economic system. This system was still socialist in name but running on empty rituals while its citizens were moonlighting in the second economy and its leaders were accumulating the capital that would help them weather the changes after 1989. Naturally, Ilus spearheads the movement to save the trees—sickly looking ones, authentic reminders of socialism. The entire initiative to preserve these sad trees as mementos of a life about to get passed on the freeway of history embodies the nostalgic temporality of late socialism. These trees, along with the entire lifestyle, are pathetic, but they are "ours." They are literal signposts of the shared sense of security one had within the shared material scarcity of socialism.

Ilus's gang of district dwellers marches out all the clichés of a good comedy to prevent the tree cutting: diversion by cleavage, courtesy of the stereotypical slutty neighborhood wife, diversion by religious procession, and finally diversion by alcohol. In the end, when the council hires an entire troop of tree cutters to slaughter all the trees at once at dawn, the residents have no choice but to occupy the trees. The tree cutters find the neighbors nesting like birds, cranking up the utopia to an entirely new level. In fact, nostalgia for the lost potential of socialist collectivism is grafted onto a potential for a capitalist future, where this kind of civil disobedience may actually happen.[41] Least believable of all, even the policeman, the representative of law enforcement, gets on board—that is, up onto a branch. Ilus's husband, Dezső, is the last one to join the group but not before yelling out, to reassure us that some things never change, that he is climbing up only to take his wife's spot so she can make him breakfast. The serial ends on this cheerful note, with Dezső frozen on the screen midclimb.

Nowhere was socialist soap production as prolific and profitable as in Czechoslovakia. Dramatic serials date back to 1959, when *Rodina Blahova* (Family Blaha) began broadcasting live once a month. A total of 280 more serial broadcasts followed during the socialist period. The most popular of these were created by the writer-director duo Jaroslav Dietl and Jaroslav Dudek during the thaw period and circulated within and beyond the region. By the 1970s, the genre settled into a one-hour format, with four serials (each with twelve to thirteen episodes) covering the entire year.[42] Dietl was a veteran of Czechoslovak television, but he was also an openminded writer well ahead of his time and little appreciated by the critical establishment despite the massive national and international success of his serials. He was keen to learn and adapt from foreign models throughout his career.[43]

His most popular soap, *Nemocnice na kraji města* (Hospital at the edge of town, 1977), drew an average viewership of 88 percent and was also a roaring success in many other Soviet bloc countries, as well as West Germany,[44] the Soviet Union, Poland, Romania, Hungary, Bulgaria, Yugoslavia, and Cuba. It was also broadcast in Austria, Switzerland, Finland, Cyprus, Australia, China, and Afghanistan.[45] *Hospital* was bought by Norddeutscher Rundfunk, who kept the East German dubbing but reedited the serial into nine fifty-eight-minute episodes rather than keeping the thirteen episodes of varying lengths. Ratings proved the international value of the program: when the station ARD broadcast it in prime time weekly in April 1980, the show reached nineteen to twenty million viewers.[46] In a major marketing coup, Czechoslovak TV coproduced a second season for West German audiences in 1981, with an investment of 2 million West German marks. While the program's original purpose was to promote socialist health care, its popularity and translatability were ironically due to its utopian depiction of the socialist hospital. The well-equipped hospital with kind doctors who care about their patients more closely resembled American medical soaps.

The soap opera genre has been called escapist or at least utopian, depicting a universe of privileged consumption.[47] The Dietl serial with the most direct gendered address, *Žena za pultem* (Women behind the counter, 1977), fully indulges in this utopianism. The protagonist, Anna Holubova, works in the delicatessen section of a grocery store, behind a stack of canned caviar; her daily interactions take place among heaps of tropical fruits and an extravagant array of cheeses, which do not accurately reflect the much more austere shopping conditions of the 1970s. But the show stands out in the first place because it was designed to demonstrate the success of state feminism.[48] The feminized workplace setting allowed the twelve-episode program to focus on a female collective and thus model women's desirable roles in socialist society. Characters and narrative arcs were determined by an ideological framework: the morally superior, helpful characters were all party members, while the antisocial, selfish characters were not—although, unlike in the earlier period of strict socialist realism, these "bad" characters were gently mocked for their consumer greed or bourgeois manners, rather than punished.[49]

Viewers were offered a range of female behaviors and were directed to identify with Anna, who begins her job as a shop assistant in the store after her divorce, embarking on a new life as a single mother of two. She is caught in a realistic struggle among her roles as a colleague, mother, and ex-wife. Anna, another socialist superwoman, demonstrates exemplary self-reliance and dignity in all three areas. Paulina Bren interprets Anna's

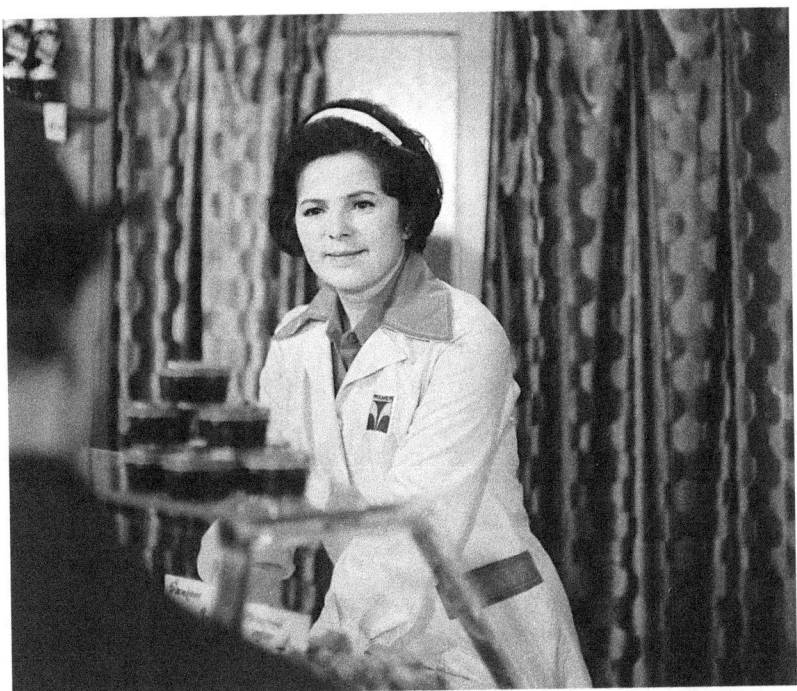
Jiřina Švorcová as the woman behind the counter.

character as a mother figure who is symbolic of all women of the nation, who were called upon to heal the collective wounds of 1968's trauma. To mark this converge between the national and nuclear family, much of the serial was first broadcast over the 1977 Christmas season.[50] Actress Jiřina Švorcová was carefully selected for the role of Anna because she was known to be a die-hard Stalinist.[51] When he was told he had to cast her, Dietl was frustrated not only because of her political leanings but also because she was too heavy, not very attractive, and ten years older than Anna's character.[52]

As elsewhere in the region, the post-1968 period of normalization had brought about a crisis of masculinity and foregrounded women's role as a major anchoring power for nationalism in Czechoslovakia.[53] Women's ratio in the workforce was 47 percent in 1971, compared with 30 to 40 percent in Austria and Germany. The socialist state invested in the idealized image of the socialist woman who is independent, desirable, and capable. While *Women* showed women doing it all with heroism and success, like other socialist drama serials, it also endorsed men's leadership positions in the public sphere and minimal obligations in the domestic sphere. Serials like *Women Behind the Counter* were surrounded by other, less popular Czechoslovak programs that demonstrated men's superior decision-making and leadership abilities in public life, such as *Man at the Town Hall* (1976) and *The Northern District* (1980).[54] One would not see men cleaning or taking care of children in such serials, although one would see them bumbling and constantly in need of female help. The socialist soap confirmed the gendered status quo of state feminism, which further naturalized the traditional division of roles while it vastly expanded women's workload. Women tended to blame their burden on the system and its failed feminism, rather than on men and nationalism,[55] in a tragic twist that helped demonize feminism as a whole and prepared the ground for the postfeminist turn.

From Socialist to Postsocialist Superwomen

Late socialist serials give us a retrospective glimpse into a gradual economic and cultural transformation that prepared for a transition to capitalism, rather than for a sudden and spectacular implosion, which came to define the narrative of socialism's demise. They show that this transformation had a gendered infrastructure carefully cultivated by party policy toward women and deployed in popular genres that hid didactic messages in realistic-utopian, fictional plots that also opened the door to unpredictable reception practices. These shows were often experimental mixes of old and new, American commercial quality and European public service broadcasting quality, in a sauce of state socialist educational propaganda. They were the unique products of an industry that was open to novelty but had not yet yielded the primacy of domestic production to a ratings- and advertising-driven market. The genre proved flexible enough for the purposes of socialist states looking for ways to accommodate their disillusioned audiences' escape from vacuous public rituals into home-based entertainment and into an emerging second economy. It also provided a surprising aesthetic continuity with the socialist realist requirements of an earlier, postwar communism, given the reliance of both socialist realism and soap opera on stock characters. The socialist soap made for a tenuous compromise with entertainment and consumerism, since too much explicit propaganda risked alienating the audience while too much realism risked releasing affective discontent and ambivalence about the regime.

Paulina Bren writes that late socialist culture resembled American culture in the 1980s, establishing a significant similarity between East and West following 1968. Bren references Lauren Berlant's characterization of a shrinking public realm and slipping government control in the United States, balanced by a growing and increasingly fragmented set of private worlds. Bren notes that this realization undermines the "existing historiography of binaries" between official versus unofficial cultures, the first and second economy, party elite versus dissident elite, and a politicized public sphere versus a depoliticized private sphere. Television consistently directs us to the gray zones in between.[56]

The structural similarities between East and West became especially prominent through the lens of TV entertainment, which was instrumental in lulling audiences' political sensibilities. Socialist dramatic serials of the 1970s and 1980s do not simply serve as historical documents for the present. They were also active social texts that shaped as much as reflected the shift of the regime from revolutionary masculinity to a domestic femininity that united and fortified the nation around the hearth of socialist lifestyle and consumption. It is clear that women were rather ambivalent heroes propped up by late socialism.

Anna behind the counter, Ilus at the helm of the housing collective, and the Polish Working Woman embody the quintessential socialist woman shouldering her double burden and increasing national responsibility. They still enjoyed some late socialist policies of redistribution directed at reproductive straight women, such as paid maternity leave, free day care, health care, and education. The late socialist transition to a private economy, however, was increasingly preparing them and real-life women behind various counters for more self-reliance and independence, anticipating the gradual postsocialist withdrawal of redistribution policies and the fortification of patriarchal-nationalist paradigms. Late socialist heroines can be retrospectively read as exemplary postfeminists in training, with a high sense of self-reliance and keen juggling abilities. Their greatest power and reward, however, was the belief in their own superpower. The opposition to Western feminism was in part justified by the perception that Eastern European women did not need an ideology based on their powerlessness. As Bren puts it, "It was superwoman in the service not only of her family but, inadvertently, also of the larger socialist family. Dietl's Anna, like so many other women, had been seduced into believing that this was her identity—her exhausting indispensability to her family, large and small."[57]

Nevertheless, late socialist serials also subverted socialist rituals by mocking their gendered underpinnings within the microcosms of the family and the neighborhood. Some 1980s serials took this subversion to surprising levels. The hit Hungarian show *Linda*, broadcast between 1984 and 1989 for three nonconsecutive seasons, was a generic hybrid of police procedural, action series, sitcom, and soap opera. Its creator, György Gát, was admittedly inspired by Jackie Chan's and Bruce Lee's early films and the subsequent surge in the popularity of martial arts. The show was so far ahead of its time in terms of its commercial theme, quasi-feminist character choices, and quality of entertainment that Gát was required to shoot three pilot episodes before the entertainment desk finally gave it a green light and ordered another fourteen episodes. The three pilot episodes were aired in 1983; seven more episodes were aired in 1986, and the last seven in 1989.

Instead of a masculine superhero, the serial is centered around a dainty but scrappy high school girl who is a master of judo and wants to be a policewoman—a queer combination of Nancy Drew and Buffy the Vampire Slayer. Nóra Görbe, Gát's wife, who played Linda, learned tae kwon do for the role. Unlike other late socialist drama serials, *Linda* skirts politics altogether. It was an immediate popular success, although never with critics. The serial had a measurable impact on young people, however: the number of women applying to work for the police rose sharply; and there was a noticeable increase in the popularity of self-defense sports as well.

Linda was so popular that viewers had a hard time parting with it in 1989. Yielding to the call of nostalgia, Görbe finally agreed to do a follow-up serial in 2000. This was very different from the original, particularly because of the protagonist's gendered transformation. In the original, Linda is a short-haired tomboy who wears minimal makeup and rides a motorbike. She incessantly mocks her clumsy puppy dog boyfriend and exploits him for various services she requires for her detective missions. She lives with her father, an actor. Postsocialist Linda is markedly more feminine. She drives a minivan, is a vegetarian, and practices the more defensive and less aggressive aikido. *Linda* has also been in regular reruns. Two commercial channels bought its broadcasting rights: RTL Klub in 1999 and Viasat in 2005. The state broadcaster also reran the series in 2003, 2010, and 2011.[58]

Another remarkable Hungarian serial that bridged and mingled the values of socialism and the postsocialist era is the long-running *Szomszé-*

Nóra Görbe as the iconic policewoman Linda.

dok (Neighbors, 1987–1999, 331 episodes). Unlike *Linda*, which imported the generic conventions and gendered representations of the anticipated future into late socialism, *Neighbors* resurrected the earnest pedagogical utopianism of the recent past, which programs of the late 1980s typically only employed as an empty format or comic reference point. While formally more of a soap opera than those programs I discussed earlier, the serial resembled the School TV program *Family Circle* in its tone and approach. As I explain in chapter 2, *Family Circle* had well-known actors dramatize common conflict situations within families, from which experts extracted lessons for viewers. While in the 1960s and 1970s such a proto-reality show was groundbreaking because it used fiction for propaganda, by 1989 fiction was the only way to influence viewers, and the paternalistic educational tone adopted by *Neighbors* had become outdated and generally swallowed by irony.

Neighbors was thus both pioneering in its form as a soap opera most closely corresponding to Western generic conventions and deeply anachronistic in its didacticism. Another housing-based "panel" drama, it follows the residents of a new block of flats on the outskirts of Budapest. Although its creator, Ádám Horváth, claims he modeled the show after *EastEnders* and other British working-class soaps, the residents fail any test of authenticity. They speak in an unnaturally overenunciated Hungarian normally reserved for the stage, have exuberant interest in current affairs, and never shy away from moralizing, acting as mouthpieces for the producer's lofty messages about peaceful coexistence and democratic participation.⁵⁹ They represent an idealized cross section of an allegedly classless society, which constructs the "masses" as refined and well-intentioned through the aspirational perspective of an intellectual class. But the intellectual spirit of the show is not that of the rebellious, youthful, oppositional intellectual; rather, it is that of a prewar, older, conservative bourgeoisie.

At the same time, this almost campily earnest soap opera displays awareness of its transitional time by making constant, postmodern references to its own status as a TV show. Many scenes create a continuity between the characters' lives and those of the actors who play them. The TV set is often on in the background to situate the narrative in the present and provide ironic commentary. For instance, in the very first episode, popular announcer Júlia Kudlik introduces the new serial *Neighbors*, immediately following *Isaura* (1976), the popular Brazilian telenovela.

Neighbors is an important historical archive, since it incorporates within its narrative arc the last months of socialism and the most momentous part of the transition to capitalism. Although it stayed on the air for ten years, there was a nostalgic quality to it to begin with because of its tendentiousness. Viewers enjoyed it as if it had already been a cult show during its first run, as fans embrace an exceptionally bad movie.⁶⁰ Eventually, TV audiences migrated to the postsocialist soap opera *Barátok közt* (Among friends), produced by the commercial network RTL Klub. Nevertheless, thanks to its cult status, *Neighbors* has been rerun several times on the state broadcaster.

Neighbors was one of a number of socialist transitional soaps set in the housing blocks. However, with its bourgeois values, forced humor, and didactic seriousness, it was the opposite of the Polish *Alternatywy 4* (4 Alternative Street), created by Stanislaw Bareja in the brief period of lax censorship after Solidarity's triumph in 1980. *Alternatywy 4* was the only serial that remained in production after martial law took over in 1981, upheld as an example to demonstrate the freedom of the media in Poland. However, it was not allowed to air until 1986–1987.⁶¹ Much like *Neighbors*, the show documents the waning years of socialism and anticipates the new system to come. But unlike *Neighbors*, and similar to Bareja's former, popular film comedies, it openly foregrounds and mocks the failings of the system through the lives of the inhabitants. Its cast of characters is almost identical to that of *Neighbors*: a surgeon, a crane operator, a goodhearted petty thief, a provincial apparatchik, a university professor, an opera singer, a primary school teacher, a factory foreman, and so forth. Instead of the top-down paternalism of *Neighbors*, however, Bareja's cast goes through a series of comic and absurd events that were inspired by Bareja's experience in political cabaret. Similar to the other transitional serials, *Alternatywy 4* enjoys a solid fan following, including younger generations, and is frequently rebroadcast on public TV.[62]

The quintessential Polish late socialist soap-serial *The Forty-Year-Old*, discussed earlier, was also resurrected in the 1990s. Twenty years later, the Karwowskis no longer represented the typical Polish family: Stefan, the father, is divorced and raising children from various relationships, only some of whom speak Polish as their native tongue. His daughter Jagoda, on the other hand, has no offspring but is married to a wealthy French businessman. As Kinga Bloch explains, the postsocialist *Forty-Year-Old* failed precisely because it correctly featured the breakdown of the ideal of the national family and the increasing individualization of society and decreasing time for community. Bloch writes that almost all viewers she interviewed, "regardless of their education and gender, regret a decrease in the series' spontaneity and sense of togetherness."[63] This is an investment not so much in the existence but in the ideal of togetherness that the show promoted, in which nostalgic remembrances anchor themselves.

It was also the investment in the utopian qualities of the soap opera that lent the Czechoslovak TV serial-soap *Nemocnice na kraji města* (Hospital on the outskirts) cult status. The serial was first, cautiously rebroadcast in 1992. Rerunning socialist serials gained more momentum after 1999, when Czech Television repeated the politically sensitive *Třicet případů majora Zemana* (Thirty cases of Major Zeman), shot in the 1970s. Petr Bednařík explains that the rebroadcast was presented along with documentary footage about life in the 1970s to demonstrate how the original serial distorted historical events.[64] The success of the rebroadcast convinced commercial stations to buy the rights to late socialist dramatic serials. In 2001, after some negotiation among networks, Czech Television bought the copyright to the first six new episodes of a sequel to *Hospital* titled *Nemocnice na kraji města po dvaceti letech* (Hospital on the outskirts twenty years later).[65] Much media hype preceded the sequel. First the original twenty episodes were rerun in 2003 to top ratings.[66] The Slovak commercial television station Markíza ran the serial almost simultaneously with Czech Television. It was also bought by the Polish TVP, the Hungarian RTL Club, and TVB-92 in Serbia and Montenegro. The lack of interest from German-speaking televisions was an unpleasant surprise. However, the new episodes' reception was not all favorable. Critics and viewers alike criticized the emphasis on contemporary issues, the quality of the dialogues, and the realism of the characters. Nevertheless, Czech television produced and released thirteen additional episodes of the serial, this time named *Nemocnice na kraji města—nové osudy* (Hospital on the outskirts—new life stories) in 2008. By this time Nova and Prima televisions had begun broadcasting new Czech hospital dramas, which posed a competition and brought ratings down to about 1.3 million viewers, despite the fact that both the script and the production values were of higher quality than those of the previous serial.

Postsocialist Postfeminism

Late socialist domestic serials registered and facilitated the actual transition between the two world systems. They married the gendered values of late socialism, which were themselves embedded in prewar bourgeois family values, with postsocialist nationalism's reaffirmation of traditional femininity and bourgeois values, on the shared ground of demonizing feminism. These serials also provide testimony to television's own function as a seismograph most responsive to socioeconomic transformation operating, as it does, in the intersection of viewer engagement and creative professional practices. Transitional serials' unique generic and aesthetic hybridity reveals the TV industry's own transformation from a state-run, relatively isolated monopoly institution catering to a homogenized national audience to a set of dispersed media institutions competing for segments of an increasingly diversified audience exposed to a massive influx of transnational, commercial TV influence.

Late socialist TV was strangely depoliticized. It was a microcosm of a regime that seemed to linger in a timeless vacuum, nostalgic for its own lost potential. In the republics of Yugoslavia, Hungary, Czechoslovakia, and Poland, in particular, this inertia fostered TV entertainment that paid lip service to the regime's crumbling principles as much as it mocked those. Serials of the 1970s and 1980s channeled party policies that put forward women as the new heroes of socialist consumer lifestyles and placed emphasis on the politics of the everyday. When the system eventually imploded in 1989, the shock was caused as much by the loss of a comatose value scheme that had perpetuated a sense of frozen time as by the political and economic overhaul that followed. Most of the new political parties that rose from the ashes of the one-party system scrambled to build legitimacy by erasing any continuity with socialism—a paradoxical process that still drives political engines in the region. Nationalism was the most immediate platform on which to build this legitimacy. However, in order to offer nationalism to voters as something authentic and opposed to socialism (which it certainly was not), it needed to be rooted in a strict, naturalized gender distribution and a tight control over women's bodies and roles.

The strategic function of gender in redeploying nationalism was the reason why Eastern Europe experienced a dramatic retrenchment in gender and sexual politics following the end of the Cold War. The 1990s made room for a variety of new (post)feminist ideas, which mingled with the legacy of state feminism in a nationalistic atmosphere. This opening has certainly ushered in new gender and family models: women can now not only do it all but can also have it all—at least if they are young, attractive, and dedicated to self-improvement as both working professionals and married mothers. On a closer look, however, the apparent synergy between postsocialism and the postsocialist version of postfeminism is neither blissful nor new.[67] The postsocialist single woman, rather than a model of female independence, tends to be seen as an overworked victim of global capitalism, who has no time to build meaningful relationships with men and is thus deprived of a fulfilling life as a mother. Traditional femininity and sexuality are employed to relegitimate a strict patriarchal nationalism, which is increasingly entangled in a neoliberal culture of consumerism. Feminine desires, encouraged by both consumerist and nationalistic discourses, block rather than support feminist politics. Outside of select academic and activist hubs, which have certainly grown since 1989, feminism is considered generally redundant at best and a swearword at worst.[68]

Nationalistic retrenchment creates its own gendered temporal and causal grid. It attributes women's potential postfeminist "empowerment" to Western degeneration caused by global media influences on "our" women. This story denies the organic continuity between postfeminism and the late socialist ethos that forced on women the "freedom" to do it all. In a similar vein, the alleged postsocialist emasculation of men has been blamed on external influences even though the crisis of masculinity flared up following the failed revolutionary efforts of 1956 and 1968, the failed competition with the West in industrial production, and the subsequent period of normalization that shifted emphasis from production to the "feminized" sphere of the socialist way of life anchored in consumption practices.

Late socialist domestic dramas bridged socialism and postsocialism either during their original run or in the form of postsocialist reruns and sequels. These serials fill some of the motivated gaps created and sustained by nationalistic amnesia. They are transitional products that, in their narrative content, constantly oscillate between the private politics of the everyday and the public politics of nationalism. They alternately poke fun at rigid, compensatory gender models and reaffirm the masculinist, heteronormative politics of nationalism. They foreground the gendered mechanism of the transition and also highlight the significance of postsocialist cultures as a crucial testing ground that should temper enthusiasm about the global benefits of postfeminism.

One could even argue that late socialist gender models were superior to postsocialist ones at least in one respect: in promoting the notion of a successful female-led collective. Even though women universally repudiated socialist state feminism and even blamed it for their double or triple burden, the community envisioned in *Women Behind the Counter*, *District 78*, and a host of other serials across the region visualized a kind of protofeminist solidarity that resonated with viewers. Postsocialist postfeminism has removed even this last thread of solidarity and revealed how postfeminism operates at its most cynical core: it takes "feminism" out of the equation and leaves behind the illusion of solidarity that manifests itself in destructive self-blame. For the majority of Eastern European women, thinking you are a superhero is not only self-destructive but also politically self-defeating.

IV • GENRES OF HUMOR

Socialist Comedy 11

Is Socialist Comedy an Oxymoron?

What's the difference between really existing socialism and
   working socialism?
Working socialism doesn't exist. Existing socialism doesn't work.
—HUNGARIAN JOKE FROM THE 1980S (AUTHOR'S TRANSLATION).
"PESTI VICCEK A SZOCIALIZMUS IDEJÉN" WEBSITE

The documentary *Exporting Raymond* follows American producer Phil Rosenthal's journey to Moscow to help adapt his sitcom *Everybody Loves Raymond* for Russian audiences. It is a comic account of getting lost in intercultural translation as Raymond's world is transformed into that of Kostya, the protagonist of the Russian version. Rosenthal is a likable guide through the oddities of Russian television production. But he is also our only guide, acting not only as producer but also as the star and commentator of what has been described in reviews as his "vanity project." As a result, we cannot help but feel for him as he is increasingly exasperated in the "chaotic, frustrating, inspiring and hilarious world of Russian relations."[1] He arrives in Moscow in the conviction that "certain things are universal.... Everyone has parents, almost everyone has siblings, most people have relationships with significant others. I've found that there can be humor in these situations." However, he says, "In Russia, I got resistance to this theory."[2]

The film sets out to prove that his theory was correct after all. It shows that, with plenty of patience, even Russians can be trained to understand and even make comedy. The film's executive producer John F. Woldenberg "theorizes" that Russia's tough history ("the kgb"!) and contemporary challenges ("organized crime"!) have made it hard for people to find humor in real life. This is allegedly why the Russian team wanted to turn the show into something over-the-top, with exaggerated performances, glamorous actors, and lavish sets. Rosenthal put it more blatantly following a screening of the film, in response to the question whether Russians could teach Americans anything about television: "No. They don't have the experience, the resources that we have. It's like the child trying to teach the adult."[3]

Let us set aside the fact that Rosenthal ignores the varied legacies of the American sitcom itself when he derives a universal, transcultural recipe of the genre from *Raymond*. It is only since the 1960s, after all, that the sitcom has come to be associated with the white middle class in the United States. Previously, sitcoms featured many more working-class, ethnic, and immigrant families.[4] However, the more important issue for my purposes here is the ethnocentric assumptions toward Russia—and, by extension, the former Soviet empire—in Rosenthal's attitude toward comedy. It is true that *Raymond* was only one of a handful of American sitcom adaptations in Russia in the late first decade of the new millenium (following *The Nanny*, *Married with Children*, and *Who's the Boss?*). However, we can safely assume the reason it was so hard to translate its humor was not that Russian audiences had no comic sophistication and were desensitized to humor in everyday life. The assumption that they had never before experienced the comic in the "absurdity of everyday interactions" is absurd in itself.[5] Soviet television had produced humorous programs from the beginning, which were consistently popular with viewers. But even beyond the genres that featured humorous entertainment, a sophisticated, satirical mode of communication permeated television even more than other socialist institutions. It absorbed and adapted to TV a way of seeing best represented by a literary tradition steeped in absurd humor, exemplified by the writings of Nikolai Gogol and Mikhail Bulgakov.

In fact, in a transhistorical perspective, humor is one of the most dependable popular weapons against authoritarian regimes. It thrives on oppression and censorship, rather than being silenced by it. This is why the early decades of socialist TV, particularly the 1960s, saw outspoken critical humor develop in the Soviet Union and, even more robustly, in Eastern Europe. By the 1980s of late socialism, nationalistic parties had co-opted their intellectual opposition and even nurtured political humor to demonstrate their own benevolence and openness to critique. As I explain in this chapter, in this semiliberalized environment of semifree speech, humor lost much of its critical edge and gradually became tame and trivial.

The "Russians" do not get to explain this history in Rosenthal's documentary because they are viewed through his condescending Cold War lens from the beginning. If they could have a voice, I speculate that they would say their resistance to *Raymond* is not because the show's humor is too sophisticated and absurd but, conversely, because it's too mundane and shallow. (They would most likely call it too "American.") From this absent point of view, the film ultimately appears to be a testament to the arrogance of Hollywood television executives. It is also a cautionary tale about projecting narratives of democratization onto the global expansion of the television industry after the Cold War. This particular "case study" features a process of format adaptation that considers the host culture a blank slate without any valuable aesthetic traditions or cultural institutions to draw on, ready to soak up American values through access to American humor.

In this chapter I first show that, rather than a government-controlled soapbox that repelled humor, much of socialist TV programming was actually perceived by audiences as comic because socialism itself was absurdly comical. Television was an instrument of absurdity as it constantly foregrounded the distance between the utopian world it depicted and the actual experience of socialist lives. After discussing the specificities of the comic register of socialist television, I step farther back and assess how TV humor concentrated around specific genres. These genres continued older traditions of cabaret and satire while they also incorporated the influence of contemporaneous European TV comedy. Comic genres return socialist television to a shared European tradition embedded in a petit bourgeois value and taste system. This European tradition survived and in some contexts flourished throughout the period and well prepared the transition to the postsocialist explosion of global entertainment. In other words, far from being an absent expression that Rosenthal assumed would have to be transplanted by American professionals, socialist TV produced specific forms of humor that had absorbed earlier generic and cultural legacies.

Comic Socialism

"What is absolute good?"
"Communism."
"And what is absolute bad?"
"The road leading to it."
—HUNGARIAN JOKE FROM THE 1980S (AUTHOR'S TRANSLATION).
"PESTI VICCEK A SZOCIALIZMUS IDEJÉN" WEBSITE

In 1984, Hungarian critic Vilmos Faragó published a series of articles in the film journal *Filmvilág* about television entertainment. In the first of these, he asks himself what kinds of programs he finds entertaining. In response, he explains that Hungarian Television divides its programming into "serious" and "entertaining" genres. While the latter consists mostly of humorous shows, he says he actually finds more humor in the "serious" category. For instance, in programs about foreign politics, behind the smooth speeches delivered by influential interviewees, he hears "the comic chatter of a world turned irrational," and behind their smooth, made-up faces he sees "the grin of a white clown." He finds humor in serious political commentaries, which offer diagnoses in a compelling fashion about "a world sunk into infantilism." He finds humor in serious TV conversations about the economy, which are peppered with jargon and mesmerize as if they were shamanic spells. He finds celebratory speeches particularly funny for their inability to say anything genuine, true, lived, and personal. He describes as amusing the scientists of the educational program *Scholarly Club*, live classical music concerts, and live theater broadcasts, which are "some of the least televisual enterprises."[6]

Looking back thirty years later, the author puts vividly what turned socialist programming absurdly comic: it was the perspective that viewers brought to their TV experience. Late socialist TV of the 1980s, in particular, operated under such a satirical gaze. Of course, satire is not necessarily funny in the sense that it produces laughter, as the sitcom does. While the sitcom is safe and predictable, "The essence of satire is that it perceives some absurdity inherent in the logic of some position and ... draws the absurdity out and isolates it, so that all can see it."[7]

In another example of the comic absurdity of late socialism, Dominic Boyer writes about the language of news in East Germany; that it was designed with the noble intention to unite the referential precision of socialist philosophers such as Lenin and Marx with the poetic quality of Goethe. The result, however, was neither but instead a kind of *Funktionärsdeutsch*, whose repetitive efforts to approximate a monologic ideal only created indeterminacy and polysemy. The effect was "like listening to reports from another planet," as one of Boyer's interviewees put it.[8]

In the next chapter, I explore in more detail the analogy between the performative, self-justifying forms of late socialist news and the ironic sensibilities generated by contemporary, late capitalist news. The range of humor in late socialism was actually much broader and deeper than oppositional satire from the beginning. Serguei Alex Oushakine describes socialist comic genres as "jokes of repression," whose mode was very different from the liberating laughter of Bakhtin's medieval carnivalesque. Rather, they uncoupled laughter from any association with happiness—an association essential for the American sitcom, which Rosenthal assumes to be universal.[9] Laughter in socialism had a community-building function, inviting only those in the know. The offer of inclusion was as important as the satisfaction over fooling censors.[10]

Oushakine laments the scarcity of scholarship on comedic forms and genres that circulated within the Soviet Union—something even more true for Eastern Europe. The typical approach to socialist humor is what Michel Foucault called the "repressive hypothesis," which assumes that censorship prevented comic genres from flourishing. Rosenthal's theorizing about the lack of Russian comedy clearly carries residues of this. Oushakine, on the other hand, tracks the history of Soviet comedy back to the film comedies of the 1930s. These were modifications of Hollywood musicals that continued the legacy of absurd humor targeting nineteenth-century state bureaucracy, such as Nikolai Gogol's (1809–1852) and Mikhail Saltykov-Shchedrin's (1826–1889) writing. They also attempted to integrate "light genres" of objectionable bourgeois origin such as cabaret, farce, and operetta with the "agit-hall" entertainment of the early Soviet Union. Equally important, as elsewhere in the Soviet-controlled region, debates about the role of comedy and satire were at the forefront of political and academic discussions throughout socialism.[11] As for television, even though socialist parties tried to steer its mainstream programming and effect toward education and, even more hopelessly, political agitation, viewers made it clear from the earliest days that they saw it as a medium of entertainment and relaxation.[12]

Cabaret and Bourgeois Humor

"What is socialism? A transition from capitalism to capitalism."
—HUNGARIAN JOKE FROM THE 1980S (AUTHOR'S TRANSLATION).
"PESTI VICCEK A SZOCIALIZMUS IDEJÉN" WEBSITE

After television got established as a mass institution in the 1950s and 1960s, every country developed similar comedy genres, which necessarily drew on presocialist forms of humor. In the Central and Eastern European countries, these presocialist forms derived from the tradition of stage cabaret and, when adapted to TV, continued to carry the generic label of "cabaret" as a fairly specific socialist TV genre.

The most influential European traditions were the French *cabaret* and German *Kabarett*. While the English equivalent of the word means musical entertainment featuring humor, comedy, song, dance, and theater, the original European phenomenon also implied political satire. The lighter, more entertaining elements and the satirical, more politicized elements coexisted in a fairly liberal environment until World War II. This peaceful combination was the key to the popularity of cabaret during the Weimar Republic: cabaret was both a medium for political expression and critique and an outlet for much-needed distraction and amusement during the years of economic crisis and war preparation. Political cabaret flourished in Germany in the Weimar period, employing distinguished writers such as Klaus Mann and Erich Kästner, only to be repressed by the Nazi regime in 1933, when German-speaking cabaret artists fled to Switzerland, Scandinavia, France, or the United States. The first cabaret in Berlin was the Überbrettl, or "Superstage" (in reference to Friedrich Nietzsche's Übermensch), founded in 1901. The first one in Munich was Die Elf Scharfrichter, also launched in 1901.[13]

Polish stage cabaret originated in Kraków: the first Polish cabaret, Zielony Balonik, or "Green Balloon," was founded there in 1905. One of its creators, Tadeusz Boy-Żeleński, was an enfant terrible of the Polish literary scene and an important figure in the "Young Poland" movement. Much of cabaret took the form of satirical short plays, which, as in Germany, included some of the leaders of Kraków's political and cultural circles. It was sophisticated entertainment, which addressed literary and cultural elites rather than broad audiences.[14]

In the Austro-Hungarian Monarchy, Budapest was a most hospitable city for cabaret. The first Hungarian-language cabaret, the Bonbonier, opened in Budapest in 1907.[15] As was the case elsewhere in the region, cabaret was a progressive space, where comedians directly responded to concurrent political events with wit and courage. The best writers of the time wrote for and performed on the stage, many of them former journalists for whom journalism and political satire were two sides of the same coin. At the end of World War I, there were about thirty cabarets in Budapest. By the end of World War II, there were about fifty, despite increasing anti-Semitism and, after 1939, mass deportations, which devastated the cabaret because most comedians were Jewish.[16] It was during these years that performers assembled a rhetorical tool kit that bypassed the attention of the pro-German police and was to be deployed successfully during socialism. These strategies included slips of the tongue, playing dumb, ambiguity, double language, and performances of overidentification.

After the war, stage cabarets reopened just before TV cabaret began in the 1950s. In the GDR, the first postwar stage cabaret, Die Distel, opened in 1953 in Berlin, while West German cabaret was concentrated around Düsseldorf, Munich, and Berlin. Stage and TV cabaret developed hand in hand and often exchanged talent, personnel, and entire shows during socialism. In Budapest, after the devastation of the war, theaters needed to be rebuilt. The first cabaret reopened as early 1945. For a few years, until communist dictatorship took over, there seemed to be a true opportunity to deploy political humor as the language of a broad public sphere, widening cabaret's niche, cosmopolitan appeal beyond the capitol. The forced communist takeover in 1949 squashed such hopes and planted mistrust against the government again. Censorship became dogmatic; it struck down on political satire and briefly banned political cabaret. Cabaret was considered by the party leadership a self-serving, cynical bourgeois pastime, which had no place in a communist society of the future.[17] In response, cabaret performers adopted forms of ironic overidentification with the regime's own rhetoric and rituals in these early years—forms that Soviet political humor was to take only in the 1970s and 1980s. Hungarian comedians of the 1950s and early 1960s, first on stage and radio and increasingly on television, demonstrated excessive rhetorical loyalty to party requirements of behavior and thinking. They memorized revolutionary slogans and songs, pointed out the moral corruption of capitalism with zeal, and celebrated factory workers for their productivity. They did so while winking at the audience, who well understood the parodic intent of these extreme performances.[18]

In socialist Hungary, political thawing began relatively early, shortly after the failed 1956 anti-Soviet revolution, when János Kádár began his long authoritarian reign as secretary general of the socialist party. Television, which became a mass medium around this time, almost immediately adapted political humor from Hungarian Radio, which had itself incorporated forms of stage cabaret. The post-1956 thawing reestablished the Budapest petite bourgeoisie of the original political cabaret as its comedic inspiration, with unspoken party approval. Television thus played a crucial role in shoring up bourgeois humor and values. In 1957, just a year after television's postwar relaunch and the crushed revolt against Soviet occupation, television broadcast a live memorial show from the Literary Stage theater dedicated to the legacy of Endre Nagy, the "godfather" of prewar political cabaret.[19] The same year saw the first New Year's cabaret, another live theatrical broadcast, which was hosted by some of the most popular comedians.[20]

In a parallel development, in Poland the first political TV cabaret was broadcast on New Year's Eve of 1960. It was so popular that people would stop dancing at New Year's Eve parties to watch it. It was followed in the 1960s by new live entertainment shows. As in Budapest, many of the political cabaret programs drew on the interwar Polish cabaret tradition. *Kabaret Starszych Panow* (Cabaret of two old men, 1958–1966) displayed nostalgia for the bygone era of prewar elegance and the sophistication of the urban intelligentsia. The program reached cult status over the years and still elicits immediate recognition among all Poles.[21] It featured two performers, who met while working for Polish Radio: Jeremi Przybora, who also wrote the script, and Jerzy Wasowski, who also wrote the music. Their sense of humor was "absurdist, sophisticated, and elegant."[22] Przybora and Wasowski played two bourgeois characters, Pan (Mr.) A and Pan B, who were dressed in dinner jackets and top hats and discussed the events of the day. Direct political references were uncommon; jokes were usually camouflaged to pass censorship.[23] True to the cabaret format, their act included a great deal of music. The show also had a range of celebrity guests, mostly actors. There were two new editions a year, each followed by many reruns. Pikulski recalls that the comedians' guiding idea was to "provide entertainment, to amuse themselves and their audiences by detaching them from the gray, boring, and ugly everyday life and rampant vulgarity."[24] In its heyday, the show was criticized for romanticizing the outdated style and sensibilities of the prewar era. The socialist youth organization rejected the program for not being sufficiently progressive and direct.[25]

Jeremi Przybora and Jerzy Wasowski, the "two old men" of *Kabaret Starszych Panow*.

The thaw period lightened TV cabaret even further. Several of the most memorable and popular programs in Poland were associated with Olga Lipinska, a theater and TV director and satirical artist, one of the few women in the world of socialist comedy. She directed and produced *Kabaret Olgi Lipinskiej* (The Olga Lipinska cabaret), a fifty-minute program that premiered in 1974 (under a different title), ran until 2005, and was resurrected in 2010. Lipinska was also involved in the creation of a New Year's Eve special edition cabaret called *Szopka noworoczna*, which summarized the past year's events in comic style. Lipinska's other TV cabaret productions include *Głupia sprawa* (Stupid thing, 1968–1970), *Gallux Show* (1970–1974), *Właśnie leci kabarecik* (The cabaret is on, 1975–1977), and *Kurtyna w górę* (Curtain up!, 1977–1981). Her cabaret was infused with the regional tradition of the absurd and surreal, particularly with the humor of the prewar Warsaw poet Konstanty Ildefons Gałczyński. Like the cabaret of the two "old men," Lipinska's programs included celebrity guests as well as musical numbers and offered cultural and social commentary, which carefully evaded direct politicizing and branded itself as "pure entertainment." In turn, it was accused of promoting bourgeois kitsch and undermining the wholesome, realistic, educational ethos of socialism.

In the Romania of the 1960s, the program *Varietati* (Varieties) was broadcast every Sunday afternoon. It featured political satire and comedy skits sandwiched within dance and music performances.[26] Other humorous and satirical variety programs included *Intalnire cu umorul si satira* (Date with humor and satire), *Umor si satira* (Humor and satire), *Intalnirea de la ora 10* (The 10 o'clock meeting), all shown on Saturday evening; and *Varietati musical-coreografice* (Musical and choreographical varieties) and *Studioul muzicii usoare* (The studio of pop music) on Sunday evenings.[27] In the GDR, the values and tastes of the Weimar period reigned supreme despite the party's concerted efforts to create a more revolutionary television and overcome the distinction between bourgeois and working-class tastes.[28] Viewers' rejection of political-artistic experiments and demand for light entertainment forced the SED to shift direction in the early 1960s from "the revolutionary, grassroots transformation of popular culture" to the nationalistic embrace of "warmed-over bourgeois values."[29]

Nevertheless, throughout the region, party leaders continued to express consternation about the TV boom of prewar light entertainment. One typical summary prepared by a party official for the Hungarian Socialist Party Committee in the spring of 1959 speculated that there are "many reasons" for bourgeois cabaret's return. "Television, even when its editors know exactly what they want, has difficulty doing something radically different in the genre of entertainment than other media do. One can only change this with collective effort," she proposes with mandatory optimism.[30] The 1966 report of the Hungarian National Council of Trade Unions also zeroed in on political cabaret in its annual assessment of TV programming: "Certain political cabaret programs are tasteless; their political content is ambiguous; and they often cause outrage among groups of more politically evolved workers."[31] Even the president of Hungarian Television and Radio at the time, István Tömpe, felt compelled to express moral caution about TV cabaret in his 1966 annual report: "We need to reduce the number of political cabaret programs. We need to ensure that political jokes elevate, rather than disrupt, the spirit of public political exchange."[32] The Agit-Prop Committee's assessment of Hungarian Television's 1970–1971 program planning declares:

> Television's production of cabaret and other comedy programs has increased a great deal. They have not succeeded in improving the content, however. This is not only because satirical topics are harder to adapt to the screen but also because the majority of these programs are based on the Budapest petite bourgeoisie's thinking. They forget about the fact that the needs of an increasingly educated working class and peasantry are more and more prominent. In addition, most of these programs are primitive, lacking authentic humor. The new plan needs to take into account changes in viewer demand; and the leadership needs to make efforts to allow class politics to prevail in humorous programs as well.[33]

But such caution increasingly got reduced to empty rhetoric. Prewar forms of variety entertainment not only survived into socialism but became progressively more frequent on TV. One obvious reason for this was that TV comedy was fed by and inherited talent from stage comedy and then radio. The three institutions existed in symbiosis throughout the socialist decades. As elsewhere, cabaret performers were predominantly Jewish. While their community was devastated by the Holocaust and subsequent emigration, most Jewish comedians also de-emphasized their ethnic heritage as the entire "Jewish question" became taboo during socialism. But what helped bourgeois comedy thrive in the first place was that its occasional edge of political satire was overshadowed by an array of light cabaret acts, including many musical numbers. The latter remained safely disconnected from the turbulent world of the 1960s, 1970s, and 1980s and adopted the depoliticized, nostalgic note often deployed in the service of the nationalistic cultural policies of socialist governments.

For instance, on May 1, 1965, *Csak a szépre emlékezem* (I only remember the good times), a typical variety program that borrowed the title of a popular romantic song dripping with nostalgia, interspersed variety acts with archival footage from old movies and postwar May Day parades for good measure, lining up older and younger performers in a summer entertainment mélange of humorous skits and crooning chansons. The only contemporaneous reference in the program, identified as "cabaret" in the generic classification of the Hungarian TV Archives, was a brief Beatles parody.[34] The rest of the content was infused with a prewar generation's taste.

Foreign observers of socialism would have been shocked by the number of these depoliticized comedy-variety entertainment programs: in Hungary alone, TV offerings included shows such as *Nemcsak a tükör görbe* (The mirror is not the only thing that's crooked, 1965), based on humorous skits written by classical and contemporary comic writers; *Pesti kabaré* (The cabaret of Budapest, 1969–1970), a four-part series that reinvigorated the bourgeois heritage of comic writing with adaptations of early-century writers Ferenc Molnár, Gáspár Heltai, and Frigyes Karinthy; the two-part *Kabaré utca* (Cabaret street, 1971); the 1970 news satire series *Sajtókabaré* (Press cabaret); *Csak férfiaknak* (Only for men, 1968), which featured a retrograde patriarchal take on gender roles within marriage; the similar *Kriminális* (Criminal, 1972); *Mondom a magamét* (1975), broadcast from Mikroszkóp Színpad (Microscope Stage), one of several Budapest theaters devoted to comedy; and a number of one-man shows typically performed by older comedians. In 1969, the series *Pest Cabaret—or What Amused Our Grandfathers* was broadcast, with the explicit intention to evoke the satirical cabaret scene of early twentieth-century Budapest.[35] A critic dubbed the program "cabaret museum" because of its intention to reproduce the authentic feel of the interwar context along with the original jokes.[36]

But even for a child of the 1970s and 1980s like myself, it was a strange experience to reconcile the regimented, centrally controlled routine and material scarcity of everyday socialism with the abundance of lewd songs, dance numbers, and vaudeville acts on TV. These were not simply in conflict with a socialist-realist aesthetic and the mission to educate the public; they felt outdated and out of place, obviously belonging to a different, more decadent era. While there must have been a demographic of older viewers who remembered the interwar and war periods and shared a taste for these acts, these programs had little to do with the everyday worlds of much of the population, especially of younger people. They were the odd packaging one had to unwrap to get to the occasional more contemporary, edgy, satirical cabaret.

New Year's Cabaret

The satirical, political branch of cabaret continued to thrive as well, although always moderated and toned down by the legacy of bourgeois variety entertainment. By the 1970s, comedians' performative leverage expanded to openly poking fun at socialist bureaucracy, at the deceitfulness of official news, or the evident shortage of consumer products. In East Germany, new forms of cabaret developed in the 1970s and 1980s, when cabaret became an important form of social criticism again. In Hungary, the popular political satire show *Parabola* began as early as 1964.[37] In a development that anticipated the merging of satire and serious news in the post–Cold War era, the participatory current affairs program *Fórum* (discussed in chapter 2) launched its satirical spin-off, *Fórum—kabaré*, with the catchphrase "Ask away—we'll answer if we can."[38] By the 1970s of the thaw, nothing rivaled the popularity of humorous programs.

I now take a closer look at the highlight of comedic programming, the annual ritual of the Hungarian New Year's cabaret program. This block of entertainment, which usually started in prime time during dinner and lasted all the way into the new year, united in perfect harmony the two main components of the original early twentieth-century stage cabaret: light entertainment with operetta segments, gags, and lewd jokes on the one hand, and political satire on the other. My focus here is on the political piece, which was the most anticipated part of the show, made palatable and digestible by the trivial merrymaking wrapped around it. The New Year's cabaret was an important television event every year, eagerly anticipated in the months leading up to it and eagerly discussed long after.

For instance, the 1964 New Year's show was titled "For Those over 20" and featured mostly cabaret skits and songs by popular stage actors and actresses, on topics such as summer vacation and foreign travel. The 1965 program block was titled "TV's Gift Calendar." It assembled parodies of typical socialist educational TV genres: of a public service program for "girls and women"; a program that taught good manners; a general advice-giving program; and others that focused on fashion, correct language use, sports, news, humor, and School TV.

Throughout the 1970s and 1980s, the last, most watched hour was devoted to comedian Géza Hofi's one-man show. Hofi embodied the voice of late socialist political cabaret, likely the most liberal of its kind in the region. His New Year's Eve stand-up specials were much awaited national celebrations and continue to be fondly recalled to this day. Hofi took on a different persona in each New Year's special, often that of a character from a popular television program, and offered a satirical analysis of the past year's main events. His performance was interspersed with parodies and songs. The "Hofi" phenomenon was a high achievement of "wink wink" political comedy. He was seen as the man of the people who speaks out loud what everyone knew but could not say. The intimacy and identification with Hofi derived from his invitation to people to fill in the blanks, finish his sentences, read what he left unsaid. His shows offered a carnivalesque mastery over the nonsense that looked like serious television.

For his 1972 New Year's twenty-five-minute show, Hofi appeared dressed as Ulysses, hero of the 1968 Italian miniseries *Odissea*, which swept European TV screens at the time. This fictional disguise allowed Hofi to borrow the world of the TV epic in order to talk allegorically about the epic failures and oddities of socialism. On a set that recalled the series, Ulysses/Hofi recounted his journey in his usual conversational street vernacular, whose distance from *Odissea*'s earnest homage to Ulysses created a comic effect. But the real, less obvious target of parody was the aspirational, artificially erudite dictum of much socialist programming. In Hofi's account, nymphs are prostitutes who work for hard currency, and Kirke becomes an allegory for failing pig farms in agricultural cooperatives. He took stabs at educational TV series and a new law about keeping dogs. He also commented on the politicization of sports matchups against Soviet opponents, weaving in some Russian-language humor, which was an ongoing source of jokes that created a language within a language and cemented collective intimacy during the entire socialist period.

On December 31, 1976, Hofi appeared in the character of a newspaper stand vendor, who explained current events summed up by press headlines. He made jokes about communist slogans that already operated as jokes, such as a literal interpretation of the cliché "the Leninist path." He pointed out the reliably unreliable nature of socialist institutions such as the outdated state phone communication system and the mistakes in the phone book. He criticized the new mass education law and his hobbyhorse, television's overzealous contributions to mass education. Because TV was dominated by educational programs, he recommended that people should pay tuition rather than a TV subscription fee. The 1977 show featured an elaborate array of television parodies, which poked fun, once again, at the educational overreach of national TV and the phony seriousness of foreign political correspondents. He inserted himself in the character of Michael Strogoff, hero of the eponymous dramatic serial running at that time, to criticize various socialist rituals, including politically sensitive issues such as Lenin and the Soviet Union and the regime's stubborn insistence on calling the 1956 anti-Soviet uprising "counterrevolution," as well as TV commercials and international sports stars such as Franz Beckenbauer, Niki Lauda, and Muhammad Ali.

These New Year's specials reproduced the best satirical spirit of prewar cabaret. They were spearheaded by the Budapest petit bourgeois everyman who evaluated politics and daily life from an oppositional standpoint, in an intimate language that confirmed a familial bond between the performer and the audience. While Hofi's comedy resurrected the most critical tradition of political cabaret, it is important to keep in mind that his annual golden hour, and the political criticism his comic persona conveyed, were also endorsed and supported by the party. This benevolent attitude meant that the regime was also in on the joke made at its own expense. Having Hofi star in the New Year's cabaret consolidated oppositional humor as a building block of late socialism's ideological architecture.

This appeared to be an architecture of ideological stagnation that would never crumble. However, currents of the presocialist past and the winds of the postsocialist future were both quietly eroding its foundations. Late socialism's TV humor was a fascinating, decadent amalgam of presocialist bourgeois tastes infused with a political tradition and elements of what was to develop into a postsocialist entertainment infused with the influence of transnational comedy formats. Television's humorous programs displayed intense cultural transformations happening within what seemed to be a paralyzed system.

12 (Post)socialist Political Satire

American television finally embraced satire in the postnetwork era. Humor had tended to take less negative forms on TV until the late 1970s; more critical kinds of social satire had been carried by print journalism and comic books. The three large TV networks preferred safer, more mainstream forms of comedy, which attracted advertisers and the largest possible audience shares. After decades of broadcasting devoted to least objectionable programming and nonoffensive forms of humor, satire has transformed from a rare mode of expression on the periphery of television into a genre that encompasses TV-land. The history of this shift has been well explored: it has been enabled by a changing technological infrastructure that allowed for a large number of channels to deliver diversified programming via cable and satellite; widespread access to technologies of production and distribution mostly thanks to the Internet; and the conglomeration and integration of ownership over multiple media platforms.[1] The establishment of Comedy Central as a distinct brand among Viacom's assets has been a milestone in this narrative. Ironically, the channel's two most defining comedy news shows, *The Daily Show with Jon Stewart* and *The Colbert Report*, galvanized political participation and civic interest to an extent far beyond what even their hosts admitted. Rather than simply providing humorous commentary on what would be assumed to remain authentic, "real" news, "fake" news has assumed the mandate to provide reliable information about matters of public interest. The amount of audience trust placed in late night news comedies reveals a corresponding erosion of trust in network news and other traditional news sources.

Television satire is a "posttrust" lens on politics, permeated by suspicion about authority. It gains particular legitimacy "when historical reality presents periods of social and political rupture (such as culture wars, actual wars, and unpopular leaders) or mind-numbing manufactured realities (such as celebrity culture, media spin, and news management)."[2] In these times, "satire becomes a potent means for enunciating critiques and asserting unsettling truths that audiences may need or want to hear."[3]

In the Eastern European region, the entire period of socialism, and arguably the entire twentieth century, was a long series of ruptures and upheavals. Satire has been an indispensable filter for public discourse. It is one in a range of "negative" or "dark" modes of expression often associated with art. These include dark humor, the grotesque, and the absurd, manifest in the work of artists from Nikolai Gogol through Eugène Ionescu to Dušan Makavejev. During the late socialist period of the 1970s and 1980s, satire flourished in socialist media. By then, principles of a utopian Marxist-Leninist social transformation had lost much of their legitimacy. However, the clichés of political communication continued to be repeated, rigidifying into their own parodies. Satirical TV simply amplified these parodies through playing back to the regime its own vacuous audiovisual performances.

In the United States, despite the corruption of the epistemological certainty of television news, the very notion of "fake news" still presupposes the existence of "real news," at least as a lost ideal projected into the past. In Eastern Europe and the Soviet Union, ever since television grew into a mass medium during the 1950s and 1960s, TV news never even pretended to be ideologically neutral. While the level of party interference varied within the region from direct censorship to relative autonomy, TV was to support the principles of socialism and educate socialist citizens. By all accounts, the migration of trust from authentic to fake news is of a global scale. The changes that have brought it about are also symptoms of a converging media world—beginning with the transnational expansion of Comedy Central itself. Satire is used worldwide as a way to amplify the absurdity of monologic news, which seeks to establish through repetition the very epistemological certainty it claims as its basis. By replaying the echoes that reverberate in the self-referential echo chamber of "serious" news, satire has created a dialogic discourse in the Bakhtinian sense in which multiple, simultaneous voices play against one another.[4]

This recent, worldwide shift was modeled by late socialist cultures. Post-socialist TV satire, then, is at once at pace with global television and builds on what is a familiar aesthetic mode of watching and communicating in the region. In fact, anthropologists Dominic Boyer and Alexei Yurchak claim that satirical modes engaged by Comedy Central and late socialist satirical media in Eastern Europe are not simply analogous but the latter anticipates the former. They note a "family resemblance" between the aesthetics and ideological context of contemporary political satire worldwide, including *The Daily Show*, *The Colbert Report*, *The Yes Men*, *The Onion*, *South Park*, faux documentary shows like *The Office*, CNNN in Australia, Sasha Baron Cohen's satirical performances on *Da Ali G Show*, and a mode of parodic overidentification they identify by the Russian term *stiob*. Stiob is an ironic aesthetic that thrived in late Soviet socialism and "differed from sarcasm, cynicism, derision or any of the more familiar genres of absurd humor" in that it "required such a degree of *overidentification* with the object, person, or idea at which [it] was directed that it was often impossible to tell whether it was a form of sincere support, subtle ridicule, or a peculiar mixture of the two."[5]

This analogy has far-reaching implications for understanding the historical trajectory and political significance of television satire in a transnational framework. It brings up the sticky question of just what "free" late capitalist media today have in common with late socialist, centralized, "freedom-deprived" media. This question is not invalidated by the obvious differences between the two, such as the fragmentation of the viewing public into multiple niche audiences as opposed to a supposedly homogeneous national audience, the different degrees in the freedom of the press, and the differences between entertainment-centered programming targeting consumers and the educational-enlightening rationalism of late socialist media targeting citizens. However, as Boyer and Yurchak argue, there are also some major underlying structural similarities that connect the two situations. The first of these is the centralization of media ownership and control. In the United States and much of the world today, despite multiplying media outlets and the democratizing potential of the Internet, the gradual retreat of the state from media regulation has effectively unified the sources of information in very few, very powerful hands. The concentration of ownership has also led to increased commercialization. Instead of being a public service, as it has been considered in the dominant tradition of European television, news gathering and sharing has become a form of entertainment for profit.[6] Expensive foreign correspondents, time-consuming fact-checking, and thorough analysis have fallen victim to the fragmentation and commodification of deregulated news production.

It was also a centralized, hierarchical infrastructure that consolidated the news in the Soviet empire into highly standardized and censored messages. Not unlike Rupert Murdoch's News Corporation, this was a multitiered empire, where national news media were continually checked to make sure they adhered to the rhetoric of socialism set forth by Moscow. While national media in the different countries demonstrated varying degrees of openness toward and sometimes even entered into collaboration with Western news services, the ultimate power over the flow of information was condensed in the highest party echelons. Boyer describes how, in the German Democratic Republic, standardized language was essential to disseminating information from Berlin to regional media centers, which then rerouted party messages to the district-level party offices that placed the news in print and electronic media. In the GDR, as elsewhere, the socialist citizen would wake up every morning to read the exact same headlines in the exact same formulation in every paper. News was provided by the single national information service, in this case the Allgemeine Deutsche Nachrichtendienst; press photos were supplied by the national news photo service, and journalist training was centralized at Karl Marx University in Leipzig. Longtime general secretary Erich Honecker personally reviewed and revised headlines daily.[7] In a similar vein, at least through the 1960s, Hungarian State Television and Radio had a single, powerful director trusted by party authorities, who also handpicked the institutions' department heads and even reporters, taking into account the candidates' ideological convictions and class backgrounds as much as their preparation or talents.[8]

Centralized control loosened quite considerably by the 1980s. As Endre Aczél, the main editor of the nightly news program *TV Hiradó* between 1985 and 1989, explained to me in an interview, some elements remained nonnegotiable, such as news about party secretary János Kádár's speeches and announcements about state ceremonies and funerals of communist leaders. However, Aczél and his team were able to negotiate the length of these "mandatory tricks" and refresh the structure and contents of the news in several other ways: they replaced the old socialist logo with a computer-generated image of a golden globe, commissioned a popular rock musician to compose new theme music, began to lead with a story about domestic instead of international affairs, and introduced the practice of including a colorful little story on a popular topic to end the broadcast.[9] At the same time, by the late 1980s party leaders were quite aware that no one took direct propaganda seriously. Even though the leaders of Television were always appointed by the party, "[party leaders] had enough intelligence to go hunting instead rather than interfere with the work of television." "It takes a high IQ to realize that there are professionals working there who understand the job much better. If anything, party representatives dealt only with administrative and financial issues. They watched the programs, said a few words occasionally, and that was that." Nevertheless, as Aczél put it, he knew that the nightly TV news was "the last piece of agitation" in the hands of the party, which "they wanted to hold onto until the last minute" because it functioned "like scripture" to the people.[10]

The daily experience of centralized news is not unlike that of the coordinated daily talking points repeated by contemporary conservative news outlets, from right-wing talk radio to Fox News. Watching the documentary *Outfoxed: Rupert Murdoch's War on Journalism* (Robert Greenwald, 2004), one feels an eerie déjà vu. The film foregrounds the strategic repetition of rhetorical formulas and carefully crafted daily messages on Fox News, which are often communicated through memos and guidelines by Murdoch and his trusted delegates. As former Fox News reporters explain, some with their faces blocked out and voices altered, the news is skewed to reflect News Corporation's conservative spirit, and at times Murdoch's own political convictions, such as his devotion to Ronald Reagan. By contrast, Geoffrey Baym remarks that, against the background of the partisan spin and highly standardized format that defines "real" news, Jon Stewart's comedic discussions with his guests strike one as "honest" and "normal."[11]

The economic and political centralization of the structure of news reporting thus produces a highly reiterative, performative rhetoric, whose goal is to render natural the very reality it creates. The scale of this development is brilliantly demonstrated by Charlie Brooker on his BBC 4 program *Newswipe*, in a parody skit entitled "How to Report the News." Brooker assumes a reporter's familiar, rehearsed voice and persona to demonstrate the clichés that secure the "authenticity" of a news story, from "a lackluster establishing shot of a significant location" to "lazy and pointless vox pops" by people in the street. This faithful adherence to the formula produces a perfectly passable news segment despite the utter lack of reported content. In a similar vein, Jon Stewart often did not need to do more than isolate and replay fragments from the political theater that is considered "real" news. It is the operation of this theater that he interrupted in his (in)famous 2004 appearance on *Crossfire*, where he broke the character he was assigned and refused to be Tucker Carlson's "clown." *The Daily Show* frequently offered montages that juxtapose instances of political talking points in the news media to foreground their coordinated orchestration, as in conservative politicians' and the news media's strategic use of the euphemisms "job creators" instead of "rich people" and "climate change" instead of "global warming." Stephen Colbert took the performance a step further, and even closer to stiob, when he inhabited the persona of a conservative talk show host.

By the 1970s and 1980s, even in relatively oppressive places such as the Soviet Union, this distancing effect moved from the margins into the center of political discourse. In the Soviet Union, stiob sensibility emerged in the context of what Boyer and Yurchak call "hypernormalization," when the structure of late Soviet authoritative discourse gradually became more formalized and self-referential.[12] This ironic mode was an expression of skepticism about political rhetoric in general, not necessarily in direct opposition to socialist propaganda. Much like *The Colbert Report*, it was successful as an outlet because it followed the official rhetoric so precisely that it was often hard to detect the parodic intent. Stiob was thus the most effective coping strategy, especially because direct confrontation would have been easily recognized and neutralized by the state. Overidentification had the additional advantage that one could reject some misguided socialist practices without having to reject the idea of communism as a whole.[13]

This way of defamiliarizing Soviet-style rhetoric was widely exercised within the region and continued well into postsocialism. One notorious instance was Russian provocateur Sergei Kuryokhin's posing as a historian on the May 17, 1991, episode of the popular cultural-historical television program *Piatoe koleso* (The fifth wheel). He gave a long lecture that supposedly revealed some previously unknown facts about Lenin, such as that he and his followers were eager consumers of certain hallucinogenic mushrooms found in Russian forests, which altered their personalities and effectively turned them into mushrooms. Because Kuryokhin's performance reproduced the rhetoric and form of authoritative televisual discourse so faithfully, the "mushroom hoax" caused temporary confusion even among educated audiences. The effect was similar to the elaborate anticorporate hoaxes staged by "The Yes Men" and to Colbert's faithful parodic emulation of Fox's Bill O'Reilly.[14]

This mode of satirical overidentification was practiced by the pop music group AVIA in the Soviet Union, the Orange Alternative (Pomarańczowa Alternatywa) movement in Poland, the literary and music performances of Dmitri Prigov, the highly ritualized daily life of the artistic group Mit'ki, the performances of "man-dog" Oleg Kulik, and the work of East Berlin's Prenzlauer Berg artists, among others.[15] Perhaps best known among these performances are those of the Russian Necrorealist collective and the originally Yugoslavian artistic-political group Neue Slowenische Kunst (NSK), both of which have continued their activities into the post–Cold War era. The main strategy of the group, which was established in Slovenia in 1984, is to reproduce both communist and capitalist rhetoric to excess, which isolates and critiques the shared rhetorical and political elements between the two. Of its "departments," Laibach, the musical group, is the most famous, ever since its first public appearance on the Slovenian cultural-political TV magazine *TV Tednik* (TV weekly) in 1983, where its members wore military uniforms and used a quote from Hitler as their inspiration for what became their "Nazi-Kunst." They later adopted a quote from Stalin as their slogan: "We, LAIBACH, are the engineers of human souls." In 1992, NSK created their own "State in Time," a global state without a territory that issues its own passport to anyone who applies and opens embassies and consulates wherever they are invited.[16] In a gesture worthy of Stephen Colbert, they developed a practice named "NSK Garda": they hire local army personnel to guard the NSK flag in the countries they visit. This reproduction of a standard nationalist ritual through interchangeable props and in the service of a fictional, deterritorialized state foregrounds the fact that nation-states and patriotism are secured by repetitive violence.[17]

The satire news program that serves as a case study for this chapter, *Heti hetes* (The weekly seven), a pun based on the fact that "seven" and "week" both translate into "hét" in Hungarian, is a weekly, hour-long news comedy show that has successfully run on the Hungarian commercial channel RTL Klub. It was modeled after the German RTL's *Sieben Tage, sieben Köpfe* (Seven days, seven heads) format. Both programs have a host read out short news bites from the previous week, after which a panel of six celebrities comment in a humorous, often satirical fashion, including short, preprepared skits or musical numbers. Some of the six guests are permanent panelists, while others are onetime or returning guests. Much like Comedy Central's satirical news shows, *Heti hetes* targets absurdities in politics and public life, which range from the silliest to the most consequential.

While the format is indeed new and thus could be attributed to the globalization and commercialization of postsocialist television industries, the program's long-standing success has more to do with Hungarian audiences' already existing familiarity with the genre of political satire and comedy. *Heti hetes* owes much of its spirit to the flourishing satirical sensibility of late socialism. However, it also shows a deep historical continuity with the older, national and regional tradition of political cabaret, discussed in the previous chapter. This legacy compels a more subtle analysis, which foregrounds the crucial importance of different national contexts on the formation and circulation of satirical humor. At the same time, *Heti hetes* also bears the effects of profound postsocialist media change in the past two decades, which makes it an illustrative example of the historical transition and convergence between socialist and capitalist political satire.

One feature that distinguishes the national context is that, in late socialist Hungary, satire was not only tolerated but had also come to function as the default mode in which to reference the socialist system in public discourse. The more of socialism's weaknesses satirists were allowed to point out, the less it all mattered. Increasing freedom of expression went along with satire's decreasing subversive edge. Perhaps this state of ambivalence is where the parallel with contemporary, global political TV satire is most noticeable. By the mid-1980s, political satire had descended into self-serving "joking around" for the most part. This was also an indication that the political and economic transition toward capitalism had been well underway in late socialist Hungary. Paradoxically, the era associated with the height of political humor in the region was simultaneously assessed by Hungarian critics of the 1980s as a state of decline and irrelevance.[18] *Heti hetes*, although a product of a much more diversified television landscape, carries the sense of ambivalence from late socialism into neoliberal capitalism, highlighting significant analogies between the two.

Boyer and Yurchak claim that the key to the analogy between the ideological contexts of late socialism and "late liberalism" is the highly monopolized conditions of discourse production in both cases.[19] The monopolization of media production, the formalization of political discourse within the news media through party, state, and corporate talking points and political theater, the increasing emphasis on modes of performance across media outlets at the expense of substantive and critical analysis or even an attempt at factuality are not mere coincidental resemblances between late socialist and late capitalist conditions. It is precisely the collapse of communism and the disappearance of the ideological threat that had propped up the self-righteousness of capitalist media during the Cold War and that in turn led to the erosion of public trust in the news. In the past two decades, late capitalist media, diplomacy, and trade have had to justify themselves through self-persuasive, repetitive references to the freedoms guaranteed by the holy market, including personal liberties and the self-explanatory "Western lifestyle," which is often collapsed into human life and democracy.[20] The loss of an absolute ideological enemy such as the Soviet Empire has created a nonrelational, universal mantra, a kind of dogma not unlike the Marxist-Leninist tenets obsessively repeated by socialist propaganda. Within the United States, this increasingly self-referential, self-justifying, performative discourse became absurd in the face of the grim realities of corporate wars and deepening economic crisis during the Bush years. Political satire has only voiced and amplified the metacommentary generated by the gap of absurdity that has opened up between rhetoric and reality.

What follows is that the analogy between the two situations that have legitimated eerily similar forms of satirical discourse is necessary to explore in order to draw up the *global* historical trajectory of contemporary television satire. Conversely, rather than a new phenomenon transplanted into postsocialism by victorious capitalism, a program such as *Heti hetes* is a linchpin between late socialist and late capitalist forms of political satire.

Late Socialist-Postsocialist Political Satire and *Heti Hetes*

György Ónodi, the creator of *Heti hetes*, said in a recent video interview: "They tried to make the same program in Poland, but canceled it after 4 episodes. This is a Hungarian program; it's Hungarian political cabaret. The way the *chanson* is French, this kind of political cabaret is ours."[21] The German show that inspired Ónodi and his team, *Sieben Tage, sieben Köpfe*, ran on RTL on Friday nights from 1996 to 2005. The program featured presenter Jochen Busse, five permanent celebrities, and one revolving guest, typically a comedian. The show was eventually canceled due to low ratings when it transpired that a team of writers produced the jokes to be delivered by the celebrities, as is also customary with American comedy programs. *Heti hetes*, however, has received consistently high ratings in Hungary since it was launched in September 1999. In 2001 it earned the Kamera Hungaria audience award in the "Most Popular TV Show" category. It has remained among the twenty-five most popular Hungarian programs and earned an audience share of 32 to 35 percent.[22] This has been the case despite its late starting time of 9:50 PM on Sunday and the fact that RTL's rival channel, TV2, has made targeted efforts to lure viewers away from the program in the same time slot.[23]

No one could accuse the show of being overly scripted, which is one important reason for its endurance. Its ad lib quality was evident when original host Jenő Csiszár began the very first program with an unwieldy sentence punctuated by awkward pauses, which he eventually brought to a close by declaring that he was not sure what exactly would happen on the new show. One of the celebrity guests interrupted the cringe-worthy silence: "It seems that we'll mostly be embarrassing ourselves." This opened the floodgate of funny banter that has since marked the program's dynamic.

Permanent *Hetes* member János Gálvölgyi speculated about the show's longevity in an interview: "The key to its success, I think, if we remove all the forced explanations, is that people are simply interested in the seven guys who sit there; they are interested in what these guys have to say about the world."[24] Audience responses, especially in online discussions, also suggest that loyalty to the show is mostly due to the long-standing popularity of its guests. Besides the basic requirement of wit, most of the seven participants combine respectable status as public personalities with distinguished careers in some form of public performance, which, in some cases, go back to the beginning of socialist television. Gálvölgyi himself is the best example. He was launched to fame as a comedian on the 1968 national television talent show *Ki Mit Tud* (Who knows what), a lavish annual event. He has been a fixture of TV comedy ever since, while also sustaining a career as a stage actor. His own humorous weekly half-hour television show, *The Gálvölgyi Show*, has been on the air since 1991, first on the national broadcaster MTV and since 1998 on RTL Klub. Along with three other permanent *Hetes* members, he was a frequent guest on the radio program *Rádiókabaré KFT*, whose regular segment "A hónap hírei" (News of the month) inspired *Heti hetes*.

Similar to Gálvölgyi, all permanent members and most of the revolving guests on the show represent the most visible segment of the witty intellectual elite. In a small nation-state such as Hungary, such an elite is intimately connected. Because this small group is constantly in the public eye, they also have an unprecedented degree of intimacy with their national audience, which solidified in the previous era of precarious political comedy. This has major consequences that are peculiar to the program and its national context: one is that the guests can afford to behave like family members or old friends with a lot of shared history. Their interaction involves constant teasing and personal digressions. For instance, the late Imre Bajor was regularly reminded of his baldness and Tivadar Farkasházy of his speech impediment. These digressions often take up much of the airtime and become the main attraction of the show, to the extent that it is hard for the host to reel in the jokes or even to get through reading the brief news articles that elicit the conversation.

The viewer accustomed to the strict professionalism of American programming would be stunned by the loose structure and personal tone of *Hetes*. But it is precisely this leisurely spontaneity and intimacy of the discussion that makes the audience connect with the seven. On the January 31, 2011, program, they had technical difficulties with the microphones. While the show is taped on Fridays following a Thursday night meeting among the guests, the final broadcast of this particular edition included the bit where the technician came in to fix the microphones, while the guests involved him in joking conversation. On the January 2, 2011, program, the host, László Jáksó, paused during his own monologue to turn to someone in the studio audience who was apparently snacking on chips from a loud, rattling bag. Far from being irritated by the incident, Jáksó noted it was "cute" that viewers felt comfortable enough to snack and asked them to share their food with the panel members. This, in turn, launched a domino of subsequent jokes.

There is another side to the familiarity that gives the show its distinctive character among the many other comedic programs that have sprung up since the end of socialism. In online discussions, viewers often criticize the fact that most of the seven are well over fifty, unattractive, and repetitive.[25] In response, the producers have made efforts to refresh the panel by including younger faces, most notably by adding András Hajós as a permanent panelist in 2004, the same year that the original host, Csiszár, was replaced by Jáksó. Hajós, a musician-comedian in his mid-forties, had established himself as the lead singer of a rock band and became one of the most familiar television personalities, having hosted several of his own talk shows, including one on the Hungarian Comedy Central.[26]

The single woman among the core panelists is Judit Hernády, a popular actress-singer who has been a regular contributor to television comedy since the 1970s. Like Gálvölgyi, she has also garnered a reputation as a serious stage actress. Her presence sets in relief the profound masculinity of the public sphere as it manifests itself on television. The other six guests embody certain comedic character functions, which no doubt originate in early cabaret: the naive one, the smartypants, the clown, the vulgar type, the sophisticated cosmopolitan, or the tolerant one. Hernády is first and foremost "the woman." As the only woman, she diligently assumes responsibility for representing all women: when the discussion becomes explicitly sexist, she comments from "the" female perspective. It is her "natural" lot and duty to talk about the personal sphere of the nuclear family. She is the only one on the panel who willingly and often speaks about herself as a parent, evoking her daughter so frequently that she is almost a virtual character on the show.

At the same time, as a respectable artist, she has also earned the right to sit at the boys' table. It is not a coincidence that she is not a stereotypically attractive woman but someone known for her resonant, deep voice and tall, masculine stature. But she is also put in a strange double position. Often the conversation is so testosterone-filled (compared with the much more self-censored sexism of U.S. television) that she has no choice but to engage in vulgarity herself—commenting on her own breasts, vagina, or sex life in a self-objectifying manner. Given Hernády's honorary status as one of the boys, it is not very surprising that Gálvölgyi talks in the interview above about "the seven guys" on the show,[27] or that Farkasházy declares about his copanelists in another interview: "This is my second family. I love these boys."[28]

This complete blindness to the sexism embedded in the fabric of the show is another constitutive feature of the national intimacy within the expanded national family embodied by the seven. While the producers have experimented with other female guests, few of them have been as successful as Hernády at mediating between the two roles (of "the woman" and of "one of the boys"). The episode in which young Roma singer Ibolya Oláh was a guest has gone down in *Hetes* history as a massive flop, with most reviews blaming Oláh for "freezing up." In fact, as a young Roma woman from a small town, she was at several degrees of remove from the old, privileged, white men of the Budapest artist world, whose "national" discourse suddenly revealed itself to be normative, elitist, white, and misogynistic. A similar episode featured thirty-something visual artist Kriszta Nagy Tereskova as a guest on the January 2, 2011, program. Tereskova, who borrowed her artist's name from the first female astronaut, assumes a public persona that could be described as critical postfeminism: she performs to excessive, ironic perfection the social norms of behavior imposed on women. In the show's tight brotherly environment (and in Hernády's absence that week), she had little opportunity to assert herself, but toward the end of the program she pointed out how cruelly the men had laughed at her. She reached out to Hajós, the youngest and presumably most enlightened of the panelists. In response, Hajós explained to her in a painfully patronizing manner that the program was not a good place for "feminist and ecohysterical" views and proceeded to call her "kitten." Despite this dismissal, this was still a rare moment of self-reflection, when the show's, and by expansion national political comedy's, underlying gendered rules were forced into articulation.

An area where the program clearly functions as a bridge between late socialist and contemporary global satire is in its cautious approach to politics. Producer Ónodi takes pains in interviews to reiterate the political neutrality of the program and defend it from accusations of leaning to the left. This tends to come through in a "protesting too much" fashion not unlike Jon Stewart's similar claims to evenhandedness.[29] Ultimately, however, even the explicitly political discussions tend to be somewhat toothless. Ónodi emphasizes that RTL Klub imposes no censorship on the show, but that it would be unnecessary anyway because he exercises self-censorship to decide what is appropriate.[30] This echoes the words of virtually all TV professionals I interviewed about their work during late socialism.

Endre Aczél, chief editor of the nightly news program *The Week* in the late 1980s, told me that "people had grown up in self-censorship."[31] The seasoned panelists of *The Weekly Seven* are also well versed in self-censorship, which, in the era of alleged free speech, is applied in two main areas: on the one hand, toward the corporate ship RTL Klub, beholden to ratings and profit, and invested in keeping its viewership as broad as possible in a small country that cannot afford niche programming. On the other hand, the participants are mindful of party politics. Given the context of an intimate familiar dynamic within the nation, the political leadership potentially swings widely every four years after state elections, rewriting laws and setting new directions for the future. Much like under socialism, media personalities need to be cautious not to offend any major political players if they want to survive these swings. Moreover, even though RTL Klub is a commercial channel, it is still subject to state regulation, which has recently tightened under the right-wing FIDESZ government's 2010 media law, an attempt to recentralize control over the media and curtail freedom of expression, which has caused an international uproar. On the show, discussion of the law and other controversial steps taken by the FIDESZ government have been couched in subtle satire and a form of doublespeak that evokes the rhetoric of the 1970s and 1980s.

An additional, historically specific aspect of the panelists' self-censorship is the deep-rooted connection between Jewishness and oppositional humor, which reaches back to early twentieth-century stage cabaret. While communism put a lid on issues of Jewishness in order to suppress an honest reckoning of Hungary's shameful Nazi alliance and active contribution to the Holocaust, the recent surge of the radical right, enabled by the Internet and local television stations such as Echo TV, has mobilized anti-Semitism among other ethnophobic-nationalist discourses in a frightening way, often lashing out at the "communist-Jewish-unpatriotic" messages spread by *The Weekly Seven*. Understandably, the panelists themselves stay clear of identifying themselves as Jews both on and off the air, in a notable difference from American Jewish comedians such as Jerry Seinfeld, Larry David, or Jon Stewart.

The Global Lessons of Late Socialist Satire

The Murdoch empire was momentarily shaken by the British phone hacking scandal that came to light in July 2011. If one needed any more justification for the parallel between the political circumstances that gave rise to satire news in late socialism and contemporary capitalism, this was certainly it. While "empire" has mostly been used metaphorically to describe News Corporation, the fact that Murdoch and his trusted executives (most notably his heir, James) had kept much of the celebrity world under secret surveillance, that they had spent massive sums of money keeping people silent about this, and that they had collaborated with the police and most likely the government, draws up even formerly unsuspected similarities with the late Soviet empire's media operations. And the international reach of corporate media power is even more extensive than that of the Kremlin within the Soviet empire.

The analogy that emerges here between late socialist and late capitalist forms of political communication shifts standard explanations of the recent popularity of political satire in the United States. Television satire is more than an effect of technological change, a marginalized outlet for leftist liberals, or a cynical corporate forum that perpetuates what it criticizes. It has an unarticulated but formative global dimension: political television is one of the terrains where the United States' changing position in the world is continually assessed. The proliferation of satire is a response to the increase in self-referential absurdity into which much political discourse has devolved since the end of the Cold War, which has only intensified since September 11, 2001. In the absence of a global antagonist, U.S. political and news media discourses have had to ground themselves in tautologies that write off socialism as a failure and confirm, through incessant repetition, that neoliberal democracy is the single guarantor of that mysterious, self-explanatory condition, "freedom." This is a mechanism not unlike socialist propaganda's incessant, self-justifying posing as the guarantor of unity, solidarity, equality, and, yes, freedom. As Serra Tinic reminds us, the growing voice of satire news and political comedy, while always grounded in specific sociohistorical contexts, inevitably leads us to this larger geopolitical situation, with its unexpected historical parallels.[32] It might even lead us to discover some unintended ethnocentrism within media studies' stubborn U.S. or Western-centrism and encourage us to revisit socialist media in more depth for its potential lessons.

AFTERWORD

Afterward

In the introduction to this book I proposed to discuss socialism and television as windows into each other. When one makes such ambitious claims at the beginning of a large research project, they are often understood to be at least somewhat intuitive and speculative. My original research agenda, which certainly had intuitive roots, grew out of a twofold dissatisfaction.

Like many other postsocialist subjects, I was first puzzled by and then became increasingly frustrated with the way the history of socialism was dismissed and generally forgotten in the victorious post–Cold War language of democracy and the free market. This forgetting not only delegitimized the memories of those whose identities were shaped under a socialist system but also severely reduced the flexibility around the interpretive frameworks that would make sense of the postsocialist transformations following 1989. To put it bluntly, one's choices have been limited to denouncing socialism and embracing the principles of entrepreneurial democracy or wallowing in nostalgia for a world system that proved itself unviable. For someone like me, whose coming-of-age coincided with the end of the Cold War and who has had firsthand experience with both socialist authoritarian and free-market capitalist societies, these choices seemed severely inadequate. They oversimplified socialism and left little room for critiquing market-based democracies, something that became even more frustrating after September 11, 2001, and the global economic recession of 2008.

At the same time, I have experienced a more local dissatisfaction with researching and teaching global media, particularly television. It seemed that the lack of resources to teach television in a truly transnational historical and theoretical context was not simply due to the Anglo-American trajectory of the field and the scarcity of adaptable research material but also to a motivated disinterest in other histories. In the case of omitting the entire existence of socialist TV, this did not appear unrelated to the dismissal of socialism as a whole as a failed experiment that could not have produced anything other than propaganda. By contrast, television became increasingly crystallized for me as precisely the area from which a different view of socialism can be extracted; and my intuition said that socialism offered vantage points from which some of the fundamental tenets of TV studies would need to be revised.

When I proposed television and socialism as windows, however, I had not anticipated how much I would learn from this crossover. This is a sorry excuse for ending up with twelve chapters—instead of the originally planned eight—but hopefully it goes some way toward justifying the relevance of this work beyond my own growing fascination. Let me recap, as succinctly as I can, the most important insights I have gleaned in the course of researching, interviewing, browsing archives, and writing about the encounter between television and socialism.

The history of socialist TV is an integral part of global television history. Socialist TV developed in synchronicity with European television from interwar experimental broadcasts through a postwar relaunch in the 1950s, to adopting the principles of educational-nationalistic broadcasting from European public service media and gradually shifting to an entertainment-focused model by the 1970s of the political thaw. Throughout this history, socialist television participated in European media flows in terms of technological, personnel, and program exchanges, joint broadcasts, and shared broadcast signals. Socialist TV's operation poses a fundamental challenge to the idea of an intractable, hierarchical Cold War divide between East and West.

Socialist TV in Eastern Europe also shows regional features, which carry even more distinct, national specificities. In fact, grasping how socialist and postsocialist TV have functioned demands a framework equally attuned to the national, regional, European, and global scales. The regional and national characteristics owe a great deal to local television industries' negotiation between the Soviet-type socialism to which they were officially beholden and the socialism of European democracies to which they had culturally belonged and wished to return.

Every genre category I examine in the book shows evidence of this multiscale negotiation. Educational-realistic programming does so most prominently as it was privileged by both Soviet and Western European socialisms. As I show through the five chapters of part I that track the pre-1989 development of these genres, while the agitational-propagandistic excess and class consciousness of such programming certainly fulfilled Soviet-type socialist-realist educational requirements, viewers' demand quickly transformed television's offerings in more entertaining, docufictional, competitive, and participatory directions across public affairs and talk shows, quiz and game shows, and crime-based programming, much as it did elsewhere in Europe. These negotiations and the hybrid programs they bore are a crucial and so far neglected part of the prehistory of reality programming, and they issue significant challenges to the ideological and economic arguments about reality formats' synergy with contemporary neoliberalism.

Socialist TV's history is not restricted to the three decades between the late 1950s and late 1980s. Its infrastructures, cultural sensibilities, program formats, and often even participants were inherited from prewar structures and carried the cultural legacies of even older phenomena sedimented into national, regional, and imperial histories. As I show in part IV, forms of socialist comedy are indebted to both the satirical-political and the lighter, entertaining forms of prewar European cabaret. In another example I discuss in part II, socialist adventure drama, the first genre to inspire domestic scripted production, revolved around characters who played key roles at pivotal moments of regional and imperial histories and whose significance was legitimated by both folk culture and high cultural, literary production. Socialist TV thus conjures up a framework that takes into joint account the histories of intra-European imperialism and nationalism, a perspective that is indispensable for making sense of the renewed imperial divisions in contemporary Europe in the wake of the European Union's expansion and the recent crisis of the Eurozone.

Socialism and socialist TV did not expire in 1989. Contemporary reality programming, which has flooded cash-deprived postsocialist TV industries, inevitably dialogues with socialist docufictional programming, a dialogue that foregrounds both the latter's relative strengths (its nonexploitative, democratizing, educational intention) and its omissions (its motivated neglect of minorities on the margins of the normatively white, masculine nation). As I also explain, forms of late socialist satire not only resonated with but also anticipated the satirical mode that has taken over news reporting worldwide since the end of the Cold War. In a similar vein, socialist superwomen who "did it all" as the anchors of domestic drama serials of the 1970s and 1980s prepared for and issued an early critique of the postfeminist politics often associated with contemporary global quality drama.

Perhaps most surprisingly, socialist TV foregrounds the extent to which socialism was embedded in a competitive structure, which was politically motivated by the Cold War contest between the two superpowers and adapted market-based economic principles for political purposes. In the chapter on socialist commercials, I discuss how the most liberalized socialist televisions of Yugoslavia and Hungary inherited advertising structures from the prewar era and sustained their own marketing activities throughout the period. Socialist commercials remain testimonies to the complexities of socialist television and have been afforded a great deal of nostalgic affection since the end of the Cold War. As I found and elaborate in part II on genres of history, nostalgia itself is a much more complicated set of phenomena and structure of feeling than the stereotyped, sad longing for a time that cannot and should not be recovered. Postsocialist nostalgia evokes the entire history of European nationalisms, and its contemporary operations reveal renewed investment in political and economic divides between East and West.

If I had not had to force myself to stop writing, the next part of the book would linger on how postsocialist television and other media revisit and rework the legacy of socialism and help us understand its continuing relevance as a political and economic resource. Because TV under socialism is still such an uncharted territory with so many surprises, it has claimed much of the book and reduced discussions of postsocialist continuities to one chapter in each of the four parts.

If I were to embark on a follow-up book to *TV Socialism*, it would be about the legacy of socialist TV worldwide. Eastern Europe is just a piece of the Soviet Empire, and a fraction of the world system that embraced socialist ideologies during the Cold War. However, this follow-up project would have to be a collective venture and a truly global collaboration. When it materializes, it will have an enormous impact on our understanding of socialism, television, and the Cold War and its aftermath. I can only hope that *TV Socialism* has contributed somewhat to the foundations of this work.

NOTES

Introduction

1. Heather Gumbert, *Envisioning Socialism: Television and the Cold War in the German Democratic Republic* (Ann Arbor: University of Michigan Press, 2014), 4.
2. Sabina Mihelj, "Understanding Socialist Television: Concepts, Objects, Methods," *VIEW: Journal of European Television History and Culture* 3, no. 5 (2014): 16.
3. Mihelj, "Understanding Socialist Television," 7–16.
4. Joe Weisberg, the creator of the series and a former CIA agent, said in an interview that he was less interested in the spy story than in the marriage in the center of the narrative. "Espionage adds drama and raises the stakes, but the thing people are going to care about is this couple and whether or not they make it. We already know how the Cold War ends. Nobody knows how this marriage will end. Plus, deep down I'm more interested in marriage than espionage." In other words, as he explains, the Cold War setting was merely a way to distinguish his story from other successful drama series about spying set in the contemporary environment of the war on terror, most notably Showtime's Homeland. This is why, Weisberg explains, Cold War iconography shows up in a campy, nostalgic fashion, as in the title sequence's juxtaposition of Cossack dancing and Jazzercise, and Karl Marx's head superimposed on that of Santa Claus. See Katie Arnold-Ratliff, "Spy

vs. Spy: A Q&A with *The Americans* Creator Joe Weisberg," *Time*, March 12, 2013, http://entertainment.time.com/2013/03/12/spy-vs-spy-a-qa-with-the-americans-creator-joe-weisberg/.
5. See also Mihelj, "Understanding Socialist Television."
6. Sari Autio-Sarasmo and Katalin Miklóssy, "Introduction: The Cold War from a New Perspective," in *Reassessing Cold War Europe*, eds. Sari Autio-Sarasmo and Katalin Miklóssy (New York: Routledge, 2011), 1–2.
7. See, for instance, Paulina Bren and Mary Neuburger, eds., *Communism Unwrapped: Consumption in Cold War Eastern Europe* (Oxford: Oxford University Press, 2012); David Crowley and Susan E. Reid, eds., *Pleasures in Socialism: Leisure and Luxury in the Eastern Bloc* (Evanston, IL: Northwestern University Press, 2010); Gumbert, *Envisioning Socialism*; Susan Gal and Gail Kligman, *Reproducing Gender: Politics, Publics and Everyday Life after Socialism* (Princeton, NJ: Princeton University Press, 2000); Shana Penn and Jill Massino, eds., *Gender Politics and Everyday Life in State Socialist East and Central Europe* (New York: Palgrave Macmillan, 2009).
8. Anikó Imre, "Postcolonial Media Studies in Postsocialist Europe," *Boundary 2* 41, no. 1 (Spring 2014): 113–134.
9. See Anikó Imre, Timothy Havens, and Katalin Lustyik, eds., *Popular Television in Eastern Europe During and Since Socialism* (New York: Routledge, 2013). The European (Post)Socialist Television History Network and its accompanying project "Television Histories in (Post)Socialist Europe" were launched in September 2013 with the goal to offer an international collaborative platform for scholars working on television histories in Eastern Europe. The network was founded by Daniela Mustata with Anikó Imre, Ferenc Hammer, Irena Reifová, and Lars Lundgren. Other recent initiatives include Sabina Mihelj's Leverhulme-funded project "Screening Socialism" and the "Television in Europe beyond the Iron Curtain" conference at the Friedrich-Alexander-Universität Erlangen-Nürnberg in December 2013. Other influential volumes, used as crucial reference points throughout this book, are Paulina Bren, *The Greengrocer and His TV: The Culture of Communism after the 1968 Prague Spring* (Ithaca, NY: Cornell University Press, 2010), on late socialist Czech television fiction; Kristin Roth-Ey, *Moscow Prime Time: How the Soviet Union Built the Media Empire That Lost the Cultural Cold War* (Ithaca, NY: Cornell University Press, 2011); Christine Evans's forthcoming book *Between Truth and Time: A History of Soviet Central Television*; Jan Čulik, ed., *National Mythologies in Central European TV Series: How J.R. Won the Cold War* (Eastbourne: Sussex Academic Press, 2013); and a special issue of *Historical Journal of Film, Radio and Television* (24, no. 3 [2014]) dedicated to television in the former GDR.
10. See Daniela Mustata, "Editorial," *VIEW: Journal of European Television History and Culture* 3, no. 5 (2014): 1–6, http://journal.euscreen.eu/index.php/view.
11. Sabina Mihelj, "The Politics of Privatization: Television Entertainment and the Yugoslav Sixties," in *The Socialist Sixties: Crossing Borders in the Second*

World, eds. Anne Gorsuch and Diane Koenker (Bloomington: Indiana University Press, 2013), 251–267.
12. Roth-Ey, *Moscow Prime Time*, 179.
13. Katalin Palyik, interview by Anikó Imre, December 2012. Katalin Palyik is an archivist at the National Audiovisual Archives (NAVA) in Budapest.
14. Document XXVI-A-9, Box 30. MTV documents, Hungarian National Document Archives.
15. Document XXVI-A-9.
16. Anikó Imre, "National History and Cross-National Television Edutainment," *Journal of Popular Film and Television* 40, no. 3 (Fall 2012): 119–130.
17. See Dominic Boyer and Alexei Yurchak, "Postsocialist Studies, Cultures of Parody and American Stiob," *Anthropology News*, November 2008, 9–10.
18. Roth-Ey, *Moscow Prime Time*, 220.
19. Roth-Ey, *Moscow Prime Time*, 279.
20. István Vágó, Endre Aczél, Katalin Szegvári, László Szabó, and Péter Dunavölgyi, interviews by Anikó Imre, Budapest, December 2012 and December 2013.
21. Ib Bondebjerg, Tomasz Goban-Klas, Michele Hilmes, Daniela Mustata, Helle Strandgaard-Jensen, Isabelle Veyrat-Masson, and Susanne Vollberg, "American Television: Point of Reference or European Nightmare?," in *A European Television History*, eds. J. Bignell and A. Fickers (New York: Blackwell, 2008), 154–183, 177–181.
22. Rüdiger Steinmetz and Reinhold Viehoff, "The Program History of Genres of Entertainment on GDR Television," *Historical Journal of Film, Radio and Television* 24, no. 3 (2004): 320.
23. Roth-Ey, *Moscow Prime Time*, 196.
24. Roth-Ey, *Moscow Prime Time*, 225.
25. István Vágó, Endre Aczél, Katalin Szegvári, László Szabó, Péter Dunavölgyi, interviews by Anikó Imre.
26. Roth-Ey, *Moscow Prime Time*, 268.
27. Roth-Ey, *Moscow Prime Time*, 268.
28. Mats Björkin and Juan Francisco Gutierrez Lozano, "European Television Audiences: Localising the Viewers," in *A European Television History*, eds. J. Bignell and A. Fickers (New York: Blackwell, 2008), 215.
29. See also Sabina Mihelj's argument against "methodological nationalism" in her "Understanding Socialist Television."
30. Sylwia Szostak, "Poland's Return to Europe: Polish Terrestrial Broadcasters and TV Fiction," *Journal of European Television History and Culture* 1, no. 2 (2012): 80.
31. Charlotte Brunsdon, "Is Television Studies History?" *Cinema Journal* 47, no. 3 (Spring 2008): 129.
32. This occurred in 1936 in Hungary and 1937 in Poland.
33. Péter Dunavölgyi, "Televízió történet Magyarországon," [The history of Hungarian television], http://dunavolgyipeter.hu/televizio_tortenet/a_magyar

_televiziozas_tortenete_az_1950-as_evekben/1957. This history, collected and maintained by television historian Péter Dunavölgyi, and aggregated at the site http://dunavolgyipeter.hu/televizio_tortenet, accounts for each year of Hungarian Television's history during socialism, starting with 1956 and currently covering events up to 1982. In subsequent notes, this work will be cited in abbreviated form as "Dunavölgyi, 1957."

34. Knut Hickethier, "Early TV: Imagining and Realising Television," in *A European Television History*, eds. J. Bignell and A. Fickers (New York: Blackwell, 2008), 55–78.
35. Dunavölgyi, "1965."
36. Marusa Pusnik and Gregor Starc, "An Entertaining (R)evolution: The Rise of Television in Socialist Slovenia," *Media Culture and Society* 30, no. 6 (2008): 777–793.
37. Horace Newcomb, ed., *Encyclopedia of Television* (London: Routledge, 2004), 640.
38. Daniela Mustata, "Television in the Age of (Post)Communism," in *Popular Television in Eastern Europe During and Since Socialism*, eds. Anikó Imre, Timothy Havens, and Katalin Lustyik (New York: Routledge, 2013), 47–64.
39. For instance, to conform to these directives, in 1968 Hungarian Television (MTV) divided its programming among different departments this way: art films and programs that promoted cultural appreciation made up 30 percent of all programs; 9 percent of broadcast time went to literary and dramatic programming; news programs, responsible for political agitation, accounted for 29 percent; youth and children's programming made up 11.5 percent; and informational programming such as nature documentaries took up 2.5 percent. In addition, a daily morning programming block called "School Television" made up 11 percent. With the addition of Friday, a sixth day of weekly programming, that year (Monday remained a nonbroadcast day devoted to work), programs were reorganized so that each weekday had a distinct educational profile. Entertainment programs were concentrated on the weekend. See Edina Horváth, "A magyar televízió müsorpolitikája—1968," Hungarian Television (MTV) Archives, http://www.tvarchivum.hu/?id=279930.
40. Idrit Idrizi, "Das magische Gerät: Die Bedeutung des Fernsehers im isolierten Albanien und für die Erforschung des albanischen Kommunismus" (paper presented at the conference "Television in Europe beyond the Iron Curtain—National and Transnational Perspectives since the 1950s," Friedrich-Alexander-Universität Erlangen-Nürnberg, December 5–7, 2013). See also Paolo Carelli, "Italianization Accomplished: Forms and Structures of Albanian Television's Dependency on Italian Media and Culture," *VIEW: Journal of European Television History and Culture* 3, no. 5 (2014): 68–78.
41. Mustata, "Television in the Age of (Post)Communism," 47–64.
42. Annemarie Sorescu-Marinkovic, "We Didn't Have Anything, They Had It All: Watching Yugoslav Television in Communist Romania" (paper presented at

the conference "Television in Europe beyond the Iron Curtain—National and Transnational Perspectives since the 1950s," Friedrich-Alexander-Universität Erlangen-Nürnberg, December 5–7, 2013).

43. Annika Lepp and Mervi Pantti, "Window to the West: Memories of Watching Finnish Television in Estonia during the Soviet Period," VIEW: Journal of European Television History and Culture 3, no. 2 (2012): 76–86.

44. Pusnik and Starc, "An Entertaining (R)evolution," 782–783.

45. Pusnik and Starc, "An Entertaining (R)evolution," 786.

46. Sabina Mihelj, keynote address (presented at the symposium "Television Histories in (Post)Socialist Europe," Stockholm, November 2013).

47. See Heather Gumbert, "Exploring Transnational Media Exchange in the 1960s," VIEW: Journal of European Television History and Culture 3, no. 5 (2014): 50–59; Thomas Beutelschmidt and Richard Oehmig, "Connected Enemies? Programming Transfer between East and West during the Cold War and the Example of East German Television," VIEW: Journal of European Television History and Culture 3, no. 5 (2014): 60–67.

48. J. Bignell and A. Fickers, "Introduction: Comparative European Perspectives on Television History," in A European Television History, eds. J. Bignell and A. Fickers (New York: Blackwell, 2008), 27.

49. Christina Adamou, Isabelle Gaillard, and Daniela Mustata, "Institutionalizing European Television: The Shaping of European Television Institutions and Infrastructures," in A European Television History, eds. J. Bignell and A. Fickers (New York: Blackwell, 2008), 91.

50. Adamou, Gaillard, and Mustata, "Institutionalizing European Television," 78–100.

51. Heidi Keinonen, "Early Commercial Television in Finland: Balancing between East and West," Media History 18, no. 2 (2012): 177–189.

52. J. Bignell and A. Fickers, "Conclusion: Reflections on Doing European Television History," in A European Television History, eds. J. Bignell and A. Fickers (New York: Blackwell, 2008), 229–256.

53. Adamou, Gaillard, and Mustata, "Institutionalizing European Television," 94.

54. Bignell and Fickers, "Conclusion," 235.

55. Keinonen, "Early Commercial Television in Finland," 177–189; Hickethier, "Early TV," 55–78.

56. See Adamou, Gaillard, and Mustata, "Institutionalizing European Television," 94; Jerome Bourdon, Juan Carlos Ibanez, Catherine Johnson, and Eggo Mueller, "Searching for an Identity for Television: Programmes, Genres, Formats," in A European Television History, eds. J. Bignell and A. Fickers (New York: Blackwell, 2008), 101–126.

57. Bignell and Fickers, "Conclusion," 233.

58. Bignell and Fickers, "Conclusion," 234.

59. Bignell and Fickers, "Introduction," 5.

60. Bignell and Fickers, "Conclusion," 235.

61. Hickethier, "Early TV," 75.

62. Bignell and Fickers, "Introduction," 24.
63. At the same time, commercial radio and the press were free to criticize the government, which ensured some pluralism of opinion. Adamou, Gaillard, and Mustata, "Institutionalizing European Television," 78–100.
64. Autio-Sarasmo and Miklóssy, "Introduction: The Cold War from a New Perspective," 1–2.
65. Bourdon et al., "Searching for an Identity for Television," 101–126.
66. See Mihelj, "Understanding Socialist Television."
67. Daphne Berdahl, "Good Bye, Lenin! Aufwiedersehen GDR: On the Social Life of Socialism," in *Post-Communist Nostalgia*, eds. Maria Todorova and Zsuzsa Gille (New York: Berghahn Books, 2012), 187.

Chapter 1. From Socialist Realism to Emotional Realism

1. Jerôme Bourdon, "Old and New Ghosts: Public Service Television and the Popular—A History," *European Journal of Cultural Studies* 7, no. 3 (2004): 284.
2. John Corner, "Presumption as Theory: 'Realism' in Television Studies," in his *Studying Media: Problems of Theory and Method* (Edinburgh: Edinburgh University Press, 1998), 68.
3. Corner, "Presumption as Theory," 70.
4. Kristin Roth-Ey, *Moscow Prime Time: How the Soviet Union Built the Media Empire That Lost the Cultural Cold War* (Ithaca, NY: Cornell University Press, 2011), 236.
5. Ferenc Pécsi, "Heti ötven órában." *Film Színház Muzsika* 1, January 4, 1969; Ferenc Pécsi, "The Television Broadcasting Policy" August 10, 1969. MSZMP APO 288f.22/1969/19.öe. Ag.350. Hungarian National Document Archives.
6. Miklós Jovánovics, "Pro and Contra Television," *Népszabadság*, September 27, 1970.
7. Tamás Szecskő, "Szórakoztatás—Műsorpolitika" [Entertainment—programming policy], *Rádió és TV Szemle* 71, no. 3 (1971): 9.
8. Szecskő, "Szórakoztatás—Műsorpolitika," 13–14.
9. Ferenc Pécsi, "Heti ötven órában," *Film Színház Muzsika*, January 4, 1969, 1.
10. For instance, Hungarian TV's annual awards, tellingly named "quality awards" (*nívódíj*), broke down like this in 1966: five went to makers of straightforward educational programs such as "School TV"; nine were awarded to makers of news and current affairs programs; and thirteen to actors for their work in poetry, literature, and theater productions. "A Rádió és televízió új nívódíjasai," *Rádió és Televízió Újság* 28 (1966).
11. Corner, "Presumption as Theory," 73.
12. See Bjørn Sørenssen, "The Polish Black Series Documentary and the British Free Cinema Movement," in *A Companion to Eastern European Cinemas*, ed. Anikó Imre (New York: Wiley-Blackwell, 2012), 183–200; John Cunningham, "Documentary and Industrial Decline in Hungary: The 'Ózd Series' of Tamás

Almási," in *A Companion to Eastern European Cinemas*, ed. Aniko Imre (New York: Wiley-Blackwell, 2012), 311–324.
13. Corner, "Presumption as Theory," 75.
14. Christine Evans, "The 'Soviet Way of Life' as Way of Feeling: Emotion and Influence on Soviet Central Television in the Brezhnev Era," forthcoming, *Cahiers du Monde Russe* 56/2–3 (2015).
15. Evans, "The 'Soviet Way of Life' as Way of Feeling."
16. Evans, "The 'Soviet Way of Life' as Way of Feeling."
17. Heather Gumbert, *Envisioning Socialism: Television and the Cold War in the German Democratic Republic* (Ann Arbor: University of Michigan Press, 2014), 149.
18. Gumbert, *Envisioning Socialism*, 150.
19. Paulina Bren, *The Greengrocer and His TV: The Culture of Communism after the 1968 Prague Spring* (Ithaca, NY: Cornell University Press, 2010), 207.
20. John Ellis, "The Performance on Television of Sincerely Felt Emotion," *Annals of the American Academy of Political and Social Science* 625 (September 2009): 104.
21. Ellis, "The Performance on Television of Sincerely Felt Emotion," 109.
22. Ellis, "The Performance on Television of Sincerely Felt Emotion," 105.
23. Interestingly, by the 1990s, irony and sarcasm became the default modes of enjoying television and politics on a global scale. I argue in chapters 11 and 12 that the world had caught up with late socialism's ironic structure of feeling.
24. Ellis, "The Performance on Television of Sincerely Felt Emotion," 111.
25. Laurie Ouellette and James Hay, *Better Living through Reality TV: Television and Post-Welfare Citizenship* (Hoboken, NJ: Wiley-Blackwell, 2008), 3.
26. Ouellette and Hay, *Better Living through Reality TV*, 3.
27. Ouellette and Hay, *Better Living through Reality TV*, 6.

Chapter 2. Tele-education

1. Elemér Hankiss, "Jegyzetek az amerikai és a magyar TV hatásmechanizmusáról: A cselekvő és merengő tévé," *Filmvilág* 8 (1982): 54–57.
2. Heather Gumbert, *Envisioning Socialism: Television and the Cold War in the German Democratic Republic* (Ann Arbor: University of Michigan Press, 2014), 2.
3. Markus Schubert and Hans-Joerg Stiehler, "A Program Structure Analysis of East German Television, 1968–74," *Historical Journal of Film, Radio and Television* 24, no. 2 (2004): 347.
4. Schubert and Stiehler, "A Program Structure Analysis of East German Television," 345.
5. Tadeusz Pikulski, *Prywatna historia telewizji publicznej* (Warsaw: Muza SA, 2002), 41.

6. Árpád Thiery, "Interview with Ferenc Pécsi, Vice President of Hungarian TV and Radio," *Népszava*, January 3, 1972.
7. Dunavölgyi, "1972."
8. Dunavölgyi, "1972."
9. Gumbert, *Envisioning Socialism*, 16.
10. A. Fickers and C. Bignell, "Introduction: Comparative European Perspectives on Television History," in *A European Television History*, eds. J. Bignell and A. Fickers (New York: Blackwell, 2008), 24.
11. Ira Wagman, "Tele-clubs and European Television History beyond the Screen," *VIEW: Journal of European Television History and Culture* 1, no. 2 (2012): 118.
12. Wagman, "Tele-clubs and European Television History beyond the Screen," 123.
13. Wagman, "Tele-clubs and European Television History beyond the Screen," 125.
14. Huszár, Tiborné, "10 éves az iskolarádió," *Rádió és TV Szemle* 2 (1973).
15. Dunavölgyi, "1959."
16. "A TV-ben hallottuk," *Rádió és Televízió Újság* 33 (1961).
17. Proposal prepared on June 28, 1962, by István Tömpe and Jenő Lugossy for the Agitation and Propaganda Committee of the Hungarian Socialist Workers' Party's Central Committee on "The Systematic Introduction of Television and Radio into Primary and Secondary Education," MOL-288f22/10 öe. MSZMP KB Agit. prop. oszt., Hungarian National Document Archives.
18. Endre Kelemen, "Mozaikok az Iskolatelevízió történetéből," *Rádió és TV Szemle* 2 (1974): 18–31.
19. See Gábor Szenes's article on School TV, *Népszabadság*, March 6, 1970.
20. György Csepeli, "Rádiónk és televíziónk közművelődési szemlélete és gyakorlata," *Rádió és TV Szemle* 6, no. 3 (1973): 5–16. This is an interview with MTV programming director György Sándor.
21. Proposal by István Tömpe and Jenő Lugossy.
22. Pikulski, *Prywatna historia telewizji publicznej*, 95. Thanks to Maria Zalewska for the translation.
23. Andrzej Kozieł, *Za chwilę dalszy ciąg programu: Telewizja Polska czterech dekad 1952–1989* (Warsaw: Oficyna Wydawnicza Aspra-Jr, 2003), 162–163.
24. Daniela Mustata, "The Power of Television: Including the Historicizing of the Live Romanian Revolution" (PhD diss., Utrecht University, 2011).
25. The Prix Jeunesse International 1970, held in Munich, awarded the main prize in the "Youth" category to an episode called "Love" in Hungarian School TV's "Parents, Children Together" series (script Katalin Benedek, director Ilona Katkics). See Dunavölgyi, "1970"; Árpád Halasi, "Iskolatelevízió," *Magyar Ifjúság*, March 18, 1967.
26. Representative Ernő Mihályfi's speech. See *Országgyűlési Napló*, Session 21, January 27, 1966.

27. Kelemen, "Mozaikok az Iskolatelevízió történetéből," 20.
28. Mustata, "The Power of Television."
29. Pikulski, *Prywatna historia telewizji publicznej*, 95–96.
30. The discussion featured Professors Elemér Sas, Lajos Jánossy, and Péter Varga. See Dunavölgyi, "1966."
31. Criticism by József Bényi in *Hajdú-Bihari Napló*, 1967. See Dunavölgyi, "1967."
32. Much like contemporary reality programs, many of the educational series were fairly politicized and highly moralizing. For instance, the 1973 Hungarian summer program "On Wheels" gave weekly lessons to the socialist public about how to drive properly, with the intention to reduce the number of accidents, particularly on summer weekends. The host's condescending tone was accompanied by images of shiny, fast Western cars breaking traffic rules and cutting off small but decent Eastern Trabants and Wartburgs. Judit Mihalik, "A *Híradó* története 1970–1990" [The history of *Híradó* 1970–1990] (PhD diss., ELTE Media Department, Budapest).
33. Lucia Gaja Scuteri, "TV as a Linguistic Issue in Yugoslavian Slovenia: A Brief Chronology from the 1960s to the 1980s" (paper presented at the conference "Television in Europe beyond the Iron Curtain—National and Transnational Perspectives since the 1950s," Friedrich-Alexander-Universität Erlangen-Nürnberg, December 5–7, 2013).
34. Mustata, "The Power of Television."
35. Mustata, "The Power of Television."
36. Pikulski, *Prywatna historia telewizji publicznej*, 96–97.
37. Dunavölgyi, "1962."
38. Dunavölgyi, "1965."
39. Its closest contemporary kin is probably something like Khan Academy on YouTube. The primary difference is that it was taught by the most distinguished university professors. See Dunavölgyi, "1969."
40. Jérôme Bourdon, "Old and New Ghosts: Public Service Television and the Popular—A History," *European Journal of Cultural Studies* 7, no. 3 (2004): 294.
41. I expand on programs with a female address in chapter 9.
42. Mustata, "The Power of Television."
43. R. J., "Politikai tanfolyam a televízióban," *Rádió és Televízió Újság* 48 (1965). 6–8.
44. Document MSZMP APO 288f.22/1969, Hungarian National Document Archives.
45. He was similar to the Polish Professor Zin, host of the show *Piorkiem i weglem*. Professor Zin would use a piece of charcoal to draw building constructions on a big piece of white paper, while discussing architectural and art history. His talent for vivid narration made his program an instant classic; he became one of the most revered TV personalities of the era, and his show remained on the air for thirty years. With thanks to Maria Zalewska for the information.

46. János Vesernyés, "Komolyzenei rovat," *Film Színház Muzsika* 5 (1969).
47. Pikulski, *Prywatna historia telewizji publicznej*, 70.
48. Pikulski, *Prywatna historia telewizji publicznej*, 92.
49. In *Magyar Nemzet*, March 10, 1965. See Dunavölgyi, "1965."
50. Dunavölgyi, "1967."
51. Kristin Roth-Ey, *Moscow Prime Time: How the Soviet Union Built the Media Empire That Lost the Cultural Cold War* (Ithaca, NY: Cornell University Press, 2011), 73.
52. B.Z.S., "Tudósklub az ifjúságról?" [Scholarly club about youth?], *Somogy Megyei Néplap*, 1969. See Dunavölgyi, "1969."
53. Mustata, "The Power of Television."
54. András Lukácsy, "Critique of *Delta*'s Broadcast of April 9, 1972." *Magyar Hírlap*, April 9, 1972.
55. Pikulski, *Prywatna historia telewizji publicznej*, 54.
56. Christine Evans, "The 'Soviet Way of Life' as Way of Feeling: Emotion and Influence on Soviet Central Television in the Brezhnev Era," *Cahiers du Monde Russe* (Spring 2015), forthcoming.
57. Michael Reufsteck and Stefan Niggemeier, *Das Fernsehlexikon: Alles über 7000 Sendungen von Ally McBeal bis zur ZDF-Hitparade* (München: Goldmann Verlag, 2005). My thanks to Greta Olson for helping me locate this source and helping me with the translation.
58. Greta Olson, "Intersections of Gender and Legal Culture in Two Women Judge Shows: Judge Judy and Richterin Barbara Salesch," in *Contemporary Gender Relations and Changes in Legal Cultures*, eds. Hanne Petersen, José María Lorenzo Villaverde, and Ingrid Lund-Andersen (Copenhagen: DJOF, 2013).
59. Csepeli, "Rádiónk és televíziónk közművelődési szemlélete és gyakorlata," 5.
60. Dunavölgyi, "1972."
61. László Rózsa's "Critique of *Fórum*", *Népszabadság*, January 18, 1969.
62. Tibor Hegedűs, "*Fórum*—belpolitikai téma: A szocialista jogalkotás, jogalkalmazás" [*Forum*—issues of domestic politics: socialist law and legislation], *Népszabadság*, May 14, 1969.
63. Dunavölgyi, "1971."
64. Gumbert, *Envisioning Socialism*, 146.
65. Gumbert, *Envisioning Socialism*, 145.
66. Gumbert, *Envisioning Socialism*, 145–146.
67. Anonymous article about *Lunch Break* in *Film Színház Muzsika* 6 (1971). See Dunavölgyi, "1971."
68. The *Radio and TV Guide* introduced the new program this way: "TV receives countless letters in which viewers ask for advice to solve various problems. Of course Television's employees aren't able to respond to every request; but they try to help with those that have broader public implications and concern the common good. This new program deals with these common issues raised by viewer letters. It also emphasizes responsibility to one another." See Dunavölgyi, "1971."

69. Dezső Radványi, "Interview", *Radio and TV Guide* 45 (1970).
70. Mariann Ember, "Hakni vagy újfajta filmezés," *Filmkultúra* 3 (1972); interview with Radványi Dezső.
71. While critics heralded the film, the Monok party leadership rejected the portrayal of the protagonist and the community and wrote a letter to István Tömpe, head of Hungarian Television, protesting the charges of systematic racism and exclusion against the Roma based on what they called the protagonist's lies. Document XXVI-A-8-a, Box 151, Hungarian National Document Archives.
72. Endre Kelemen, "Interview," *Filmesház*, December 2013, Budapest.
73. Conversation with Endre Kelemen.
74. Conversation with Endre Kelemen.
75. Conversation with Endre Kelemen.
76. Conversation with Endre Kelemen.

Chapter 3. Crime Appeal

1. As Deborah Jermyn does in her book-length discussion on *Crimewatch*; see Deborah Jermyn, *Crime Watching: Investigating Real Crime TV* (New York: I. B. Tauris, 2007), 172.
2. Jérôme Bourdon, Juan Carlos Ibáñez, Catherine Johnson, and Eggo Mueller, "Searching for an Identity for Television: Programmes, Genres, Formats," in *A European Television History*, eds. J. Bignell and A. Fickers (New York: Blackwell, 2008), 114.
3. Bourdon et al., "Searching for an Identity for Television," 113.
4. Bourdon et al., "Searching for an Identity for Television," 116.
5. Bourdon et al., "Searching for an Identity for Television," 117.
6. Jonathan Bignell, "Transatlantic Spaces: Production, Location and Style in 1960s–1970s Action-Adventure TV Series," *Media History* 16, no. 1 (2010): 56.
7. Bignell, "Transatlantic Spaces," 55.
8. Roger Moore visited Budapest and was interviewed on the nightly news in 1971. See Dunavölgyi, "1971."
9. Uwe Breitenborn, "'Memphis Tennessee' in Borstendorf: Boundaries Set and Transcended in East German Television Entertainment," *Historical Journal of Film, Radio and Television* 24, no. 3 (2004): 394.
10. Tamas Garai, "Milyen sorozatokat lathatunk a TV-ben?," *Fejér Megyei Hírlap*, January 24, 1985.
11. Petr A. Bílek, "The 30 Cases of Major Zeman: Domestication and Ideological Conversion of a James Bond Narrative in the Czech TV Serial Context of the 1970s," in *National Mythologies in Central European TV Series: How J.R. Won the Cold War*, ed. Jan Čulík (Brighton: Sussex Academic Press, 2013), 49.
12. Bílek, "The 30 Cases of Major Zeman," 50.
13. Bílek, "The 30 Cases of Major Zeman," 52.
14. Bílek, "The 30 Cases of Major Zeman," 52.

15. See Christine Evans, "'Spiritual Coauthorship': *Seventeen Moments of Spring* and the Soviet TV Miniseries," in her forthcoming book *Between Truth and Time: A History of Soviet Central Television*.
16. Evans, "'Spiritual Coauthorship.'"
17. Evans, "'Spiritual Coauthorship.'"
18. Evans, "'Spiritual Coauthorship.'"
19. This is particularly relevant in the case of Vladimir Putin's reliance on socialist television in boosting Russian imperial nationalism.
20. Bourdon et al., "Searching for an Identity for Television," 115.
21. Bourdon et al., "Searching for an Identity for Television," 114–115.
22. Bourdon et al., "Searching for an Identity for Television," 116.
23. My thanks to Irena Reifová for the research and information.
24. With thanks to Daniela Mustata for the research and information.
25. The number 997 is a Polish police emergency telephone number.
26. "Premiera Magazynu 997," TVP website, http://www.tvp.info/2901062/magazyn/kartka-z-kalendarza/premiera-magazynu-997/.
27. With thanks to Maria Zalewska for the research and information.
28. *Rádió és Televízió Újság* 49 (1965); Dunavölgyi, "1965."
29. *Magyar Nemzet*, December 15, 1965.
30. *Népszava*, July 30, 1966.
31. Géza Németi, *Rádió és Televízió Újság* 16 (1969). See Dunavölgyi, "1969."
32. "B.G.," *Magyar Nemzet*, April 19, 1969.
33. László Szabó, interview by Anikó Imre, December 2013.
34. Szabó, interview by Anikó Imre.
35. Szabó, interview by Anikó Imre.
36. Szabó, interview by Anikó Imre.
37. Szabó, interview by Anikó Imre.
38. Szabó, interview by Anikó Imre.
39. It makes sense that he is now finding himself to the left of the current far-right, ultranationalistic government.
40. Szabó, interview by Anikó Imre.
41. Gergő Olajos, interview by Anikó Imre, July 25, 2013.
42. As an indication of just how exceptional the program was among socialist conditions, Olajos reveals that he actually did not watch it growing up because his parents did not let him. What is more, László Szabó did not let his own children watch it!
43. Olajos says public television does not have enough money for thorough and regular viewer surveys. The last broadcast of the 2013 season was watched by 100,000 people among individuals aged eighteen to forty-nine. Olajos, interview by Anikó Imre.
44. If we add video game transplants, as happened with *World's Wildest Police Videos*, the confusion increases exponentially. Jermyn, *Crime Watching*, 176.

Chapter 4. The Great Socialist Game (Show)

1. Jérôme Bourdon, "Old and New Ghosts: Public Service Television and the Popular—A History," *European Journal of Cultural Studies* 7, no. 3 (2004): 287.
2. Bourdon, "Old and New Ghosts," 287.
3. Dunavölgyi, "1967."
4. István Vágó, interview by Anikó Imre, December 18, 2013.
5. Sari Autio-Sarasmo and Katalin Miklóssy, "Introduction: The Cold War from a New Perspective," in *Reassessing Cold War Europe*, eds. Sari Autio-Sarasmo and Katalin Miklóssy (New York: Routledge, 2011), 6.
6. Christine Evans, "'KVN Is an Honest Game': The Problem of Authority on *Club of the Merry and Resourceful*, 1961–1971," in her forthcoming book *Between Truth and Time: A History of Soviet Central Television*.
7. Pia Koivunen, "The World Youth Festival as an Arena of the 'Cultural Olympics' in Meanings of Competition in Soviet Culture in the 1940s and 1950s," in *Competition in Socialist Society*, eds. Katalin Miklóssy and Melanie Ilic (London: Routledge, 2014).
8. Christine Evans, "Song of the Year and Soviet Mass Culture in the 1970s," *Kritika: Explorations in Russian and Euroasian History* 12, no. 3 (Summer 2011): 622.
9. Evans, "Song of the Year and Soviet Mass Culture," 624.
10. Evans, "Song of the Year and Soviet Mass Culture," 619–620.
11. Koivunen, "The World Youth Festival."
12. Koivunen, "The World Youth Festival."
13. Claudia Dittmar, "GDR Television in Competition with West German Programming," *Historical Journal of Film, Radio and Television* 24, no. 3 (2004): 328.
14. Dittmar, "GDR Television," 317.
15. Uwe Breitenborn, "'Memphis Tennessee' in Borstendorf: Boundaries Set and Transcended in East German Television Entertainment," *Historical Journal of Film, Radio and Television* 24, no. 3 (2004): 392.
16. Ruediger Steinmetz and Reinhold Viehoff, "The Program History of Genres of Entertainment on GDR Television," *Historical Journal of Film, Radio and Television* 24. no. 3 (2004): 320.
17. Dittmar, "GDR Television," 322.
18. Dittmar, "GDR Television," 329.
19. Dittmar, "GDR Television," 334–335.
20. Dittmar, "GDR Television," 327.
21. Dittmar, "GDR Television," 337.
22. Dittmar, "GDR Television," 336.
23. With the exception of the BBC; see Bourdon, "Old and New Ghosts," 288.
24. Noémi Dóra Dankovics, "Játékmesterek és vetélkedőműsorok a magyar televíziózás történetében" [Quiz show hosts and game shows in the history

of Hungarian television] (PhD diss., Budapest College of Communication and Business, 2012).
25. Breitenborn, "'Memphis Tennessee' in Borstendorf," 391.
26. Bourdon, "Old and New Ghosts," 288.
27. Dittmar, "GDR Television," 339.
28. Daniela Mustata, "The Power of Television: Including the Historicizing of the Live Romanian Revolution" (PhD diss., Utrecht University, 2011); see chap. 4, "Reassembling a History of Romanian Television Programmes."
29. Dunavölgyi, "1966."
30. András Budai, "A Magyar Rádió és Televízió nemzetközi kapcsolatai," in *Tanfolyamok, Előadások a Televízióról* (Budapest: MRT Tömegkommunikációs Kutatóközpont, 1970).
31. János Gulyás, secretary of Vörös Csillag (Red Star) Tractor Factory's Eger division. Document MSZMP APO 288f.22./1968/15.ö.e. AG 10/120, Hungarian National Document Archives. No exact date is indicated.
32. Response to Gulyás by Jenő Gerencsér from the Hungarian Socialist Workers' Party's Agitation and Propaganda Division, Document MSZMP APO 88f.22./1968/15.ö.e. AG 10/120/3 from 04.16.1968, Hungarian National Document Archives.
33. Dunavölgyi, "1967."
34. Alexandru Matei, "The Golden Stag Festival in Ceausescu's Romania (1968–1971)," *View* 1, no. 2 (2013).
35. Evans, "Song of the Year and Soviet Mass Culture."
36. Evans, "Song of the Year and Soviet Mass Culture."
37. This is why it caused no ethical conundrum that, like other stages of public participation, sports were centralized and top athletes were paid a salary by the state.
38. Evans, "'KVN Is an Honest Game.'"
39. Evans, "'KVN Is an Honest Game.'"
40. Kristin Roth-Ey, *Moscow Prime Time: How the Soviet Union Built the Media Empire That Lost the Cultural Cold War* (Ithaca, NY: Cornell University Press, 2011), 246.
41. Evans, "'KVN Is an Honest Game.'"
42. Roth-Ey, *Moscow Prime Time*, 248.
43. Roth-Ey, *Moscow Prime Time*, 253.
44. Evans, "'KVN Is an Honest Game.'"
45. Roth-Ey, *Moscow Prime Time*, 257.
46. Roth-Ey, *Moscow Prime Time*, 259.
47. Evans, "'KVN Is an Honest Game.'"
48. Evans, "'KVN Is an Honest Game.'"
49. Roth-Ey, *Moscow Prime Time*, 260.
50. Evans, "'KVN Is an Honest Game.'"
51. Evans, "'KVN Is an Honest Game.'"

52. Evans, "Song of the Year and Soviet Mass Culture."
53. Dunavölgyi, "1964."
54. "A nyolcvan év nem érdem—interjú Vitray Tamással," http://www.origo.hu/teve/20121031-vitray-tamas-a-nyolcvan-ev-nem-erdem.html.
55. Dunavölgyi, "1971."
56. Vera Vajk, "Fekete fehér, igen, nem," *Népszava*, February 17, 1970.
57. Breitenborn, "'Memphis Tennessee' in Borstendorf," 399.
58. Announcement in *Rádió és TV újság* 6 (1962).
59. Assessment of Hungarian Television's work by the Komárom County Committee of the Hungarian National Front, Document 288f.22/163/12.öe—MSZMP KB Agitációs és Propaganda Osztálya, Hungarian National Document Archives.
60. Announcement in *Rádió és TV újság* 6 (1962).
61. Announcement in *Rádió és TV újság* 31 (1966).
62. Miklós Végh, "Critique," *Rádió és TV újság*, April 18, 1971.
63. Pál Bélley, "Critique," *Magyar Hírlap*, April 19, 1971.
64. Evans, "'KVN Is an Honest Game.'"
65. Evans, "'KVN Is an Honest Game.'"
66. Evans, "'KVN Is an Honest Game.'"
67. Evans, "'KVN Is an Honest Game.'"
68. Evans, "'KVN Is an Honest Game.'"
69. Clip from the show (courtesy of Maria Zalewska), https://www.youtube.com/watch?v=lqU1qYBxWpI.
70. The show aired for the first time in 1967 and stayed on the air until 1969. There were only eighteen episodes in total.
71. Tadeusz Pikulski, *Prywatna historia telewizji publicznej* (Warsaw: Muza SA, 2002), 73.
72. Bourdon, "Old and New Ghosts," 288.
73. Miklós Pálos, "Interview with László Grétsy," *Hétfői Hírek*, February 27, 1971.
74. H.T., "Világirodalmi vetélkedő egyetemi fokon" [Academic quiz show about world literature], *Esti Hírlap*, February 2, 1965.
75. Dunavölgyi, "1966."
76. Dunavölgyi, "1966."
77. Survey published in *Rádió és TV újság* 5 (1967).
78. Dunavölgyi, "1971."
79. Dunavölgyi, "1970."
80. Vágó, interview by Anikó Imre.
81. László Halász, "Játék-műveltség-vetélkedők," *Magyar Rádió és Televízió Szemle* 2 (1971): 15–22.
82. Halász, "Játék-műveltség-vetélkedők," 15–22.
83. Dunavölgyi, "1970."
84. Dunavölgyi, "1970."

Chapter 5. Postsocialist Ethno-Racial Reality TV

1. See, for instance, V. Stetka, "Globalization, Reality TV and Cultural Inclusion: The Case of the 2005 Czech Search for Superstar," *EastBound* 1 (2009): 1–20, http://eastbound.eu/2009/stetka; G. Turner, "Cultural Identity, Soap Narrative, and Reality TV," *Television and New Media* 6, no. 4 (2005): 415–422; S. Waisbord, "McTV: Understanding the Global Popularity of Television Formats," *Television and New Media* 5, no. 2 (2004): 359–383; M. Aslama and M. Pantti, "Flagging Finnishness: Reproducing National Identity in Reality Television," *Television and New Media* 8, no. 1 (2007): 49–67.
2. John Ellis, "The Performance on Television of Sincerely Felt Emotion," *Annals of the American Academy of Political and Social Science* 625 (September 2009): 110.
3. J. Ladányi and I. Szelényi, *Patterns of Exclusion: Constructing Gypsy Ethnicity and the Making of an Underclass in Transitional Societies of Europe* (New York: Columbia University Press, 2006), 1–8.
4. The iconic moment of shattering this illusion, usually realized in the course of travel to the West, has been dramatized in a number of films by Eastern European auteurs, most memorably in Krzysztof Kieślowski's *White* (1994), which can be read as a racial allegory: the Polish man's revenge for being deprived of his whiteness (embodied in his masculinity) by his French ex-wife and, by extension, Western Europe. See Anikó Imre, "Postcolonial Media Studies in Postsocialist Europe," *Boundary* 2 41, no. 1 (Spring 2014): 113–134.
5. On the relationship between race and ethnicity, see P. Gilroy, "Race Ends Here," *Ethnic and Racial Studies* 21, no. 5 (1998): 838–847.
6. S. Murray and Laurie Ouellette, "Introduction," in *Reality TV: Remaking Television Culture*, eds. Laurie Ouellette and S. Murray (New York: New York University Press, 2004), 6.
7. Murray and Ouellette, "Introduction," 6.
8. See Laurie Ouellette and James Hay, *Better Living through Reality TV: Television and Post-Welfare Citizenship* (Hoboken, NJ: Wiley-Blackwell, 2008). For an excellent example of studies that redirect attention from issues specific to postwelfare societies, see Marwan Kraidy, *Reality Television and Arab Politics: Contention in Public Life* (Cambridge: Cambridge University Press, 2009).
9. Zala Volčič, "Fame on the Farm: Class and Celebrity on Slovene Reality TV," in *Real Class: Ordinary People and Reality Television across National Spaces*, eds. Helen Wood and Beverly Skeggs (London: BFI, 2012).
10. See M. Stewart, *The Time of the Gypsies* (Oxford: Westview Press, 1997); Ladányi and Szelényi, *Patterns of Exclusion*; Anikó Imre, "Global Entertainment and the European 'Roma Problem,'" *Third Text* 20, no. 6 (2006): 659–670.
11. See Anikó Imre, "Roma Music and Transnational Homelessness," *Third Text* 22, no. 3 (2008): 325–336.

12. "Botrányos TV2 műsor," *Népszabadság* online, March 4, 2003, http://www.nol.hu/cikk/389740/.
13. "Ugyanakkor megtudhatjuk azt is, milyen egy bazi nagy roma buli Győzike módra," RTL Klub online, January 27, 2005, http://www.online.rtlklub.hu/Győzike/?id=0501168298.
14. RTL Klub and TV2 both began broadcasting in 1997 and have dominated the Hungarian television market ever since. They both specialize in producing reality formats and broadcasting American fictional programming. RTL Klub is owned by the RTL Group, Europe's largest content producer for television and radio, majority-owned by German media conglomerate Bertelsmann.
15. "RTL Group Annual Report, 2005," RTL Group web page, http://www.rtlgroup.com/files/AR2005_RTLGroup_COMPLETE.pdf.
16. RTL Group audited results year ended December 31, 2005. See RTL Group web page, http://www.rtlgroup.com/files/Full_Audited_Results_Doc_15032006doc.pdf..
17. "Szenzáció," 2005, http://www.est.hu/cikk/47650/szenzacio_gyozike_lekorozte_a_baratokat/r0409.
18. D. Kompare, "Extraordinarily Ordinary: *The Osbournes* as 'an American Family,'" in *Reality TV: Remaking Television Culture*, eds. Laurie Ouellette and S. Murray (New York: New York University Press, 2004).
19. Kompare, "Extraordinarily Ordinary."
20. Depicting ethnic minorities as essentially emotional—rather than rational— beings is a recognizable racist discourse, and one that has been attributed to Gypsies as far back as the nineteenth century. As W. Willems puts it, "They were said to live by nature's clock and react instinctively to external impulses." See W. Willems, *In Search of the True Gypsy: From Enlightenment to Final Solution* (London: Frank Cass, 1997), 50.
21. John Corner, "Performing the Real: Documentary Diversions," *Television and New Media* 3, no. 3 (2002): 255–269.
22. Alexander Dhoest, "'The Pfaffs Are Not Like the Osbournes': National Inflections of the Celebrity Docusoap," *Television and New Media* 6, no. 2 (2004): 224–245.
23. Dhoest, "'The Pfaffs Are Not Like the Osbournes,'" 224–225.
24. *Hot top 100 sztár: A száz legfontosabb magyar híresség* (Budapest: Euromedia BT, 2008).
25. "Gáspár Győző szerepei: György Péter szerint kiszabadult a szellem a palackból—Az RTL Klub hajlik a folytatásra," *Népszabadság* online, January 6, 2006, http://www.nol.hu/cikk/389740/.
26. János Daróczi is a member of a family well known for their Roma activism. He is editor of the *Roma Magazin* weekly TV show devoted to Roma issues, on MTV (Hungarian National Television).
27. L. Kürti, "Media Wars: Cultural Dialogue and Conflict in Hungarian Popular Broadcasting," in *Fondazione Eni Enrico Mattei Series Index*, SUSDIV,

paper 8 (January 2008), http://www.feem.it/Feem/Pub/Publications/EURODIVpapers/default.htm.

28. The exception is the half-Roma character of Nóra on the popular prime-time soap opera *Barátok közt* (Between friends), which marks the first Roma presence in fictional programming. G. Bernáth and V. Messing, "Roma szappanopera karakter a *Barátok közt*-ben: Az első fecske," *Médiakutató*, spring 2001. http://www.mediakutato.hu/cikk/2001_01_tavasz/01_roma_szereplo_a_baratok_koztben

29. V. Messing, *In a White Framework: The Representation of Roma in the Hungarian Press* (Frankfurt: VDM Verlag, 2008).

30. V. Munk, "Sztárság, elméletben," *Médiakutató*, Spring 2009, http://mediakutato.hu/cikk/2009_01_tavasz/01_sztarsag_elmeletben/01.html.

31. Ágnes Jenei, "Neotelevízió: Válság vagy megújulás?," *Médiakutató*, spring 2006. http://www.mediakutato.hu/cikk/2006_01_tavasz/03_neotelevizio/

32. Of course, the emergence of the familiar, everyday celebrity has a crucial economic underpinning: cash-strapped postsocialist media economies are constrained to the production of nonscripted programming. The circulation of cheap formats is at least partly responsible for the global shift toward what Graeme Turner calls the "demotic turn" in celebrity culture, which, Zala Volčič explains in her excellent analysis of the Slovenian program *The Celebrity Farm*, well describes the cultural and economic context of postsocialist television celebrity. See Volčič, "Fame on the Farm."

33. He speaks with a strong regional accent that is also marked as ethnic and punctuated by Romani expressions.

34. Kürti, "Media Wars," 17.

35. The initial ads for the *Győzike* program, along with the opening credits, used music from Kusturica's film about a vivacious Roma wedding, *Black Cat White Cat*. *Győzike* has been heavily promoted along ethnic lines, using Gypsy stereotypes to publicize the show. See "Romakép-zavar," *Heti válasz*, June 23, 2005, http://www.romapage.hu/hirek/hircentrum-forummal/article/75165/169/page/3/, and "Botrányos TV2 műsor."

36. Indeed, after receiving some complaints about the show's Gypsy stereotyping, RTL Klub issued a statement insisting that it was not a "Roma show" but a "comedy reality show": "The *Győzike* show is not Roma, but is rather an entertainment program, which, if it is influential in any way, certainly doesn't deepen, but rather reduces discrimination." Péter Kolosi, RTL Klub program manager, quoted in "Gáspár Győző szerepei."

37. "GyőzikeTv. Fórum," http://forum.sg.hu/forum.php3?azonosito=gyozike.

38. See Kürti, "Media Wars."

39. See J. Hartley, "Democratainment," in *The Television Studies Reader*, eds. Robert C. Allen and Annette Hill (London: Routledge, 2004), 524–533; M. Hills, *Fan Cultures* (London: Routledge, 2002); Henry Jenkins, *Fans, Bloggers and Gamers: Media Consumers in a Digital Age* (New York: New York University

Press, 2006); Liesbet van Zoonen, "Imagining the Fan Democracy," *European Journal of Communication* 19, no. 1 (2004): 39–52.
40. A. Appadurai, *Fear of Small Numbers: An Essay on the Geography of Anger* (Durham, NC: Duke University Press, 2006), 51.
41. Appadurai, *Fear of Small Numbers*, 51.
42. Appadurai, *Fear of Small Numbers*, 44–45.
43. A well-respected cultural critic, for instance, talks about "parasite media" in the highbrow literary and cultural journal *Èlet és Irodalom* (Life and literature), using the *Győzike* show as his chief example. See P. György, *Èlet és Irodalom* 49, no. 22 (June 3, 2006), http://www.es.hu/pd/display.asp?channel=MUBIRALAT0522&article=2005-0605-2241-12PHRS.
44. Jenei, "Neotelevízió."
45. L. Kolozsi, "Smink nélkül: Kultúra a képernyőn," *Filmvilág* 5 (2005), http://www.filmvilag.hu/xista_frame.php?cikk_id=8258.
46. B. Skeggs, "The Making of Class and Gender through Visualizing Moral Subject Formation," *Sociology* 39, no. 5 (2005): 968.
47. Skeggs, "The Making of Class and Gender," 961.
48. Erzsébet Bori, "Cigányutak: Roma dokumentumfilm," *Filmvilág* 6 (2005), http://www.filmvilag.hu/xista_frame.php?cikk_id=8270.
49. See András Fáy, "Mónika, avagy a buta ország," *Èlet és Irodalom* 45, no. 23 (2001), http://www.es.hu/index.php?view=doc;3445; S. Varró, "Romák a képernyön: Sötét hírek," *Filmvilág* 6 (2005): 6, http://www.filmvilag.hu/xista_frame.php?cikk_id=8272; Zsuzsa Darab, "Pop, tabu, satöbbi: A hét föbün a televízióban," *Filmvilág* 2 (2008), http://www.filmvilag.hu/xista_frame.php?cikk_id=9262; Kolozsi, "Smink nélkül."
50. See B. Skeggs, H. Wood, and N. Thumin, "'Oh Goodness, I Am Watching Reality TV': How Methods Make Class in Audience Research," *European Journal of Cultural Studies* 22, no. 1 (2009): 5–24; B. Skeggs, H. Wood, and N. Thumin, "Making Class through Moral Extension on Reality TV," 2007, http://www9.umu.se/medfak/cgf/bev%20warwick%20with%20edits%20_2_.pdf, accessed May 11, 2009.
51. Munk, "Sztárság, elméletben."
52. Annabel Tremlett, "Why Must Roma Minorities Be Always Seen on the Stage and Never in the Audiences? Children's Opinions of Reality Roma TV," in *Popular Television in Eastern Europe During and Since Socialism*, eds. Aniko Imre, Timothy Havens, and Katalin Lustyik (New York: Routledge, 2013), 241–258.
53. For example, in 2007, Kaposvár University carried out a survey among fifteen hundred primary school students in the region to gauge the relationship children had with education and the community. When asked whom the children considered their role model, a third of them reported Győzike. See "Hmmm . . . —Győzike a példaképe minden harmadik somogyi általános iskolásnak," February 9, 2007, http://www.mtv.hu/magazin/cikk.php?id=183025.

54. D. Buckingham, "What Are Words Worth? Interpreting Children's Talk about Television," *Cultural Studies* 5, no. 2 (1991): 243.
55. A. Imre, "National Intimacy: Social Networking Sites and Post-Socialist Public Culture," *European Journal of Cultural Studies* 12, no. 2 (2009): 219–234.
56. See, for instance, this excerpt: http://frumusete.protv.ro/video-elena-marghidan-este-de-nerecunoscut/20327/pagina-12.html. I am grateful to Elena Panican for this information.
57. I thank Alice Bardan for information on *Satra*.
58. *Pestiside*, June 26, 2007, http://www.pestiside.hu/20070626/hungo-celeb-roundup-pako-survives-triple-media-assassination-attempt/.
59. See the interview here: http://www.youtube.com/watch?v=5uUHjPHCiJU&feature=PlayList&p=8E4B7D1D5E0CEC47&playnext_from=PL&playnext=1&index=30.
60. http://africanexaminer.com/blog2/2008/02/13/nigerian-singer-in-trouble-for-praising-hitler/.
61. István Vágó, interview by Anikó Imre, December 18, 2013.

Chapter 6. The Historical Adventure Drama

1. John Ellis, *Visible Fictions* (London: Routledge, 1982), 5.
2. See Géza Hofi's memorable parody of the series *Rózsa Sándor* (1971, dir. Miklós Szinetár), inspired by the mythical adventures of the eponymous nineteenth-century Hungarian outlaw.
3. Sonja De Leeuw, Alexander Dhoest, Juan Francisco Gutierrez Lozano, François Heinderyckx, Anu Koivunen, and Jamie Medhurst, "TV Nations or Global Medium? European Television between National Institution and Window on the World," in *A European Television History*, eds. J. Bignell and A. Fickers (New York: Blackwell, 2008), 134.
4. De Leeuw et al., "TV Nations or Global Medium?," 139.
5. De Leeuw et al., "TV Nations or Global Medium?," 141.
6. Alexander Dhoest, "Quality and/as National Identity: Press Discourse on Flemish Period TV Drama," *European Journal of Cultural Studies* 7, no. 3 (2004): 311.
7. Dhoest, "Quality and/as National Identity," 318.
8. See Anikó Imre, "Eastern Westerns: Socialist Edutainment or National Transvestism," *New Review of Film and Television Studies* 9, no. 2 (June 2011): 152–169.
9. Joep Leerssen, John Neubauer, Marcel Cornis-Pope, Biljana Markovic, and Dragan Klaic, "The Rural Outlaws of East-Central Europe," in *History of the Literary Cultures of East-Central Europe: Junctures and Disjuncture in the 19th and 20th Centuries*, vol. 4, *Types and Stereotypes*, eds. Marcel Cornis-Pope and John Neubauer (Amsterdam: John Benjamins, 2010), 407–440.
10. Rákóczi's portrait is on the five-hundred-forint banknote in Hungary, his statues pepper the landscape, and there is no town that would not have streets and schools named after him.

11. The term *kuruc* is used to denote armed anti-Habsburg rebels in the Kingdom of Hungary between 1671 and 1711.
12. László Deák-Sárosi, "Nemzeti kalandfilm-sorozatunk," *Filmkultúra* (2006), http://www.filmkultura.hu/regi/2006/articles/essays/tenkes.hu.html.
13. Deák-Sárosi, "Nemzeti kalandfilm-sorozatunk."
14. Jutta Rassloff, "Juraj Janosik," in *History of the Literary Cultures of East-Central Europe: Junctures and Disjuncture in the 19th and 20th Centuries*, vol. 4, *Types and Stereotypes*, eds. Marcel Cornis-Pope and John Neubauer (Amsterdam: John Benjamins, 2010), 441–456.
15. Rassloff, "Juraj Janosik," 441–456.
16. Martin Vortruba, "Hang Him High: The Elevation of Janosik to an Ethnic Icon," *Slavic Review* 65, no. 1 (2006): 24–44.
17. Rassloff, "Juraj Janosik," 441–456.
18. Vortruba, "Hang Him High," 24–44.
19. "It may be said then that the theme of the haiduc-outlaw was a powerful influence over the emergence of the vernacular literatures of South-Eastern (and Eastern) Europe, involving an intense back-and-forth of literary activities and influences—from country to country, from East to West and vice versa, and from metropolitan, printed 'high' literature to performative balladry." See Neubauer et al., "The Rural Outlaws of East-Central Europe."
20. Vortruba, "Hang Him High," 24–44.
21. Rassloff, "Juraj Janosik," 441–456.
22. Rassloff, "Juraj Janosik," 441–456.
23. A. Jäckel, "Mihai Viteazul/Michael the Brave, Sergiu Nicolaescu, Romania, 1970–71," in *The Cinema of the Balkans*, ed. D. Iordanova (London: Wallflower Press, 2006), 78.
24. D. Petrescu, "The Alluring Facet of Ceaușescu-ism: Nation-Building and Identity Politics in Communist Romania, 1965–1989," *New Europe College Yearbook* 11 (2003): 258.
25. Others include the Yugoslavian *Boj na Kosovu* (The Battle of Kosovo, Sotra, 1989), the Bulgarian *Vreme na nasilie* (Time of violence, Staikov, 1988), and the Albanian *Balada e Kurbinit* (Ballad of Kurbini, Çashku, 1990). See Jäckel, "Mihai Viteazul/Michael the Brave," 83.
26. The reference most likely includes a targeted stab at neighboring Romania, given the clashing claims over the territory of Transylvania in both countries' national histories.
27. Rassloff, "Juraj Janosik," 441–456.

Chapter 7. Postsocialist Nostalgia and European Historical Drama

1. See Amy Holdsworth, "Television Resurrections: Television and Memory," *Cinema Journal* 47, no. 3 (2008): 137; Milly Buonanno, *Italian TV Drama and Beyond: Stories from the Soil, Stories from the Sea* (Bristol: Intellect, 2002), 199.

2. John Ellis, "Television and History," *History Workshop Journal* 56 (Fall 2003): 181.
3. Gary R. Edgerton, "Introduction: Television as a Historian: A Different Kind of History Altogether," in *Television Histories: Shaping Collective Memory in the Media Age*, eds. G. Edgerton and Peter C. Rollins (Louisville: University Press of Kentucky, 2001), 1.
4. Edgerton, "Introduction," 5.
5. Edgerton, "Introduction," 1. See Ann Gray Buonanno and Erin Bell, "History on Television: Charisma, Narrative and Knowledge," *European Journal of Cultural Studies* 1, no. 1 (2007): 113–133.
6. Edgerton, "Introduction," 3.
7. Jérôme Bourdon, Juan Carlos Ibáñez, Catherine Johnson, and Eggo Mueller, "Searching for an Identity for Television: Programmes, Genres, Formats," in *A European Television History*, eds. J. Bignell and A. Fickers (New York: Blackwell, 2008), 118.
8. Bourdon et al., "Searching for an Identity for Television," 103.
9. In 2004 alone, local fiction broadcast by private channels increased by 158 hours in 2004 (from 39 percent in 2003 to 41 percent). In 2007, the share of European fiction broadcast was between 40 and 50 percent in Finland (49.7 percent), Switzerland (44.3 percent), and the Netherlands (43.9 percent). It was between 30 and 40 percent in nine countries and lower than 30 percent in three: Sweden (29.3 percent), Denmark (19 percent), and Luxembourg (0.5 percent). "Eurofiction 2005," http://www.obs.coe.int/about/oea/pr/eurofiction2005.html.
10. "Eurofiction 2005."
11. José Carlos Rueda Laffond, Carlota Coronado Ruiz, Catarina Duff Burnay, Amparo Guerra Gómez, Susana Díaz Pérez, and Rogério Santos, "Parallel Stories, Differentiated Histories: Exploring Fiction and Memory in Spanish and Portuguese Television," *VIEW: Journal of European Television History and Culture* 3, no. 2 (2012): 37–44.
12. Buonanno, *Italian TV Drama and Beyond*, 119.
13. Buonanno, *Italian TV Drama and Beyond*, 118.
14. Buonanno, *Italian TV Drama and Beyond*, 201.
15. Buonanno, *Italian TV Drama and Beyond*, 210.
16. Buonanno, *Italian TV Drama and Beyond*, 214.
17. Buonanno, *Italian TV Drama and Beyond*, 224.
18. Buonanno, *Italian TV Drama and Beyond*, 213.
19. Buonanno, *Italian TV Drama and Beyond*, 207.
20. Buonanno, *Italian TV Drama and Beyond*, 208.
21. Havens, Bottando, and Thatcher write that American product continues to account for nearly 70 percent of all worldwide trade in television programs, and the trade deficit between the EU and the United States in audiovisual products continues to hover above $7 billion per year. See Timothy Havens,

Evelyn Bottando, and Matthew S. Thatcher, "Intra-European Media Imperialism: Hungarian Program Imports and the Television without Frontiers Directive," in *Popular Television in Eastern Europe Before and Since Socialism*, eds. Anikó Imre, Timothy Havens, and Kati Lustyik (New York: Routledge, 2012), 123–140.

22. Havens, Bottando, and Thatcher, "Intra-European Media Imperialism," 140.
23. Sylwia Szostak, "Poland's Return to Europe: Polish Terrestrial Broadcasters and TV Fiction," *Journal of European Television History and Culture* 1, no. 2 (2012): 91.
24. Szostak, "Poland's Return to Europe," 91.
25. For more details, see Anikó Imre, "Eastern European Cinema from *No End* to the End (As We Know It)," in *The Blackwell Companion to East European Cinemas*, ed. Anikó Imre (New York: Blackwell, 2012) 1–22.
26. http://www.kordafilmstudio.hu/?scr=news,ch&action=shownews&id=83. Accessed November 3, 2014.
27. Jack Rapke, "Question-and-Answer Session at School of Cinematic Arts" (University of Southern California, Los Angeles, April 2011).
28. Rapke, "Question-and-Answer Session at School of Cinematic Arts."
29. Dominic Boyer likens postsocialist nostalgia to Bakhtin's heteroglossia to illustrate its complexity. See Dominic Boyer, "From Algos to Autonomos: Nostalgic Eastern Europe as Postimperial Mania," in *Post-Communist Nostalgia*, eds. Maria Todorova and Zsuzsa Gille (New York: Berghahn Books, 2010), 19. See also Zala Volčič and Mark Andrejevic, "Commercial Nationalism on Balkan Reality TV," in *The Politics of Reality Television: Global Perspectives*, eds. Marwan Kraidy and Katherine Senders (London: Routledge, 2010), 113–126.
30. Zsuzsa Gille, "Postscript," in *Post-Communist Nostalgia*, eds. Maria Todorova and Zsuzsa Gille (New York: Berghahn Books, 2010), 279.
31. Dominic Boyer, "*Ostalgie* and the Politics of the Future in Eastern Germany," *Public Culture* 18, no. 2 (2006): 363.
32. Boyer, "*Ostalgie* and the Politics of the Future in Eastern Germany," 365.
33. Boyer, "*Ostalgie* and the Politics of the Future in Eastern Germany," 367.
34. Or *Gebildeten*, as they were called in German. See Boyer, "From Algos to Autonomos."
35. See Joep Leerssen, "Nationalism and the Cultivation of Culture," *Nations and Nationalism* 12, no. 4 (2006): 559–578.
36. Anikó Imre, "Love to Hate: National Intimacy and Racial Intimacy on Reality TV in the New Europe," *Television and New Media* 16.2 (2015): 103–130.
37. See Tania Modleski, "Femininity as Mas(s)querade: A Feminist Approach to Mass Culture," in *Feminism: Critical Concepts in Literary and Cultural Studies*, ed. Mary Evans (New York: Routledge, 2000), 322–332; Andreas Huyssen, "Mass Culture as Woman: Modernism's Other," in *After the Great Divide: Modernism, Mass Culture, Postmodernism*, ed. Andreas Huyssen (Bloomington: Indiana University Press, 1986), 44–64.

38. The study revolves around the Czech series *Vyprávěj*, which revisits shared socialist memories.
39. Irena Carpentier Reifová, Kateřina Gillárová, and Radim Hladík, "The Way We Applauded: How Popular Culture Stimulates Collective Memory of the Socialist Past in Czechoslovakia—the Case of the Television Serial *Vyprávěj* and Its Viewers," in *Popular Television in Eastern Europe During and Since Socialism*, eds. Anikó Imre, Timothy Havens, and Katalin Lustyik (New York: Routledge, 2012), 199–221. As the authors show, television not only makes history an important part of its programming but also stimulates collective memory among diverse groups of viewers thanks to its capacity for personalization and narrativization.
40. Boyer "*Ostalgie* and the Politics of the Future in Eastern Germany," 372.
41. Boyer, "*Ostalgie* and the Politics of the Future in Eastern Germany," 372.
42. Boyer, "From Algos to Autonomos," 23.
43. Gerd Gemünden, "Nostalgia for the Nation: Intellectuals and National Identity in Unified Germany," in *Acts of Memory: Cultural Recall in the Present*, eds. Mieke Bal, Jonathan Crewe, and Leo Spitzer (Hanover, NH: Dartmouth University Press, 1999), 123.
44. Gemünden, "Nostalgia for the Nation," 127.
45. Maya Nadkarni, "'But It's Ours': Nostalgia and the Politics of Authenticity in Post-Socialist Hungary," in *Post-Communist Nostalgia*, eds. Maria Todorova and Zsuzsa Gille (New York: Berghahn Books, 2010), 204.
46. Bourdon et al., "Searching for an Identity for Television," 101–126.
47. Maria Todorova, "Introduction: From Utopia to Propaganda and Back," in *Post-Communist Nostalgia*, eds. Maria Todorova and Zsuzsa Gille (New York: Berghahn Books, 2010), 7.
48. Todorova, "Introduction," 9.
49. See Charlotte Brunsdon, "Is Television Studies History?," *Cinema Journal* 47, no. 3 (2008): 127–134; Holdsworth, "Television Resurrections," 137–143.
50. Kateryna Khinkulova, "Hello, Lenin? Nostalgia on Post-Soviet Television in Russia and Ukraine," VIEW: *Journal of European Television History and Culture* 1, no. 2 (2012): 94–104. Although one suspects that this televisual Eurocentrism is also appropriated by national parties and governments, it serves retrograde, ultranationalist directions.
51. Ekaterina Kalinina, "Nostalgia Channel: Virtual Life in the Soviet Past" (paper presented at the symposium "Television Histories in (Post)Socialist Europe," Södertörn University, Sweden, November 7, 2013).
52. "USSR Meets YouTube," http://www.independent.co.uk/news/media/ussr-meets-youtube-in-russian-web-nostalgia-project-1830421.html.
53. "Dankó rádió—indul a nóta rádió," http://www.sat-tv-radio.hu/friss-hirek/danko-radio-indul-a-nota-radio.html?Itemid=2.
54. "Csatornanézettség—2011: Az 50 legnézettebb hazai TV adó," http://sorozatwiki.hu/news.php?readmore=55921.

55. Zala Volčič, "Yugo-Nostalgia: Cultural Memory and Media in the Former Yugoslavia," *Critical Studies in Media Communication* 24, no. 1 (2007): 21–38.
56. Dina Iordanova, "Balkan Wedding Revisited," http://www.cas.umn.edu/assets/pdf/WP981.PDF. Accessed November 3, 2013.
57. Iordanova, "Balkan Wedding Revisited."
58. Irena Reifová, "Rerunning and 'Rewatching' Socialist TV Drama Serials: Post-Socialist Czech Television Audiences between Commodification and Reclaiming the Past," *Critical Studies in Television* 4, no. 2 (2009): 57.
59. Reifová, "Rerunning and 'Rewatching' Socialist TV Drama Serials," 60.
60. Uwe Breitenborn, "'Memphis Tennessee' in Borstendorf: Boundaries Set and Transcended in East German Television Entertainment," *Historical Journal of Film, Radio and Television* 24, no. 3 (2004): 396.
61. Holdsworth, "Television Resurrections," 137.
62. Daphne Berdahl, "*Good Bye Lenin!* Aufwiedersehen GDR: On the Social Life of Socialism," in *Post-Communist Nostalgia*, eds. Maria Todorova and Zsuzsa Gille (New York: Berghahn Books, 2010), 177–180.

Chapter 8. Commercials as Time-Space Machines

1. Heather Gumbert, "Shoring Up Socialism: Transnational Media Exchange and Cultural Sovereignty in the GDR" (paper presented at the conference "Television in Europe beyond the Iron Curtain—National and Transnational Perspectives since the 1950s," Friedrich-Alexander-Universität Erlangen-Nürnberg, December 5–7, 2013).
2. Gumbert, "Shoring Up Socialism"; Thomas Beutelschmidt, "East German TV and Global Transfers" (paper presented at the conference "Television in Europe beyond the Iron Curtain—National and Transnational Perspectives since the 1950s," Friedrich-Alexander-Universität Erlangen-Nürnberg, December 5–7, 2013); Richard Oehmig, "Mission Impossible? Die Exportbemühungen des Fernsehens der DDR im Spiegel außenpolitischer und ökonomischer Implikationen" (paper presented at the conference "Television in Europe beyond the Iron Curtain—National and Transnational Perspectives since the 1950s," Friedrich-Alexander-Universität Erlangen-Nürnberg, December 5–7, 2013).
3. "Soviet TV Advertisements from the 1970s and 1980s," http://boingboing.net/2013/02/17/soviet-tv-advertisements-from.html.
4. "The Only Anthology of Retro Soviet TV Commercials," http://www.retrosovietads.com/.
5. Tadeusz Pikulski, *Prywatna historia telewizji publicznej* (Warsaw: Muza SA, 2002), 29.
6. Pikulski, *Prywatna historia telewizji publicznej*, 28.
7. Sabina Mihelj, "Socialist Television in a Transnational Perspective: Challenges and Opportunities" (paper presented at the symposium "Television Histories in (Post)Socialist Europe," Stockholm, November 2013).

8. Ilona Pócsik, interview by Anikó Imre, December 2013.
9. "Az RTV Belkereskedelmi Igazgatóság tevékenysége 1968–88 között" [Report on the activities of Hungarian Television and Radio's Commercial Department 1968–88], internal departmental correspondence, courtesy of Ilona Pócsik.
10. "Az RTV Belkereskedelmi Igazgatóság tevékenysége 1968–88 között."
11. Annemarie Sorescu-Marinković, "'We Didn't Have Anything, They Had It All': Watching Yugoslav Television in Communist Romania" (paper presented at the conference "Television in Europe beyond the Iron Curtain—National and Transnational Perspectives since the 1950s," Friedrich-Alexander-Universität Erlangen-Nürnberg, December 5–7, 2013).
12. Annika Lepp and Mervi Pantti, "Window to the West: Memories of Watching Finnish Television in Estonia during the Soviet Period," *VIEW: Journal of European Television History and Culture* 3, no. 2 (2012): 76–86.
13. Gumbert, "Shoring Up Socialism"; Beutelschmidt, "East German TV and Global Transfers"; Oehmig, "Mission Impossible?"
14. György Varga, "Műsoron a hirdetés," *Figyelő*, September 30, 1970.
15. Anecdotal evidence shows that in Hungary, recognizing old commercials has become a popular party game at company gatherings.
16. Zala Volčič, "Yugo-Nostalgia: Cultural Memory and Media in the Former Yugoslavia," *Critical Studies in Media Communication* 24, no. 1 (2007): 21–38.
17. Diana Georgescu, "'Ceaușescu Hasn't Died": Irony as Countermemory in Post-Socialist Romania," in *Post-Communist Nostalgia*, eds. Maria Todorova and Zsuzsa Gille (New York: Berghahn Books, 2010), 154–166.
18. Maya Nadkarni, "'But It's Ours': Nostalgia and the Politics of Authenticity in Post-Socialist Hungary." in *Post-Communist Nostalgia*, eds. Maria Todorova and Zsuzsa Gille (New York: Berghahn Books, 2010), 197.
19. Nadkarni, "'But It's Ours,'" 201.
20. Alexei Yurchak, *Everything Was Forever Until It Was No More: The Last Soviet Generation* (Princeton, NJ: Princeton University Press, 2005), 46.
21. Quoted in Irena Reifová, "Rerunning and 'Rewatching' Socialist TV Drama Serials: Post-Socialist Czech Television Audiences between Commodification and Reclaiming the Past," *Critical Studies in Television* 4, no. 2 (2009): 59. Also see Susan Stewart, *On Longing: Narratives of the Miniature, the Gigantic, the Souvenir, the Collection* (Durham, NC: Duke University Press, 1999).

Chapter 9. Women and TV

1. Lynn Spigel, *Welcome to the Dreamhouse: Popular Media and Postwar Suburbs* (Durham, NC: Duke University Press, 2001), 5.
2. Janet Thumim, "Women at Work: Popular Drama on British Television c. 1955–1960," in *Small Screens, Big Ideas: Television in the 1950s*, ed. Janet Thumim (London: I. B. Tauris, 2002), 207–222.

3. Lynne Joyrich, "All That Television Allows: TV, Melodrama, Postmodernism and Consumer Culture," in *Private Screenings: Television and the Female Consumer*, eds. Lynn Spigel and Denise Mann (Minneapolis: University of Minnesota Press, 1992), 240.
4. Joyrich, "All That Television Allows," 244.
5. Elihu Katz and Rowan Howard-Williams, "Did Television Empower Women? The Introduction of Television and the Changing Status of Women in the 1950s," *Journal of Popular Television* 1, no. 1 (2013): 19.
6. Katz and Howard-Williams, "Did Television Empower Women?," 11.
7. Katz and Howard-Williams, "Did Television Empower Women?," 13.
8. Beverle Houston, "Viewing Television: The Metapsychology of Endless Consumption," in *Phenomenological Approaches to Popular Culture*, eds. M. Carroll and E. Tafoya (Bowling Green, OH: Bowling Green State University Press, 2000), 203–220.
9. Thumim, "Women at Work," 220.
10. Katz and Howard-Williams, "Did Television Empower Women?," 18.
11. Michael Kackman, "Quality Television, Melodrama and Cultural Complexity," *Flow*, March 5, 2010, http://flowtv.org/2010/03/flow-favorites-quality-television-melodrama-and-cultural-complexity-michael-kackman-university-of-texas-austin/.
12. See Hana Cervinkova, "Postcolonialism, Postsocialism and the Anthropology of East-Central Europe," *Journal of Postcolonial Writing* 48 (2012): 156; Narcis Tulbure, "Introduction to Special Issue: Global Socialisms and Postsocialisms," *Anthropology of Eastern Europe Review* 27, no. 2 (2009): 4.
13. See Heather Gumbert, *Envisioning Socialism: Television and the Cold War in the German Democratic Republic* (Ann Arbor: University of Michigan Press, 2014); Paulina Bren, *The Greengrocer and His TV: The Culture of Communism after the 1968 Prague Spring* (Ithaca, NY: Cornell University Press, 2010); Kristin Roth-Ey, *Moscow Prime Time: How the Soviet Union Built the Media Empire That Lost the Cultural Cold War* (Ithaca, NY: Cornell University Press, 2011).
14. On representative writings in (post)socialist studies of women and gender, see Zillah Eisenstein, "Eastern European Male Democracies: A Problem of Unequal Equality," in *Gender Politics and Post-Communism*, eds. N. Funk and M. Mueller (New York: Routledge, 1993), 303–330; Agnieszka Graff, "The Return of the Real Man: Gender and E.U. Accession in Three Polish Weeklies," 2005, http://www.iub.edu/~reeiweb/events/2005/graffpaper.pdf; Djurdja Knezevic, "Affective Nationalism," in *Transitions, Environments, Translations: Feminism in International Politics*, eds. J. W. Scott, C. Kaplan, and D. Keates (London: Routledge, 2004), 65–71; Anikó Imre, "Lesbian Nationalism," *Signs* 33, no. 2 (2007): 255–282; Laurie Occhipinti, "Two Steps Back? Anti-Feminism in Eastern Europe," *Anthropology Today*, 12, no. 6 (1996): 13–18; Barbara Einhorn, *Cinderella Goes to the Market: Citizenship, Gender and Women's Movements in East Central Europe* (London: Verso,

1993); Susan Gal and Gail Kligman, *Reproducing Gender: Politics, Publics and Everyday Life after Socialism* (Princeton, NJ: Princeton University Press, 2000); Shana Penn and Jill Massino, eds., *Gender Politics and Everyday Life in State Socialist East and Central Europe* (New York: Palgrave Macmillan, 2009); Éva Fodor, "Smiling Women and Fighting Men: The Gender of the Communist Subject in State Socialist Hungary," *Gender and Society* 16, no. 2 (2002): 240–263; Susan Zimmermann, "Gender Regime and Gender Struggle in Hungarian State Socialism," *Aspasia* 4 (2010): 1–24.

15. The exceptions are equally significant here; see the work of Zala Volčič, Karmen Erjavec, Nadia Kaneva, Elza Ibroscheva, and a handful of others.
16. See Fodor, "Smiling Women and Fighting Men," 240–263.
17. See Fodor, "Smiling Women and Fighting Men," 240–263; Zimmermann, "Gender Regime and Gender Struggle," 1–24.
18. Dunavölgyi, "1957."
19. Bren, *The Greengrocer and His TV*, 160.
20. Roth-Ey, *Moscow Prime Time*, 202. This was reinforced in a 1970s survey conducted by Polish Radio and Television. See Dunavölgyi, "1970."
21. Roth-Ey, *Moscow Prime Time*, 203.
22. Margit Benkő, "Életmód és Tévénézés," *Kultúra és közösség* 3 (1986): 32–33.
23. See Bren, *The Greengrocer and His TV*, 191.
24. "Kapok ide, kapok oda—Pörkölődik az ing nyaka—Ég a rántás fut a tej!—csodálatos egy találmány—Egy baja van: hogy nézni kell." See Dunavölgyi, "1959."
25. Daniela Mustata, e-mail to Anikó Imre, September 13, 2013.
26. Hungarian Socialist Workers' Party Central Committee, MOL—288f 22/1959 6.öe./23. MSZMP KP, Agitációs és Propaganda Osztály (Department of Agitation and Propaganda files), Hungarian National Document Archives.
27. Christine Evans, "The 'Soviet Way of Life' as Way of Feeling: Emotion and Influence on Soviet Central Television in the Brezhnev Era," *Cahiers du Monde Russe* 56/2–3 (2015), forthcoming.
28. Evans, "The 'Soviet Way of Life' as Way of Feeling."
29. Roth-Ey, *Moscow Prime Time*, 243.
30. Evans, "The 'Soviet Way of Life' as Way of Feeling."
31. Tadeusz Pikulski, *Prywatna historia telewizji publicznej* (Warsaw: Muza SA, 2002), 54.
32. Pikulski, *Prywatna historia telewizji publicznej*, 54.
33. See Dunavölgyi, "1969."
34. Ferenc Erőss, "Critique," *Rádió és TV Szemle* (5) 1962.
35. "Megnéztük," *Rádió és TV Újság* 10 (1963).
36. Bren, *The Greengrocer and His TV*, 112.
37. Christine Evans, "Song of the Year and Soviet Mass Culture in the 1970s," *Kritika: Explorations in Soviet and Euroasian History* 12, no. 3 (2011): 622.
38. Evans, "Song of the Year and Soviet Mass Culture in the 1970s," 624.
39. Fodor, "Smiling Women and Fighting Men," 251.

40. Fodor, "Smiling Women and Fighting Men," 249.
41. Zimmermann, "Gender Regime and Gender Struggle," 11.
42. Zimmermann, "Gender Regime and Gender Struggle," 11.

Chapter 10. Socialist Soaps

1. As Paulina Bren points out, this was not an isolated strategy. Under Brazil's military rule, Globo teamed up with the government to showcase upscale lives in telenovelas as a sign of modernization and upward mobility. See Paulina Bren, *The Greengrocer and His TV: The Culture of Communism after the 1968 Prague Spring* (Ithaca, NY: Cornell University Press, 2010), 125.
2. Ien Ang and Jon Stratton, "The End of Civilization as We Knew It: *Chances* and the Postrealist Soap Opera," in *To Be Continued . . . Soap Operas Around the World*, ed. Robert C. Allen (London: Routledge, 1995), 122–144.
3. Ib Bondebjerg, Tomasz Goban-Klas, Michele Hilmes, Daniela Mustata, Helle Strandgaard-Jensen, Isabelle Veyrat-Masson and Susanne Vollberg, "American Television: Point of Reference or European Nightmare?," in *A European Television History*, eds. J. Bignell and A. Fickers (New York: Blackwell, 2008), 154–183.
4. See Sabina Mihelj, "Television Entertainment in Socialist Eastern Europe: Between Cold War Politics and Global Developments," in *Popular Television in Eastern Europe During and Since Socialism*, eds. Anikó Imre, Timothy Havens, and Katalin Lustyik (London: Routledge, 2012), 13–29.
5. Idrit Idrizi, "Das magische Gerät: Die Bedeutung des Fernsehers im isolierten Albanien und für die Erforschung des albanischen Kommunismus" (paper presented at the conference "Television in Europe beyond the Iron Curtain—National and Transnational Perspectives since the 1950s," Friedrich-Alexander-Universität Erlangen-Nürnberg, December 5–7, 2013).
6. As it is widely known, Ceaușescu built his legitimacy on currying favor with Western countries. He visited with Nixon and even gained most favored nation status in the United States in 1975.
7. Bondebjerg et al., "American Television," 177–178.
8. János Horvát, "Külföldi műsorok a magyar képernyőn," *Pártélet*, August–September 1986, 89–93.
9. "Kozonsegtisztelo televizio," *Magyar Hirlap*, August 20, 1986.
10. Horvát, "Külföldi műsorok a magyar képernyőn," 89–93.
11. L.G., "Másfélből kettő," *Magyar Nemzet*, September 20, 1988.
12. "Beszélgetés a műholdas televíziózásról: Megnyíló égi csatorna," *HVG*, November 8, 1986.
13. Horvát, "Külföldi műsorok a magyar képernyőn," 90.
14. Such was the case with the 1977 miniseries *Washington: Behind Closed Doors*, a historical drama about the Nixon administration. On the one hand, it was aired in most socialist countries because it contained internal criticism of the capitalist system. On the other hand, it demonstrated the people's will to

impeach the president elected by the people. See Horvát, "Külföldi műsorok a magyar képernyőn," 91.

15. Heather Gumbert, "Shoring Up Socialism: Transnational Media Exchange and Cultural Sovereignty in the GDR" (paper presented at the conference "Television in Europe beyond the Iron Curtain—National and Transnational Perspectives since the 1950s," Friedrich-Alexander-Universität Erlangen-Nürnberg, December 5–7, 2013).
16. Stewart Anderson, "Modern Viewers, Feudal Television Archives: How to Study German Fernsehspiele of the 1960s from a National Perspective," *Critical Studies in Television* 5, no. 2 (2010): 92–104.
17. Thomas Beutelschmidt and Henning Wrage, "'Range and Diversity' in the GDR?: Television Drama in the Early 1970s," *Historical Journal of Film, Radio and Television* 24, no. 3 (2004): 441–454.
18. Beutelschmidt and Wrage, "'Range and Diversity' in the GDR?," 443.
19. Beutelschmidt and Wrage, "'Range and Diversity' in the GDR?," 445.
20. Markus Schubert and Hans-Jeorg Stiehler, "A Program Structure Analysis of East German Television, 1968–1974," *Historical Journal of Film, Radio and Television* 24, no. 4 (2004): 345–353.
21. Beutelschmidt and Wrage, "'Range and Diversity' in the GDR?," 446.
22. Beutelschmidt and Wrage, "'Range and Diversity' in the GDR?," 448.
23. Laura Voloncs, "Rólunk Szól: 'A Szabó család' mint a kádári Magyarország kordokumentuma," *Médiakutató*, Spring 2010, http://www.mediakutato.hu/cikk/2010_01_tavasz/02_szabo_csalad.
24. Information courtesy of Nevena Dakovic, December 2013.
25. Bondebjerg et al., "American Television," 162.
26. Following some experiments with the genre, Central Television returned to the historical serial formula. See Simon Huxtable, presentation at workshop "Rethinking Socialist TV: Viewers, Genres, Messages" at the annual convention of the Association for Slavic and East European Studies, San Antonio, TX, November 2014.
27. Christine Evans, "'The 'Soviet Way of Life' as Way of Feeling: Emotion and Influence on Soviet Central Television in the Brezhnev Era," *Cahiers du Monde Russe* (Spring 2015), forthcoming.
28. Bren, *The Greengrocer and His TV*, 130.
29. During his decade in office (1970–1980), First Secretary Edward Gierek had an ambitious plan to raise living standards. Unfortunately, this was financed by massive borrowing, which then largely accounted for Poland's economic collapse in the 1980s. "Edward Gierek Obituary," *Telegraph*, July 31, 2001, http://www.telegraph.co.uk/news/obituaries/1335845/Edward-Gierek.html. Thanks to Maria Zalewska for research and translation.
30. It is part of a cycle of Polish satirical soaps produced in the 1970s and 1980s, including *Alternatywy 4* (4 Alternative Street, 1986); *Wojna Domowa* (Civil war, 1965–1966), *Daleko od Szosy* (Far from the highway, 1976), and *Jan Serce* (John Heart, 1982); Kinga Bloch, "The Life and Afterlife of a Socialist Media

Friend: On the Long-Term Cultural Relevance of the Polish TV Series 'Czterdziestolatek,'" *VIEW Journal* 2, no. 3 (2013): 88–98.

31. Bloch, "The Life and Afterlife of a Socialist Media Friend," 88–98.
32. Information courtesy of Maria Zalewska, September 2013.
33. Sabina Mihelj, "The Politics of Privatization: Television Entertainment and the Yugoslav Sixties," in *The Socialist Sixties: Crossing Borders in the Second World*, eds. Anne Gorsuch and Diane Koenker (Bloomington: Indiana University Press, 2013), 251–267.
34. Nevena Dakovic and Aleksandra Milanovic, "Socialist Family Sitcom: Bridging the East-West Divide in the 1970s" (paper presented at the conference "Television in Europe beyond the Iron Curtain—National and Transnational Perspectives since the 1950s," Friedrich-Alexander-Universität Erlangen-Nürnberg, December 5–7, 2013).
35. By the mid-1970s, practically all women of working age were fully employed, and proportions in education were equal between sexes. But this of course did not mean reduction of domestic responsibilities, although the state did help out with maternal leave, free child care centers, reduced meals, and laundry services. This disappeared after 1989. See Eva Fodor, "Smiling Women and Fighting Men: The Gender of the Communist Subject in State Socialist Hungary," *Gender and Society* 16, no. 2 (2002): 245.
36. Fodor, "Smiling Women and Fighting Men," 249.
37. Fodor, "Smiling Women and Fighting Men," 257.
38. Fodor, "Smiling Women and Fighting Men," 250.
39. Fodor, "Smiling Women and Fighting Men," 251.
40. Fodor, "Smiling Women and Fighting Men," 246.
41. Although it has been recirculated so many times in film and on TV that it is almost clichéd. It is especially popular in comedic representations. *The Simpsons* had an "occupy the trees" episode, and in a 2013 episode of the popular ABC sitcom *Modern Family*, Cam sits in a tree to save it from being cut down.
42. Bren, *The Greengrocer and His TV*, 126.
43. Dietl's serials clearly forced the party to reassess its relationship to viewers. Dietl placed great emphasis on success measured in terms of ratings: nine million viewers at least (out of a population of 15 million) was the beginning of success for him. Paulina Bren gives a detailed account of his trajectory, from the 1975 *Hamr Dynasty* about forced agricultural collectivization through his prolific annual output of new soaps. See Bren, *The Greengrocer and His TV*, 133.
44. Bren, *The Greengrocer and His TV*, 144.
45. Petr Bednařík, "The Production of Czechoslovakia's Most Popular Television Serial *The Hospital on the Outskirts* and Its Post-1989 Repeats," *VIEW Journal* 2, no. 3 (2013): 27–36.
46. Bednařík, "The Production of Czechoslovakia's Most Popular Television Serial," 27–36.

47. Christine Geraghty, "Soap Opera and Utopia," in *Cultural Theory and Popular Culture: A Reader*, ed. John Storey (Harlow, UK: Pearson Press, 1994), 246–254.
48. Jakub Machek, "'The Counter Lady' as a Female Prototype: Prime Time Popular Culture in 1970s and 1980s Czechoslovakia," *Media Research*, 16, no. 1 (2010): 44.
49. Machek, "'The Counter Lady' as a Female Prototype," 44.
50. Bren, *The Greengrocer and His TV*, 164.
51. Bren, *The Greengrocer and His TV*, 174.
52. Bren, *The Greengrocer and His TV*, 175.
53. Bren, *The Greengrocer and His TV*, 169.
54. Machek, "'The Counter Lady' as a Female Prototype," 48.
55. Machek, "'The Counter Lady' as a Female Prototype," 47.
56. Bren, *The Greengrocer and His TV*, 7–9.
57. Bren, *The Greengrocer and His TV*, 176.
58. Apats Gábor, "Linda huszonöt éve sikított először," *Origo*, July 12, 2009, http://www.origo.hu/teve/20090709-linda-sorozat-tortenete-gorbe-noraval-szerednyey-belaval-bodrogi-gyulaval.html.
59. Ferenc Hammer, "Coy Utopia: Politics in the First Hungarian TV Soap," in *Popular Television in Eastern Europe During and Since Socialism*, eds. Anikó Imre, Timothy Havens, and Katalin Lustyik (New York: Routledge, 2012), 222–240.
60. János Szegő, "Időszerű anakronizmus—a 'Szomszédok' húsz éve," *Népszabadság*, November 6, 2009, http://www.nol.hu/lap/tv/20091106-lombikbabok?ref=sso.
61. Dorota Ostrowska, "The Carnival of the Absurd: Stanislaw Bareja's *Alternatywy 4* and Polish Television in the 1980s," in *Popular Television in Eastern Europe During and Since Socialism*, eds. Anikó Imre, Timothy Havens, and Katalin Lustyik (New York: Routledge, 2012), 68.
62. Ostrowska, "The Carnival of the Absurd," 77–78.
63. Bloch, "The Life and Afterlife of a Socialist Media Friend," 88–98.
64. Bednařík, "The Production of Czechoslovakia's Most Popular Television Serial," 27–36.
65. 18.2 percent for the first episode, which increased to 31 percent, or 2.6 million viewers, for the twentieth episode. The first new episode received a 46.8 percent rating and an audience share of 77.2 percent, which never dropped below 60 percent. Most viewers were women, mostly older, urban, fairly established and educated. See Bednařík, "The Production."
66. Bednařík, "The Production of Czechoslovakia's Most Popular Television Serial," 27–36.
67. For an excellent summary of the problems of postsocialist postfeminism, see Ksenija Vidmar-Horvat, "The Globalization of Gender: *Ally McBeal* in Post-Socialist Slovenia," *European Journal of Cultural Studies* 8, no. 2 (2005): 239–255.

68. On the state of academic feminism, see Krassimira Daskalova, "Introduction: The Birth of a Field: Women's and Gender Studies in Central, Eastern and Southeastern Europe," *Aspasia* 4 (2010): 155–205. On the academic and mainstream resistance of feminism, see Helena Goscilo and Yana Hashamova, "Introduction," *Aspasia* 4 (2010): 94–102.

Chapter 11. Socialist Comedy

1. "Exporting Raymond," press kit, 2011.
2. "Exporting Raymond."
3. Phil Rosenthal, "Q&A" (meeting at the Television Symposium, University of Southern California, Los Angeles, April 2011).
4. Andrea Press, "Gender and Family in Television's Golden Age and Beyond," *Annals of the American Academy of Political and Social Science* 625, no. 1 (September 2009): 139–150.
5. "Exporting Raymond."
6. Vilmos Faragó, "Magyar Általános Szórakoztató," *Filmvilág* 1 (1984): 59–60, http://filmvilag.hu/xereses_frame.php?cikk_id=6554.
7. J. Gray, J. P. Jones, and E. Thompson, "The State of Satire, the Satire of State," in *Satire TV: Politics and Comedy in the Post-Network Era*, eds. J. Gray, J. P. Jones, and E. Thompson (New York: New York University Press, 2009), 13.
8. Dominic Boyer writes that the news was the result of a careful calculation of social engineering, whose goal was to change collective consciousness. This project, Boyer argues, while obviously a part of the larger scheme of international socialism, also revived the nineteenth-century German cultural bourgeoisie's desire to create a national consciousness among all the peoples who shared the German language as their main connection. Socialist media were to complete the paradoxical project of manufacturing the *Volk* on whose preexistence the entire concept of a national consciousness was based. See Dominic Boyer, "Censorship as Vocation: The Institutions, Practices, and Cultural Logic of Media Control in the German Democratic Republic," *Comparative Studies in Society and History* 45 (2003): 523.
9. Serguei A. Oushakine, "Introduction: Jokes of Repression," *East European Politics and Societies* 25, no. 4 (November 2011): 655.
10. Oushakine, "Introduction," 656.
11. Serguei A. Oushakine, "'Red Laughter': On Refined Weapons of Soviet Jesters," *Social Research* 79, no. 1 (Spring 2012): 189–216.
12. This was particularly true in the most liberal socialist countries. Sabina Mihelj references a 1963 Serbian survey that shows that programs containing music, humor, and sports had the highest viewer ratings and that, in the 1960s, programs with a humorous address had the highest appeal in all of Yugoslavia. According to a representative poll conducted in Serbia in

May 1967, as many as 68.2 percent of viewers wanted television programs to contain more "humorous-satirical programs"—by far the most sought-after genre type—while only 6.3 percent opted for more information and 10.8 for more educational programs. On the little screen, even otherwise apolitical forms of entertainment, those centered on depictions of private life and mythologized recollections of World War II, tended to leave room for subtle criticism and ironic humor. In Yugoslavia, the comic twists and turns of everyday life depicted in the comic serial *Theater in the House* (1973–1984) and *Vruć vetar* (Hot wind, 1980) occasionally poked fun at the seamy underbelly of Yugoslav affluence, including unemployment and reliance on mass labor migration to the West. Likewise, the Soviet variety show *The Pub of 13 Chairs* regularly included stand-up comedy stints parodying the shortcomings of Soviet society, such as the scarcity of consumer goods and the mismatch between political visions and everyday life. See Sabina Mihelj, "The Politics of Privatization: Television Entertainment and the Yugoslav Sixties," in *The Socialist Sixties: Crossing Borders in the Second World*, eds. Anne Gorsuch and Diane Koenker (Bloomington: Indiana University Press, 2013), 251–267.

13. "Cultures of Drink: Song, Dance, Alcohol and Politics in 20th Century German Cabarets," https://courses.cit.cornell.edu/his452/Alcohol/germancabaret.html. Accessed on November 8, 2013.
14. Thanks to Maria Zalewska for the research.
15. G. Apats, "Szeszélyes évadok," 2007, http://www.origo.hu/teve/20071130-100-eves-a-magyar-kabare-szeszelyes-evszakok-tortenete.html.
16. Z. Rick, "A pesti kabarék a II. világháború idején," 2008, http://www.mazsike.hu/pesti+kabarek+a+ii+vilaghaboru+idejen.html.
17. Á. Alpár, "A pesti kabaré," 2011, http://tbeck.beckground.hu/szinhaz/htm/25.htm.
18. Faragó, "Magyar Általános Szórakoztató," 59–60.
19. Dunavölgyi, "1957."
20. Dunavölgyi, "1957."
21. Tadeusz Pikulski, *Prywatna historia telewizji publicznej* (Warsaw: Muza SA, 2002), 74.
22. Marek Haltof, *Polish National Cinema* (Oxford: Berghahn Books, 2002), 140.
23. Pikulski, *Prywatna historia*, 75.
24. Pikulski, *Prywatna historia*, 74.
25. Pikulski, *Prywatna historia*, 75.
26. Silviu Brucan, "Idila mea cu televiziunea," in *Viziune-Tele* (TVR Directia de Logistica si Memorie, 1996), 41.
27. Daniela Mustata, "Reassembling a History of Romanian Television Programmes," in "The Power of Television: Including the Historicizing of the Live Romanian Revolution" (PhD diss., Utrecht University, 2011).
28. Heather Gumbert, *Envisioning Socialism: Television and the Cold War in the*

German Democratic Republic (Ann Arbor: University of Michigan Press, 2014), 156.
29. Gumbert, *Envisioning Socialism*, 157.
30. In the summer of 1959, Mrs. K.I., party secretary for the TV Union, prepared a report for the Central Committee. See Dunavölgyi, "1959."
31. Report from the National Council or Labor Unions, "Vélemények a Televízió munkájáról," March 29, 1966, 288f 22/1966/agit/73/3, Hungarian National Document Archives.
32. Report about the Work of Television prepared by the President of Hungarian Television, "Jelentés a Televízió munkájáról," March 31, 1966, 288f 22/1966/11 ö.e, agit/375, Hungarian National Document Archives.
33. Document from 1970, 288f 41/130 ö.e Ag 897, Agitációs Propaganda Bizottság, Hungarian National Document Archives.
34. Transcript provided by Hungarian TV Archives, May 1, 1965.
35. Dunavölgyi, "1969."
36. Anna Vilcsek, "Critique," *Magyar Nemzet*, April 30, 1969.
37. Dunavölgyi, "1964."
38. Dunavölgyi, "1969."

Chapter 12. (Post)socialist Political Satire

1. See G. Baym, "'The Daily Show': Discursive Integration and the Reinvention of Political Journalism," *Political Communication* 22 (2005): 259–276; J. Gray, J. P. Jones, and E. Thompson, "The State of Satire, the Satire of State," in *Satire TV: Politics and Comedy in the Post-Network Era*, eds. J. Gray, J. P. Jones, and E. Thompson (New York: New York University Press, 2009), 3–36.
2. Gray, Jones, and Thompson, "The State of Satire," 15.
3. Gray, Jones, and Thompson, "The State of Satire," 15.
4. See Amber Day, "And Now . . . The News? Mimesis and the Real in *The Daily Show*" in *Satire TV: Politics and Comedy in the Post-Network Era*, eds. J. Gray, J. P. Jones, and E. Thompson (New York: New York University Press, 2009), 85–103; Baym, "The Daily Show," 266.
5. Dominic Boyer and Alexei Yurchak, "AMERICAN STIOB: Or, What Late-Socialist Aesthetics of Parody Reveal about Contemporary Political Culture in the West," *Cultural Anthropology* 25, no. 2 (2010): 179–221.
6. Baym, "The Daily Show," 261.
7. D. Boyer, "Censorship as Vocation: The Institutions, Practices, and Cultural Logic of Media Control in the German Democratic Republic," *Comparative Studies in Society and History* 45 (2003): 511–545.
8. M. Zalán, "A magyar rádió és televízió belső felépítése és szerkezete," internal report no. 753.3, 1966, Open Society Archives, Budapest.
9. This is something Aczél directly borrowed from British TV in his previous

job as foreign correspondent from London. Endre Aczél, interview by Anikó Imre, December 2013.
10. Aczél, interview by Anikó Imre.
11. Baym, "The Daily Show," 272.
12. Dominic Boyer and Alexei Yurchak, "Postsocialist Studies, Cultures of Parody and American Stiob," *Anthropology News*, November 2008, 9–10.
13. See Boyer and Yurchak, "Postsocialist Studies," 9–10.
14. Boyer and Yurchak, "AMERICAN STIOB," 179–221.
15. Boyer and Yurchak, "AMERICAN STIOB," 179–221.
16. Natasa Kovačević, "Late Communist and Postcommunist Avant-Garde Aesthetics: Interrogations of Community," in *Postcommunism, Postmodernism, and the Global Imagination*, ed. C. Muraru (New York: Columbia University Press, 2009), 211–230.
17. Kovačević, "Late Communist and Postcommunist Avant-Garde Aesthetics," 211–230.
18. M. Faragó, "Puha humor," *Filmvilág* 9 (1984): 62–63, http://filmvilag.hu/xereses_frame.php?cikk_id=6339; György Csepeli, "A televíziós szórakoztatásról," *Filmvilág* 1 (1984): 59–60, http://filmvilag.hu/xereses_frame.php?cikk_id=6554; A. Kristóf, "A kabaré alkonya," *Filmvilág* 1 (1980): 56–57, http://filmvilag.hu/xereses_frame.php?cikk_id=8028.
19. Boyer and Yurchak, "AMERICAN STIOB," 4.
20. Boyer and Yurchak, "AMERICAN STIOB," 4.
21. "Az utolsó Heti hetes," NOL TV, June 12, 2010, http://www.noltv.hu/video/2678.html.
22. "Heti nézettség: Legyűrte az RTL Klubot a Tv2," *Origo*, December 7, 2010.
23. "Verebest is bevetik a Heti hetes ellen," *Origo*, February 12, 2010, http://www.origo.hu/teve/20100212-verebest-is-bevetik-a-heti-hetes-ellen.html.
24. G. Apats, "Gálvölgyi János: A Heti hetes arra jó, hogy ne hülyüljek el," *Origo*, February 17, 2011, http://www.origo.hu/teve/20110217-interju-galvolgyi-janossal-a-madach-szinhaz-szineszevel-a-galvolgyi-show.html.
25. See Fórum "Nézed a Heti Hetest?," http://www.hoxa.hu/?p1=forum_tema&p2=21887&p4=0; http://www.sg.hu/listazas.php3?id=967998509&order=reverse&index=1.
26. "Csak egy nap: Bekukucskáltunk a Heti Hetes kulisszái mögé," *Blikk*, February 25, 2008, http://www.blikk.hu/blikk_csakegynap/20080225/bekukucskaltunk_a_heti_hetes_kulisszai_moge/.
27. Apats, "Gálvölgyi János."
28. "Az utolsó Heti hetes," NOL TV.
29. "Hajós András lesz a Heti hetes új bohóca," *Velvet Kommandó*, September 1, 2004, http://velvet.hu/celeb/hetiheto901/; C. Kalmár, "Nem a Heti hetestől várják a választ," *Origo*, September 10, 2009, http://www.origo.hu/teve/20090910-nem-a-heti-hetestol-varjak-a-valaszt-onodi-gyorgy.html.
30. Kalmár, "Nem a Heti hetestől várják a választ."

31. Aczél, interview by Anikó Imre.
32. Serra Tinic, "Speaking 'Truth' to Power? Television Satire, Rick Mercer Report, and the Politics of Place and Space," in *Satire TV: Politics and Comedy in the Network Era*, eds. J. Gray, J. P. Jones, and E. Thompson (New York: New York University Press, 2009), 168.

BIBLIOGRAPHY

Aczél, Endre. Interview by Anikó Imre. December 2012 and December 2013.
Allen, Robert C., ed. *To Be Continued . . . Soap Operas around the World*. London: Routledge, 1995.
Allen, Robert C., and Annette Hill, eds. *The Television Studies Reader*. London: Routledge, 2004.
Anderson, Stewart. "Modern Viewers, Feudal Television Archives: How to Study German *Fernsehspiele* of the 1960s from a National Perspective." *Critical Studies in Television* 5, no. 2 (2010): 92–104.
Appadurai, A. *Fear of Small Numbers: An Essay on the Geography of Anger*. Durham, NC: Duke University Press, 2006.
Autio-Sarasmo, Sari, and Katalin Miklóssy, eds. *Reassessing Cold War Europe*. New York: Routledge, 2011.
Bal, Mieke, Jonathan Crewe, and Leo Spitzer, eds. *Acts of Memory: Cultural Recall in the Present*. Hanover, NH: Dartmouth University Press, 1999.
Balada e Kurbinit. Dir. Kujtim Çashku, 1990.
Baym, G. "'The Daily Show': Discursive Integration and the Reinvention of Political Journalism." *Political Communication* 22 (2005): 259–276.
Bednařík, Petr. "The Production of Czechoslovakia's Most Popular Television Serial *The Hospital on the Outskirts* and Its Post-1989 Repeats." *VIEW Journal of European Television History and Culture* 2, no. 3 (2013): 27–36.
Bélley, Pál. "Critique." *Magyar Hírlap*, April 19, 1971.

Benkő, Margit. "Életmód és Tévénézés." *Kultúra és közösség* 3 (1986): 32–44.

"Beszelgetes a muholdas televiziozasrol. Megnyilo egi csatorna." *HVG*, November 8, 1986.

Beutelschmidt, Thomas. "East German TV and Global Transfers." Paper presented at the conference "Television in Europe beyond the Iron Curtain—National and Transnational Perspectives since the 1950s," Friedrich-Alexander-Universität Erlangen-Nürnberg, December 5–7, 2013.

Beutelschmidt, Thomas, and Henning Wrage. "'Range and Diversity' in the GDR?' Television Drama in the Early 1970s." *Historical Journal of Film, Radio and Television* 24, no. 3 (2004): 441–454.

Beutelschmidt, Thomas, and Richard Oehmig. "Connected Enemies? Programming Transfer between East and West during the Cold War and the Example of East German Television." *VIEW: Journal of European Television History and Culture* 3, no. 5 (2014): 60–67.

"B.G." *Magyar Nemzet*, April 19, 1969.

Bignell, Jonathan. "Transatlantic Spaces: Production, Location and Style in 1960s–1970s Action-Adventure TV Series." *Media History* 16, no. 1 (2010): 53–65.

Bignell, J., and A. Fickers, eds. *A European Television History*. New York: Blackwell, 2008.

Bloch, Kinga. "The Life and Afterlife of a Socialist Media Friend: On the Long-Term Cultural Relevance of the Polish TV Series 'Czterdziestolatek.'" *VIEW Journal of European Television History and Culture* 2, no. 3 (2013): 88–98.

Boj na Kosovo. Dir. Zdravko Šotra, 1989.

Bourdon, Jérôme. "Old and New Ghosts: Public Service Television and the Popular—A History." *European Journal of Cultural Studies* 7, no. 3 (2004): 283–304.

Boyer, Dominic. "Censorship as Vocation: The Institutions, Practices, and Cultural Logic of Media Control in the German Democratic Republic." *Comparative Studies in Society and History* 45 (2003): 511–545.

———. "*Ostalgie* and the Politics of the Future in Eastern Germany." *Public Culture* 18, no. 2 (2006): 363

Boyer, Dominic, and Alexei Yurchak. "AMERICAN STIOB: Or, What Late-Socialist Aesthetics of Parody Reveal about Contemporary Political Culture in the West." *Cultural Anthropology* 25, no. 2 (2010): 179–221.

———. "Postsocialist Studies, Cultures of Parody and American Stiob." *Anthropology News*, November 2008: 9–10.

Breitenborn, Uwe. "'Memphis Tennessee' in Borstendorf: Boundaries Set and Transcended in East German Television Entertainment." *Historical Journal of Film, Radio and Television* 24, no. 3 (2004): 391–402.

Bren, Paulina. *The Greengrocer and His TV: The Culture of Communism after the 1968 Prague Spring*. Ithaca, NY: Cornell University Press, 2010.

Bren, Paulina, and Mary Neuburger, eds. *Communism Unwrapped: Consumption in Cold War Eastern Europe*. Oxford: Oxford University Press, 2012.

Brucan, Silviu. "Idila mea cu televiziunea." In *Viziune-Tele* (TVR Directia de Logistica si Memorie, 1996), 41.

Brunsdon, Charlotte. "Is Television Studies History?" *Cinema Journal* 47, no. 3 (2008): 127–137.

Buckingham, D. "What Are Words Worth? Interpreting Children's Talk about Television." *Cultural Studies* 5, no. 2 (1991): 228–245.

Budai, András. "A Magyar Rádió és Televízió nemzetközi kapcsolatai." In *Tanfolyamok, Előadások a Televízióról*, 23–34. Budapest: MRT Tömegkommunikációs Kutatóközpont, 1970.

Buonanno, Ann Gray, and Erin Bell. "History on Television: Charisma, Narrative and Knowledge." *European Journal of Cultural Studies* 1, no. 1 (2007): 113–133.

Buonanno, Milly. *Italian TV Drama and Beyond: Stories from the Soil, Stories from the Sea*. Bristol: Intellect, 2002.

Carelli, Paolo. "Italianization Accomplished: Forms and Structures of Albanian Television's Dependency on Italian Media and Culture." *VIEW: Journal of European Television History and Culture* 3, no. 5 (2014): 68–78.

Carroll, M., and E. Tafoya, eds. *Phenomenological Approaches to Popular Culture*. Bowling Green, OH: Bowling Green State University Press, 2000.

Cervinkova, Hana. "Postcolonialism, Postsocialism and the Anthropology of East-Central Europe." *Journal of Postcolonial Writing* 48 (2012): 155–163.

Corner, John. "Performing the Real: Documentary Diversions." *Television and New Media* 3, no. 3 (2002): 255–269.

———. "Presumption as Theory: 'Realism' in Television Studies." In *Studying Media: Problems of Theory and Method*, 68–75. Edinburgh: Edinburgh University Press, 1998.

Cornis-Pope, Marcel, and John Neubauer, eds. *History of the Literary Cultures of East-Central Europe: Junctures and Disjuncture in the 19th and 20th Centuries. Vol. 4, Types and Stereotypes*. Amsterdam: John Benjamins, 2010.

Crowley, David, and Susan E. Reid, eds. *Pleasures in Socialism: Leisure and Luxury in the Eastern Bloc*. Evanston, IL: Northwestern University Press, 2010.

Csepeli, György. "Rádiónk és televíziónk közművelődési szemlélete és gyakorlata." *Rádió és TV Szemle* 6, no. 3 (1973): 5–16.

Čulík, Jan, ed. *National Mythologies in Central European TV Series: How J.R. Won the Cold War*. Brighton: Sussex Academic Press, 2013.

Dakovic, Nevena, and Aleksandra Milanovic. "Socialist Family Sitcom: Bridging the East-West Divide in the 1970s." Paper presented at the conference "Television in Europe beyond the Iron Curtain—National and Transnational Perspectives since the 1950s," Friedrich-Alexander-Universität Erlangen-Nürnberg, December 5–7, 2013.

Dankovics, Noémi Dóra. "Játékmesterek és vetélkedőműsorok a magyar televíziózás történetében." PhD diss., Budapest College of Communication and Business, 2012.

Daskalova, Krassimira. "Introduction. The Birth of a Field: Women's and Gender

Studies in Central, Eastern and Southeastern Europe." *Aspasia* 4 (2010): 155–205.

Dhoest, Alexander. "'The Pfaffs Are Not Like the Osbournes': National Inflections of the Celebrity Docusoap." *Television and New Media* 6, no. 2 (2004): 224–245.

———. "Quality and/as National Identity: Press Discourse on Flemish Period TV Drama." *European Journal of Cultural Studies* 7, no. 3 (2004): 305–324.

Dittmar, Claudia. "GDR Television in Competition with West German Programming." *Historical Journal of Film, Radio and Television* 24, no. 3 (2004): 327–343.

Document MSZMP APO 288f.22/1969. Hungarian National Document Archives.

Document from 1970, 288f 41/130 ö.e Ag 897. Agitációs Propaganda Bizottság. Hungarian National Document Archives.

Document 288f.22/163/12.öe—MSZMP KB Agitációs és Propaganda Osztálya. Hungarian National Document Archives.

Document XXVI-A-8-a, Box 151. Hungarian National Document Archives.

Document XXVI-A-9, Box 30. MTV documents, Hungarian National Document Archives.

Dunavölgyi. Péter. Interview by Anikó Imre. December 2012 and December 2013.

———. "A magyar televíziózás története." http://dunavolgyipeter.hu.

Edgerton, G., and Peter C. Rollins, eds. *Television Histories: Shaping Collective Memory in the Media Age*. Louisville: University Press of Kentucky, 2001.

Einhorn, Barbara. *Cinderella Goes to the Market: Citizenship, Gender and Women's Movements in East Central Europe*. London: Verso, 1993.

Ellis, John. "The Performance on Television of Sincerely Felt Emotion." *Annals of the American Academy of Political and Social Science* 625 (September 2009): 103–115.

———. "Television and History." *History Workshop Journal* 56 (Fall 2003): 278–285.

———. *Visible Fictions*. London: Routledge, 1982.

Ember, Mariann. "Hakni vagy újfajta filmezés." *Filmkultúra* 3 (1972).

Erőss, Ferenc. "Critique." *Rádió és TV Szemle* 5 (1962).

Evans, Christine. *Between Truth and Time: A History of Soviet Central Television*. Forthcoming.

———. "Song of the Year and Soviet Mass Culture in the 1970s." *Kritika: Explorations in Russian and Euroasian History* 12, no. 3 (Summer 2011): 617–645.

———. "The 'Soviet Way of Life' as Way of Feeling: Emotion and Influence on Soviet Central Television in the Brezhnev Era." *Cahiers du Monde Russe* 56/2–3 (2015), forthcoming.

Evans, Mary, ed. *Feminism: Critical Concepts in Literary and Cultural Studies*. New York: Routledge, 2000.

Fodor, Eva. "Smiling Women and Fighting Men: The Gender of the Communist Subject in State Socialist Hungary." *Gender and Society* 16, no. 2 (2002): 240–263.

Funk, N., and M. Mueller, eds. *Gender Politics and Post-Communism*. New York: Routledge, 1993.
G., L. "Masfelbol ketto." *Magyar Nemzet*, September 20, 1988.
Gal, Susan, and Gail Kligman. *Reproducing Gender: Politics, Publics and Everyday Life after Socialism*. Princeton, NJ: Princeton University Press, 2000.
Garai, Tamas. "Milyen sorozatokat lathatunk a TV-ben?" *Fejér Megyei Hírlap*, January 24, 1985.
Gerencsér, Jenő. Document MSZMP APO 88f.22./1968/15.ö.e. AG 10/120/3 from 04.16.1968. Hungarian National Document Archives.
Gilroy, P. "Race Ends Here." *Ethnic and Racial Studies* 21, no. 5 (1998): 838–847.
Gorsuch, Anne, and Diane Koenker, eds. *The Socialist Sixties: Crossing Borders in the Second World*. Bloomington: Indiana University Press, 2013.
Goscilo, Helena, and Yana Hashamova. "Introduction." *Aspasia* 4 (2010): 94–102.
Gray, J., J. P. Jones, and E. Thompson, eds. *Satire TV: Politics and Comedy in the Post-network Era*. New York: New York University Press, 2009.
Gulyás, János. Document MSZMP APO 288f.22./1968/15.ö.e. AG 10/120. Hungarian National Document Archives.
Gumbert, Heather. *Envisioning Socialism: Television and the Cold War in the German Democratic Republic*. Ann Arbor: University of Michigan Press, 2014.
———. "Exploring Transnational Media Exchange in the 1960s." *VIEW: Journal of European Television History and Culture* 3, no. 5 (2014): 50–59.
———. "Shoring Up Socialism: Transnational Media Exchange and Cultural Sovereignty in the GDR." Paper presented at the conference "Television in Europe beyond the Iron Curtain—National and Transnational Perspectives since the 1950s," Friedrich-Alexander-Universität Erlangen-Nürnberg, December 5–7, 2013.
Halász, László. "Játék-műveltség-vetélkedők." *Magyar Rádió és Televízió Szemle* 2 (1971): 15–22.
Haltof, Marek. *Polish National Cinema*. Oxford: Berghahn Books, 2002.
Hankiss, Elemér. "Jegyzetek az amerikai és a magyar TV hatásmechanizmusáról: A cselekvő és merengő tévé." *Filmvilág* 8 (1982): 54–57.
Hegedűs, Tibor. "*Fórum*—belpolitikai téma: A szocialista jogalkotás, jogalkalmazás." *Népszabadság*, May 14, 1969.
"Heti nézettség: Legyűrte az RTL Klubot a Tv2." *Origo*, December 7, 2010.
Hills, M. *Fan Cultures*. London: Routledge, 2002.
Holdsworth, Amy. "Television Resurrections: Television and Memory." *Cinema Journal* 47, no. 3 (2008): 137–144.
Horvát, János. "Külföldi műsorok a magyar képernyőn." *Pártélet*, August–September 1986, 89–93.
Hot top 100 sztár: A száz legfontosabb magyar híresség. Budapest: Euromedia BT, 2008.
Huyssen, Andreas, ed. *After the Great Divide: Modernism, Mass Culture, Postmodernism*. Bloomington: Indiana University Press, 1986.

Hungarian Socialist Workers' Party Central Committee. Document MOL—288f 22/1959 6.öe./23. MSZMP KP, Agitációs és Propaganda Osztály (Department of Agitation and Propaganda files). Hungarian National Document Archives.

Idrizi, Idrit. "Das magische Gerät: Die Bedeutung des Fernsehers im isolierten Albanien und für die Erforschung des albanischen Kommunismus." Paper presented at the conference "Television in Europe beyond the Iron Curtain—National and Transnational Perspectives since the 1950s," Friedrich-Alexander-Universität Erlangen-Nürnberg, December 5–7, 2013.

Imre, Anikó, ed. *The Blackwell Companion to East European Cinemas*. New York: Blackwell, 2012.

———, ed. *A Companion to Eastern European Cinemas*. New York: Wiley-Blackwell, 2012.

———. "Eastern Westerns: Socialist Edutainment or National Transvestism." *New Review of Film and Television Studies* 9, no. 2 (June 2011): 152–169.

———. "Global Entertainment and the European 'Roma Problem.'" *Third Text* 20, no. 6 (2006): 659–670.

———. "Lesbian Nationalism." *Signs* 33, no. 2 (2007): 255–282.

———. "Love to Hate: National Intimacy and Racial Intimacy on Reality TV in the New Europe." *Television and New Media* 16.2 (2015): 103–130.

———. "National History and Cross-National Television Edutainment." *Journal of Popular Film and Television* 40, no. 3 (Fall 2012): 119–130.

———. "National Intimacy: Social Networking Sites and Post-socialist Public Culture." *European Journal of Cultural Studies* 12, no. 2 (2009): 219–234.

———. "Postcolonial Media Studies in Postsocialist Europe." *Boundary 2* 41, no. 1 (Spring 2014): 113–134.

———. "Roma Music and Transnational Homelessness." *Third Text* 22, no. 3 (May 2008): 325–336.

Imre, Anikó, Timothy Havens, and Katalin Lustyik, eds. *Popular Television in Eastern Europe During and Since Socialism*. New York: Routledge, 2012.

Iordanova, Dina., ed. *The Cinema of the Balkans*. London: Wallflower Press, 2006.

J., R. "Politikai tanfolyam a televízióban." *Rádió és Televízió Újság* 48 (1965): 6–8.

Jenkins, Henry. *Fans, Bloggers and Gamers: Media Consumers in a Digital Age*. New York: New York University Press, 2006.

Jermyn, Deborah. *Crime Watching: Investigating Real Crime TV*. New York: I. B. Tauris, 2007.

Jovánovics, Miklós. "Pro and Contra Television." *Népszabadság*, September 27, 1970.

Kalinina, Ekaterina. "Nostalgia Channel: Virtual Life in the Soviet Past." Paper presented at the symposium "Television Histories in (Post)Socialist Europe," Södertörn University, Stockholm, Sweden, November 7, 2013.

Kállai, E. ed. *The Gypsies/the Roma in Hungarian Society*. Budapest: Regio Press, 2002.

Katz, Elihu, and Rowan Howard-Williams. "Did Television Empower Women? The Introduction of Television and the Changing Status of Women in the 1950s." *Journal of Popular Television* 1, no. 1 (2013): 7–24.

Keinonen, Heidi. "Early Commercial Television in Finland: Balancing between East and West." *Media History* 18, no. 2 (2012): 177–189.

Kelemen, Endre. "Interview." *Filmesház*, December 2013.

———. "Mozaikok az Iskolatelevízió történetéből." *Rádió és TV Szemle* 2 (1974): 18–31.

Khinkulova, Kateryna. "Hello, Lenin? Nostalgia on Post-Soviet Television in Russia and Ukraine." *VIEW: Journal of European Television History and Culture* 1, no. 2 (2012): 94–104.

Kozieł, Andrzej. *Za chwilę dalszy ciąg programu: Telewizja Polska czterech dekad 1952–1989*. Warsaw: Oficyna Wydawnicza Aspra-Jr, 2003.

"Kozonsegtisztelo televizio." *Magyar Hirlap*, August 20, 1986.

Kraidy, Marwan. *Reality Television and Arab Politics: Contention in Public Life*. Cambridge: Cambridge University Press, 2009.

Kraidy, Marwan, and Katherine Senders, eds. *The Politics of Reality Television: Global Perspectives*. London: Routledge, 2010.

Ladányi, J., and I. Szelényi. *Patterns of Exclusion: Constructing Gypsy Ethnicity and the Making of an Underclass in Transitional Societies of Europe*. New York: Columbia University Press, 2006.

Laffond, José Carlos Rueda, Carlota Coronado Ruiz, Catarina Duff Burnay, Amparo Guerra Gómez, Susana Díaz Pérez, and Rogério Santos. "Parallel Stories, Differentiated Histories: Exploring Fiction and Memory in Spanish and Portuguese Television." *VIEW: Journal of European Television History and Culture* 1, no. 3 (2013): 37–44.

László, Rózsa. "Critique of *Fórum*." *Népszabadság*, January 18, 1969.

Leerssen, Joep. "Nationalism and the Cultivation of Culture." *Nations and Nationalism* 12, no. 4 (2006): 559–578.

Lepp, Annika, and Mervi Pantti. "Window to the West: Memories of Watching Finnish Television in Estonia during the Soviet Period." *VIEW: Journal of European Television History and Culture* 3, no. 2 (2012): 76–86.

Lukácsy, András. "Critique of *Delta*'s Broadcast of April 9, 1972." *Magyar Hírlap*, April 9, 1972.

Machek, Jakub. "'The Counter Lady' as a Female Prototype: Prime Time Popular Culture in 1970s and 1980s Czechoslovakia." *Media Research* 16, no. 1 (2010): 31–52.

Magyar Nemzet, December 15, 1965.

Matei, Alexandru. "The Golden Stag Festival in Ceausescu's Romania (1968–1971)." *VIEW The Journal of European History and Culture* 1, no. 2 (2013).

"Megnéztük." *Rádió és TV Újság* 10 (1963).

Messing, V. *In a White Framework: The Representation of Roma in the Hungarian Press*. Frankfurt: VDM Verlag, 2008.

Mihalik, Judit. "A *Híradó* története 1970–1990." PhD diss., ELTE Media Department, Budapest.

Mihályfi, Ernő. *Országgyűlési Napló*, Session 21, January 27, 1966.

Mihelj, Sabina. "Socialist Television in a Transnational Perspective: Challenges and Opportunities." Paper presented at the symposium "Television Histories in (Post)Socialist Europe," Södertörn University, Stockholm, Sweden, November 2013.

Miklóssy, Katalin, and Melanie Ilic, eds. *Competition in Socialist Society*. London: Routledge, 2014.

Muraru, C., ed. *Postcommunism, Postmodernism and the Global Imagination*. New York: Columbia University Press, 2009.

Mustata, Danaiela. "Editorial." *VIEW: Journal of European Television History and Culture* 3, no. 5 (2014): 1–6.

———. "The Power of Television: Including the Historicizing of the Live Romanian Revolution." PhD diss., Utrecht University, 2011.

National Council on Labor Unions. "Vélemények a Televízió munkájáról." March 29, 1966. 288f 22/1966/agit/73/3. Hungarian National Document Archives.

Németi, Géza. *Rádió és Televízió Újság* 16 (1969).

Népszava, July 30, 1966.

Newcomb, Horace, ed. *Encyclopedia of Television*. London: Routledge, 2004.

Occhipinti, Laurie. "Two Steps Back? Anti-feminism in Eastern Europe." *Anthropology Today* 12, no. 6 (1996): 13–18.

Oehmig, Richard. "Mission Impossible? Die Exportbemühungen des Fernsehens der DDR im Spiegel außenpolitischer und ökonomischer Implikationen" Paper presented at the conference "Television in Europe beyond the Iron Curtain—National and Transnational Perspectives since the 1950s," Friedrich-Alexander-Universität Erlangen-Nürnberg, December 5–7, 2013.

Olajos, Gergő. Interview by Anikó Imre. July 25, 2013.

Ouellette, Laurie, and James Hay. *Better Living through Reality TV: Television and Post-welfare Citizenship*. Hoboken, NJ: Wiley-Blackwell, 2008.

Ouellette, Laurie, and S. Murray, eds. *Reality TV: Remaking Television Culture*. New York: New York University Press, 2004.

Oushakine, Serguei A. "Introduction: Jokes of Repression." *East European Politics and Societies* 25, no. 4 (November 2011): 655–657.

———. "'Red Laughter': On Refined Weapons of Soviet Jesters." *Social Research* 79, no. 1 (Spring 2012): 189–216.

Pálos, Miklós. "Interview with László Grétsy." *Hétfői Hírek*, February 27, 1971.

Palyik, Katalin. Interview by Anikó Imre. December 2012.

Pécsi, Ferenc. "Heti ötven órában." *Film Színház Muzsika*, January 4, 1969, 1–3.

———. "The Television Broadcasting Policy," August 10, 1969. MSZMP APO 288f.22/1969/19.öe. Ag.350. Hungarian National Document Archives.

Penn, Shana, and Jill Massino, eds. *Gender Politics and Everyday Life in State Socialist East and Central Europe*. New York: Palgrave Macmillan, 2009.

"Pesti viccek a szocializmus idején." http://ketezer.hu/2006/07/pesti-viccek-a-szocializmus-idejen/.

Petersen, Hanne, José María Lorenzo Villaverde, and Ingrid Lund-Andersen, eds. *Contemporary Gender Relations and Changes in Legal Cultures*. Copenhagen: DJOF, 2013.

Petrescu, D. "The Alluring Facet of Ceausescu-ism: Nation-Building and Identity Politics in Communist Romania, 1965–1989." *New Europe College Yearbook* 11 (2003): 241–272.

Pikulski, Tadeusz. *Prywatna historia telewizji publicznej*. Warsaw: Muza SA, 2002.

Pócsik, Ilona. Interview by Anikó Imre. December 2013.

President of Hungarian Television. Report about the Work of Television, "Jelentés a Televízió munkájáról." March 31, 1966. 288f 22/1966/11 ö.e, agit/375. Hungarian National Document Archives.

Press, Andrea. "Gender and Family in Television's Golden Age and Beyond." *Annals of the American Academy of Political and Social Science* 625, no. 1 (September 2009): 139–150.

Pusnik, Marusa, and Gregor Starc. "An Entertaining (R)evolution: The Rise of Television in Socialist Slovenia." *Media Culture and Society* 30, no. 6 (2008): 777–793.

Rádió és TV újság 6 (1962).

Rádió és Televízió Újság 49 (1965).

"A rádió és televízió új nívódíjasai." *Rádió és Televízió Újság* 28 (1966).

Rádió és TV újság 31 (1966).

Rádió és TV újság 5 (1967).

Radványi, Dezső. "Interview." *Radio and TV Guide* 45 (1970).

Rapke, Jack. "Question-and-Answer Session at School of Cinematic Arts." University of Southern California, Los Angeles, April 2011.

Reifová, Irena. "Rerunning and 'Rewatching' Socialist TV Drama Serials: Postsocialist Czech Television Audiences between Commodification and Reclaiming the Past." *Critical Studies in Television* 4, no. 2 (2009): 53–71.

Reufsteck, Michael, and Stefan Niggemeier. *Das Fernsehlexikon: Alles über 7000 Sendungen von Ally McBeal bis zur ZDF-Hitparade*. Munich: Goldmann Verlag, 2005.

Rosenthal, Phil. "Q&A." Meeting at the Television Symposium, University of Southern California, Los Angeles, April 2011.

Roth-Ey, Kristin. *Moscow Prime Time: How the Soviet Union Built the Media Empire That Lost the Cultural Cold War*. Ithaca, NY: Cornell University Press, 2011.

Rózsa Sándor. Dir. Miklós Szinetár, 1971.

S., B. Z. "Tudósklub az ifjúságról?" *Somogy Megyei Néplap*, 1969.

Schubert, Markus, and Hans-Joerg Stiehler. "A Program Structure Analysis of East German Television, 1968–74." *Historical Journal of Film, Radio and Television* 24, no. 2 (2004): 345–353.

Scott, J. W., C. Kaplan, and D. Keates, eds. *Transitions, Environments, Translations: Feminism in International Politics*. London: Routledge, 2004.

Scuteri, Lucia Gaja. "TV as a Linguistic Issue in Yugoslavian Slovenia: A Brief Chronology from the 1960s to the 1980s." Paper presented at the conference "Television in Europe beyond the Iron Curtain—National and Transnational Perspectives since the 1950s," Friedrich-Alexander-Universität Erlangen-Nürnberg, December 5–7, 2013.

Skeggs, Beverly, H. Wood, and N. Thumin, "'Oh Goodness, I Am Watching Reality TV': How Methods Make Class in Audience Research," *European Journal of Cultural Studies* 22, no. 1 (2009): 5–24.

Skeggs, B. "The Making of Class and Gender through Visualizing Moral Subject Formation." *Sociology* 39, no. 5 (2005).

Sorescu-Marinkovic, Annemarie. "'We Didn't Have Anything, They Had It All': Watching Yugoslav Television in Communist Romania." Paper presented at the conference "Television in Europe beyond the Iron Curtain—National and Transnational Perspectives since the 1950s," Friedrich-Alexander-Universität Erlangen-Nürnberg, December 5–7, 2013.

Spigel, Lynn. *Make Room for TV: Television and the Family Ideal in Postwar America*. Chicago: University of Chicago Press, 1992.

———. *Welcome to the Dreamhouse: Popular Media and Postwar Suburbs*. Durham, NC: Duke University Press, 2001.

Spigel, Lynn, and Denise Mann, eds. *Private Screenings: Television and the Female Consumer*. Minneapolis: University of Minnesota Press, 1992.

Steinmetz, Rüdiger, and Reinhold Viehoff. "The Program History of Genres of Entertainment on GDR Television." *Historical Journal of Film, Radio and Television* 24, no. 3 (2004): 317–325.

Stewart, M. *The Time of the Gypsies*. Oxford: Westview Press, 1997.

Stewart, Susan. *On Longing: Narratives of the Miniature, the Gigantic, the Souvenir, the Collection*. Durham, NC: Duke University Press, 1999.

Storey, John, ed. *Cultural Theory and Popular Culture: A Reader*. Harlow, UK: Pearson Press, 1994.

Szabó, László. Interview by Anikó Imre. December 2012 and December 2013.

Szecskő, Tamás. "Szórakoztatás—Műsorpolitika." *Rádió és TV Szemle* 71, no. 3 (1971): 5–27.

Szegvári, Katalin. Interview by Anikó Imre. December 2012 and December 2013.

Szenes, Gábor. "School TV." *Népszabadság*, March 6, 1970.

Szostak, Sylwia. "Poland's Return to Europe: Polish Terrestrial Broadcasters and TV Fiction." *Journal of European Television History and Culture* 1, no. 2 (2012): 79–92.

"A TV-ben hallottuk." *Rádió és Televízió Újság* 33 (1961).

T., H. "Világirodalmi vetélkedő egyetemi fokon." *Esti Hírlap*, February 2, 1965.

Thiery, Árpád. "Interview with Ferenc Pécsi, Vice President of Hungarian TV and Radio." *Népszava*, January 3, 1967.

Thumim, Janet, ed. *Small Screens, Big Ideas: Television in the 1950s*. London: I. B. Tauris, 2002.

Tiborné, Huszár. "10 éves az iskolarádió." *Rádió és TV Szemle* 2 (1973).

Todorova, Maria, and Zsuzsa Gille, eds. *Post-communist Nostalgia*. New York: Berghahn Books, 2010

Tömpe, István, and Jenő Lugossy. "The Systematic Introduction of Television and Radio into Primary and Secondary Education." MOL-288f22/10 öe. MSZMP KB Agit. prop. oszt. Hungarian National Document Archives.

Tulbure, Narcis. "Introduction to Special Issue: Global Socialisms and Postsocialisms." *Anthropology of Eastern Europe Review* 27, no. 2 (2009): 2–18.
Vágó, István. Interview by Anikó Imre. December 2012 and December 2013.
Vajk, Vera. "Fekete fehér, igen, nem." *Népszava*, February 17, 1970.
Varga, György. "Műsoron a hirdetés." *Figyelő*, September 30, 1970.
Végh, Miklós. "Critique." *Rádió és TV újság*, April 18, 1971.
Vesernyés, János. "Komolyzenei rovat." *Film Színház Muzsika* 5 (1969).
Vidmar-Horvat, Ksenija. "The Globalization of Gender: *Ally McBeal* in Post-Socialist Slovenia." *European Journal of Cultural Studies* 8, no. 2 (2005): 239–255.
Vilcsek, Anna. "Critique," *Magyar Nemzet*, April 30, 1969.
Volčič, Zala. "Yugo-Nostalgia: Cultural Memory and Media in the Former Yugoslavia." *Critical Studies in Media Communication* 24, no. 1 (2007): 21–38.
Vortruba, Martin. "Hang Him High: The Elevation of Janosik to an Ethnic Icon." *Slavic Review* 65, no. 1 (2006): 24–44.
Vreme na nasilie. Dir. Ludmil Staikov, 1988.
Wagman, Ira. "Tele-clubs and European Television History beyond the Screen." *VIEW: Journal of European Television History and Culture* 1, no. 2 (2012).
White. Dir. Krzysztof Kieślowski, 1994.
Willems, W. *In Search of the True Gypsy: From Enlightenment to Final Solution*. London: Frank Cass, 1997.
Wood, Helen, and Beverly Skeggs, eds. *Real Class: Ordinary People and Reality Television across National Spaces*. London: BFI, 2012.
Yurchak, Alexei. *Everything Was Forever until It Was No More: The Last Soviet Generation*. Princeton, NJ: Princeton University Press, 2005.
Zalán, M. "A magyar rádió és televízió belső felépítése és szerkezete." Internal report no. 753.3, 1966. Open Society Archives, Budapest.
Zimmermann, Susan. "Gender Regime and Gender Struggle in Hungarian State Socialism." *Aspasia* 4 (2010): 1–24.
Zoonen, Liesbet van. "Imagining the Fan Democracy." *European Journal of Communication* 19, no. 1 (2004): 39–52.

INDEX

Aczél, Endre, 245–246, 254
advertising, 15, 92, 99, 113, 168, 174–183, 191. *See also* commercials
Africa, 110–111, 125–127
agitation, 35
Aktenzeichen XY . . . ungelöst, 66–67, 72–78
Alternatywy 4, 220–221
Albania, 14–15, 201
American television, 2, 3, 11, 13, 17–18, 20, 23, 28, 41–42, 56, 66–68, 73, 83–84, 93, 112–114, 117, 134, 142, 156, 158, 165, 179, 181, 187–188, 200–203, 214, 216, 228–229, 242–243, 250, 253, 255
America's Most Wanted, 66
announcer, 168, 193
archives, 6, 7, 23, 61, 79
art, 33–34, 42, 46, 52–53, 104, 107, 142, 163, 189
audiences, 10–12, 23, 28, 32, 37, 43, 49–50, 52–53, 58–59, 64–65, 69, 76, 83, 91–95, 99–100, 107–109, 113–114, 118–123, 151–152, 187, 191–192, 199, 201, 216–217, 230, 241–243, 251; and research, 163–164, 176, 182; and ratings, 202, 204, 213–214, 251–252, 254
Austria, 157, 214–215

British Broadcasting Corporation (BBC), 28, 34, 43, 45, 66, 196, 203
Belgium, 13, 44, 116, 136–137, 157
Borgias, The, 159–160
Brezhnev, Leonid, 9, 35
broadcast, live, 11, 14, 94–95, 111; signals, 14–15
Bulgaria, 15, 92, 178, 200, 204, 214
bourgeois, 8, 22, 106, 117, 220, 222, 229, 231–238, 241

cabaret, 22, 134, 148, 168, 229, 231–241, 249–250, 255; New Year's, 40, 52, 234–235, 239–241, 259

capitalism, 2, 9, 14–15, 21–22, 30–31, 33, 35, 76, 83–85, 88–91, 94–96, 134, 161, 181–183, 213, 216, 220, 223, 231, 233, 244, 248–250, 255
Ceaușescu, Nicolae, 9, 13, 15, 18, 90, 92, 140, 149, 178–179, 181–182, 201
celebrity, 83, 91–92, 94, 97, 102, 106–107, 109–129, 150–151, 248, 250
censorship, 9, 18–19, 78, 80, 94, 133, 140, 151, 231, 233–234, 243, 253–254
class, social, 36, 46, 49–50, 109, 111, 113–129, 134, 147, 163, 187, 230–238, 259
Colbert Report, The, 242, 244, 247–248
Cold War, the, 1–3, 6, 12, 17–18, 20–21, 47, 52, 61, 67, 76, 79, 81, 150, 156, 160–162, 164–165, 171–173, 182, 190, 201, 223, 229, 239, 250, 256–258, 260; and competition, 10, 84–91, 107, 112, 260
colonization, 110, 121, 126, 149, 157, 164. *See also* imperialism
comedy, 6, 8, 11, 19, 22, 51–52, 95, 168, 200, 227–256; and news, 22, 238–239, 245–256, 259
Comedy Central, 242–244, 249, 252
commercials, 15, 22–23, 150, 173–183, 260. *See also* advertising
competition, 10, 20, 35, 57, 68, 85, 94–107, 174, 180, 197, 223, 259; and market, 33, 156–159, 176; and music, 91–93 and reality TV, 27; and sports, 14, 93–98, 100–105. *See also* Cold War
consumerism, 22, 51, 84, 87, 92, 96, 99, 116, 134, 153, 160–163, 173, 175, 187–188, 190, 197, 199, 207, 214, 216, 222–223, 239
consumption, 85, 114–115, 150, 172–182, 200, 217
courtroom drama, 56
Croatia, 16, 140, 206
crime appeal programs, 22, 66–82, 259
Crimewatch UK, 66, 72–73, 82
criticism, 112
Családi kör, 50, 61–65, 197
cultural studies, 6, 82, 189, 205

Czechoslovakia, 13–14, 33, 37, 69–71, 73, 84, 86, 92–93, 137, 139, 146–147, 152, 159, 171, 182, 202, 204, 210, 213–216, 221–222
Czech Republic, the, 171–172, 221–22
Czterdziestolatek, 205–207, 221
Cuba, 214

Daily Show with Jon Stewart, The, 242, 244, 246–247, 254–255
Dallas, 200–201
Denmark, 13
Dietl, Jaroslav, 213, 217
District 78 (A 78-as körzet), 207–213, 224
docufiction, 8, 44, 60–65, 72, 82, 195–197, 259
documentary, 22, 28, 31, 34–35, 42, 54–55, 60–61, 70, 108–109, 112, 114, 116, 123, 169, 195–196
drama serial, 6, 8, 11, 15, 19, 22, 34, 170–171, 188, 198–224, 260
Dziedzic, Irena, 55, 194

East Germany. *See* GDR, 88–89, 176; and TV programming, 8, 14, 17, 19, 21, 28–65, 84, 91, 98, 100–104, 107–108, 141, 156, 190, 192, 199, 201, 230, 238–240, 243, 258–259; and taste, 52, 99, 101–106, 137, 144–145
emotion, 9, 23, 34–35, 41, 54, 56–57, 61–62, 65, 108, 111, 113, 115, 134, 173–183, 190, 194, 199
Estonia, 15, 174, 179–180, 204
ethnicity, 109–110, 114, 127, 196. *See also* race
Europe, 86, 101, 110, 128, 144, 155–173, 179, 182, 229, 232, 240, 258–260; Western, 8, 11–17, 20–21, 28, 33–34, 43, 49, 65–68, 83–86, 90, 93, 101, 136, 142, 146–147, 175–177, 180, 200–201
European Broadcasting Union, 16–17
European Union, the, 5, 110, 156, 158–159, 165, 172, 259; and Audiovisual Media Services Directive, 158–159
Exporting Raymond, 227–230

feminism, 187–190, 197–198, 204–206, 209, 214–216, 222–224, 254; post-, 22, 190, 198, 200, 205, 209, 222–224, 254, 260
Fernsehgericht Tagt, Das, 56
FIDESZ, 65, 80, 168–170, 254–255
film, 7, 9, 10, 12, 22, 29, 32, 42, 48, 52–54, 68, 89, 102, 104, 136, 138, 140–141, 145, 148–151, 158–160, 166, 169–170, 193, 231
Finland, 13, 15, 17, 157, 179–180, 214
Fórum, 57–59, 239
Fox News, 246, 248
France, 13, 19, 43, 66, 73, 101, 137, 157, 200, 232, 250

game show, 11, 22, 28, 42, 43, 53, 83–108, 259
GDR, 2, 9, 13–14, 37, 42, 56, 58–59, 68, 84, 88–90, 93, 97, 99, 144, 164–165, 171, 174, 180, 202, 204, 214, 233, 236, 239, 245, 248
gender, 22, 49, 54, 60–61, 63–64, 95, 100, 111, 142, 163, 187–226, 252–254
Germany, 16–17, 19, 43–44, 66, 70, 171, 232; West, 14, 58, 68, 72–74, 78, 88–89, 136–137, 147, 156–157, 162, 164–166, 180, 200, 202, 214–215, 233, 250
Gierek, Edward, 205–206
globalization, 113, 120, 122, 127–128, 249
Great Britain, 13, 30, 38, 66–68, 72, 117, 136, 156–157, 200, 202
Greece, 13, 17, 19
Győzike, 111–125, 127–129
Gurza, Jerzy, 205
Gypsy. *See* Roma
Gyula Vitéz, 134, 148–153

Habsburg Empire, 15, 109, 139–140, 178
Heti hetes, 248–255
historical drama, 6, 67, 133–172, 199, 203
Hitler, Adolf, 157, 248
Hofi, Géza, 40, 52, 148, 239–241
Hollywood, 34–35, 67, 150, 159–160
Honecker, Erich, 9, 42, 88, 202, 245

humor, 28, 32, 38, 226–256; political, 22, 204–214, 241–256
Hungary, 7, 8, 11, 13–16, 23, 32–34, 37, 40–54, 56–57, 59–60, 67, 74–81, 84, 86, 91–92, 96–98, 101–102, 104, 109–124, 126, 137, 139–153, 159, 162, 168–171, 173, 176–180, 191–192, 196–198, 200–204, 207–214, 218, 220–222, 233–234, 236–239, 245, 248, 260

imperialism, 110, 128, 137, 154, 161, 164, 200, 259; and postimperial, 164–167. *See also* colonization
India, 43–44, 188
International Broadcasting Union, 16
International Youth Festival. *See* World Youth Festival
Intervision, 13, 17, 84
Ireland, 13, 157
Isaura, 74, 200, 220
Italy, 13–16, 43, 66, 156–159, 175, 201

James Bond, 69–70
Janosik, 135, 141–148
journalism, 10, 42, 59, 72, 74, 77, 99, 121–122, 233, 242

Kant, Immanuel, 46
Kádár, János, 7, 9, 51, 58, 78–79, 170, 209, 234, 245
Kékfény, 67, 74–82
Khrushchev, Nikita, 85, 87, 92, 197
Ki Mit Tud, 57, 97–98, 251
Kobieta pracująca, 205, 217
Kudlik, Julia, 54–55, 220
KVN, 53, 93–96, 98–99, 192

Lapin, Sergei, 9, 95
Lenin, 35, 41
Leont'eva, Valentina, 35, 55, 193
lifestyle, 213, 217, 222, 250; and television, 197–199, 200, 203, 206
Linda, 218–220
Lipinska, Olga, 194, 235–236

literature, 9, 10, 12, 29, 32, 42, 44, 48, 52–53, 102–104, 112, 136–138, 140, 146–147, 163, 165–167, 189, 228, 232, 259
Lithuania, 204

MAFILM, 60, 149, 160, 178
marketing, 173–183, 260
melodrama, 187–188, 210
memory, 23, 155, 161, 171, 178–181
Michael Strogoff, 40
Michael the Brave, 140, 149–150
migration, 110
Mit dem Herzen dabei, 37
music, 11, 29, 42, 52, 57, 84, 91–93, 141–142, 145, 168, 170, 179, 202, 210, 230, 234, 236–237, 246, 248

Naše malo misto, 206
nationalism, 12, 15, 17, 31–32, 36, 38, 44, 65, 85–87, 89, 92–94, 96, 101–102, 104–109, 115–129, 133–154, 162–172, 181, 189–190, 193–194, 215–216, 222–224, 237, 248, 252–253, 258–260
Nemocnice na kraji města, 213–214, 221–222
neoliberalism, 111, 120, 169, 223, 249, 256, 259
Netherlands, the, 66, 72
nostalgia, 3, 12, 22–23, 31, 38, 65, 70–72, 74, 80, 135, 137, 153, 174, 179, 213, 218, 221–222, 234, 237, 257, 260; and Ostalgie, 164–165; and Yugo-nostalgia, 170–171; postsocialist, 155–172, 178, 180–183
news, 8, 16, 19, 31, 35, 40, 42–43, 70, 79–81, 88, 116, 169, 195, 202, 231, 243–245, 249, 260; and current affairs, 42, 79, 196–197, 200, 202
Newswipe, 246–247

Olajos, Gergő, 80–81
Organisation Internationale de Radio-diffusion et de Télévision, 16–17
Osbournes, The, 113–116, 127
Ottoman Empire, the, 109, 138, 139, 149
Ot vsei dushi, 35–37, 55, 194
outlaw, 139–141

Passendorfer, Jerzy, 141, 147
Pepereczko, Marek, 142–143
Pfaffs, De, 116, 127
Pócsik, Ilona, 176–178
poetry, 53, 102–104, 231
Poland, 13, 33, 37, 42, 45, 47, 49, 52–53, 55–56, 69, 73, 84, 86, 92–93, 100, 137, 139, 141–148, 159, 175, 194, 200, 203–205, 207, 209, 214, 217, 220–222, 232, 234, 248, 250
Polizeiruf 110, 67–68, 89
Portugal, 13, 44, 157
postsocialism, 1, 2, 4–6, 12, 19, 21–22, 31, 38, 92, 105–106, 109–129, 135, 144, 155–172, 174, 190, 198, 207, 218, 220–224, 241–258, 260
Pozorište u kući, 206–207
Prisma, 58
propaganda, 2, 6, 8, 14, 19, 29, 35–36, 39, 46, 50–51, 57, 69, 81, 91, 103, 133, 140, 148, 168, 176, 182, 192, 195, 203–204, 216, 246–247, 250, 256, 258–259
public service announcement, 174, 181
public service broadcasting, 2, 4, 7, 11, 14, 17–18, 20–21, 28, 29, 34, 39, 44, 56, 65, 72, 80–82, 83–84, 89–90, 116, 156–157, 168, 170–172, 175, 181, 200, 216, 245, 258
Putin, Vladimir, 167

quality television, 27, 52, 63, 109, 112, 122, 136, 158, 160, 167, 216, 260
quiz show. *See* game show

race, 108–129, 163, 165, 169. *See also* ethnicity
radio, 7, 8, 42–44, 46, 49, 63, 90, 145, 169–170, 175–177, 203, 233–234, 237, 251
realism, 21, 27–65, 127, 150, 259; socialist, 29, 30, 147, 190, 195, 259; emotional, 34–38, 61–65, 108, 216
reality TV, 6, 27, 28–84, 96, 99, 104, 108–129, 158, 163, 167, 259
Roma, the, 61, 108–129, 163

Romania, 9, 13, 15, 18, 45, 46, 48–50, 54, 73, 86, 90, 92, 112, 125, 139, 140, 146, 149, 162, 169, 178–181, 192, 201, 214, 236
Russia, 94, 146, 167, 180, 201, 227–230, 248

Saint, The, 67–68, 150
Satra, 125
School TV, 40–64, 239
science, 45–48, 51–52, 54
satellite, 14, 20, 134, 156, 169, 197, 242
self-improvement, 48, 65
Serbia, 140–141, 169–170, 179, 206, 221
Seventeen Moments of Spring, 70–72, 167
Showtime, 159–160
sitcom. *See* situational comedy
situational comedy, 6, 134, 218, 227, 230–231
Slovakia, 141, 145–148, 153, 169, 221
Slovenia, 13, 16, 48, 139, 175, 248
soap opera, 6, 22, 62, 112, 114, 116, 134, 159, 190, 198–224
Song of the Year (Pesnia goda), 87, 92
Soviet Union, the, 3, 7, 9, 10–16, 18, 31, 35–37, 53, 58, 69–71, 78, 86–88, 92–96, 98—100, 134, 167, 174, 191–193, 197, 201, 204, 214, 228–231, 233–234, 240–241, 243, 245, 247–248, 250, 255
Spain, 13, 66, 157, 159
sports, 14, 42, 93–98, 100–105, 168, 175, 179, 201, 239–241
spy drama, 3, 67–70, 76, 81
Stalin, Josef, 35, 94, 134, 190, 215, 248
Starszych Panow, 234–235
stiob, 244, 247
Sweden, 13, 66
Switzerland, 157, 232
Szabó család, A, 203
Szabó, Gyula, 144
Szabó, László, 75–82
Szomszédok, 207, 220

Táncdalfesztivál, 91–93
Tatort, 68–69
talent show, 32, 97–100
telenovela, 157

television, and folk culture, 133–153, 169, 259; studies, 4, 19, 30, 82, 172, 258; transnational, 12, 18, 66–67, 81, 133–154, 157–161, 222, 241, 243–244, 258; and youth, 46–49, 52–54, 98–99, 121–123, 140
television format, 27, 28, 36, 38–39, 58, 67–68, 72–73, 83, 85, 89, 91–92, 94, 106–108, 112–129, 157, 200, 204, 241, 246, 259
Tenkes kapitánya, A, 135, 140–148, 151, 153
theater, 12, 34, 48, 52, 94–96, 111, 136, 230, 232–234, 237–238
Thirty Cases of Major Zeman, The, 69–71, 171, 221
Tito, Josip Broz, 16, 175, 181

Ukraine, the, 167, 169

Vágó, István, 94, 96, 104, 106, 107, 129
variety show, 42, 53, 83, 89–90, 100, 168, 236–238
Vertov, Dziga, 32
Vitray, Tamás, 96, 152
VVV, 93–95

Westerns, 143–144; and DEFA, 144, 171
whiteness, 109–110, 112, 121–126, 128–129
Wij, heren van Zichem, 136–137
women and television, 44, 49–50, 54, 60, 63–65, 72, 76, 95, 100, 187–224, 253–254
Women Behind the Counter, 202, 214–216, 224
World War II, 13, 16, 43, 53, 60, 70, 112, 137, 157–158, 165, 167, 196, 203, 232–233, 238
World Youth Festivals, 87, 94, 97

Yugoslavia, 7, 14–16, 33, 37, 48, 58, 86, 158, 170, 173, 175, 178–180, 200, 203, 206–207, 214, 222, 248, 260

Zimmermann, Eduard, 72–73, 78
Zin, Wiktor, 47

www.ingramcontent.com/pod-product-compliance
Lightning Source LLC
Chambersburg PA
CBHW070751230426

43665CB00017B/2327